# SELinux by Example

## Using Security Enhanced Linux

Frank Mayer, Karl MacMillan, David Caplan

PRENTICE
HALL

Upper Saddle River, NJ • Boston • Indianapolis • San Francisco
New York • Toronto • Montreal • London • Munich • Paris
Madrid • Cape Town • Sydney • Tokyo • Singapore • Mexico City

Much of the structure and organization, and portions of the detailed content, of this book are based on material from Tresys Technology, LLC, their training courses, and their open source tools. Used with permission.

The publisher offers excellent discounts on this book when ordered in quantity for bulk purchases or special sales, which may include electronic versions and/or custom covers and content particular to your business, training goals, marketing focus, and branding interests. For more information, please contact:

    U.S. Corporate and Government Sales
    (800) 382-3419
    corpsales@pearsontechgroup.com

For sales outside the United States, please contact:

    International Sales
    international@pearsoned.com

This Book Is Safari Enabled

The Safari, Enabled icon on the cover of your favorite technology book means the book is available through Safari Bookshelf. When you buy this book, you get free access to the online edition for 45 days. Safari Bookshelf is an electronic reference library that lets you easily search thousands of technical books, find code samples, download chapters, and access technical information whenever and wherever you need it.

To gain 45-day Safari Enabled access to this book:

- Go to http://www.prenhallprofessional.com/safarienabled
- Complete the brief registration form
- Enter the coupon code TVGH-6RDI-7RCZ-Z6IZ-C7HZ

If you have difficulty registering on Safari Bookshelf or accessing the online edition, please e-mail customer-service@safaribooksonline.com.

Visit us on the Web: www.prenhallprofessional.com

Library of Congress Cataloging-in-Publication Data

Mayer, Frank, 1961-
  SELinux by Example : Understanding Security Enhanced Linux / Frank Mayer, Karl MacMillan, David Caplan.
    p. cm.
  Includes bibliographical references and index.
  ISBN 0-13-196369-4 (pbk. : alk. paper) 1. Linux. 2. Operating systems (Computers) 3. Computer networks--Security measures. I. MacMillan, Karl, 1975- II. Caplan, David, 1963- III. Title.
  QA76.76.O63M3738 2006
  005.8--dc22

        2006012657

ISBN 0-13-196369-4

Text printed in the United States on recycled paper at R.R. Donnelley & Sons in Crawfordsville, Indiana
First printing, August 2007

# SELinux by Example

# Prentice Hall
# Open Source Software Development Series
## Arnold Robbins, Series Editor

### *"Real world code from real world applications"*

Open Source technology has revolutionized the computing world. Many large-scale projects are in production use worldwide, such as Apache, MySQL, and Postgres, with programmers writing applications in a variety of languages including Perl, Python, and PHP. These technologies are in use on many different systems, ranging from proprietary systems, to Linux systems, to traditional UNIX systems, to mainframes.

The **Prentice Hall Open Source Software Development Series** is designed to bring you the best of these Open Source technologies. Not only will you learn how to use them for your projects, but you will learn *from* them. By seeing real code from real applications, you will learn the best practices of Open Source developers the world over.

**Titles currently in the series include:**

*Linux® Debugging and Performance Tuning: Tips and Techniques*
Steve Best
0131492470, Paper, © 2006

*Understanding AJAX: Using JavaScript to Create Rich Internet Applications*
Joshua Eichorn
0132216353, Paper, © 2007

*Embedded Linux Primer*
Christopher Hallinan
0131679848, Paper, © 2007

*SELinux by Example*
Frank Mayer, David Caplan, Karl MacMillan
0131963694, Paper, © 2007

*UNIX to Linux® Porting*
Alfredo Mendoza, Chakarat Skawratananond, Artis Walker
0131871099, Paper, © 2006

*Linux Programming by Example: The Fundamentals*
Arnold Robbins
0131429647, Paper, © 2004

*The Linux® Kernel Primer: A Top-Down Approach for x86 and PowerPC Architectures*
Claudia Salzberg, Gordon Fischer, Steven Smolski
0131181637, Paper, © 2006

*To our wives Barbara, Sawyer, and Kimberly*

# Contents

# Acknowledgments

Everyone who ever wrote a book says it was a lot of work, but as we discovered, you really do not understand how much work until you try. Even with three authors, we could never have finished this book without help from many people. Tresys Technology gave us great latitude to work on this book even to the occasional determent of our "real work." Tresys also generously allowed us to use its training materials as the basis for most of this book.

Although we (the authors) are actively involved in the development of SELinux, it is truly a community effort. Many, many people contributed to this book indirectly through their active involvement in the SELinux open source community. Chief among this community is Stephen "Smoogle" Smalley, who is truly an amazing engineer. Not only is he the heart of the SELinux development community, he finds a way (and time!) to be highly active in all aspects of the constantly expanding SELinux development projects. Our most common way to understand some "subtle nuance in SELinux" was to "ask Steve."

Stephen, along with two colleagues from Tresys, Christopher Pebenito and Joshua Brindle, provided invaluable insights through their detailed reviews of our manuscript. We would also like to thank Arnold Robbins, the series editor for this book, for his insightful comments from an engineer not immersed in the SELinux community. Much of this book is based on various training materials we've developed at Tresys over the years. Contributors to these materials include James Athey, Chad Sellers, Spencer Shimko, Christopher Pebenito, and Joshua Brindle. We would also like to thank all the engineers who sat through any of these training seminars for their useful feedback.

We would especially like to thank Catherine Nolan, our editor at Pearson Education, who enthusiastically started this project and remained committed through our many outline and schedule changes. Denise Mickelsen, editorial assistant, also did a great job helping us through the final stages of publication. We would also like to thank the rest of the team at Pearson Education including Suzette Ciancio and Heather Fox (marketing team), Gina Kanouse (Production supervisor), and Alan Clements (cover design).

Finally, we would especially recognize our loving families, our wives Barbara, Sawyer, and Kimberly, and our children Alexandra, Jessica, Samuel, and Rachel. We love you all for the support and encouragement you gave us (and the missing nights and weekends you allowed us).

# About the Authors

**Frank Mayer** is cofounder and Chief Technology Officer of Tresys Technology, and has 23 years of experience in the design, development, and analysis of secure operating systems. He has been an active contributor to SELinux for six years, and has initiated and participated in the development of many new SELinux innovations and tools. He also chairs the annual SELinux Symposium. Frank has published many papers on secure and trustworthy operating systems, and has also explored security in parallel computing, networks, and enterprise applications.

**Karl MacMillan** is an active contributor in the SELinux community and has led the development of many important SELinux features. He is also a sought after speaker and consultant, and has helped many individuals and organizations understand and apply strong computer security with SELinux. Previous to his work on SELinux, Karl made important contributions in the fields of pattern recognition and evolutionary computing as applied to document and audio recognition, where he has numerous published papers.

**David Caplan** is a senior security engineer at Tresys Technology with over 20 years of experience in computer security and a wide range of other programming- and software-related areas. He has worked with SELinux for six years as a contributor to many of the SELinux-related open source projects and has led multiple efforts in analyzing and constructing SELinux policy for a variety of systems.

# Preface

This book is based on our many years of working with, deploying, and helping evolve *Security Enhanced Linux* (SELinux). We have also created technical courses on SELinux, and in our teaching experience we have found that it is difficult to introduce entirely new and foreign notions of computer security to a new audience. In this book, we think we achieved a good balance between conceptual overview versus concrete, hands-on examples.

Another challenge with this book is that SELinux is a new technology; although it has been incorporated into mainstream Linux distributions, it is still evolving. We and others have many innovative ongoing research and development projects to enhance SELinux in many ways. In this book, we face the challenge of describing a moving target. Fortunately, the core concepts of SELinux are fairly well established, and at least the kernel portion of the security enhancements are changing at a manageable pace. For the newer work, we describe the emerging technologies we believe are most important.

## Audience

This book is primarily aimed at the person who most needs to make use of the security enhancements that SELinux brings to Linux. As you will see, this person is primarily interested in understanding, writing, modifying, and/or managing SELinux policies. You are such a person if you want to use SELinux to enhance the security of your application, system, or network.

To make effective use of this book, you should have a good understanding of Linux/UNIX systems. The more familiar you are with the interworkings of the Linux kernel and key services, the easier it will be for you to understand the security object model that SELinux uses. However, as long as you have good working knowledge of Linux, its conventions, and filesystem layout, and/or its programming paradigms, you should have no problem with the material of this book.

Users of systems that include SELinux (for example, Red Hat Enterprise Linux, Fedora Core, Gentoo, and Debian) will also find this book helpful. Although most users and system administrators will not likely write SELinux policy, understanding the SELinux policy language and security model will give you greater insights into the power of SELinux to afford you greater security.

## What You Will Learn

This book is all about writing SELinux security policies to make effective use of the security enhancements SELinux brings to Linux. That sounds simple, but in reality, you have to learn new ideas and understand the SELinux policy language before you can help you understand how to *effectively* use these enhancements.

We divide the book into three parts around the learning steps you, as a student of SELinux, will traverse. The specific topics are as follows:

- **Part I**

  Overview of mandatory access control

  Type enforcement concepts and applications

  SELinux architecture and mechanisms

- **Part II**

  Details of the SELinux native policy language syntax and semantics

  Object labeling in SELinux

- **Part III**

  Two primary methods developed to build SELinux policies: the example policy and the reference policy

  Impacts of SELinux on system administration

  How to write policy modules for SELinux

Our goal is to help you understand the details involved in SELinux so that you can create secure systems. Given the young nature of SELinux, we necessarily provide you with all the gory details of the low-level policy language. Remember, however, that much work is ongoing to make it easier to build secure systems without knowing all the low-level details. Where appropriate, we discuss this evolving work and help you understand how to write *secure* policies that can pass the scrutiny of independent review.

Each chapter concludes with a summary of the key points we discuss in the chapter and exercises to reinforce your understanding of these points. Exercises range from thought experiments, to hands-on exploration, to modification of real security policies. They all will help enhance your understanding of SELinux.

## Summary of Chapters

We divided this book into three parts, each of which contains several chapters:

*Part I, "SELinux Overview."* This part provides the background of SELinux evolution and an overview of its security concepts and architecture.

> *Chapter 1, "Background."* In this chapter, we discuss the evolution of access control in operating systems, kinds of access control mechanisms, their strengths and weaknesses, and the kind of access control SELinux brings to Linux.

> *Chapter 2, "Concepts."* In this chapter, we provide a conceptual overview of SELinux security mechanisms in the form of a detailed tutorial. This chapter is a good, concise discussion of the security enhancements SELinux brings to Linux.

> *Chapter 3, "Architecture."* In this chapter, we provide an overview of the SELinux architecture and implementation and an overview of the policy language architecture.

*Part II, "SELinux Policy Language."* This part contains a detailed description of the entire SELinux policy language syntax and semantics. Each chapter addresses a portion of the language. This part of the book can be viewed as a policy language reference.

> *Chapter 4, "Object Classes and Permissions."* In this chapter, we describe how SELinux controls kernel resources using object classes and defines fine-grained permissions to those object classes.

*Chapter 5, "Type Enforcement Policy."* In this chapter, we describe all the core policy language rules and statements that enable us to write a type enforcement policy. Type enforcement is the central access control feature of SELinux.

*Chapter 6, "Roles and Users."* In this chapter, we discuss the SELinux role-based access control mechanism and how roles and users in the policy language support the type enforcement policy.

*Chapter 7, "Constraints."* In this chapter, we discuss the constraint feature of the SELinux policy language, which is a means to provide restrictions within the policy that support the type of enforcement policy.

*Chapter 8, "Multilevel Security."* In this chapter, we describe the policy language features that allow for optional multilevel security access controls in addition to the core type of enforcement access controls.

*Chapter 9, "Conditional Policies."* In this chapter, we discuss an enhancement to the policy language that enables us to make portions of the type enforcement policy conditional on Boolean expressions whose values can be changed during the course of operation on a production system.

*Chapter 10, "Object Labeling."* In this chapter, we finish our discussion of the policy language by examining how objects are labeled and how we manage those labels in support of SELinux-enhanced access control.

*Part III, "Creating and Writing SELinux Security Policies."* In this final part, we show you how to make use of the policy language, discussing methods for building security policies and insights into administering an SELinux system and writing and debugging SELinux policy modules.

*Chapter 11, "Original Example Policy."* In this chapter, we discuss the example policy, which is a method (source files, build tools and conventions, and so on) for building an SELinux policy that has evolved over the years from the original example policy released with SELinux by the National Security Agency. Fedora Core 4 and Red Hat Enterprise Linux come standard with policies based on the example policy.

*Chapter 12, "Reference Policy."* In this chapter, we discuss a new method for building an SELinux policy that provides all the features of the example policy along with support for emerging SELinux technology. The more recent Fedora Core 5 uses reference policy as its policy foundation.

*Chapter 13, "Managing an SELinux System."* In this chapter, we discuss how SELinux impacts the administration of a Linux system.

*Chapter 14, "Writing Policy Modules."* In this final chapter, we bring all that you have learned throughout the book into a guided tour on writing a policy module for both the example and reference policies.

*Appendixes.* We have included several appendixes with additional reference material:

*Appendix A, "Obtaining SELinux Sample Policies."* This appendix provides instructions on how to obtain the sample policy source files we discuss in this book.

*Appendix B, "Participation and Further Information."* This chapter lists sources of additional information on SELinux and describes how you can further participate in the development of SELinux.

*Appendix C, "Object Class Reference."* This chapter provides a detailed dictionary of all SELinux kernel object classes and associated permissions.

*Appendix D, "SELinux Commands and Utilities."* This chapter provides a summary of utilities and third-party tools available to help with developing SELinux policies and managing SELinux systems.

## How to Use This Book

Rarely does one read a technical book cover to cover. Most people want to understand a particular item or begin exploring the technology as soon as possible. Although reading the book cover to cover is certainly an option, we also recommend an alternative strategy.

Thoroughly read and understand Part I (Chapters 1–3); this part provides you with the necessary background and conceptual insights to understand SELinux. In particular, carefully read and study Chapter 2. You may want to skim Part II (Chapters 4–10) to get a sense of the content of these chapters. These chapters are loaded with the details of the SELinux policy language. For most people, there are too many details to absorb as part of a strategy to first learn about SELinux. As a strategy, you might want to carefully read Chapter 5 and skim Chapters 4 and 10. These chapters cover the SELinux policy language elements that are most used by policy writers. Finally, read the chapters of Part III (Chapters 11–14) that address the issues in which you are interested. Use Part II as a reference as you read these chapters.

## Sidebars, Notes, Warnings, and Tips

We make extensive use of sidebars and notes throughout this book to provide additional information or emphasis on certain items. We also include a number of warnings and tips. Following are the conventional purposes for each of these within this book:

- **Sidebars.** We use sidebars primarily for two purposes. First, we use them for additional information that is not directly covered within the main text of the chapter. For example, we use sidebars to highlight differences between various versions of SELinux or to discuss in detail a particular concept that might be of interest to the reader. We also use sidebars to document the complete syntax of all SELinux policy language statements throughout Part II. These syntax sidebars provide a quick reference for the various policy language elements.

- **Notes.** We use notes to provide additional emphasis on certain points. Usually notes are short items of additional clarification or detail.

- **Warnings.** Warnings are used much like notes except that they emphasize something that requires additional caution or strong emphasis.

- **Tips.** Tips provide quick hints and suggestions about how to perform a given function or make something easier.

## Typographical Conventions

All technical books must use some form of typographical convention to better communicate with the reader. This is especially true due to heavy overloading of terminology, and SELinux is no different. In general, we use italics to introduce a *key concept* at the point where we define the concept (usually first use or near the first use). We also use *italics* for emphasis. For a particularly **strong point of emphasis,** we use a bold font.

Throughout this book, we use a fixed-width font for any SELinux policy language element (`allow`), user commands (`ps`, `ls`), or anything you would type or see on the computer.

For longer listings that show commands and their output, we use the Bourne shell standard prompts of # (for root shells) and $ (for ordinary user shells). User input (that is, something that you type) is also in bold and fix-width fonts in listings. For example:

```
# ls -lZ /etc/selinux/
-rw-r--r--  root   root    system_u:object_r:selinux_config_t config
drwxr-xr-x  root   root    system_u:object_r:selinux_config_t strict
drwxr-xr-x  root   root    system_u:object_r:selinux_config_t targeted
```

When referring to library functions or system calls, we use the convention of including empty parentheses, such as `execve()`. We also use this convention for policy macros that take arguments, such as `domain_auto_trans()`. When referring you to the Linux manual page for additional information on a command or function, we use the convention of italics for the command or function and enclose the manual section within parentheses; for example, *make*(1), *execve*(2).

## Where to Get SELinux

SELinux is supported in several Linux distributions, including Red Hat Enterprise Linux, Red Hat Fedora Core, Gentoo, and Debian. Fedora Core has been the central platform around which the SELinux community has tested and integrated most of its innovations. *Red Hat Enterprise Linux, version 4* (RHEL4), is the first large commercial distribution to fully support a version of SELinux. Nearly everything we discuss in this book is relevant to RHEL4 and other Linux distributions.

We chose to base this book on *Fedora Core 4* (FC4), which is a version of Fedora Core released *after* RHEL4. Everything we discuss should work on an FC4 system. During the eight months it took us to write this book, FC4 evolved, was tested, and released. As we finish this book, *Fedora Core 5* (FC5) was just released. FC5 incorporates many new SELinux innovations, many of which the authors had a principle role in developing. The new FC5 features are probably a good indicator of what is likely to show up in RHEL5. As much as practical, throughout this book we note new *features* and capabilities available in FC5 and not in FC4. Also, where applicable, we note features in FC4 that are not supported in the older RHEL4.

If you are an enterprise user or developer, you are likely using RHEL4 or planning to use RHEL5. We currently use RHEL4 for our enterprise developments and products. If you are an SELinux developer or early adopter, you are probably using a version of Fedora Core or some other distribution. In all cases, this book should provide you extensive information about how to use SELinux and develop SELinux policies.

## How to Get the Book's Sample Policies

Throughout this book, we give example pieces of SELinux policies. These examples are based on the *strict Fedora Core 4* policy as distributed by Red Hat. We discuss this policy in more detail in Chapter 11. FC4 comes standard with a *targeted* (and *not* strict) policy, so you must go through additional steps to get the policy upon which our examples are based. In Part III, we broaden our perspective on sample policies to include other types of policies. We provide instructions in Appendix A on how to get the sources for all the various sample policies we discuss in this book.

# Part I

# SELinux Overview

1

# Chapter 1

# Background

**In this chapter**

*Security Enhanced Linux* (SELinux) is an exciting new technology for securing our computer networks and systems. In a real sense, it represents the culmination of nearly 40 years of operating system security research. For the first time, we have a powerful, flexible, mandatory access control mechanism incorporated into a mainstream, widely distributed operating system. In this chapter, we provide a brief overview of the history of secure operating system research as a means to motivate and set into perspective the value that SELinux brings to today's computer security challenges.

## 1.1 The Inevitability of Software Failure

Appropriately enough, we derive the title of this first section of a book on SELinux from a paper[1] that the principal creators of SELinux coauthored before the SELinux project was even started. The authors of that paper pointed out that software is flawed, and that too much of the software being developed assumes that applications can enforce security without the support of the underlying operating systems. As they note:

> The necessity of operating system security to overall system security is undeniable ... If it fails to meet this responsibility, system-wide vulnerabilities will result.

A design that tries to create security without the support of the underlying operating system is a "fortress built upon sand"[2] with no secure foundation upon which to sit.

---

1  P. Loscocco, S. Smalley, P. Muckelbauer, R. Taylor, S. Turner, J. Farrell. *The Inevitability of Failure: The Flawed Assumption of Security in Modern Computing Environments.* In Proceedings of the 21st National Information Systems Security Conference, pp. 303–314, October 1998, available at www.nsa.gov/selinux/papers/inevit-abs.cfm.

2  D. Baker. *Fortresses Built Upon Sand.* In Proceedings of the New Security Paradigms Workshop, pp. 148–153, 1996.

In the years since that paper was published in 1998, the problem of flawed application software has become practically an everyday news headline. Rarely does a week go by that some new virus, computer theft, or system vulnerability is not announced. The fact of life in the computer era is that application software is flawed and will remain flawed. We certainly applaud the efforts to make software better and more reliable, but flaws will undoubtedly remain an ongoing problem for the foreseeable future. Some people will always try to exploit these flaws. Our challenge as a community is to find ways to have secure systems knowing that flawed application software will always exists. We cannot meet this challenge successfully without first finding firm ground upon which to build (that is, the operating system).

Thus we find the goal of SELinux: specifically, to promulgate a better form of operating system security. As we discuss in this book, the state of the art in operating system security is inadequate. We as a computer security community have known this for nearly 40 years. We have conducted much research but have had limited success improving this situation for mainstream operating systems. Finally, with SELinux, we believe real progress has been made in a way that we will prove lasting. SELinux is indeed a *security enhancement* to the Linux operating system. This enhancement can effectively mitigate the problem of flawed application software, including those flaws not yet discovered or created. This same enhancement can also enforce many security goals, ranging from data confidentiality to application integrity to improved robustness.

With SELinux, we have made a great stride toward moving our "fortress" off the shifting sands on which it currently sits.

## 1.2 The Evolution of Access Control Security in Operating Systems

Early operating systems had little or no security; a user could access any file or resource just by knowing how to name the resource. Fortunately, it was not long before access control mechanisms began to emerge to provide some sense of security. The predominant type of access control we have today is called *discretionary access control* (DAC). The primary feature of DAC is that individual users, often a resource "owner," can specify who may or may not access the resource. As you will see, DAC has some fundamental security weaknesses that are intrinsic to its nature. To overcome these weaknesses, the computer security community has been trying to develop useful *mandatory access control* (MAC) mechanisms. MAC is intended to avoid the weaknesses of DAC while providing the security required. Unfortunately, creating a useful MAC mechanism that is secure yet flexible enough to address a wide range of problems has proven difficult. The primary value that SELinux brings to Linux is a flexible, configurable MAC mechanism. In the remainder of this section, we explore the strengths and weaknesses of various DAC and MAC mechanisms, as a means to provide a context for understanding the true value that SELinux provides.

## 1.2.1 The Reference Monitor Concept

To understand access control, you must have an appreciation for the *reference monitor concept.* The U.S. Department of Defense led the early research into operating system security in the 1970s and 1980s. A key early report from that work, the so-called Anderson Report,[3] defined for the first time this fundamental model for characterizing access control in operating systems (see Figure 1-1).

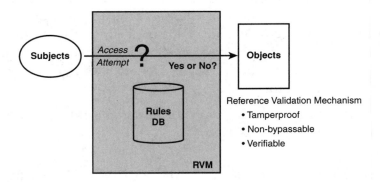

**FIGURE 1-1**
The reference monitor concept

---

3  Anderson, James P. Computer Security Technology Planning Study, Volume II, ESD-TR-73-51, Vol. II, Electronic Systems Division, Air Force Systems Command, Hanscom Field, Bedford, MA 01730 (Oct. 1972), available at http://csrc.nist.gov/publications/history/ande72.pdf.

In a reference monitor, the operating system isolates passive resources into distinct *objects* such as files and active entities such as running programs into *subjects*. The reference monitor mechanism (called a *reference validation mechanism*) would then validate access between subjects and objects by applying a security policy as embodied in a set of access control rules. In this manner, program access to system resources such as files can be limited to those accesses that accord with the security policy. Access control decisions are based on *security attributes* associated with each subject and object that represents the subject's/object's security-related characteristics. For example, in standard Linux, subjects (that is, processes) have real and effective user identifiers, and objects (for example, files) have access permission modes that are used to determine whether a process may open a file.

Other than implementing the security policy, the fundamental design goals of an implementation of the reference monitor concept are that it be:

- Tamper-proof (cannot be maliciously changed or modified)
- Nonbypassable (subjects cannot avoid the access control decisions)
- Verifiable (it is correct and implementation of the security policy can be demonstrated)

Nearly all operating systems implement some form of a reference monitor and can be characterized in terms of subjects, objects, and security policy rules. In standard Linux, subjects are generally processes, and objects are the various system resource used for information sharing, storage, and communication (files, directories, sockets, shared memory, and so on). In Linux, as in most other popular operating systems, the security policy rules enforced by the reference monitor (that is, the kernel) are fixed and hard-coded, whereas the security attributes that these rules use for validation (for example, access modes) can be changed and assigned. Standard Linux security is a form of DAC security.

## 1.2.2 The Problem with Discretionary Access Control

As noted, DAC is a form of access control that usually allows authorized users (via their programs such as a shell) to change the access control attributes of objects, thereby specifying whether other users have access to the object. A simple form of DAC might be file passwords, where access to a file requires the knowledge of a password created by the file owner (and distributed by word of mouth to other users authorized to view the file). Most DAC mechanisms are based on user-identity access control attributes. Nearly all modern operating systems have some form of user-identity-based DAC. In Linux, the *owner-group-world permission mode* mechanism is prevalent and well known. Likewise, a more general *access control list* mechanism is also common.

All DAC mechanisms have a basic weakness in that they fail to recognize a fundamental difference between human users and computer programs. DAC typically tries to emulate an ownership concept where; for example, file owners have the right to specify access to files and only give access to other users they trust to access the file.[4] Assuming that you can trust the human user (arguably an invalid proposition in general), the way computers work does not directly model the real world. Simply put, users rely on software, not of their own creation, to perform functions on the computer. So, we are not really giving users the ability to grant and use access. Instead, we are giving software programs this capability. As has become obvious in the age of the Internet, programs are often full of flaws or are downright malicious. This is the problem with *Trojan horses,* first recognized in the 1970s, of which today's modern viruses, worms, and spyware are just variants. In short, if a user is authorized access, that really means programs are authorized that access, and if programs are authorized that access, malicious programs will have that same access.

DAC assumes a benign environment where all programs are trustworthy and without flaws. Although the early computer research community, which largely lived in an academic world and from which so much of our current technology evolved, might have wished for such an environment; in reality, however, we know of no such benign computer environment in the entire history of computer science. Human nature will always have those who exploit weakness in flawed software.

## 1.2.3 The Origins of Mandatory Access Control

Throughout the 1970s and 1980s, significant energy was exerted to address the problem of malicious and flawed software. The goal was to achieve MAC, where the basis of access control decisions was not at the discretion of individual users or even system administrators. We wanted to implement an *organizational security policy* to

---

4   This is where the word discretion comes from. Owners use their discretion to grant or not grant access.

control access to objects that could not be affected by the actions of individual programs. The military funded most of this work, which focused on protecting the *confidentiality* of classified government data. In particular, the most common MAC mechanisms implemented to date address the problem of multilevel security, a simplified form of which is shown in Figure 1-2.

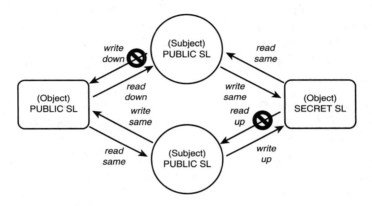

**FIGURE 1-2**
Multilevel security model

*Multilevel security* (MLS) is typically based on a formal model called the *Bell-LaPadula model.*[5] In the MLS model, all subjects and objects are labeled with a security level. In our example, we have a PUBLIC and a SECRET sensitivity level. The levels represent the relative sensitivity of the data and the clearance of the user on whose behalf the subjects are operating (SECRET being data of "higher" sensitivity than PUBLIC). In MLS, subjects can always read and write objects at the same sensitivity. In addition, subjects can read lower-level objects ("read down") and write higher-level objects ("write up"). However, a subject may never read higher-level objects ("no read up") nor write lower-level objects ("no write down"). The idea being that information can flow from lower levels to higher levels, but not the reverse, thereby protecting the confidentiality of the higher-level data.

---

5   This model is actually captured in a set of three papers written in 1973 and an interpretation of these papers for the Multics operating system written in 1976. The Multics interpretation paper is the easiest to read of the set. See David E. Bell and Leonard J. LaPadula, *Secure Computer System: Unified Exposition and MULTICS Interpretation*, MTR-2997 Rev. 1, The MITRE Corporation, Bedford, MA 01730 (Mar. 1976); also ESD-TR-75-306, rev. 1, Electronic Systems Division, Air Force Systems Command, Hanscom Field, Bedford, MA 01731, available at http://csrc.nist.gov/publications/history/bell76.pdf.

MLS was a radical change in the way we thought about access control. No longer are data owners arbitrarily determining who may access objects. Further, we could now have strong security assuming most software was untrusted, because the information flow rules prevent inappropriate data access. In MLS, the organization decides via fixed rules how data may be shared regardless of the desires of individual users (and more important, the programs they run). MLS is by far the most implemented MAC mechanism to date and is still prevalent in several niche operating systems. MAC mechanisms similar to MLS have also been contemplated and built, all of which share a common theme of implementing a small number of fixed security properties.

The primary weakness of MLS is the fact that it implements a single security goal (that is, protecting the confidentiality of sensitive data using the model of government classified documents) in a strict, inflexible manner. Not all operating system security concerns are related to data confidentiality, and of those that are, most are not amenable to the rigid and simple model of classified government documents (including many, if not most, government systems dealing with classified data). To expand upon this goal in MLS (and similar MAC mechanisms), subjects must be given privilege to work outside the security policy (that is, violating the principle of nonbypassability) and trusted not to violate the intent of the policy. This inflexibility and narrow focus has kept MLS and similar MAC mechanisms from achieving broad appeal.

## 1.2.4 A Better Form of Mandatory Access Control

SELinux implements a flexible MAC mechanism called *type enforcement* (TE). As you will see, type enforcement provides strong mandatory security in a form that is adaptable to a large variety of security goals, concurrently. Type enforcement provides a means to control access down to the individual program level, in a manner that allows an organization to define a security policy appropriate for their systems. In type enforcement, all subjects and objects have a *type identifier* associated with them. To access an object, the subject's type must be authorized for the object's type, regardless of the user identity of the subject.

What makes the SELinux approach superior to a straight MLS solution is that the rules governing type-based access control are not predefined nor hard-coded in the kernel. By default, SELinux allows no access. An organization can develop any number of rules specifying what is allowed, making SELinux adaptable to a wide variety of security policies.

The collection of rules that determine allowed access for a system is called an *SELinux policy*. Physically, an SELinux policy is a special file that contains all the rules that the SELinux kernel will enforce. The policy file is compiled from a set of source files. As you will see, SELinux policies can vary from system to system. During the boot process, the policy is loaded into the kernel, where it is then used as the basis for access control decisions.

> NOTE  The term *policy* is greatly overloaded in the computer security field. Throughout this chapter, we use the term to refer to general definitions of an organization security goals and objectives. However, SELinux also uses *policy* to refer to the set of rules (and the file that contains them) that are loaded into the kernel for access enforcement. We try to avoid confusion by limiting the overloading use of this word (although we cannot completely avoid this problem). Where its use is ambiguous, we explicitly write *SELinux policy* to avoid confusion.

SELinux brings flexible type enforcement along with a form of *role-based access control* and the optional addition of traditional MLS to Linux. This flexible and adaptable MAC security, built in to the mainstream Linux operating system, is what makes SELinux such a promising technology for improved security.

## 1.2.5 The Evolution of SELinux

SELinux has its origins in high-assurance operating system security and micro-kernel research from the 1980s. These two research threads came together in a project called *Distribute Trusted Mach* (DTMach), which merged the experiences of earlier research projects (LOCK, which involved a form of type enforcement in a high-assurance security kernel; and Trusted Mach, which incorporated multilevel security controls into the Mach microkernel). The U.S. National Security Agency's research organization participated in the DTMach effort and continued its participation through a number of subsequent secure microkernel projects. This work eventually resulted in a new security architecture, called *Flask,* that supported a more flexible and dynamic type of enforcement mechanism.[6]

---

6  R. Spencer, S. Smalley, P. Loscocco, M. Hibler, D. Andersen, and J. Lepreau. "The Flask Security Architecture: System Support for Diverse Security Policies." In Proceedings of the Eighth USENIX Security Symposium, pp. 123–139, August 1999.

The various platforms upon which this work was performed were research micro-kernels not in wide market use. The NSA recognized a need to expose this technology to a broader community in hopes of demonstrating its viability and gaining broader support for its use. In the summer of 1999, the NSA began to implement the Flask security architecture in the Linux kernel. In December 2000, the NSA made its first public release of this work, called Security Enhanced Linux. Being implemented in a popular mainstream operating system, SELinux started to attract the attention of the Linux community. SELinux was originally released as a collection of kernel patches for the 2.2.x kernel.

Following the 2001 Linux Kernel Summit in Ottawa, Canada, the *Linux Security Module* (LSM)[7] project was started to create a flexible framework for the Linux kernel that allowed different security extensions to be added to Linux. The NSA and the SELinux community were major contributors to this effort, with SELinux helping to drive many of the requirements for LSM. Concurrent with the LSM effort, NSA started to adapt SELinux to use the LSM framework. The core LSM features were integrated into the mainline Linux kernel starting in August 2002, and were incorporated into the Linux 2.6 kernel. By August 2003, the NSA, with growing open source community help, had completed its migration of SELinux to the LSM framework, resulting in the inclusion of SELinux in the main Linux 2.6 kernel. SELinux had become a fully functional LSM module included in the core Linux code set.

Several Linux distributions began using the SELinux features in the 2.6 kernel to various degrees, but the primary effort to make SELinux ready for the enterprise was via the Red Hat-sponsored Fedora Core project. The NSA and Red Hat started a joint effort to integrate SELinux as part of the mainstream Fedora Core Linux distribution. Prior to Red Hat's interest, SELinux was always an add-on set of packages that required significant expertise to integrate. Red Had took the initiative (and business risks) to make SELinux a part of a mainstream distribution, complete with modified user-space tools and services and enhanced security enabled by default. Starting with Fedora Core 2 and continuing with Fedora Core 3, SELinux and its supporting infrastructure and tools were improved for mainstream use. In early 2005, Red Hat released its *Enterprise Linux version 4* (REL4) with SELinux as a fully enabled by default security enhancement. SELinux and mandatory access control had reached the mainstream operating system market at last.

---

7   See http://lsm.immunix.org.

SELinux is still a relatively new and complex technology, and significant research and development is continuing to improve its utility. We discuss much of these emerging developments throughout this book.

## 1.3 Summary

- Application software is flawed and will remain flawed for the foreseeable future. Nonetheless, we must find ways to create secure systems despite these inevitable flaws. Real security cannot be achieved without better underlying operating system security. The goal of SELinux is to provide this improved security in a mainstream operating system (that is, Linux).

- The reference monitor concept is a common means of describing access control in operating systems. In a reference monitor, resources are encapsulated into distinct objects, and accesses between subjects (that is, processes) and objects are mediated by the reference validation mechanism according to the system security policy.

- Operating systems have two forms of access control: *discretionary access control* (DAC) and *mandatory access control* (MAC). Standard Linux security is a form of DAC. SELinux adds a flexible, configurable MAC to Linux.

- DAC has a fundamental weakness in that it is subject to a variety of malicious software attacks. MAC is a way to avoid these weaknesses. Most MAC features implemented so far are a form of multilevel security modeled after governmental classification controls.

- SELinux implements a more flexible form of MAC called type enforcement and an optional form of multilevel security.

## Exercises

1. Set up an SELinux system and install the strict example policy using the instructions in Appendix A, "Obtaining SELinux Sample Policies."

# Chapter 2

# Concepts

**In this chapter**

The details of the SELinux access control mechanism and policy language are extensive and fully described in later chapters. However, the basic concepts and goals of SELinux are fairly simple. In this chapter, we examine the security concepts of SELinux and the motivations behind these concepts. Gaining a conceptual understanding is necessary to effectively use and apply SELinux access controls. This chapter focuses on the primary access control feature of SELinux, *type enforcement* (TE), although we also briefly discuss the optional multilevel security mechanism.

## 2.1 Security Contexts for Type Enforcement

All operating system access control is based on some type of access control attribute associated with objects and subjects. In SELinux, the access control attribute is called a *security context*. All objects (files, interprocess communication channels, sockets, network hosts, and so on) and subjects (processes) have a single security context associated with them. A security context has three elements: user, role, and type identifiers. The usual format for specifying or displaying a security context is as follows:

```
user:role:type
```

The string identifiers for each element are defined in the SELinux policy language, which we discuss in greater detail later. For now, just understand that a valid security context must have one valid user, role, and type identifier, and that the identifiers are defined by the policy writer. The namespaces for each identifier are orthogonal. (So, for example, it is possible, but not usually advisable, to have the same string identifier for a user, a role, and a type.)

> **Examining Security Contexts**
>
> SELinux modifies many system commands by adding the -z option to display the security contexts of objects and subjects. For example, `ls -z` shows the security contexts of file system objects and `ps -z` shows the security contexts of processes. Another useful command is `id`, which shows the security context of your shell (that is, your current user, role, and type). The following, for example, shows the security context of a shell on a running SELinux system:
>
> ```
> $ id -z
> joe:user_r:user_t
> ```
>
> You can use these commands to explore your own SELinux system as we walk through the examples in this chapter.

## 2.1.1 Comparing SELinux with Standard Linux

At this point, it is useful to compare the access control attributes on standard Linux with those of SELinux. For simplicity, we stick to common filesystem objects such as files and directories. In standard Linux, the access control attributes of subjects are the real and effective user and group IDs associated with all processes via the process structure in the kernel. These attributes are protected by the kernel and set via a number of controlled means, including the login process and setuid programs. For objects (for example, files), the inode of the file contains a set of access mode bits and file user and group IDs. The former controls access based on three sets of read/write/execute bits, one each for file owner, file group, and everyone else. The latter determines the file owner and group to decide which set of bits to use on a given access attempt.

As noted, in SELinux, the access control attributes are always the security context triple. All objects and subjects have an associated security context. Where standard Linux uses the process user/group IDs, the file's access mode, and the file user/group IDs to grant or deny access, SELinux uses the security contexts of a process and the object the process accesses. More specifically, because the primary access control feature of SELinux is type enforcement, the type identifier from the security context is used to determine access.

NOTE   SELinux *adds* type enforcement to standard Linux. This means that both the standard Linux and enhanced SELinux access controls must be satisfied to access an object. So, for example, if we have SELinux write access to a file but we do not have w permission on the file, we cannot write the file.

Table 2-1 summarizes the comparison of standard Linux and the added SELinux security attributes and access control.

TABLE 2-1
Comparison of Standard Linux and Security-Enhanced Linux Access Control

|  | Standard Linux | SELinux Added |
|---|---|---|
| **Process security attributes** | Real and effective user and group IDs | Security context |
| **Object security attributes** | Access modes and file user and group IDs | Security context |
| **Basis for access control** | Process user/group ID and file's access modes based on file's user/ group ID | Permissions allowed between process type and file type |

## 2.1.2 More on Security Contexts

The security context is a simple, consistent access control attribute. In SELinux, the type identifier is the primary part of the security context that determines access. For historical reasons, the type of a process is often called a *domain*. The use of "domain" and "domain type" to mean the type of a process is so common and pervasive that we do not attempt to avoid using the term *domain*. In general, consider domain, domain type, subject type, and process type to be synonymous.

The user and role identifiers in a security context have little impact in the access control policy for type enforcement except for constraint enforcement, which we discuss in Chapter 7, "Constraints." For processes, user and role identifiers are more interesting because they are used to control the association of types with user identifiers and thus with Linux user accounts (more on this later). For objects, however, user and role identifiers have nearly no use. As a convention, the role of an object is usually `object_r`, and the user of an object is usually the user identifier of the process that created the object. They have no effect on access control.

Finally, be aware of the differences between the user ID in standard Linux security and the user identifier in a security context. Technically, these are completely orthogonal identifiers, used separately by the standard and security-enhanced access control mechanisms, respectively. Any relationship between these two is strictly provided via the login process according to conventions not directly enforced by the SELinux policy.

## 2.2 Type Enforcement Access Control

In SELinux, all access must be explicitly granted. SELinux allows *no access by default,* regardless of the Linux user/group IDs. Yes, this means that there is no default superuser in SELinux, unlike root in standard Linux. The way access is granted is by specifying access from a subject type (that is, a domain) and an object type using an `allow` rule. An `allow` rule has four elements:

- *Source type(s)*   Usually the domain type of a process attempting access
- *Target type(s)*   The type of an object being accessed by the process
- *Object class(es)*   The class of object that the specified access is permitted
- *Permission(s)*   The kind of access that the source type is allowed to the target type for the indicated object classes

As an example, take the following rule:

```
allow user_t bin_t : file {read execute getattr};
```

This example shows the basic syntax of a TE allow rule. This rule has two type identifiers: the *source* (or subject or domain) type, `user_t`; and the *target* (or object) type, `bin_t`. The identifier `file` is the name of an *object class* defined in the policy (in this case, representing an ordinary file). The *permissions* contained within the braces are a subset of the permissions valid for an instance of the file object class. The translation of this rule would be as follows:

A process with a domain type of `user_t` can read, execute, or get attributes for a file object with a type of `bin_t`.

As we discuss later, permissions in SELinux are substantially more granular than in standard Linux, where there are only three (rwx). In this case, read and execute are fairly conventional; getattr is less obvious. Essentially, getattr permission to a file allows a caller to view (not change) attributes such as date, time, and *discretionary access control* (DAC) access modes. In a standard Linux system, a caller may view such information on a file with only search permission to the file's directory even if the caller does not have read access to the file.

Assuming that user_t is the domain type of an ordinary, unprivileged user process such as a login shell process, and bin_t is the type associated with executable files that users run with the typical security privileges (for example, /bin/bash), the rule might be in a policy to allow users to execute shell programs such as the bash shell.

> NOTE    There is no significance to the _t in the type identifier name. This is just a naming convention used in most SELinux policies; a policy writer can define a type identifier using any convenient convention allowed by the policy language syntax.

Throughout this chapter, we often depict allowed access using symbols: circles for processes, boxes for objects, and arrows representing allowed access. For example, Figure 2-1 depicts the access allowed by the previous allow rule.

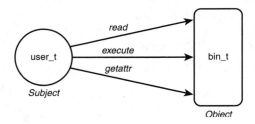

**FIGURE 2-1**
A depiction of an allow rule

### 2.2.1 Type Enforcement by Example

SELinux `allow` rules such as the preceding example are really all there is to granting access in SELinux. The challenge is determining the many thousands of accesses one must create to permit the system to work while ensuring that only the necessary permissions are granted, to make it as secure as possible.

To further explore type enforcement, let's use the example of the password management program (that is, `passwd`). In Linux, the password program is trusted to read and modify the shadow password file (`/etc/shadow`) where encrypted passwords are stored. The password program implements its own internal security policy that allows ordinary users to change only their own password while allowing root to change any password. To perform this trusted job, the password program needs the ability to move and re-create the shadow file. In standard Linux, it has this privilege because the password program executable file has the *setuid bit* set so that when it is executed by anyone, it runs as `root` user (which has all access to all files). However, many, many programs can run as `root` (in reality, all programs can potentially run as `root`). This means, any program (when running as `root`) has the potential to modify the shadow password file. What type enforcement enables us to do is to ensure that only the password program (or similar trusted programs) can access the shadow file, regardless of the user running the program.

Figure 2-2 depicts how the password program might work in an SELinux system using type enforcement.

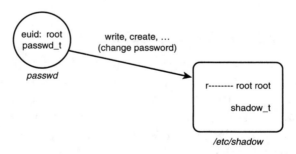

```
allow passwd_t shadow_t : file {ioctl read write create getattr
setattr lock relabelfrom relabelto append unlink link rename};
```

FIGURE 2-2
Type enforcement example: passwd program

In this example, we defined two types. The `passwd_t` type is a domain type intended for use by the password program. The `shadow_t` type is the type for the shadow password file. If we examine such a file on disk, we would see something like this:

```
# ls -Z /etc/shadow
-r------   root    root    system_u:object_r:shadow_t   shadow
```

Likewise, examining a process running the password program under this policy would yield this:

```
# ps -aZ
joe:user_r:passwd_t     16532 pts/0     00:00:00 passwd
```

For now, you can ignore the user and role elements of the security context and just note the types.

Examine the `allow` rule in Figure 2-2 The purpose of this rule is to give the `passwd` process' domain type (`passwd_t`) the access to the shadow's file type (`shadow_t`) needed to allow the process to move and create a new shadow password file. So, in reexamining Figure 2-2, we see that the depicted process running the password program (`passwd`) can successfully manage the shadow password file because it has an effective user ID of `root` (standard Linux access control) *and* because a TE `allow` rule permits it adequate access to the shadow password file's type (SELinux access control). Both are necessary, neither is sufficient.

### 2.2.2 The Problem of Domain Transitions

If all we had to do was provide allowed access for processes to objects such as files, writing a TE policy would be straightforward. However, we have to figure out a way to securely run the right programs in a process with the right domain type. For example, we do not want programs not trusted to access the shadow file to somehow execute in a process with the `passwd_t` domain type. This could be disastrous. This problem brings us to the issue of *domain transitions*.

To illustrate, examine Figure 2-3, in which we expand upon the previous password program example. In a typical system, a user (say Joe) logs in, and through the magic of the login process, a shell process is created (for example, running `bash`). In standard Linux security, the real and effective user IDs (that is, `joe`) are the same.[1] In our example SELinux policy, we see that the process type is `user_t`, which is intended to be the domain type of ordinary, untrusted user processes. As Joe's shell runs other programs, the type of the new processes created on Joe's behalf will keep the user_t domain type unless some other action is taken. So how does Joe change passwords?

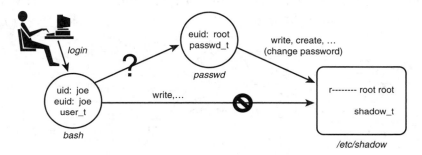

**FIGURE 2-3**
The problem of domain transitions

We would not want Joe's untrusted domain type user_t to have the capability to read and write the shadow password file directly because this would allow any program (including Joe's shell) to see and change the contents of this critical file. As discussed previously, we want only the password program to have this access, and then only when running with the passwd_t domain type. So, the question is how to provide a safe, secure, and unobtrusive method for transitioning from Joe's shell running with the user_t type to a process running the password program with the passwd_t type.

## 2.2.3 Review of SetUID Programs in Standard Linux Security

Before we discuss how to deal with the problem of domain transitions, let's first review how a similar problem is handled in standard Linux where the same problem of providing Joe a means to securely change his password exists. The way Linux solves this problem is by making passwd a setuid to the root program. If you list the password program file on a typical Linux system, you see something like this:

```
# ls -l /usr/bin/passwd
-r-s-x-x  1 root root 19336 Sep  7 04:11 /usr/bin/passwd
```

---

1   To be precise, Joe would not be a user ID. Rather, the string joe is used to determine the user ID (which is an integer number) from the password file (/etc/passwd). For ease of explanation, we skip that intermediate step and just use the string identifiers in our examples.

Notice two things about this listing. First the s in the x spot for the owner permission. This is the so-called *setuid bit* and means that for any process that executes this file, its effective UID (that is, the user ID used for access control decisions) will be changed to that of the file owner. In this case, root is the file owner, and therefore when executed the password program will always run with the effective user ID of root. Figure 2-4 shows these steps.

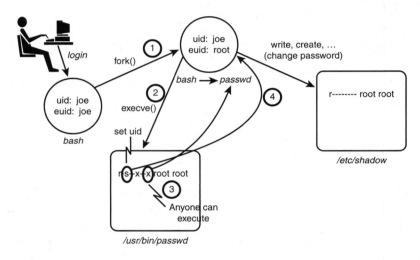

FIGURE 2-4
Password program security in standard Linux (setuid)

What actually happens when Joe runs the password program is that his shell will make a fork() system call to create a near duplicate of itself. This duplicate process still has the same real and effective user IDs (joe) and is still running the shell program (bash). However, immediately after forking, the new process will make an execve() system call to execute the password program. Standard Linux security requires that the calling user ID (still joe) have x access, which in this case is true because of the x access to everyone. Two key things happen as a result of the successful execve() call. First, the shell program running in the new process is replaced by the password program (passwd). Second, because the setuid bit is set for owner, the effective user ID is changed from the process' original ID to the file owner ID (root in this case). Because root can access all files, the password program can now access the shadow password file and handle the request from Joe to change his password.

Use of the setuid bit is well established in UNIX-like operating systems and is a simple and powerful feature. However, it also illustrates the primary weakness of standard Linux security. The password program needs to run as root to access the shadow file. However, when running as root, the password program can effectively access any system resource. This is a violation of the central security engineering principal of *least privilege.* As a result, we must trust the password program to be benign with respect to all other possible actions on the system. For truly secure applications, the password program requires an extensive code audit to ensure it does not abuse its extra privilege. Further, when the inevitable unforeseen error makes its way into the password program, it presents a possible opportunity to introduce vulnerabilities beyond accessing the shadow password file. Although the password program is fairly simple and highly trusted, think of the other programs (including login shells) that may and do run as root with that power.

What we would really like is a way to ensure least privilege for the password program and any other program that must have some privilege. In simple terms, we want the password program to be able to access only the shadow and other password-related files plus those bare-minimum system resources necessary to run; and we would like to ensure that no other program but the password (and similar) programs can access the shadow password file. In this way, we need only evaluate the password (and similar) programs with respect to its role in managing user accounts and need not concern ourselves with other programs when evaluating security concerns for user account management.

This is where type enforcement comes in.

## 2.2.4 Domain Transitions

As previously shown in Figure 2-2, the `allow` rule that would ensure that `passwd` process domain type (`passwd_t`) can access the shadow password file. However, we still have the problem of domain transitions described earlier. Providing for secure domain transition is analogous to the concept of setuid programs, but with the strength of type enforcement. To illustrate, let's take the setuid example and add  type enforcement (see Figure 2-5).

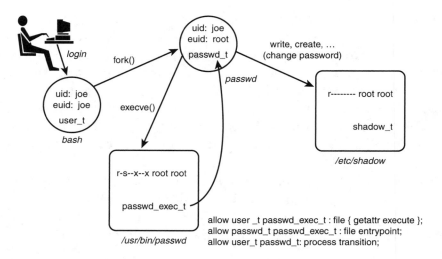

**FIGURE 2-5**
Passwd program security in SELinux (domain transitions)

Now our example is more complicated. Let's examine this figure in detail. First notice that we have added the three types we showed previously, namely Joe's shell domain (user_t), the password program's domain type (passwd_t), and the shadow password file type (shadow_t). In addition, we have added the file type for the passwd executable file (passwd_exec_t). For example, listing the security context for the password program on-disk executable would yield a result something like this:

```
# ls -Z /usr/bin/passwd
-r-s-x-x  root  root  system_u:object_r:passwd_exec_t  /usr/bin/passwd
```

Now we have enough information to create the TE policy rules that allow the password program (and presumably only the password program) to run with the passwd_t domain type. Let's look at the rules from Figure 2-5. The first rule is as follows:

```
allow user_t passwd_exec_t : file {getattr execute};
```

What this rule does is allow Joe's shell (user_t) to initiate an execve() system call on the passwd executable file (passwd_exec_t). The SELinux execute file permission is essentially the same permission as x access for files in standard Linux.

(The shell "stats" the file before trying to execute, hence the need for `getattr` permission, too.) Recall our description of how a shell program actually works. First it forks a copy of itself, including identical security attributes. This copy still retains Joe's shell original domain type (`user_t`). Therefore, the execute permission must be for the original domain (that is, the shell's domain type). That is why `user_t` is the source type for this rule.

Let's now look at the next allow rules from Figure 2-5:

```
allow passwd_t passwd_exec_t : file entrypoint;
```

This rule provides *entrypoint access* to the `passwd_t` domain. The `entrypoint` permission is a rather valuable permission in SELinux. What this permission does is define which executable files (and therefore which programs) may "enter" a domain. For a domain transition, the new or "to-be-entered" domain (in this case, `passwd_t`) must have `entrypoint` access to the executable file used to transition to the new domain type. In this case, assuming that only the `passwd` executable file is labeled with `passwd_exec_t`, and that only type `passwd_t` has `entrypoint` permission to `passwd_exec_t`, we have the situation that only the password program can run in the `passwd_t` domain type. This is a powerful security control.

> WARNING   The concept of `entrypoint` permission is extremely important. If you did not fully understand the preceding example, please re-read it again before proceeding.

Let's now look at the final rule:

```
allow user_t passwd_t : process transition;
```

This is the first `allow` rule we have seen that did not provide access to file objects. In this case, the object class is `process`, meaning the object class representing processes. Recall that all system resources are encapsulated in an object class. This concept holds for processes, too. In this final rule, the permission is `transition` access. This permission is needed to allow the type of a process' security context to change. The original type (`user_t`) must have `transition` permission to the new type (`passwd_t`) for the domain transition to be allowed.

These three rules together provide the necessary access for a domain transition to occur. For a domain transition to succeed, all three rules are necessary; alone, none is sufficient. Therefore, a domain transition is allowed only when the following three conditions are true:

1. The process' new domain type has `entrypoint` access to an executable file type.

2. The process' current (or old) domain type has `execute` access to the entry point file type.

3. The process' current domain type has `transition` access to the new domain type.

When all three of these permissions are permitted in a TE policy, a domain transition may occur. Further, with the use of the `entrypoint` permission on executable files, we have the power to strictly control which programs can run with a given domain type. The `execve()` system call is the only way to change a domain type,[2] giving the policy writer great control over an individual program's access to privilege, regardless of the user who may be invoking the program.

Now the issue is how does Joe indicate that he wants a domain transition to occur. The above rules allow only the domain transition; they do not require it. There are ways that a programmer or user can explicitly request a domain transition (if allowed), but in general we do not want users to have to make these requests explicitly. All Joe wants to do is run the password program, and he expects the system to ensure that he can. We need a way to have the system initiate a domain transition by default.

## 2.2.5 Default Domain Transitions: type_transition Statement

To support domain transitions occurring by default (as we want in the case of the password program), we need to introduce a new rule, the *type transition rule* (`type_transition`). This rule provides a means for the SELinux policy to specify default transitions that should be attempted if an explicit transition was not requested. Let's add the following `type transition` rule to the `allow` rules:

```
type_transition user_t passwd_exec_t : process passwd_t;
```

---

2   To be precise, a recent change to SELinux provides a means for a process, with necessary privilege, to change its security context without an `execve()` call. In general, without strong justification, this mechanism, described in Chapter 5, "Type Enforcement," should not be used because it greatly weakens the strength of type enforcement.

The syntax of this rule differs from the `allow` rule. There are still source and target types (`user_t` and `passwd_exec_t`, respectively) and an object class (`process`). However, instead of permissions, we have a third type, the *default type* (`passwd_t`).

`Type_transition` rules are used for multiple different purposes relating to default type changes. For now, we are concerned with a `type_transition` rule that has `process` as its object class. Such rules cause a default domain transition to be attempted. The `type_transition` rule indicates that, by default on an `execve()` system call, if the calling process' domain type is `user_t` and the executable file's type is `passwd_exec_t` (as is the case in our example in Figure 2-5), a domain transition to a new domain type (`passwd_t`) will be attempted.

The `type_transition` rule allows the policy writer to cause default domain transitions to be initiated without explicit user input. This makes type enforcement less obtrusive to the user. In our example, Joe does not want to know anything about access control or types; he wants only to change his password. The system and policy designer can use `type_transition` rules to make these transitions transparent to the user.

> NOTE  Remember that a `type_transition` rule causes a domain transition to be attempted by default, but it *does not allow it*. You must still provide the three types of access required for a domain transition to successfully occur, whether it was initiated by default or as a result of the user's explicit request.

## 2.3 The Role of Roles

SELinux also provides a form of *role-based access control* (RBAC). The RBAC feature of SELinux is built upon type enforcement; access control in SELinux is primarily via type enforcement. Roles limit the types to which a process may transition based on the role identifier in the process' security context. In this manner, a policy writer can create a role that is allowed to transition into a set of domain types (assuming the type enforcement rules allow the transition), thereby defining the limits of the role. Take our password program example in Figure 2-5. Although according to the type enforcement rules, the password program can be executed by the `user_t` domain type to enter the new `passwd_t` domain, Joe's role must also be allowed to be associated with the new domain type for the transition to occur. To illustrate, we extend the password program example in Figure 2-6.

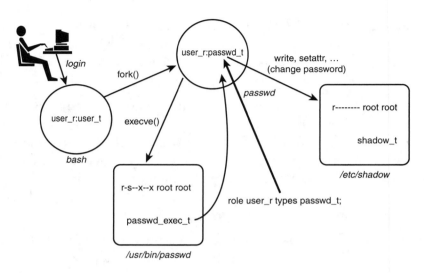

**FIGURE 2-6**
Roles in domain transitions

We have added the role portion (user_r) of the security contexts for the processes depicted. We also added a new rule, specifically the *role statement:*

```
role user_r type passwd_t;
```

The role statement declares role identifiers and associates types with the declared role. The previous statement declares the role user_r (if it has not already been declared in the policy) and associates the type passwd_t with the role. What this association means is that the passwd_t type is allowed to coexist in a security context with the role user_r. Without this role statement, the new context joe:user_r:passwd_t could not be created, and the execve() system call would fail, even though the TE policy allows Joe's type (user_t) all the necessary access.

A policy writer can define roles that are further constrained and then associate these roles to specific users. For example, imagine that in our policy we also create a role called restricted_user_r, identical to user_r in all regards except that it is not associated with the passwd_t type. Thus, if Joe's role is restricted_user_r instead of user_r, Joe would not be authorized to run the password program even though the TE rules would allow his domain type the access.

Chapter 6, "Roles and Users," discusses in detail the purposes of roles in SELinux and in particular how they are created and associated with users.

## 2.4 Multilevel Security in SELinux

Type enforcement is far and away the most important *mandatory access control* (MAC) mechanism that SELinux introduces. However, in some situations, primarily for a subset of classified government applications, traditional *multilevel security* (MLS) MAC coupled with type enforcement is valuable. In recognition of these situations, SELinux has always had some form of MLS capability included. The MLS features are optional and generally the less important of the two MAC mechanisms in SELinux. For the vast majority of security applications, including many if not most classified data applications, type enforcement is the best-suited mechanism for enhanced security. Nonetheless, the addition of MLS enhances security for some applications.

The basic concept of MLS was introduced in Chapter 1, "Background;" actual implementations of MLS are more involved. The *security level* used by MLS systems is a combination of a hierarchical *sensitivity* and a set (including the null set) of non-hierarchical *categories*. These sensitivities and categories are used to reflect real information confidentiality or user clearances. In most SELinux policies, the sensitivities (s0, s1, ...) and categories (c0, c1, ...) are given generic names, leaving it to user-space programs and libraries to assign user-meaningful names. (For example, s0 might be associated with UNCLASSIFIED and s1 with SECRET.)

To support MLS, the security context is extended to include security levels as such these:

```
user:role:type:sensitivity[:category,...][-sensitivity[:category,...]]
```

Notice that the MLS security context must have at least one security level (which is composed of a single sensitivity and zero or more categories), but can include two security levels. These two security levels are called *low* (or *current* for processes) and *high* (or *clearance* for processes), respectively. If the high security level is missing, it is considered to be the same value as the low (the most common situation). In practice, the low and high security levels are usually the same for most objects and processes. A range of levels is typically used for processes that are considered *trusted subjects* (that is, a process trusted with the ability to downgrade information) or multilevel objects such as directories that might contain objects of differing security levels. For purposes of this overview, assume that all processes and objects have a single security level.

The MLS rules for accessing objects are much the same as discussed in Chapter 1, except that security levels are not hierarchical but rather governed by a *dominance relationship.* Unlike equality where a level is either higher than, equal to, or lower than another level, in a dominance relationship, there is a fourth state called *incomparable* (also known as *noncomparable;* see the definition of *incomp* in the following list). What causes security levels to be related via dominance rather than equality are the categories, which have no hierarchical relationship to one another. As a result, the four dominance operators that can relate two MLS security levels are as follows:

*dom:*  (*dominates*) SL1 *dom* SL2 if the sensitivity of SL1 is *higher or equal to* the sensitivity of SL2, *and* the categories of SL1 are a *superset* of the categories of SL2.

*domby:*  (*dominated by*) SL1 *domby* SL2 if the sensitivity of SL1 is *lower than or equal to* the sensitivity of SL2, *and* the categories of SL1 are a *subset* of the categories of SL2.

*eq:*  (*equals*) SL1 *eq* SL2 if the sensitivity of SL1 and SL2 are *equal, and* the categories of SL1 and SL2 are the *same set.*

*incomp:*  (*incomparable* or *noncomparable*) SL1 *incomp* SL2 if the categories of SL1 and SL2 cannot be compared (that is, neither is a subset of the other).

Given the domain relationship, a variation of the Bell-La Padula model is implemented in SELinux where a process can "read" an object if its current security level *dominates* the security level of the object, and "write" an object if its current security level *is dominated by* the security level of the object (and therefore read and write the object only if the two security levels are *equal*).

The MLS constraints in SELinux are in addition to the TE rules. If MLS is enabled, both checks must pass (in addition to standard Linux access control) for access to be granted. Chapter 8, "Multilevel Security," discusses the SELinux optional MLS features.

## 2.5 SELinux Features Familiarization

At this time, it is worthwhile to play with an SELinux system a little. For our examples, we use a *Fedora Core 4* (FC4) distribution with the strict policy. Most of these examples should also work on *Red Hat Enterprise Linux version 4* (RHEL4) or *Fedora Core 5* (FC5). You might also be able to work with other distributions, although there may be differences. Appendix A, "Obtaining SELinux Sample

Policies," describes how to obtain the policy files and other materials we use as examples throughout this book and how to configure your system accordingly.

---

### Running in Permissive Mode

SELinux can run in permissive mode, where the access checks occur; but instead of denying unallowed access, it simply audits them. This mode is useful when first learning about SELinux, and you may want to start exploring the system in this mode. Of course, permissive mode should not be used in operational systems if you want the enhanced access security of SELinux. Note that some utilities are found in `/usr/sbin`, which is not normally in a regular user's path.

The simplest way to check the current mode of SELinux is to run the `getenforce` command. To set the system in permissive mode, run the command `setenforce 0`. (You must be logged in as `root` in the `sysadm_t` domain to change the system to permissive mode.) To return it to enforcing mode, run the command `setenforce 1`. (Because you are in permissive mode, you just need to be logged in as root to change the system to enforcing mode.)

We have already mentioned the `-Z` option added to some system commands. Commands such as `ls` and `ps` display the security contexts of files and processes. As an exercise, run the commands `ps xZ` and `ls -Z /bin` and examine the various security contexts for running processes and executable files.

---

## 2.5.1 Revisiting the Passwd Example

Throughout this chapter, we used the example of the shadow password file and the password program. If you examine the security context of these two files, their types should be `shadow_t` and `passwd_exec_t`, respectively. As discussed previously, `passwd_exec_t` is the entrypoint type for the `passwd_t` domain. To witness how the process of domain transitions work, walk through the following set of commands. You need two terminal windows or virtual consoles to do this walkthrough.

In the first window, run the `passwd` command:

---

```
$ passwd
Changing password for user joe.
Changing password for joe
(current) UNIX password:
```

This starts the password program and prompts for the user's current password. Do not enter the password, but instead switch to the second terminal. In the second terminal, su to root and then run the ps command:

```
$ su
Password:
Your default context is root:sysadm_r:sysadm_t.

Do you want to choose a different one? [n]
# ps axZ|grep passwd
user_u:user_r:passwd_t              4299 pts/1     S+     0:00 passwd
```

As you can see, the type of the running password program is passwd_t, as we would expect given the rules described in the examples earlier in this chapter.

> NOTE   In a strict policy such as the one we use for our examples, a normal user (that is, a user running a shell in the user_t domain) does not have permission to read many /proc/pid entries, and as such the passwd process would not show up in the ps axZ output. That is why you need to su to root first.

## 2.5.2 Perusing the Policy File

In FC4 systems, the binary file containing the kernel policy is located in the well-known directory /etc/selinux/. The configuration file (config) in that directory indicates the policy to be used and loaded on boot. You can also configure the system to boot in permissive mode in this file. For our exercises, we are using FC4's strict policy, which (if installed according to Appendix A) should be here:

    /etc/selinux/strict/policy/policy.[ver]

The version of the policy reflects the version of the SELinux policy compiler (checkpolicy). In our example, the version is 19. Configuring an SELinux system and creating a kernel policy file from policy sources are discussed in greater detail in Part III, "Creating and Writing SELinux Security Policies." For now, we want to look around inside the policy to see what is there.

A useful tool for examining the contents of a policy is the policy analysis tool *apol* created by Tresys Technology and distributed in a package of SELinux tools called SeTools (see Appendix D, "SELinux Commands and Utilities"). The SeTools package is included on most SELinux distributions. Run the command apol to determine whether the tool is present on your system. If not, Appendix D provides information on how to obtain the SeTools package.

The `apol` (for "analyze policy") tool is a sophisticated SELinux policy analysis tool that we use throughout the book to examine SELinux policies. For now, we want to use some of its basic features to examine aspects of the policy file. Run `apol` and open the strict policy file. Under the menu **Query > Policy Summary**, you can view a summary of the policy statistics (see Figure 2-7).

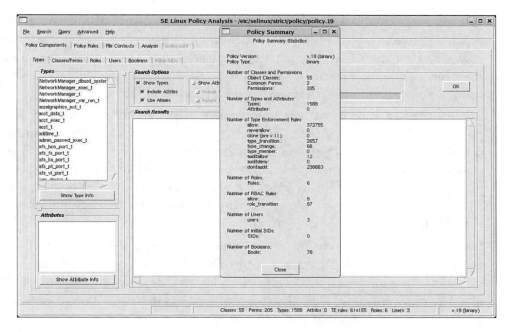

**FIGURE 2-7**
Policy summary using apol

`Apol` has a series of major tabs (Policy Components, Policy Rules, Analysis, and so on) that enable you to search and analyze a policy in various ways. Take some time to explore the Policy Components and Policy Rules tabs and become familiar with both portions of the policy we discussed in this chapter and the `apol` tool itself. You will find it useful throughout Part II, "SELinux Policy Language," to use `apol` to examine your policy and follow along with the examples.

## 2.6 Summary

- SELinux access control is based on a security context associated with all system resources including processes. The security context contains three elements: user, role, and type identifiers. The type identifier is the primary basis for access control.

  In SELinux, type enforcement is the primary access control feature. Access is granted between subjects (that is, processes) and objects by specifying `allow` rules that have the subject's type (also called a domain type) as the source and the object's type as the target. Access is granted for specified object classes using a fine-grained set of permissions defined for each object class.

  One of the key benefits of type enforcement is the ability to control which programs may run with a given domain type, thereby allowing access control down to individual programs (rather than the less-secure level of a user). The capability for a program to enter into a domain (that is, run with a given process type) is called domain transition and is tightly controlled by SELinux `allow` rules. SELinux also allows domain transitions to occur automatically through the `type_transition` rule.

- SELinux does not directly use the role identifiers in a security context for access control. Instead, all access is controlled based on types. Roles are used to associate the allowed domain types into which a process running on behalf of a user may transition. This allows sets of type enforcement allowed capabilities to be grouped together and authorized for a user as a role.

- SELinux provides an optional MLS access control mechanism that provides further access restrictions for a certain class of data sensitivity applications. The MLS features are built upon the TE mechanism. MLS also extends the security context to include a current (or low) security level and an optional high (or clearance) security level.

## Exercises

1. What is a "domain" and how is it related to or different from a type?

2. What are the access control attributes used by SELinux type enforcement security to control access? What portion of the attribute is used by type enforcement for access control?

3. Let's assume that we have a file named `datafile` with the following security attributes:

   `-r-xr-xr-x root root system_u:object_r:data_t datafile`

   Let's also assume that your shell process type is `user_t` and that type has all access permissions for file objects of type `data_t`. Can you read and/or write this file? Why or why not?

4. For SELinux to allow a domain transition, a number of access permissions must be allowed among three types. What are the access permissions required and between what types? What do the types represent?

5. In answering Question 4, was a `type_transition` rule required? Why or why not?

6. In SELinux, a role is not used as a basis for access control, but it can prevent a domain transition from succeeding. How and why?

Extra credit: Examine the SELinux configuration file `/etc/selinux/config`. What are the possible states in which SELinux can run and what do each mean? How do the settings in this file differ from using the `setenforce` command?

# Chapter 3

# Architecture

## In this chapter

This chapter provides an overview of the SELinux design and its policy language. The SELinux architecture reflects its origins in secure microkernel research. It integrates itself into the kernel using the *Linux Security Module* (LSM) framework. This architecture is also extensible into user-space servers. The SELinux policy language is flexible, allowing an organization to implement a variety of security goals via mandatory access controls.

## 3.1 The Kernel Architecture

SELinux provides enhanced access control over all kernel resources. In its current form, SELinux is incorporated into the kernel via the LSM framework.

### 3.1.1 LSM Framework

The idea behind the LSM framework is to allow security modules to plug into the kernel that can further restrict the default Linux identity-based *discretionary access control* (DAC) security. LSM provides a set of *hooks* in the kernel system call logic. These hooks are usually placed *after* the standard Linux access checks but before the actual resource is accessed by the kernel on behalf of the caller. Figure 3-1 illustrates the basic LSM framework.

SELinux is loaded into the kernel as an LSM module and is consulted for additional access validation before the access attempt is allowed.

One of the ramifications of the LSM framework is that SELinux is consulted only if standard Linux access checks succeed. In practice, this has no negative affect on the access control policy because SELinux access control can be more restrictive than standard Linux DAC and not override the DAC decision. However, the LSM framework can affect the audit data collected by SELinux. For example, if you want to use the SELinux audit data to observe all access denials, be aware that in most cases SELinux will not be consulted, and therefore cannot audit, if the denial is a result of standard Linux security.

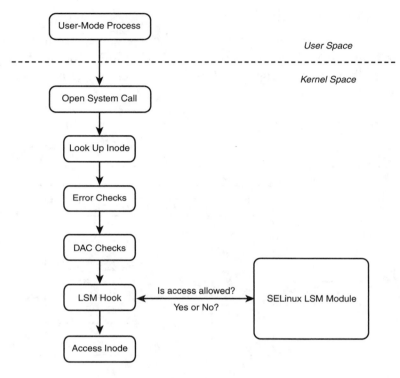

**FIGURE 3-1**
LSM hook architecture[1]

The LSM framework is comprehensive, and the hooks are scattered throughout the kernel. Each LSM hook translates into one or more access permissions for one or more object classes. Understanding object access permissions in SELinux is in large part related to understanding the LSM hooks. Chapter 4, "Object Classes and Permissions," discusses object classes and permissions in detail.

---

1  C. Wright, C. Cowan, S. Smalley, J. Morris, and G. Kroah-Hartman. "Linux Security Modules: General Security Support for the Linux Kernel," in proceedings of the 11th USENIX Security Symposium, August 2002, available at http://lsm.immunix.org/lsm_doc.html.

## 3.1.2 SELinux LSM Module

The SELinux kernel architecture reflects the Flask architecture, which was designed for a microkernel environment. The Flask architecture has three primary components, as illustrated in Figure 3-2: security server, object managers, and the access vector cache.

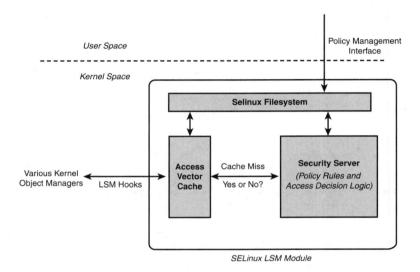

FIGURE 3-2
SELinux LSM module architecture

The Flask design makes a strong distinction between security policy decision making and enforcement functions. Policy decision making is the job of the *security server*. The name security server reflects SELinux's micorkenel roots, where the policy decision role was encapsulated in a userspace server. In Linux, the security server for kernel objects is located in the SELinux LSM module. The policy used for the security server is embodied in a set of rules that is loaded via the policy management interface. These rules can differ from system to system, making SELinux highly adaptable to various organizational security goals. The architecture is designed such that the security server could be completely replaced with logic that implements an entirely new access control policy without changing the rest of the architecture. In practice, new security servers are not needed because type enforcement provides sufficient flexibility for almost any access control security policy.

*Object managers* are responsible for enforcing the policy decisions of the security server for the set of resources they manage. For the kernel, you can think of object managers as kernel subsystems that create and manage kernel-level objects. Examples of kernel object managers include the filesystem, process management, and System V *interprocess communication* (IPC). In the LSM architecture, the object managers are represented by the LSM hooks; these hooks are scattered throughout the kernel subsystems and call the SELinux LSM module for access decisions. The LSM hooks then enforce those decisions by allowing or denying access to the kernel resource.

The third component of the SELinux architecture is the *access vector cache* (AVC). The AVC caches decisions made by the security server for subsequent access checks and thus provides significant performance improvements for access validation. The AVC also provides the SELinux interfaces for the LSM hooks and hence with the kernel object managers.

The AVC is invalidated when a policy is loaded, thereby keeping the cache coherent. However, SELinux does not fully implement access revocation on policy change. This is no worse than standard Linux, which does not access revocation at all. In standard Linux, if you have a file descriptor, you can use it regardless of the change in file access mode. In SELinux, for objects such as files where access is validated on all attempts to use (for example, every read system call is checked against the policy and not just open calls), access revocation works fine. Just having a file descriptor does not mean access to the file will be granted. For some resources, however, such as memory mapped-files and connection-oriented sockets, access is validated only when the resource is initially accessed and not on subsequent use. In these cases, existing access is not revoked. We expect that there will be further research to improve access revocation in SELinux.

## 3.2 Userspace Object Managers

One of the powerful features of the SELinux architecture is that it can be applied to userspace resources and to kernel resources. Indeed, its origins were in microkernel research where most resource management was performed by userspace servers. Examples of userspace servers in Linux that can be enhanced to enforce access control over their resources include the X server and database services. Each of these servers provides abstract resources (windows, tables, and so on) over which mandatory security could be provided. This section examines two ways that the SELinux architecture supports userspace servers.

## 3.2.1 Kernel Support for Userspace Object Managers

A simple way SELinux supports userspace objects is directly via the kernel security server, as depicted in Figure 3-3.

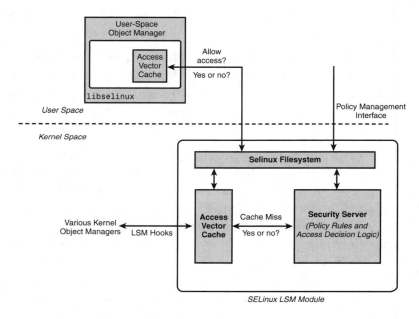

**FIGURE 3-3**
Userspace object managers using kernel security server

In this method, the userspace object manager behaves much like the kernel object managers. The kernel security server contains the entire security policy, and the userspace object manager must query the kernel for access control decisions. The primary difference is that userspace object managers cannot use the kernel AVC. Each server must have its own, separate AVC that stores the past decisions it has requested from the kernel. The AVC functionality for userspace servers is contained in the library `libselinux`.

Another difference is that userspace object managers do not have LSM hooks, which are a kernel-space concept. Instead, the object manager has internal interfaces with its AVC inside `libselinux`. The AVC handles cache misses and queries the kernel on behalf of the object manager.

Although straightforward, this method for supporting userspace object managers has a number of weaknesses. First, to use type enforcement, object managers must define object classes that represent their resources. For example, a database server might define object classes that include database, table, schema, entry, and so on. For kernel resources, object classes are fixed and correspond to hard-coded class off-sets defined in SELinux LSM module header files. The relationship of class defini-tions in the policy and with those in the kernel code results in an unfortunate dependency between the userspace policy and the code. Specifically, two userspace servers must be careful not to both use the same object class offset in the kernel. The kernel provides no way to manage this possible conflict.

The second weakness with this approach is that kernel security server is manag-ing policy for object classes for object managers that are not in the kernel. This increases storage cost within the kernel for abstraction not related to the kernel and can negatively impact the cost of kernel policy validation for AVC misses.

## 3.2.2 Policy Server Architecture

To address the weaknesses of using the kernel security server for userspace object managers and to enhance the security capabilities of SELinux, an effort is ongoing to build userspace support for userspace object managers. This project has two pri-mary goals and a number of secondary goals. The primary goals are as follows:

- Provide better support for user-space object managers by providing a *user-space security server* that makes access decisions for the user portion of the policy

- Provide fine-grained access control for the policy itself by building a *policy management server* that is a userspace object manager whose object classes rep-resent portions of the policy

Collectively, these two servers are referred to as the *policy server.* Figure 3-4 depicts the architecture of the policy server.

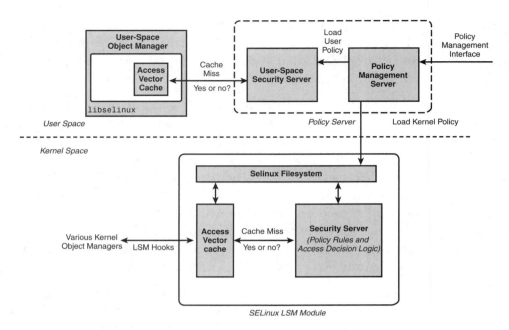

FIGURE 3-4
SELinux policy server architecture

In the policy server architecture, all manipulation and management of the over-all *system policy* is controlled through the *policy management server* (PMS). The PMS is itself a userspace object manager in that it creates object classes representing policy resources and enforces a fine-grained access control policy over those resources. This feature alone provides significant security enhancement for SELinux. Previously, access control to the policy was an all-or-nothing proposition; you either could write the policy file or not. With the PMS, you can now allow access to portions of the policy and limit access to others. For example, the SELinux policy can allow user management tools to add users and make role assignments, but not change type enforcement `allow` rules. Better yet, you can authorize a database server to change *type enforcement* (TE) rules relating to its object classes and types, but not those of the kernel. Internally, the PMS is designed to use another recent new feature of SELinux, *loadable policy modules,* which we describe later in this chapter.

The second major function of the PMS is to split the system policy into kernel and user portions and load them respectively into the kernel security server and *userspace security server* (USSS). In this way, the kernel is not made aware of rules and object classes of concern only to userspace object managers. Userspace object managers query the USSS and not the kernel. AVCs in various userspace object managers register with the USSS (and not the kernel) for policy update and cache coherency functions.

The policy server architecture has a number of strengths in addition to the removal of the kernel's responsibility for userspace resources and the fine-grained access for policy management. Because the PMS is a running server, we can extend its interface to allow remote network access for distributed policy management. The PMS and USSS are designed to allow for runtime registration of object classes, breaking the code dependency for userspace object managers that exists in the kernel. The difference between the two approaches is masked by `libselinux` providing backward compatibility with existing work. Finally, the PMS and USSS are designed as separate services to allow for one or both to be used without the other. For example, in a system where fine-grained policy access control is unnecessary, the USSS could be used alone to support other userspace object servers.

At the time of this writing, the policy server work is under development and not fully integrated into any distributions. You can check the status of this work at http://sepolicy-server.sourceforge.net.

## 3.3 SELinux Policy Language

Chapter 2, " Concepts," presented an overview of the SELinux security concepts and introduced some of the policy language concepts. In the previous section, you saw how the policy is used in the SELinux architecture. For kernel resources, the policy is loaded into the SELinux LSM module security server and used to make access control decisions. One strength of SELinux is that its policy rules are not static. Rather, someone (or many ones) must write the policy and ensure that it reflects the desired security goals. Fundamentally, this book is all about how to write SELinux policies (and how to make sure they are good policies). Using and applying SELinux is all about writing and understanding policies.

In Part II of this book, we take you through each major portion of the policy and discuss the policy language syntax and semantics in detail. In this section, we provide an overview of how a policy is constructed and compiled and show you how to build a policy from the strict policy we use as an example throughout this book.

### 3.3.1 The Native SELinux Policy Language Compiler

The primary way to construct a policy file for the kernel is to compile it from a *source policy file* using the `checkpolicy` program. This source file, which itself is constructed in several steps, is typically named `policy.conf`. Checkpolicy checks the source policy file for syntax and semantic correctness and writes the results in a form (called a *binary policy file*) that is readable by the kernel policy loader (`load_policy`). The language syntax supported by `checkpolicy` is the native, primitive language supported by SELinux. You can think of the `checkpolicy` language as analogous to assembly language. Higher-level languages and other more abstract ways to create policies are being developed, and some of these are discussed later in this book. For now, we focus on the native policy language and construction of policy for enforcement by the kernel.

Figure 3-5 illustrates the primary sections of a policy source file expected by `checkpolicy`.

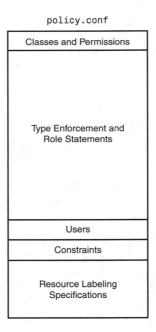

FIGURE 3-5
Organization of policy source file (policy.conf)

The first section of a policy source file defines the object classes to the security server. This section also defines the permissions for each object class. For the kernel, these classes are directly related to kernel source files. In general, as an SELinux policy writer you would never change or modify the object class and permission definitions. We discuss the specific object classes and their associated permissions in Chapter 4.

The next section contains the type enforcement statements, which is by far the largest portion of an SELinux policy. This is the section that policy writers spend most of their time writing. It contains all the type declarations and all the TE rules (including all `allow`, `type_transition`, and other TE rules). We discuss types and the core TE rules in detail in Chapter 5, "Type Enforcement." The TE section often contains thousands of type declarations and tens of thousands of TE rules. This section also contains rules and declarations for roles and users in the policy. Roles and users, which are supporting concepts to type enforcement, are discussed further in Chapter 6, "Roles and Users." Some recent enhancements to the TE policy section, specifically conditional policies, are discussed in Chapter 9. "Conditional Policies."

The next section of a policy source file contains the constraints. Constraints provide a means of further limiting the TE policy beyond what the TE rules permit. The *multilevel security* (MLS) policy, for example, is implemented as a set of constraints. We discuss constraints in Chapter 7, "Constraints," and MLS in Chapter 8, "Multilevel Security."

The last section of a policy file contains labeling specifications. All objects must be labeled with a security context for SELinux to enforce access control. This section tells SELinux how to treat filesystems for the purpose of labeling and contains the rules for labeling transient objects that are created at runtime. A separate related mechanism, called a *file contexts file,* is used to initialize the security context labeling of files, directories, and other objects on permanent filesystems. These and other topics relating to object labeling are discussed in Chapter 10, "Object Labeling."

> ### Examining the policy.conf File
>
> As with the binary policy file created by `checkpolicy` (`policy.[ver]`), you can use the Tresys `apol` tool to view, search, and analyze the contents of the `policy.conf` file. The `policy.conf` file is more abstract than the binary file format, which often makes it an easier target for policy analysis and debugging. Also, the `policy.conf` file is closest in form to the original source modules and therefore the best form for tracking back bugs to the original source file. In any case, both are equivalent and should reflect the same security policy.

## 3.3.2 Source Policy Modules in a Monolithic Policy

A common type of SELinux policy today is a *monolithic* policy. This is a policy that is constructed as a single binary policy file by `checkpolicy` that is directly loaded into the kernel. Because SELinux policies are usually quite large and complex, like software, they are constructed in terms of smaller units called modules. There are a couple of different means to make a policy modular. The original and still widely used method, called *source modules,* supports the development of a monolithic policy. Source modules are combined as text files through a combination of shell scripts, `m4` macros, and `Makefiles` that together create a crude higher-level language. The policy modules are essentially concatenated together into a single large source file (that is, `policy.conf`) that is then compiled by `checkpolicy` into a binary file readable by the kernel.

## 3.3.3 Loadable Policy Modules

A new method for creating a modular policy is called *loadable modules,* which uses recent extensions to `checkpolicy` and a module compiler (`checkmodule`) to construct loadable policy modules compiled independently of each other. Loadable modules are also the basis for the policy server discussed earlier in this chapter. In the loadable module case, there is no longer a monolithic binary policy constructed; instead, a (expectedly smaller) core subset of the policy is constructed called the *base module.* You create the base module much like you create the monolithic policy. With loadable modules, however, you can streamline the base module, including only rules relating to the core operating system. The rest of the policy is created as separate loadable modules. You can add all other policy rules in a modular fashion when you install their associated software package.

Loadable modules introduce policy syntax changes that are designed to ease the division of the policy into separate, individually distributable policy modules. These changes differ for base and nonbase modules. The base module uses the same policy language as monolithic policies with minor additions. Nonbase (that is, loadable) modules use a subset of the standard policy language with several additional language features. The subset of the policy language includes most of the type enforcement, role, and user statements. The additional language features are used to manage dependencies between modules. We discuss the languages changes resulting form loadable modules in detail using sidebars throughout Part II.

*Fedora Core 5* (FC5) has adopted the loadable module infrastructure for future versions. In this book, we primarily discuss the monolithic policy approach and language, but we do use sidebars to discuss the newer loadable modules features.

### 3.3.4 Building and Installing Monolithic Policies

As you read through the remainder of this book, you will likely want to experiment with SELinux policy writing. You will need to compile your modifications into a complete policy file and experiment with your modifications by loading the new policy into the kernel and experiencing the resulting changes in the kernel's access control enforcement. Before you can complete these actions, we must introduce the basic means of building and installing kernel security policies.

> TIP Remember that if you install your policy, the kernel will immediately begin to enforce access based on the rules in the policy. While you are learning about SELinux and experimenting with the language, you may end up causing programs to crash due to lack of access. We suggest you experiment with policy writing with the system in permissive mode (`setenforce 0`) until you become more familiar with the policy language and its ramifications. Of course, you should always run production systems in enforcing mode (`setenforce 1`).

The example policy build method (see Chapter 11, "Original Example Policy") is a typical way that a policy is constructed. Figure 3-6 shows this type of construction.

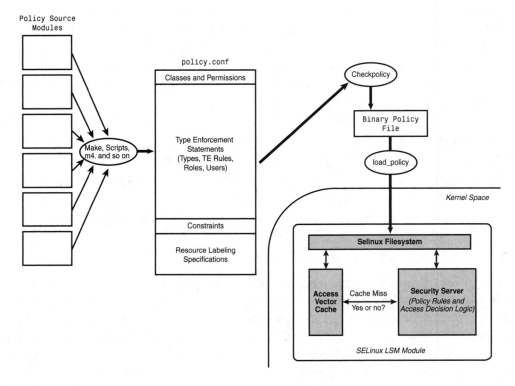

**FIGURE 3-6**
Build and load process for SELinux policy using source modules

Starting from the left side of this figure, you have the source files for the policy broken down into many tens of individual source modules. Later in the book, we talk about various conventions for organizing these modules in the example policy. For now, just understand that these files are combined through a combination of scripts and macro processors into the single `policy.conf` file, which is a complete and syntactically correct statement of a SELinux source policy. You then compile the source policy using `checkpolicy` into a binary policy file (assuming no errors!) appropriate for the kernel. The `load_policy` program is then used to load the binary policy file into the kernel, which then enforces access control based on the policy rules.

At this point in this book, you might find this process overwhelming and confusing, especially in light of our discussion of means to construct a policy other than source modules to build policy. Don't panic; we just want you to get a sense of the overall process. Policy source directories usually have a `Makefile` that automates this process for you. In the policy we use in Part II, which if installed correctly should be in `/etc/selinux/strict/src/policy/`, the interesting make targets are as follows:

*policy*      Make `policy.conf` and `policy.[ver]` locally to test the compilation and check for error.

*install*     Do everything that `make policy` does plus install the binary policy file such that it will be loaded into the kernel at boot time and the policy configuration files.

*load*        Do everything that `make policy` does plus immediately load the binary policy file into the kernel as the active access control policy and install the `file_contexts` file.

So, for example, `make policy` will perform all the steps in Figure 3-6 except the last step (install the binary policy and load it into the kernel).

Feel free to experiment with the various `make` targets in our example policy; just be careful about doing a `make install` or `make load` because this will change the access control enforcement on your system.

## 3.4 Summary

- SELinux is implemented as an LSM module in the kernel. SELinux uses LSM hooks throughout the kernel to control access to kernel resources. Access decisions are made by the SELinux security server, which is part of the SELinux LSM module. The security policy enforced by the security server is loaded into the kernel via a privileged userspace interface. The AVC provides performance improvement for access validation.

  The SELinux framework also supports userspace object managers through the `libselinux` library. In its basic form, the kernel security server directly provides access validation, whereas the library contains a per-process AVC. This approach requires the kernel to hold the policy for all userspace managers and to be aware of all userspace object classes.

- The emerging policy server architecture enhances support for userspace object managers by providing a userspace security server that will enforce all portions of the policy relating to userspace objects, thereby relieving the kernel of its need to know of userspace object classes and policy rules. The policy server will also provide fine-grained access control to the policy itself, allowing greater distribution of policy management authority.

- SELinux policies tend to be large and complex, necessitating the need for them to be constructed as a collection of modules. A common method is to use source modules, where all modules are built as part of a single, monolithic module. This is the method used in Red Hat Enterprise Linux 4 and Fedora Core 4, and the one we assume in Part II.

- A second modularity approach provides for loadable modules, where policy pieces can be constructed largely independent of other modules, and combined at install time on a running system. In the case of loadable modules, a base module is created in a manner similar to a monolithic policy, but with the expectation that the base module can be smaller and focused on the core operating system. Additional software packages will have their portion of the policy installed as separate loadable modules. This is the method being adopted by FC5.

  `Checkpolicy` is the policy compiler that takes a complete policy source file (`policy.conf`) and validates the syntax and semantics of the file and creates a binary policy file. In the case of loadable modules, `checkpolicy` compiles the base policy module, and the program `checkmodule` compiles the individual loadable modules.

## Exercises

1.  In the LSM framework, which check usually occurs first, the standard Linux access checks or the SELinux checks? Why?

2.  In the kernel, how do SELinux object managers and LSM hooks relate?

3.  When a new policy is loaded into the kernel, the access vector cache (AVC) is invalidated. Why do you think that is necessary?

4.  Although SELinux does not fully implement access revocation on policy change, for objects such as regular files it does. Standard Linux access con-

trol does not implement access revocation for regular files. Explain the reasons for this difference.

5. Why do you think userspace object managers cannot use the kernel access validation cache like they do the kernel security server?

6. In the policy server architecture, would it ever make sense to have a userspace object manager without the policy management server? Why or why not?

Extra credit: Go to the example policy source directory and `make policy` to create the `policy.conf` (source) and `policy.[ver]` (binary) policy files. Use `apol` to examine the number of `allow` rules in each file and notice the large difference. Any ideas what might be the cause of that difference?

# Part II

# SELinux Policy Language

# Chapter 4

# Object Classes and Permissions

**In this chapter**

This chapter covers object classes and permissions defined in SELinux. We discuss the policy language statements that define object classes and permissions the kernel supports and provide an overview of the kernel object classes standard in a SELinux system. Appendix C, "Object Classes and Permissions," includes a detailed listing of each standard SELinux object class and its associated permissions.

## 4.1 Purpose of Object Classes in SELinux

Object classes and their associated permissions are the basis for access control in SELinux. Object classes represent categories of resources such as files and sockets, and permissions represent accesses to those resources such as reading or sending. Understanding object classes and permissions is a difficult aspect of SELinux because it requires both SELinux and Linux knowledge.

An object class represents all resources of a certain kind (for example, files or sockets). An instance of an object class (for example, a specific file or socket) is simply called an object. Often the terms *object class* and *object* are used interchangeably, but it is important to understand the difference. Object class refers to the entire category of resources (files); object refers to a specific instance of the object class (/etc/passwd).

As discussed in Chapter 2, "Concepts," access to objects is expressed in the policy through permissions to object classes that have a specified type(s). To illustrate, let's consider an `allow` rule from Chapter 2:

```
allow user_t bin_t : file {read execute getattr};
```

In this rule, processes with the type `user_t` (that is, the source or subject) are allowed to read, execute, and get attributes for all objects of class `file` that have the target type (`bin_t`) in their security context. The object class `file` specifies the category of resource, and `bin_t` specifies which instances of that category of resources to which this rule applies (that is, those file objects that have the type `bin_t`). It does not apply to objects that have `bin_t` type that are not of `file` class nor to file objects that do not have `bin_t` as their type.

The permissions in this rule—`read`, `execute`, and `getattr`—define the access allowed to those objects by subjects (implicitly process objects) that have the type `user_t`. Each of these permissions, which must be valid for the file object class, represent some form of access to the objects. (For example, the `read` permission is required to use the `open(2)` system call to open a file for reading, use the `read(2)` system call on an opened file, and so on.) The set of permissions defined for an object class (also called an *access vector*) represents all the possible access that can be allowed to the resources represented by that object class.

The set of object classes available depends on the version of SELinux and its Linux kernel. Over time, new and different object classes have evolved to address new and changed features of the kernel. For example, newer versions of the Linux kernel have introduced a new Netlink-specific socket for controlling the audit framework.[1] For those kernels that support the Netlink socket, there is an SELinux object class with appropriate permissions defined.

## 4.2 Defining Object Classes in SELinux Policy

A policy must include declarations for all object classes and permissions supported by the SELinux kernel and other object managers. In general, we, as policy writers, are not concerned with creating new objects classes; however, we need to understand the object classes that are defined to write effective SELinux policies. It is useful to understand the object class and permission declaration syntax because it allows us to understand the supported object classes and permissions in the policy version we are using.

---

### Adding New Object Classes and Permissions

Adding new object classes and changing the permissions on existing object classes are complex tasks that should normally be undertaken only when changing the actual system code itself. Unlike other aspects of the SELinux policy language, object classes and permissions are closely tied to the implementation details of Linux, particularly the kernel. In fact, object classes and permissions are designed to represent as accurately as possible the resources implemented by the system. For this reason, it makes sense to change the object classes or permissions that match a corresponding change in the system.

---

1 Information about and source code for the Linux audit framework and tools is available at http://people.redhat.com/sgrubb/audit/.

An example of the type of change that would warrant a change in the object classes and permissions is the addition of a new form of *interprocess communication* (IPC) to the kernel. In this case, an entirely new category of resource is being added, likely with new or expanded system calls, and a new object class would likely be required to accurately represent the semantics of this resource.

Adding or changing object classes or permissions requires changes both to the policy and to the system code that will enforce access control based on the new object classes or permissions. Simply adding an object class or permission to the policy without changing the code will likely have no effect other than wasting kernel memory.

Basically, for the target audience of this book (SELinux policy writers and administrators), you should never change the object class and permission definitions.

---

## 4.2.1 Declaring Object Classes

Object classes are declared using the *class declaration statement.* The class declaration statement simply declares an object class name and nothing else. For example, we declare an object class for directories (named `dir`) with the following statement:

```
class dir
```

The class declaration statement consists of the keyword `class` followed by the class name. Notice that the class declaration statement does not end in a semicolon like many other policy statements. You can see the full syntax for the class statement in the sidebar on page 63.

Object class names have a separate namespace. It is possible, but generally poor policy writing practice, to have object classes, permissions, types, and so on all have the same name.

---

### Class Declaration Statement Syntax

The class declaration statement allows you to declare object class names. The full syntax of the class declaration statement is as follows:

class *class_name*

`class_name`   An identifier for the object class. The identifier can be any length and can contain ASCII letters or numbers.

Class declarations are valid only in monolithic policies and base loadable modules. They are not valid in conditional statements and non-base loadable modules.

---

## 4.2.2 Declaring and Associating Object Class Permissions

There are two methods of declaring permissions. The first is called *common permissions* and allows us to create permissions that we associate with an object class as a group. Common permissions are useful when similar object classes (for example, files and symbolic links) share a set of access permissions. The second method is called *class-specific permissions* and allows us to declare permissions specific to that object class alone. As you will see, some object classes have only class-specific permissions, some have only common permissions, and some have both.

### 4.2.2.1 Common Permissions

The *common permission statement* allows the creation of sets of permissions that we associate as a group with two or more object classes. The full syntax of the common permission statement is shown in the sidebar on page 64. For example, the UNIX philosophy of "everything is a file" means that many file-related object classes have a common set of permissions. A common permission statement to declare these file-related permissions in SELinux is as follows:

---

```
common file
{
     ioctl
     read
     write
     create
     getattr
     setattr
     lock
```

```
    relabelfrom
    relabelto
    append
    unlink
    link
    rename
    execute
    swapon
    quotaon
    mounton
}
```

This statement declares a common permission set called `file` and defines it as a set of permissions called `ioctl`, `read`, `write`, `create`, and so on. A common permission statement by itself has no effect; it is only when we associate a set of common permissions with an object class that they are useful.

As with object classes, common permission names are declared in their own namespace. This can lead to some confusion if we are not careful. For example, as illustrated in the preceding examples, we have both an object class and a common permission named `file`. Although the names are the same, they are in fact two distinct and very different components of the policy.

---

### Common Permission Statement Syntax

The common permission statement allows you to declare a common permission name that has a set of permissions that can be associated with an object class as a group. Common permissions can be associated with multiple object classes. The full syntax for the common permission statement is as follows:

`common common_name { perm_set }`

`common_name`   An identifier for the common permissions. The identifier can be any length and can contain ASCII letters, numbers, a dash (-), or a period ( . ).

`perm_set`   One or more permission identifiers in a space-separated list. The identifiers can be any length and contain ASCII letters, numbers, a dash (-), or a period ( . ).

A common permission set is associated with an object class using the access vector statement.

Common permission statements are valid only in monolithic policies and base loadable modules. They are not valid in conditional statements and non-base loadable modules.

---

## 4.2.2.2 Associating Permissions with Object Classes

We associate permissions with an object class using the *access vector statement*. The full syntax for the access vector statement is shown in the sidebar on page 66. We use the access vector statement to associate common and class-specific permissions. For example, the following statement associates a single class-specific permission with the object class `dir`:

```
class dir { search }
```

As this example shows, the access vector statement looks similar to the class declaration statement (a similarity attributable to the reuse of the keyword `class`). The class declaration and access vector statements are distinct despite beginning with the same keyword. The access vector statement must provide a previously declared object class name (`dir`) and then provide one or more permissions. In this partial example, we define a single, class-specific permission (`search`). Notice that this statement also does not end in a semicolon.

The previous access vector statement would result in the `dir` object class having one class-specific permission: `search`. In general, you would see multiple permissions for an object class, as follows:

```
class dir { search add_name remove_name }
```

This example associates three class-specific permissions with the object class `dir`. We can also associate common permissions using the optional `inherits` keyword in the access vector statement. For example, the `dir` object class is one of several object classes that are "file-like" and share common permissions with other file-like classes. The following access vector statement is a complete access vector statement for `dir` associating the common permission `file`, shown previously, along with several class-specific permissions unique to directories:

```
class dir
inherits file
{
        add_name
        remove_name
        reparent
        search
        rmdir
}
```

As this example illustrates, we use the keyword `inherits` followed by the name of a previously declared common permission set (`file`) to associate all the common file permissions with `dir`. The result of this statement is that the valid permissions for the object class `dir` are all those defined earlier for the common permission `file` and the five permissions specific to `dir`.

It is possible to have an object class that has only common permissions. For example, the access vector statement for the object class for symbolic link files (`lnk_file`) is this:

```
class lnk_file inherits file
```

This statement results in the class `lnk_file` having only those permissions defined in the common permission `file` and no others.

Likewise, it is possible to have object classes with only class-specific permissions (that is, no common permissions). For example, the access vector statement for the object class representing file descriptors (`fd`) has a single class-specific permission allowing use of a file descriptor:

```
class fd { use }
```

---

### Access Vector Statement Syntax

The access vector statement associates permissions with a previously declared object class. The full syntax for the access vector statement is as follows:

```
class class_name [ inherits common ]   [{ perm_set } ]
```

| | |
|---|---|
| *class_name* | A previously declared object class name. |
| *common* | A previously declared common permission set name. |
| *perm_set* | One or more permission identifiers in a space-separated list. The identifiers can be any length and contain ASCII letters, numbers, or a period ( . ). |

At a minimum, either one *common* or a *perm_set* must be specified, but both can be provided. The resulting permissions for the object class are the union of the common permissions and the *perm_set*.

Access vector statements are valid only in monolithic policies and base loadable modules. They are not valid in conditional statements and non-base loadable modules.

---

## 4.3 Available Object Classes

This chapter provides an overview of the kernel object classes available in *Fedora Core 4* (FC4). Our goal is to describe the object classes and how the system resources are mapped to those object classes. Appendix C provides a reference for all object classes and their associated permissions. The most difficult part of writing good policy is understanding the semantics of the object classes and permissions and the implications of those semantics in the context of an application policy on a particular system.

An FC4 system has more than 40 kernel object classes representing all the resources provided by the kernel. The number of object classes illustrates a basic philosophy in SELinux to represent the kernel resources as completely and accurately as possible. The richness and complexity of Linux means that this accurate representation is necessarily rich and complex itself. This complexity may seem daunting, but it is necessary to give SELinux the flexibility to fully address the security challenges facing Linux. Tools and technology are emerging that use the richness of SELinux to provide sophisticated security without the user needing to be aware of the underlying complexity.

To ease understanding, we divide the kernel object classes into four categories: file-related, network-related, System V IPC, and miscellaneous.

### 4.3.1 File-Related Object Classes

The first category of object classes are those related to files and other resources stored in filesystems. These are often the most familiar object classes to most users. Included in this category are all the object classes that can be associated with persistent, on-disk filesystems and with in-memory filesystems, such as proc or sysfs.

In UNIX-like systems, an underlying concept is that "everything is a file." This is in many ways true, but it obscures the fact that not all "files" are the same. In reality, a modern UNIX-like system such as Linux has special files for devices, and IPC, in addition to standard files used for the storage of data. SELinux accurately represents this more detailed view of the kernel. Table 4-1 summarizes the file-related object classes.

TABLE 4-1
File-Related Object Classes

| Object Class | Description |
| --- | --- |
| blk_file | Block files |
| chr_file | Character files |
| dir | Directories |
| fd | File descriptors |
| fifo_file | Named pipes |
| file | Ordinary files |
| filesystem | Filesystem (for example, an actual partition) |
| lnk_file | Symbolic links |
| sock_file | UNIX domain sockets |

The object classes file and dir represent ordinary files and directories, respectively. Ordinary files are those files that store data; they are the most familar objects on most systems. Directories, which are a special file in Linux, are unique because they can contain other objects.

The lnk_file object class represents symbolic links. It is important in many situations to distinguish between regular files and symbolic links to prevent common attacks. Malicious processes and users can create symbolic links that cause a process to access or modify files other than those intended. The separate lnk_file object class allows policies to be written that prevent these types of attacks.

The object classes fifo_file and sock_file represent special files used for IPC. The fifo_file object class represents fifo files, also called named pipes. The sock_file object class controls the ability to create, access, and so on the file-related object associated with a UNIX domain socket. We discuss the UNIX domain socket object classes and their relationships to socket files in the next section.

In Linux, devices are accessed through special files that are commonly found in the /dev/ directory. These files represent, through major and minor device numbers, block and character devices. Character devices are those devices that programs read or write data to or from as a stream of bytes. Block devices are those devices that require data to be passed in larger blocks. The `chr_file` and `blk_file` object classes represent character and block devices, respectively.

The final two object classes in this category, filesystems and file descriptors, are not typically considered objects in Linux. The `filesystem` object class represents a mounted filesystem. This object class controls global operations such as mounting or querying quotas. For example, using the `filesystem` object class, we can allow only mounting of filesystems that support the storage of security contexts. All filesystems of a particular type (for example, `ext3`) get a default label defined in the policy with the `fs_use` statement, which is described in Chapter 10, "Object Labeling." That default type may be overridden when the partition is mounted with the `context mount` option, also described in Chapter 10.

File descriptors are handles, representing opened file-related objects, stored within processes. Although distinct from the file-related objects they represent in kernel data structures, it is common to think of file descriptors *as* the underlying file-related object. Indeed, standard Linux access control does not provide access control over file descriptors separately from that of the underlying object. This strategy ignores the fact that file descriptors are distinct resources that can be passed between processes, most commonly when a child inherits the file descriptors from its parent. This inheritance is not always desirable, and admonishments to reduce file descriptor inheritance appear in many Linux programming guides, particularly for daemons. To address this and other issues, we have the `fd` object class, which represents file descriptors in SELinux. Using this object class it is possible to prevent the usage of file descriptors passed or inherited between processes. It is important to note, however, that the permission to use a file descriptor is not sufficient to access the underlying file-related object; the process must also have the associated permission on the underlying object.

## 4.3.2 Network-Related Object Classes

The network-related object classes represent network resource such as network interfaces, various types of sockets, and hosts. The current object classes are sufficient to allow comprehensive control over networking on a single system. Further enhancements in this area, such as labeled network packets, are likely in the future.[2] Table 4-2 summarizes the network- and socket-related object classes.

---

2  Morris, James. *Directions in SELinux Networking*. Presentation at the Linux Kernel Networking Summit, 2005. Slides available at http://people.redhat.com/jmorris/slides/ns2005.pdf.

TABLE 4-2
Network-Related Object Classes

| Object Class | Description |
| --- | --- |
| association | IPsec security association |
| key_socket | Sockets that are of protocol family PF_KEY, used for key management in IPsec |
| netif | Network interface (for example, eth0) |
| netlink_audit_socket | Netlink socket for controlling auditing |
| netlink_dnrt_socket | Netlink socket for controlling DECnet routing |
| netlink_firewall_socket | Netlink socket for creating user space firewall filters |
| netlink_ip6fw_socket | Netlink socket for creating user space firewall filters |
| netlink_kobject_uevent _socket | Netlink socket for receiving kernel event notifications in user space |
| netlink_nflog_socket | Netlink socket for receiving Netfilter logging messages |
| netlink_route_socket | Netlink socket for controlling and managing network resources such as the routing table and IP address |
| netlink_selinux_socket | Netlink socket for receiving notices of policy load, enforcement mode toggle, and AVC cache flush |
| netlink_tcpdiag_socket | Netlink socket for monitoring TCP connections |
| netlink_socket | All other Netlink sockets |
| netlink_xfrm_socket | Netlink socket for getting, maintaining, and setting IPsec parameters |
| node | Host represented by an IP address or range of addresses |
| packet_socket | Raw sockets where the protocol is implemented in userspace |
| rawip_socket | IP sockets that are neither TCP or UDP |
| socket | All other sockets |

| Object Class | Description |
|---|---|
| tcp_socket | TCP sockets |
| udp_socket | UDP sockets |
| unix_dgram_socket | IPC datagram sockets on a local machine (UNIX domain) |
| unix_stream_socket | IPC stream sockets on a local machine (UNIX domain) |

The node, netif, packet_socket, rawip_socket, tcp_socket, udp_socket, and socket object classes control typical access to the network. The netif object class represents network interfaces. Each named network interface (for example, eth0, eth1, and so on) is represented by an instance of the netif object class. Remote hosts on the network, identified by IP address or range, are represented by the node object classes. Using the node object class, we can limit the hosts (via IP address) to which a process may interact over the network. The various socket object classes listed previously represent the kinds of socket by protocol. Successfully sending or receiving network data requires permissions on all the relevant netif, node, and socket object class instances.

The standard networking sockets are divided by protocol (as determined on creation by the socket(2) system call). The different socket object classes allow us to limit the type of packets an application can send or receive. This is particularly helpful in limiting the capability of applications to send raw packets. The object classes tcp_socket and udp_socket represent sockets for TCP and UDP, respectively. The rawip_socket object class represents sockets for sending raw IP packets and the packet_socket object class represents sockets for sending any other type of raw packet. All other sockets are represented by the socket object class.

Communication using *IP Security* (IPsec) has additional resources represented by the object classes association and key_socket. An IPsec security association is a connection that affords security services to the traffic that it carries. The association object class repesents IPsec associations. IPsec requires the management of keys through a key management (PF_KEY) socket, which is represented by the key_socket object class.

Local communications on Linux boxes can be accomplished using UNIX domain sockets (PF_UNIX). These sockets are commonly used for local IPCs. Connection-oriented sockets, also called stream sockets, are represented by the unix_stream_socket object class; datagram sockets are represented by the unix_dgram_socket object class. UNIX domain sockets can be associated with a special file in a filesystem to allow other applications to easily connect to the socket. This file is represented by the sock_file object class, a file-related object class described earlier.

The final group of sockets in SELinux are the Netlink sockets. These sockets were originally developed to provide a standard means of configuring networking in Linux.[3] They are now used to communicate a variety of information between kernel and userspaces. There are several object classes representing Netlink sockets based on protocol type, and the generic netlink_socket for any remaining protocols without a specific object class.

### 4.3.3 System V IPC Object Classes

The IPC-related object classes represent System V IPC resources (see Table 4-3). The msgq and msg object classes represent message queues and the messages in a message queue. The sem object class represents semaphores. The shm object class represents shared memory segments. Note that access to global system information about all System V IPC resources is controlled by a permission on the system class.

TABLE 4-3
IPC-Related Object Classes

| Object Class | Description |
|---|---|
| ipc | Deprecated; no longer used |
| msg | Messages within a message queue |
| msgq | Message queues |
| sem | Semaphores |
| shm | Shared memory segment |

---

3  Horman, Neil. *Understanding and Programming with Netlink Sockets.* http://people.redhat.com/nhorman/papers/netlink.pdf.

### 4.3.4 Miscellaneous Object Classes

Table 4-4 lists a number of remaining object classes that do not easily fit into one of the other categories.

The `capability` object class represents process capabilities in the standard Linux access control model. This object class allows SELinux to control the capabilities granted to "root" processes. Examples of these capabilities include the ability to override the discretionary access controls (permissions modes) and send raw network packets. This object class and its permissions allow control over whether a process may use a capability it already has been granted by standard Linux.

The remaining two object classes, `security` and `system`, represent access to special resources of the SELinux security server and the system, respectively. They are unique in that there is only ever one instance of each of these object classes, reflecting that there is ever only one security server and system.

TABLE 4-4
Miscellaneous Object Classes

| Object Class | Description |
| --- | --- |
| capability | Privileges that are implemented as capabilities in Linux |
| process | Processes which are also objects in SELinux |
| security | SELinux security server in the kernel |
| system | System as a whole |

## 4.4 Object Class Permission Examples

To provide a greater understanding of how permissions control access to system resources, let's further discuss the permissions for two object classes: `file` and `process`. We provide a detailed description of all permissions for each object class in Appendix C.

---

Access Revocation

The revocation of previously granted access is an important part of creating a flexible and dynamic security mechanism. Revocation is needed either when the policy changes or when the security context of an object is changed. For example, if the security context of a file is changed, processes that have that file open may no longer be allowed the same access to the file by the new policy. Mechanically, the system would have to revoke any existing access to the file if that access is not consistent with the change. Ensuring access revocation in all circumstances is a difficult task for any complex operating system.

SELinux supports revocation in many circumstances and provides much more access revocation support than standard Linux. For example, file access is checked on every read and write to a file; so if the security context of the file changes, the access is revoked on the next read or write attempt.

There are circumstances where access is not revoked (for example, with memory-mapped file access and outstanding asynchronous I/O requests). It is likely that revocation support will increase in SELinux, but it is unlikely that full coverage can be achieved. This is partly due to the nature of the UNIX *application programming interfaces* (APIs), partly due to community resistance to invasive changes to certain kernel subsystems, and partly due to the inherent complexity of the task.

In general, you can avoid most revocation issues by designing systems that do not relabel objects. SELinux provides permissions (`relabelfrom` and `relabelto`) to restrict this ability.

---

## 4.4.1 File Object Class Permissions

Table 4-5 lists the permissions for the `file` object class. Most of the permissions are common to all file-related object classes; only `execute_no_trans`, `entry-point`, and `execmod` are specific to the `file` object class (these are marked with a an asterisk, *).

There are three categories of permissions for the file object class: permissions that map directly to standard Linux access control permissions, extensions of the standard Linux permissions, and SELinux-specific permissions.

TABLE 4-5
File Object Class Permissions

| Permission | Description |
|---|---|
| append | Append to file contents (that is, opened with O_APPEND flag). |
| create | Create new file. |
| entrypoint* | File can be used as the entry point of the new domain via a domain transition. |
| execmod* | Make executable a file mapping that has been modified (implied by a copy-on-write). |
| execute | Execute; corresponds to x access in standard Linux. |
| execute_no_trans* | Execute file in the caller's domain (that is, without a domain transition). |
| getattr | Get attributes for file, such as access mode (for example, stat, some ioctls). |
| ioctl | ioctl(2) system call requests not addressed by other permissions. |
| link | Create hard link to file. |
| lock | Set and unset file locks. |
| mounton | Use as mount point. |
| quotaon | Allow file to be used as a quota database. |
| read | Read file contents; corresponds to r access in standard Linux. |
| relabelfrom | Change the security context from the existing type. |
| relabelto | Change the security context to the new type. |
| rename | Rename a hard link. |
| setattr | Change attributes for file such as access mode (for example, chmod, some ioctls). |
| swapon | Deprecated; was used to allow file to be used for paging/swapping space. |
| unlink | Remove hard link (delete). |
| write | Write file contents; corresponds to w access in standard Linux. |

### 4.4.1.1 Standard Linux Permissions

The permissions `read`, `write`, and `execute` correspond loosely to the standard Linux permissions read, write, and execute (that is, r, w, and x). There are some differences from the standard permission checks. In standard Linux, access is usually checked only when the file is opened. In SELinux, access is checked on every use when feasible. The `read` and `write` permissions are checked both at file open and on each subsequent read or write operation. The `read` permission covers the ability to read a file in its entirety. It includes the permissions to access the file in a random access manner. The `write` permission includes the permission to write to a file, including appending. Like `read` permission, `write` permission covers random access writing. The `read` and `write` permissions are also checked when a file is memory mapped, for example, `mmap(2)` system call, or the protections on an existing mapping are changed with `mprotect(2)` system call.

The `execute` permission controls the ability to execute the file using the `execve(2)` system call. It is required regardless of whether there is a domain transition (see `exec_no_trans` below). The `execute` permission is also required to successfully use a file as a shared library.

### 4.4.1.2 Extensions to the Standard Linux Access Control

One of the benefits of SELinux is that it provides additional permissions that give a finer granularity of control than what is available with standard Linux.

In standard Linux, the ability to create a file is governed by the ability to write to the containing directory. In SELinux, the `create` permission directly controls the ability to create a file of a specific SELinux type. Using this permission, we can allow a domain type to create files of type `etc_t`, but not of type `shadow_t`. Like many permissions in SELinux, the file `create` permission is necessary but not sufficient. For example, the creating domain type must also have permission to create objects in the containing `dir` object and the permissions to `create` permission the `file` object. We likely require `write` permission for the object class to which we give `create` permission for any practical application.

The ability to view or modify file attributes, including permission modes and ownership information, is controlled separately with the `getattr` and `setattr` permissions. The `getattr` permission controls the reading of file attributes (for example, using the `stat(2)` system call). The `setattr` permission controls the writing of file attributes (for example, using the `chmod(2)` system call).

Locking files, either via the `flock(2)` or `fnctl(2)` system calls, is controlled by the `lock` permission. No other permissions are required to obtain the lock, though practically you are required to have `read`, `write`, or `append` permission to obtain a file descriptor to pass to the relevant locking system call.

It is often useful to allow append-only access to a file. For example, it is important that log files can never be overwritten to prevent attackers from erasing evidence. SELinux provides the separate `append` permission, which strongly enforces the `O_APPEND` mode for open. Allowing a domain type `append` permissions without `write` permissions means that process with that domain type can only add data to a file.

Just as creation is controlled separately with the `create` permission, creating and removing hard links to a file is controlled with the `link` and `unlink` permissions. In Linux, files can be referenced by one or more names, called hard links. There is no "real" name for a file; all hard links are equally valid names for a file. There are many security implications to this semantic of Linux filesystems. Unlinking a file, which is controlled by the `unlink` permission, is essentially deleting a file (although if there are multiple hard links that file will in fact not be deleted, just that name). Likewise, linking a file, controlled by the `link` permission, is really creating a new name for a file. The ability to change the name of a hard link, using the `rename(2)` system call, is controlled by a third permission, `rename`. All three hard link-related permissions require additional permissions on the effected directories to successfully complete.

The final extended permissions for files are `mounton`, `quotaon`, and `swapon`. The `mounton` permission controls the ability to mount (`mount(2)` system call) using the file as a mount point. It is more common to use directories as a mount point; when performing bind mounts (`MS_BIND`), however, it is possible to use a file as a mount point. The `quotaon` permission controls the use of a file to store quota information. When turning quotas on using the `quotactl(2)` system call (`Q_QUO-TAON`), the path of the file used to store the quota information is provided. The calling process domain type must have `quotaon` permission to that file to successfully complete the system call.

### 4.4.1.3 SELinux Specific Permissions

There are five SELinux specific permissions for files: `relabelfrom`, `relabelto`, `execute_no_trans`, `entrypoint`, and `execmod`.

The `relabelfrom` and `relabelto` permissions control the capability of a domain type to change the type of a file from one type to another type, respectively. To successfully relabel a file, a domain type must have `relabelfrom` permission for `file` objects of the current type and `relabelto` permission for `file` objects of the new type. Notice that these permissions do not allow control over the exact pairs of permissions; a domain can relabel from any type for which it has `relabelfrom` permission to any type for which it has `relabelto` permission. It is possible to add contraints on relabeling, as you will see with the `validatetrans` rule in Chapter 7, "Constraints." Relabeling objects is a potentially dangerous operation to the security of the system and should be tightly controlled.

The `execute_no_trans` permission allows a domain to execute a file without a domain transition. This permission is not sufficient to execute a file; the `execute` permission is also required. Without the `execute_no_trans` permission, a process may execute only the file with a domain transition. We want to exclude `execute_no_trans` permission if we want to ensure that an execution will always cause a domain transition (or fail). For example, when the login process executes a shell for a user login, we always want the shell process to transition *from* the privileged login domain type.

The `entrypoint` permission, which we discussed in the description of domain transitions in Chapter 2, controls the ability to use the executable file to allow a domain type transition. The `execute`, `execute_no_trans`, and `entrypoint` permissions allow fine-grained control over what code can execute with what domain type. SELinux's capability to control the domain type of individual programs is a primary reason for its capability to provide strong yet flexible security.

The `execmod` permission controls the ability to execute memory-mapped files that have been modified in the process memory. This is most useful in preventing shared libraries from being modified within a process. Without this permission, if a memory mapped file is modified in memory, the process will no longer be able to execute the file.

## 4.4.2 Process Object Class Permissions

Table 4-6 list the process object class permissions. Unlike the file permissions, many of the process permissions do not directly correspond to standard Linux access controls as Linux does not traditionally treat processes as formal objects.

**TABLE 4-6**
Process Object Class Permissions

| Permissions | Description |
|---|---|
| dyntransition | Allow a process to dynamically transition to a new context. |
| execheap | Make the heap executable. |
| execmem | Make executable an anonymous mapping or private file mapping that is writable. |
| execstack | Make the process stack executable. |
| fork | Fork into two processes. |
| getattr | Get attributes of a process through the /proc/[pid]/attr/ directory. |
| getcap | Get Linux capabilities allowed for this process. |
| getpgid | Get group process ID of process. |
| getsched | Get priority of process. |
| getsession | Get session ID of process. |
| noatsecure | Disable secure mode environment cleansing. Allows process to disable secure mode feature of glibc on execve(2). |
| ptrace | Trace program execution of parent or child. |
| rlimitnh | Inherit process resource limits on execve(2). |
| setcap | Set Linux capabilities allowed for this process. |
| setcurrent | Set the current process context. This is the first capability checked when a process tries to perform a dynamic domain transition. |
| setexec | Override the default context for the next execve(2). |
| setfscreate | Allow a process to set the context of an object created by the process to something other than the default context. |
| setpgid | Set group process ID of process. |
| setrlimit | Change process hard resource limits. |
| setsched | Set priority of process. |
| share | Allow state sharing with cloned or forked process. |
| siginh | Inherit signal state on execve(2). |

*continues*

TABLE 4-6
Process Object Class Permissions (continued)

| Permissions | Description |
|---|---|
| sigkill | Send SIGKILL signal. |
| sigchld | Send SIGCHLD signal. |
| signal | Send a signal other than SIGKILL, SIGSTOP, or SIGCHLD. |
| signull | Test for existence of another process without sending a signal. |
| sigstop | Send SIGSTOP signal. |
| transition | Transition to a new context on execve(2). |

### 4.4.2.1 Process Creation

The fork permission controls the ability of a process to use the fork(2) system call. This system call creates a copy of the process that differs only in its process identifier and resource utilization data. The security context of a process does not change as the result of forking. Forking is usually the first step in executing a new program. Controlling the ability of a process to fork limits its ability to use system resources and can potentially prevent certain types of denial-of-service attacks.

Three additional permissions control the sharing of state on process transition. The share permission controls sharing of process state, such as file descriptors and memory address space, on a execve(2) system call. The siginh permission controls the inheritance of signal state, including any pending signals. Finally, the rlimitnh permission controls the inheritance of resource limits from the parent process.

### 4.4.2.2 Process Domain Type Transition

As described for domain transitions in Chapter 2 , the transition permission controls the ability of a process in one domain to transition into another via the execve(2) system call. A domain transition can occur, if allowed, automatically as a result of a type_transition rule or when explicitly requested. The ability to request an explicit transition is controlled by the setexec permission. Programmatically, this request is made by writing to a special file in the proc filesystem. This procedure is abstracted in the setexeccon(3) library function. The ability to see the currently requested transition for the next call to execve(2) system call is controlled by the getattr permission.

The noatsecure permission causes the kernel to not set the secure mode of glibc on a domain transition. In secure mode, glibc cleanses the process environment, including powerful environment variables such as LD_PRELOAD. Without cleansing the environment the source domain can potentially control critical aspects of the target domain. Allowing the noatsecure permission is especially dangerous when the domain transition is into a more privileged domain.

The dyntransition permission is similar to the transition permission but controls the ability to change the domain type on a process at any time,[4] not just when executing an application. This permission is much more dangerous than the transition permission because it allows the starting domain to always execute arbitrary code in the new domain. For this reason, the dyntransition permission can safely be used only to transition to a domain with a strict subset of the access of the starting domain. Otherwise, the perceived protection of the domain change is false, and any access granted to the target domain must be assumed to be accessible to the starting domain.

> WARNING The ability to change the process domain type arbitrarily using the dyntransition permission for process object class breaks the important property of label tranquility. In SELinux, label tranquality simply means that in a running system, after an object is created, its type will not change. Although there always exists a need for trusted operating system components to occasionally change types of objects, SELinux has traditionally tightly controlled type changes for processes with the domain transition concept. The introduction of dyntransition permission breaks this property, which greatly complicates any security analysis of the policy. *We highly recommend that you never use this permission unless you are writing userspace object managers or other SELinux extensions.*

---

4   The only limitation to when dynamic context transitions can occur is that they cannot occur while a process has more than one thread running. This is to prevent a multithreaded process from having a different security context for each thread, which is an even weaker domain separation than offered by the current dynamic context transition. You can find the discussion of dynamic context transitions that occurred when it was introduced into SELinux at www.nsa.gov/selinux/list-archive/0411/9364.cfm. Included is information about multithreaded applications and dynamic context transitions.

The `setcurrent` permission for the `dyntransition` permission is analogous to the `setexec` permission for the `transition` permission. It controls the ability to request the change of the process domain type. Successfully changing the domain type requires the `dyntransition` permission in addition to the `setcurrent` permission. Like `setexec`, the request is made by writing to a special file in the proc filesystem. This procedure is abstracted in the `setcon(3)` library function.

### 4.4.2.3 File Creation

Like domain transitions, the setting of the security context of file-related objects created by a process can either be automatic, through inheritance or `type_transition` rules, or explicit. A program explicitly sets the context for file-related objects by writing to special files in the proc filesystem. This procedure is abstracted in the `setfscreatecon(3)` library call. The `setfscreate` permission controls the ability to make this explicit request. Like `setexeccon`, the ability to see the current state of the filesystem object context request is controlled by the `gettattr` permission.

### 4.4.2.4 Process Signaling

The ability to signal processes can be powerful because it potentially allows for the termination or stopping of processes. In addition, signaling can be used to transfer information between two processes. The `sigchld`, `sigkill`, and `sigstop` permissions control the ability to send the SIGCHLD, SIGKILL, and SIGSTOP signals, respectively. The `signull` permission controls the ability to send a null signal, for example, by passing 0 as the signal argument for the `kill(2)` system call. Finally, the `signal` permission controls the ability to send all other signals.

There are a couple reasons why some signals have an explicit permission defined and the rest are grouped under the general `signal` permission. Two signal, SIGKILL and SIGSTOP, were given an explicit permission because they cannot be blocked by a process. The SIGCHLD signal has its own permission primarily because it is used pervasively (for example, often from every process to `init`). The rest have the same security properties, so they were grouped under the `signal` permission.

### 4.4.2.5 Process Attributes

The ability to query or set the scheduling priority and policy for a process is controlled by the `getsched` and `setsched` permissions. Setting scheduling priority and policy, particularly setting the SCHED_FIFO policy, with the `sched_setscheduler(2)` system call can allow a process to take up possibly unlimited amounts of CPU time. This can be used to for denial-of-service attacks.

The process group and session identifiers control many aspects of a process' interaction with its environment, including terminal handling and signal delivery. The `getpgid` and `setpgid` permissions control the querying and setting of the process group identifier for the process. The `getsession` permission controls querying of the session identifier.

The `getcap` and `setcap` permissions control querying and setting Linux capabilities for the process. To successfully set a capability, the capability must also be allowed for the `capability` object class labeled with the domain type of the process.

Resource limits, such as the maximum core dump size or CPU time, are set using the `setrlimit(2)` system call. The `setrlimit` permission controls the ability to set hard resource limits.

### 4.4.2.6 Executing Writable Memory

As mentioned during the discussion of the `execmod` permission of the `file` object class, the ability to execute writable segments of memory is a source of many security concerns. To help address these concerns the `execmem`, `execstack`, and `execheap` permissions were created. They control the creation of executable anonymous mappings, stacks, and heaps, respectively. The enforcement of the permissions relies on additional software, such as ExecShield,[5] hardware features, such as NX.[6]

---

5   ExecShield is a Red Hat-developed kernel patch to control memory execution and add other security features. It is included in all Fedora releases and Red Hat Enterprise Linux since version 3. See www.redhat.com/f/pdf/rhel/WHP0006US_Execshield.pdf for a description.

6   NX is a hardware feature that accomplishes many of the same goals as ExecShield. A description is available at http://en.wikipedia.org/wiki/NX_bit.

## 4.5 Exploring Object Classes with Apol

`Apol` offers a variety of features for browsing and querying object classes and permissions. Under the Policy Components tab is the Classes/Perms tab, which allows browsing and searching all object classes, common permissions, and unique permissions. Figure 4-1, shows `apol` with this tab displayed. On the left are all the object classes, common permissions, and permissions. On the right is an interface that enables you to search for object classes or permissions.

Double-clicking a policy component in the lists on the left displays detailed information about the component. For example, double-clicking an object class displays its access vector; double-clicking a permission displays all the object classes with which it is associated.

The search interface enables you to search for object classes or permissions using regular expressions. For example, in Figure 4-1, we performed a search for all object classes that contain "file" as part of their name. We did not set options to include the class-specific permissions or to expand common permissions in the result. As you can see in the Search Results window, `apol` is showing the object class `file` including the class-specific permissions and the expanded common permissions. This is a convenient method to obtain a full list of the permissions associated with an object class.

Most other features in `apol` that interact with object classes, including the rule searching and automated analyses features, which allow filtering of results based on object classes and permissions. For example, Figure 4-2 shows a search for rules referring to the object class `file`.

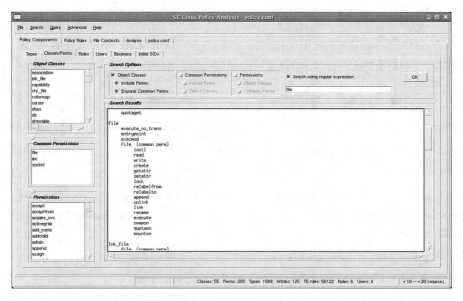

**FIGURE 4-1**
Apol displaying object classes, common permissions, and permissions

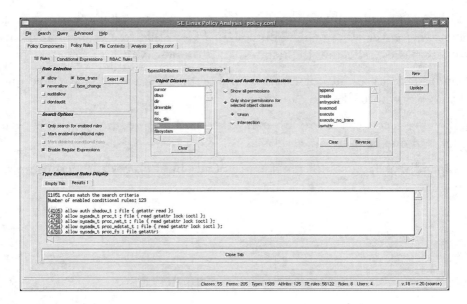

**FIGURE 4-2**
Apol displaying a search for rules with the object class file

## 4.6 Summary

- Object classes and permissions are the basis for access control in SELinux, both as part of the policy language and for the access enforcement mechanism in the kernel.

- Object classes represent system resources such as files, process, directories, and sockets. There is a corresponding object class for every kind of system resource.

- Permissions represent access to system resources. Each object class has a defined set of permissions called an access vector.

  Object classes are declared using the class declaration statement (`class`).

  Permissions are associated with object classes using the access vector statement (also `class`).

- Two types of permissions are defined in SELinux: common permissions and class-specific permissions.

- Common permissions are a set of permissions shared by more than one object class. They are associated with the object classes as a group using the access vector statement.

- SELinux provides object classes and permissions to accurately and comprehensively cover all system resources. In FC4, this results in more than 40 object classes, reflecting the richness and complexity of Linux.

- Understanding all the object classes and permissions requires a detailed understanding of both SELinux and Linux.

- Allowing access to accomplish many tasks in Linux requires multiple permissions on one or more object classes.

- Appendix C has a complete reference of all object classes and permissions.

## Exercises

1. Create a common permission set named `socket` with the permissions `read`, `write`, `bind`, `connect`, and `listen`.

2. Associate the common permissions `socket` and the class-specific permissions `connecto` and `acceptfrom` with the object class declared in Question 2.

3. Write an `allow` rule that allows the domain `httpd_t` to append to a file of type `httpd_log_t`, but not write.

4. Write the necessary allow rules to allow the domain `httpd_t` to execute files of type `bin_t`. Include the ability to request an explicit domain transition but not the ability to execute without transition. Assume that the appropriate rules giving transition and entrypoint are already present in the policy.

# Type Enforcement

The majority of a SELinux policy is made up of several rules that together we call the type enforcement rules. These rules control allowed access, many aspects of default transition labeling, auditing, and invariant assertion checking. In this chapter, we examine the type enforcement rules in detail along with the statements to define and declare the types used by these rules.

## 5.1 Type Enforcement

The majority of a SELinux policy is a set of statements and rules that collectively define the *type enforcement* (TE) policy. A well-defined, strict TE policy can contain tens of thousands of TE rules. The large number of TE rules is not surprising because they express *all* the allowed access to resources exposed by the Linux kernel. This means, for example, that every access attempt by every process to every file succeeds only if there is at least one TE rule allowing that access. If we think about the number of processes and resources on a modern Linux system, we will understand why TE rules can be numerous. When we add the audit configuration and labeling controlled by TE rules, it is not uncommon for a highly restrictive SELinux policy to contain tens of thousands of rules, although smaller policies are also common. In Part III, we discuss methods for managing and building this large set of rules; for now let's understand how the TE rules work.

The sheer number of TE rules can make understanding SELinux policies challenging, but the rules themselves are not complex. There are a relatively few varieties, and they all fall into two basic categories: *access vector* (AV) and type rules. We use AV rules to allow or audit access between two types. We use the *type rules* to control default labeling decisions under certain circumstances.

As their name implies, TE rules operate on *types,* which are associated with all resources via a security context. The policy language includes additional statements that allow us to define types and related policy components.

An important concept of SELinux is that TE rules associate privileges and accesses with programs, *not* users. All the SELinux policy language features we discuss in this chapter deal with the access of *subjects* (normally running programs) to *objects* (files, dir, sockets, and so on). This focus on programs for access control decisions is important and one of the primary benefits of SELinux. It allows the SELinux policy author to make decisions about access based on the function and security properties of programs in addition to the total access that a user needs to accomplish tasks. A program can be restricted to the minimum access permissions required to function properly, so that even if it malfunctions or has been exploited, the security of the system as a whole is not necessarily compromised. For example, if the policy for a Web server prevents it from modifying the files it displays, then even if the server is exploited, the TE policy can prevent the exploited server from changing those files. This limits the threat of defacing a Web site through a vulnerability in the Web server. The security of the system in this example is largely maintained even in the face of an exploited application. Only the exploited application is affected, and it is limited to the access we defined in the policy.

Users are not entirely ignored by SELinux. It is possible for the policy to specify multiple domain types (and thus differing sets of privilege) for the same program based on the user who runs the program. This allows for the concept of roles, which we discuss further in Chapter 6, "Roles and Users." Nonetheless, the level of access control is still based on the program's domain type and not the user's privileges.

The implications of the shift of focus from users to programs can hardly be understated; it allows us to address some of the fundamental challenges in computer security. The benefits are clear, but it does require thinking about access control in a way that is new to many people. As you read this chapter, it will help if you keep the focus on program access in mind. Additionally, if you are uncertain about the basic concepts of type enforcement, you should review Chapter 2, "Concepts," before continuing. In this chapter, we provide the details necessary to enable you to write TE rules; we assume that you understand the basic concepts of SELinux and type enforcement as discussed in Chapter 2.

## 5.2 Types, Attributes, and Aliases

*Types,* as you might guess from the term *type enforcement,* are the basic building blocks for TE rules. SELinux primarily uses types to determine what access is allowed. Attributes and aliases are policy features that ease the management and use of types. We use *attributes* to refer to a group of types with a single identifier. For the most part, the policy language allows us to use attributes in place of types in TE rules. *Aliases* are a convenience mechanism that allows us to define alternate names for a type. The alias identifier and the type identifier are treated identically as far as the policy is concerned.

## 5.2.1 Declaring Types

We must explicitly declare a type identifier using the `type` statement before using it. SELinux has no predefined types; we must explicitly declare them all. For example, suppose we want to declare a type (`httpd_t`) we intend to use as the domain type for a Web server and another type (`http_user_content_t`) we intend to apply to user data files that the Web server needs to access to display their content. We make these declarations using the `type` statement. For example:

```
type httpd_t;
type http_user_content;
```

Once declared, we can use types in security contexts, TE rules, and other policy statements where required. You can see the full syntax for the type statement in the sidebar on page 92.

---

### Type Statement Syntax

You use the `type` statement to declare types and optionally, associated alias names and attributes with the type. The full syntax for a type declaration is as follows:

`type` *type_name* [ `alias` *alias_set* ] [, *attribute_set*] `;`

| | |
|---|---|
| *type_name* | An identifier for the type. The identifier can be any length and can contain ASCII characters, numbers, an underscore (_), or a period (.). |
| *alias_set* | One or more alias identifiers. Alias identifiers have the same naming restrictions as type identifiers. If more than one alias identifier is specified, a space-separated list enclosed in braces ({  }) is used (for example, `alias { aliasa_t aliasb_t }`). |
| *attribute_set* | One or more previously declared attribute identifiers. If more than one attribute is specified, a comma-separated list is used (for example, `type bin_t, file_type, exec_type;`). |

Type statements are valid in monolithic policies, base loadable modules, and nonbase loadable modules. They are not valid in conditional statements.

---

## 5.2.2 Types and Attributes

As you might imagine, a large, complex policy may have many hundreds or thousands of types to represent all of the different resources on a system. The *Fedora Core 4* (FC4) targeted policy, for example, which is deliberately relatively small, declares more than 800 types. Combine this with the fact that all access is denied unless explicitly allowed means that directly expressing all the allowed access between types would be verbose. This is where attributes help in the policy language. Attributes can be thought of in two ways: 1) as a property or characteristic of a type, or 2) as a group of types. In either case, the mechanism is the same.

Suppose we want to allow a backup application to have read access to all files. We start by creating a domain type of the backup application (`backup_t`) and giving that type allowed access to every type associated with any file:

```
type backup_t;

allow backup_t httpd_user_content_t : file read;
allow backup_t shadow_t : file read;
# additional rules granting read access to every other type used with file objects
```

Here we give the domain type `backup_t` access to two file types: our `httpd_user_content_t` example from earlier; and the type `shadow_t`, which we expect to be the type of the `/etc/shadow` file. Both are on-disk files that a backup application must read.

To complete this example, we would have to write a rule for every other type used for any file. Depending on how many of the hundreds of declared types are ever used with a file object, we would need hundreds of allow rules to give the backup application the necessary access (one for each type). Further, every time we add a file type to the policy, we would have to remember to add an allow rule for `backup_t`. This is a tedious and error-prone process. Attributes makes this kind of "group access" easier to specify. By defining an attribute that we associate with all the file types and then granting access to that attribute (rather than the individual types), we can give `backup_t` the necessary access with a single rule.

We declare attributes with the `attribute` statement, as follows:

```
attribute file_type;
```

This statement declares an attribute called `file_type`. Types and attributes share the same namespace, so it is not possible to have a type and an attribute with the same name. Assuming that we associated the attribute `file_type` with all appropriate types, we can then allow `backup_t` read access to both of these files with a single allow rule:

```
allow backup_t file_type : file read;
```

> NOTE Whereas it is common to append a _t to all type names, the common convention for attributes is to have no additional suffix added to the name. Because types and attributes share the same name space, this makes it easier to recognize a type from an attribute when writing and examining TE rules.

Now instead of hundreds of `allow` rules, we have a single rule that grants the same access. When this policy is compiled, this rule will automatically be expanded to the hundred of rules necessary to control access based on the various file types. More important, when we define a new type for files, all we have to do is associate the new type with the `file_type` attribute and the domain type `backup_t` will automatically be given read access.

The full syntax for the attribute statement can be seen in the following sidebar.

---

### Attribute Statement Syntax

You use the `attribute` statement to declare attributes. The full syntax of the attribute statement is as follows:

`attribute attribute_name;`

`attribute_name`    An identifier for the attribute. The identifier can be any length and can contain ASCII characters, numbers, an underscore (_), or a period ( . ) .Attributes are in the same namespace as types and aliases and therefore cannot have the same name as another type or alias.

Attribute statements are valid in monolithic policies, base loadable modules, and non-base loadable modules. They are not valid in conditional statements.

---

## 5.2.3 Associating Types and Attributes

So far, we discussed how to define types and attributes but not how to associate the two. Types are most commonly associated with attributes when the types are declared using the `type` statement. For example, we can associate the attribute `file_type` with the type `httpd_user_content_t` by changing the type declaration to the following:

```
type httpd_user_content_t, file_type;
```

The common way to describe this declaration is that the type `httpd_user_content_t` *has* the `file_type` attribute. Mechanically, this statement adds the type `httpd_user_content_t` to the group of types that "have" the `file_type` attribute, but conceptually it also changes the nature of the `httpd_user_content_t` type such that it now "has" access permissions based on an attribute, and not just on permissions granted to the type itself.

Just as `httpd_user_content_t` comes to represent files served by the Web server through use, attributes gain meaning through consistent use. In this example, we are creating an attribute, `file_type`, which means all file types used on permanent storage. Thus, we as policy writers can write rules for access to "all files" without having to explicitly address each and every file type.

Types are not limited to one attribute, and in normal use it is common for a type to have several associated attributes. For example, we can create the attribute `httpdcontent` for all files intended to be available through the Web server. The types that have the `httpdcontent` attribute would likely be a subset of the types with the `file_type` attribute. To extend our earlier example, let's look at the following statements:

```
type httpd_user_content_t, file_type, httpdcontent;
type shadow_t, file_type;

allow backup_t file_type : file read;
allow httpd_t httpdcontent : file read;
```

We have now added two attributes to the `http_user_content_t` type, `file_type` (indicating this is a type of an on-disk file) and `httpdcontent` (indicating that this type is to be read by the Web server). For the more privileged type `shadow_t`, we associated only the attribute `file_type` (because allowing the Web server to display the shadow password file does not seem like a good idea!). We also have two `allow` rules giving the Web server and the backup program the access they need for the types associated with each attribute. The result is that the Web server (`httpd_t`) can read all files with the `httpdcontent` attribute but not other files such as `shadow_t`. On the other hand, the backup application (`backup_t`) can read all files that have the `file_type` attribute.

No practical limit applies to the number of attributes that a type can have and, just as with types, we can define as many or as few attributes as we want within reason.

> NOTE   At the time of this writing, the coded limit to the number of types and attributes we may define is $2^{32}$ identifiers. This is the size limit supported by the version of SELinux released with *Red Hat Enterprise Linux, version 4* (RHEL4). By the time this book is published, that size will likely be changed to $2^{16}$ identifiers (due to a significant optimization of SELinux memory usage). However, in practical terms, the number of types we can define is probably at most a few thousand (because the number of associated TE rules would likely become unwieldy). So, even the most complicated policy we have seen has had fewer than two thousand types and attributes declared.

In addition to associating attributes with types using the `type` statements, we can associate attributes to types using the `typeattribute` statement. This statement allows us to associate attributes to types separately from their declaration, potentially in another part of the policy that is in a separate file. For example, take our `type` statement for `http_user_content_t` from above:

```
type httpd_user_content_t, file_type, httpdcontent;
```

The following `type` and `typeattribute` statements are equivalent to the single `type` statement:

```
# The following two statements...
type httpd_user_content_t;
typeattribute httpd_user_content_t file_type, httpdcontent;

# are equivalent to the following single statement.
type httpd_user_content_t, file_type, httpdcontent;
```

> TIP   For the first time, we used a comment in our policy statement. For the policy compiler, the pound symbol (#) indicates a comment. All text following the pound symbol to the end of the line is ignored by the compiler.

It may not be clear from this example why the `typeattribute` statement is needed, but as you read in later chapters, the flexibility given by this statement will become clear. Basically, this statement allows us define a type in one place and associate attributes in another, increasing the language flexibility and allowing stronger modularity in the design of policy source files.

The full syntax for the `typeattribute` statement can be seen on page 97.

> WARNING   Attributes are a convenient feature of the policy language, but they can be dangerous. Associating an attribute with a type can potentially allow a large amount of access to that type. This access may or may not be appropriate; it depends on our security goals. For example, associating a domain type with an attribute will likely give that type a large amount of access, the impact of which you may not fully understand. This is often similar to granting a process a powerful privilege. You should be certain that the access for the attribute is warranted for the associated type and be careful about the impacts of future TE rules that reference that attribute.

---

### Typeattribute Statement Syntax

The `typeattribute` statement allows you to associate previously declared type and attributes. You can use this statement to associate an attribute with a type when the association is not done as part of the type declaration. The full syntax for the typeattribute statement is as follows:

typeattribute *type_name attrib_names*;

*type_name*  The name of the type to which to add the attributes. The type must be declared separately using a type statement and only one type may be specified.

*attrib_names*  One or more previously declared attribute identifiers. If more than one attribute is specified, a comma-separated list is used (for example, `typeattribute bin_t file_type, exec_type;`).

`Typeattribute` statements are valid in monolithic policies, base loadable modules, and non-base loadable modules. They are not valid in conditional statements.

---

## 5.2.4 Aliases

Aliases are alternate names used to refer to a type. We can use an alias anywhere that we would use a type name, including TE rules, security contexts, and labeling statements. Aliases are typically used for compatibility when making policy changes. For example, an older policy might refer to the type `netscape_t`. An updated policy might switch to the type name to `mozilla_t`, but provide `netscape_t` as an alias to allow older modules to correctly compile.

We declare aliases in one of two ways. The first method is as part of the type declaration using the `type` statement. We can declare the type `mozilla_t` with the alias `netscape_t` by using the `alias` keyword in the `type` statement, as follows:

```
type mozilla_t alias netscape_t, domain;
```

Notice that the alias declaration comes before the attributes for the type.

We can also declare aliases separately from the type declaration using the `typealias` statement. The following statements are equivalent to the single `type` statement above:

```
# These two statements are equivalent...
type mozilla_t, domain;
typealias mozilla_t alias netscape_t;

# to the following single statement.
type mozilla_t alias netscape_t, domain;
```

The `typealias` statement is useful when the structure of the policy makes it difficult to declare the alias as part of the type declaration. We can see the full syntax for aliases as part of `type` statements in the sidebar on page 92 and the full syntax for `typealias` in the sidebar on page 98.

### Typealias Statement Syntax

The `typealias` statement allows you define an alias name for a type. This is an alternative method to defining the alias as part of the type declaration using the type statement. The full syntax for the `typealias` statement is as follows:

typealias *type_name* alias *alias_names*;

*type_name*   The name of the type to which to add the aliases. Types must be declared separately using the `type` statement, and only one type may be specified.

`alias_names`    One or more alias identifiers. Alias identifiers have the same naming restrictions as type identifiers. If more than one alias identifier is specified, a space-separated list enclosed in braces (`{ }`) is used (for example, `{ aliasa_t aliasb_t }`).

`Typealias` statements are valid in monolithic policies, base loadable modules, and non-base loadable modules. They are not valid in conditional statements.

---

### Domain Types and Other Kinds of Types

In Chapter 2, you learned that types used on processes are sometimes called "domain types." Throughout this book, we also often use other adjectives in front of the word *type,* such as "file type" and "directory type." All these adjectives simply refer to the way that the types are used and do not reflect any special treatment of the type in the policy language. A file type, for example, is simply a way to refer to a type used as part of the security context for files. In reality, the type could be used for other object classes, too; there is nothing intrinsic to the language that makes a type a file type or a domain type. All the types in SELinux are exactly the same and can be used to label any object class instance if the appropriate access is present.

This means, for example, that a domain type such as httpd_t could be used on both a process and a file with the addition of a few rules. Traditionally, this dual use has been avoided in SELinux policies, mainly for clarity. But, in some circumstances, we have used a type as both a domain type and a file type. The distinction is completely up to the policy writer.

In the case of domain types, however, there are some technical reasons to not use these types for files and directories. In Linux, every process has files and directories automatically created in /proc/ by the kernel. These objects are used to get and set properties about these processes. In SELinux, the type of the process is automatically used for these files and directories. That would mean that for a process with type httpd_t, if the *process ID* (PID) of the process were 1000, the directory /proc/1000/ and all of its files and directories would also have the type httpd_t. If the type httpd_t was also used for regular files, that would mean that granting access for other domain types to regular files of type httpd_t would also grant access to the files and directories in /proc/, with potentially unwanted side effects.

## 5.3 Access Vector Rules

AV rules are those rules that specify their meaning in terms of access permissions[1] for object classes. The SELinux policy language currently supports four types of AV rules:

| | |
|---|---|
| `allow` | Specifies access allowed between two types |
| `dontaudit` | Specifies access denial messages to not record |
| `auditallow` | Specified access allowed events to record |
| `neverallow` | Specifies access permissions that may never be granted by any `allow` rule |

We examine each of these rules, their common and unique syntax and semantics, and examples of their usage in the remainder of this section. The common syntax for all AV rules is shown in the sidebar on page 107.

### 5.3.1 Common AV Rule Syntax

Although each of these AV rules has a different purpose, they all have the same basic syntax. Each rule contains five elements:

- *Rule name*      `allow`, `dontaudit`, `auditallow`, or `neverallow`
- *Source type(s)*      The type(s) being granted access, usually the domain type of a process attempting access
- *Target type(s)*      The type(s) of an object to which the source is being granted access
- *Object class(es)*      The class(es) of object(s) that the specified access is permitted
- *Permission(s)*      The specific access permissions that the source is allowed to the target type for the indicated object classes (also called the access vector)

A simple AV rule has one source type, target type, object class, and permission. We have seen many examples of such AV rules in our earlier `allow` rule examples, such as the following:

```
allow user_t bin_t : file execute;
```

---

1   In the code, the set of permissions for an object class are represented by a bit mask called an access vector, hence the term *access vector rule*.

This `allow` rule has the source type `user_t`, target type `bin_t`, object class `file`, and permission `execute`. This rule is commonly read as "allow user_t to execute files of type bin_t."

All four AV rules have exactly the same syntax with a different rule name keyword. For example, we could convert the previous example into an `auditallow` rule by simply replacing the rule name:

```
auditallow user_t bin_t : file execute;
```

We will discuss the meaning of this rule later; what is important at the moment is to understand that the syntax is exactly the same.

### 5.3.1.1 AV Rule Keys

Within the kernel, all the AV rules are uniquely identified by a triplet of source type, target type, and object class. This triplet is called a *key* for its use as a hash table and cache key within the policy data structures. Recall from Chapter 3, "Architecture," that rules are stored and looked up by this key. When a process makes an access attempt, the SELinux LSM module is queried for the allowed access based on this key.

So, what happens when there is more than one AV rule with the same key (that is, same source type, target type, and object class)? For example, consider a policy with the following rules:

```
allow user_t bin_t : file execute;
allow user_t bin_t : file read;
```

Are processes of type `user_t` allowed `read` or `execute` access to files of type `bin_t`? The answer is both; all rules with the same key are combined by `checkpolicy`. The compiled policy will contain a single rule with both the `execute` and `read` permissions, and both will be allowed by the security server. All the AV rules are additive in this way.

WARNING   Each subsequent AV rule in a policy that has the same keys as a previous AV rule `adds` permissions to the ultimate rule compiled into the policy. There is no concept of `removing` permissions granted by another rule. So be careful; although you might have written a nice tight rule in one part of the policy, another rule elsewhere in a policy (possibly for an attribute that is associated with your type) might grant additional permissions.

### 5.3.1.2 Using Attributes in AV Rules

Although the AV rules that we have seen so far have been simple, the syntax supports many ways to list types, object classes, and permissions, giving us flexibility and often making the rule statements more concise.

In the simple form of the rules in the previous examples, the rules have referred directly to the source type (`user_t`) and the target type (`bin_t`). It is often convenient, however, to refer to multiple types in the source or target of the rules. One way to refer to multiple types is to use attributes. We can use an attribute anywhere we can use a type in AV rules.

For example, suppose we defined an attribute (`exec_type`) that we plan to associate with all file types that an ordinary user program (indicated by the domain type `user_t`) may execute. Now we can change our above example to refer to the attribute `exec_type` rather than an explicit type such as `bin_t`, as shown here:

```
allow user_t exec_type : file execute;
```

Unlike the previous example, this rule does not directly reflect what will be enforced by the kernel. Rules that include attributes will be expanded within the kernel into a separate key for each type associated with the attribute. If there were 20 file types associated with the attribute `exec_type`, for example, the kernel AVC may end up with 20 keys and associated rules, each one granting `execute` access for `file` object class to the type `user_t` for each of the 20 file types associated with the attribute `exec_type`.

We can also use attributes as the source of an AV rule, or for both the source and target of the rule. For example, suppose we also created an attribute (`domain`) that we associated with all domain types (including `user_t`), and that we want to allow all domain types the ability to execute file types that have the attribute `file_type`. We can achieve this goal with a single rule:

```
allow domain exec_type : file execute;
```

To better illustrate the rule expansion concept, suppose that our policy associated the `domain` attribute with the types `user_t` and `staff_t`, and the `exec_type` attribute with the file types `bin_t`, `local_bin_t`, and `sbin_t`. Thus, the single rule above would be the equivalent to the following explicit rules:

```
allow user_t bin_t : file execute;
allow user_t local_bin_t : file execute;
allow user_t sbin_t : file execute;
allow staff_t bin_t : file execute;
allow staff_t local_bin_t : file execute;
allow staff_t sbin_t : file execute;
```

### 5.3.1.3 Multiple Types and Attributes in AV Rules

We are not limited to a single type or attribute for the source and target fields. Rather, we can also list multiple types or attributes as source and target. When there is more than one type or attribute, a space-separated list enclosed in braces is used, as follows:

```
allow user_t { bin_t sbin_t } : file execute;
```

In this rule, the target is both `bin_t` and `sbin_t`. Rules with multiple types or attributes in the source or target are expanded in the same ways as single attributes. In the previous example, the kernel policy would contain two keys, one each for the type target types.

We can mix types and attributes for either source or target fields, or both. For example, the following rule is perfectly legal:

```
allow {user_t domain} {bin_t file_type sbin_t} : file execute ;
```

It is fine if we explicitly list a type and an attribute that the type has. In this case, we have essentially listed the type twice. The kernel will resolve the redundancy and include only one instance of the rule for each combination of source and target types.

### 5.3.1.4 The Special Type self

The policy language has a reserved word `self` that acts like a type when used in the target field of an AV rule. For example, the following two rules are equivalent:

```
# These two rules are equivalent to each other
allow user_t user_t : process signal;
allow user_t self : process signal;
```

The keyword `self` simply means to instantiate a rule for each source type, so that the source and target are the same. In the preceding example, the second rule just creates a key with the source and target both `user_t`.

Let's look at a slightly more complicated example:

```
allow {user_t staff_t} self : process signal;
```

In this example, the rule creates two rules, one each for each source type. This rule is exactly equivalent to the following two rules:

```
# These two rules...
allow user_t user_t : process signal;
allow staff_t staff_t : process signal;

# are equivalent to the following single rule.
allow {user_t staff_t} self : process signal;
```

Notice that when using `self`, the equivalent rules are created only for each source type and themselves. In particular, `user_t` is given no access to `staff_t` and vice versa.

> NOTE You may use only the special type `self` in the target field of AV rules. In particular, you cannot use `self` as the source of an AV rule or in a type rule. Further, you cannot declare a type or attribute with `self` as its identifier.

The use of `self` is particularly valuable when using attributes or large lists of types and attributes as the source of an AV rule. For example, suppose we want every domain to be able to signal itself. We might want to write a rule such as this:

```
allow domain domain : process signal; # Not what we really want
```

Although this rule provides the desired access (every domain type would be able to signal itself), it would also allow every domain type to signal *every other domain type*. This unintended effect could be a security disaster. By using the `self` keyword, we can ensure that each domain type only gets access to itself, as follows:

```
allow domain self : process signal; # This is what we intended
```

### 5.3.1.5 The Negation Special Operator

The final syntax for types in AV rules is *type negation*. This syntax is useful for removing a type from a list of types and is most commonly used to remove a type from an attribute in a given rule. This is done by prepending the negation operator, -, to the beginning of the type name. For example, we could allow all domain types to execute all file types with the `exec_type` attribute except for `sbin_t` with the following rule:

```
allow domain { exec_type -sbin_t } : file execute;
```

This rule would expand as if the `exec_type` attribute did not contain the type `sbin_t` for this one rule.

Type negation is not order dependent; if a type is subtracted, it will not be expanded even if it comes before the attribute was listed. The following, for example, is semantically equivalent to the preceding example:

```
allow domain { -sbin_t exec_type } : file execute;
```

### 5.3.1.6 Specifying Object Classes and Permissions in AV Rules

AV rules can also contain lists of object classes and permissions. The syntax is, as with types, a space-separated list enclosed in braces, as follows:

```
allow user_t bin_t : { file dir } { read getattr };
```

This rule would result in two keys, one for each object class, just as with source or target types. This preceding rule is exactly equivalent to the following two rules:

```
# These two rules...
allow user_t bin_t : file { read getattr };
allow user_t bin_t : dir { read getattr };

# are equivalent to the following single rule.
allow user_t bin_t : { file dir } { read getattr };
```

Notice that the object classes are expanded, but each rule has the same list of permissions. This means that all the listed permissions must be valid for all the object classes. We will sometimes have to create two distinct rules with the same source and target types but different object classes because the permission lists are not valid for all classes. For example, if we look at the permissions for `file` and `dir` object class, we will notice that many of them are the same, but some are not. (The permissions valid for both are a result of the use of common permissions, as discussed in Chapter 4, "Object Classes and Permissions.")

Suppose, for example, we want to write a rule to give a form of "read" access for both object classes. The following rule is not valid:

```
# An invalid rule because search is not valid for the object class file
allow user_t bin_t : { file dir } { read getattr search };
```

Although `read` and `getattr` are common permissions for both `dir` and `file` object classes, the `search` permission is valid only for `dir` object class. Because `checkpolicy` cannot create a key that gives `file` class an invalid permission (`search`), we would get an error when trying to compile a policy with this rule. Our only recourse in this case is to create two rules, such as these:

```
# Two rules are needed when permissions are not valid for
# both object classes
allow user_t bin_t : file { read getattr };
allow user_t bin_t : dir { read getattr search } ;
```

### 5.3.1.7 Special Permission Operators for AV Rules

We can use two special operators for listing permissions in AV rules. The first special operator is a *wildcard operator* (*). The wildcard operator includes all permissions for an object class:

```
allow user_t bin_t : { file dir } *;
```

This rule will expand into all of the permissions for `file` and `dir`.

The wildcard operator syntax differs subtly from explicitly listing all the permissions for the object classes. With the wildcard operator, all permissions are included for each object class individually, regardless of whether they are valid for all the object classes. This makes it possible to use the wildcard operator in rules with multiple object classes, even if those object classes have different permissions. So, for example, the above rule would safely handle the permissions that are only valid for `dir` object class and not `file` class, unlike the earlier example.

The second special operator makes it possible to include all the permissions *not* listed using the *complement operator* (~):

```
allow user_t bin_t : file ~{ write setattr ioctl };
```

When compiled, this rule allows all the permissions for the `file` object class except `write`, `setattr`, and `ioctl`. Similar to the wildcard operator, complement expands the permission lists individually for each listed object class.

> WARNING   Be advised that the proper and allowed use of all three special operators (negation, wildcard, and complement) has evolved and changed over the past few years. Many recent versions of `checkpolicy` will allow these operators to be used in places other than those listed here. For example, `checkpolicy` versions, including that released with RHEL4, allow the wildcard operator (\*) to be used for types.
>
> Recent improvements to the compiler have tightened the allowed use for these operators to be consistent with the rules previously discussed. The primary exception is that the wildcard operator may be used for types in `neverallow` rules, but no other TE rule. In general, if you use these operators as discussed herein, you will be safe.

---

### Common Access Vector Rule Syntax

The full common syntax for AV rules is as follows:

*rule_name*   *type_set*   *type_set* : *class_set*   *perm_set* ;

*rule_name*   The name of the access vector rule. Valid rule names are allow, `auditallow`, `auditdeny`, `dontaudit`, or `neverallow`.

*type_set*    One or more types and/or attributes. There is a separate *type_set* for the source and target types of the rules. Multiple types and attributes are specified using a space-separated list enclosed in braces ({ })—for example, { bin_t sbin_t }. Types can be excluded from the list by prepending - to the type name (for example, { exec_type -sbin_t }). The keyword `self` can be used in the target type field either alone or as part of a list of types and attributes. `Self` cannot be used in the source type field. `Neverallow` rules also support the wildcard operator (`*`) to include all types and the complement operator (`~`) to include all types `except` those explicitly listed.

*class_set*     One or more object classes. Multiple object classes must be enclosed in braces (`{  }`)—for example, `{ file lnk_file }`.

*perm_set*     One or more permission. All permissions must be valid for all object classes in the *class_set*. Multiple permissions must be enclosed in braces (`{  }`)—for example, `{read create}`. The wildcard operator (`*`) is used to specify all permissions for all object classes. The complement operator (`~`) is used to specify all permissions `except` those explicitly listed.

All AV rules are valid in monolithic policies, base loadable modules, and non-base loadable modules. All AV rules except auditdeny and neverallow rules are valid in conditional statements.

## 5.3.2 Allow Rules

By now you have seen many examples of `allow` rules in this and previous chapters. The `allow` rule is the most common rule in a policy and implements the primary purpose of an SELinux policy (that is, to allow access).

As discussed, we use `allow` rules to specify all permissions that will be granted at runtime. They are the only means to allow permissions in an SELinux policy. Remember, *no access is allowed by default.* We specify access between two lists of types, the source and target, in terms of permissions for the listed object classes, as follows:

```
allow user_t bin_t : file { read execute };
```

This rule allows any process whose security context has the type `user_t` to have `read` and `execute` permissions to any ordinary file whose security context has the type `bin_t`. `Allow` rules share all of the common AV rules syntax and do not have any additional syntax.

If this example were the only `allow` rule in our policy with this source type, target type, and object class, no other access would be granted to files with the type of bin_t. For example, user_t would not be able to write files of type bin_t.

Allow rules, like all AV rules, are cumulative and the actual access allowed for a given subject-target-class key is the union of all the allow rules that refer to that key. For example, these two sets of rules are equivalent:

```
# These two rules...
allow user_t bin_t : file read;
allow user_t bin_t : file write;

# are equivalent to (and redundant with) this single rule.
allow user_t bin_t : file { read write };
```

### 5.3.3 Audit Rules

SELinux has extensive facilities for logging, or auditing, access attempts that are either allowed or denied by the policy. The audit messages, often called "AVC messages," give detailed information about an access attempt, including whether it was allowed or denied, the security context of the source and target, and other details about the resources involved in the access attempt. The messages, which are similar to other kernel messages and are usually stored in log files under /var/log, are an indispensable tool for policy development, system administration, and system monitoring. In this chapter, we examine the policy features that enable us to configure which access attempts will generate audit messages. Part III provides more information about how to use audit messages to debug and understand policies.

By default, SELinux does *not* record any access checks that are allowed but records *all* access checks that are denied. These defaults are not surprising; on most systems, thousands of accesses per second are allowed, but few accesses are denied. The allowed accesses are, by the fact that they were allowed, expected and usually do not require auditing. The denied accesses are usually, but not always, unexpected, and auditing them helps an administrator to monitor for policy bugs and/or possible intrusion attempts. The policy language allows us to override portions of these defaults to suppress audit messages for expected access denials and to generate audit messages for access attempts that were allowed.

SELinux provides two AV rules that allow us to control which access attempts are audited: dontaudit and auditallow. These two rules are the policy mechanism that enable us to change these auditing defaults. The dontaudit rule is the most commonly used. It specifies which access denials should not be audited, overriding the SELinux default behavior to audit all access denials.

> WARNING    Access denials are audited only if the denial was
> made by SELinux. Recall from Chapter 3 that LSM module hook
> functions are usually called only if the access passes the standard
> Linux discretionary access control checks. This means that if an
> access was denied because of the standard Linux access checks,
> SELinux is not even aware of the access attempt and cannot gen-
> erate an audit message. If you need to audit all denied accesses
> regardless of why the access is denied, you must directly use the
> kernel audit system included in the 2.6.x series of kernels. See the
> man pages for *auditd*(8) and *auditctl*(8).

For example, consider this:

```
dontaudit httpd_t etc_t : dir search;
```

This rule specifies that when processes of type `httpd_t` are denied `search` permission on directories of type `etc_t`, the denial should not be audited, overriding
the default behavior. We might write this rule if processes with type `httpd_t`
attempt to search directories of type `etc_t` (presumably `/etc/`) but function properly when this access is not granted. You will find Linux/UNIX applications often
exhibit this type of behavior; that is, they attempt access they do not need yet work
fine when the access is denied.

The `dontaudit` rule is useful when we want to mask audit denial messages that
are expected, usually due to expected behavior of an application. The `dontaudit`
rule allows us to avoid granting unnecessary access (because the application works
without the access, it is unnecessary by any definition) without a large number of
expected audit messages filling the system logs. As we said, this type of behavior is
all too common.

---

### Auditdeny Rule

Earlier versions of SELinux supported an `auditdeny` rule. These rules were used
for a similar purpose to the dontaudit rules. Although still supported by the policy language, an `auditdeny` rule is seldom, if ever, seen in policies. The rule is
deprecated, and we suggest you do not attempt to use it. The `dontaudit` rule,
coupled with the default behavior of recording all access denials, is the desired
method for controlling access denial auditing.

---

The other audit rule, `auditallow`, allows us to control the auditing of allowed access attempts. Unlike denied access, allowed access is not recorded by default. For example, let's look at the following rule:

```
auditallow domain shadow_t : file write;
```

This rules specifies that when a process with a type that has the `domain` attribute successfully obtains `write` access to files of type `shadow_t`, the allowed access is audited. The `auditallow` rule is useful to audit accesses that are an important security event. Examples of access that are likely to have an `auditallow` rule include writing to the shadow password file (as the above rule does) or reloading a new policy into the kernel.

Remember, audit rules let us override the default auditing settings. The `allow` rule specifies which access is allowed. The `auditallow` rule does not allow access; it enables only auditing of allowed permissions.

> NOTE   Auditing is different in permissive and enforcing modes. When running in enforcing mode, audit messages are generated every time there is an allowed or denied access that the policy states should be audited up to a rate limit (this can be set with *auditctl*(8)). In permissive mode, only the first access attempt is logged until the next policy load or toggle of the enforcing mode. Permissive mode is most often used for policy development, and this auditing mode helps reduce the size of the log.

## 5.3.4 Neverallow Rules

The final AV rule is the `neverallow` rule. We use this rule to state invariant properties specifying certain accesses that may never be permitted by an `allow` rule. You might wonder why this rule exists, because access is denied by default. The reason is to aid policy writing by noting certain undesired permissions, thereby preventing the accidental inclusion of these permissions in our policy. Recall that an SELinux policy is likely to contain tens of thousands of rules. It is quite possible to accidentally grant an access we did not want to grant. The `neverallow` rule helps prevent this situation. For example, consider this rule:

```
neverallow user_t shadow_t : file write;
```

This `neverallow` rule would prevent us from adding a rule to the policy that allows `user_t` to write to files of type `shadow_t` by generating a compile error. This rule does not remove access, it just generates compile errors. The `neverallow` rule is to state important properties about our policy before we start writing `allow` rules. The `neverallow` rules prevent us from inadvertently including permissions that we did not intend.

The `neverallow` rule supports some additional syntax that the other AV rules do not. In particular, the source and target type lists in `neverallow` rules can contain the wildcard (*) and complement (~) operators. These operators work just as they do for permission lists in the rest of the AV rules (see the section "Special Permission Operators for AV Rules," earlier in this chapter).

For example, look at the following rule:

```
neverallow * domain : dir ~{ read getattr };
```

This rule states that no `allow` rule may grant any type any access except `read` and `getattr` access (that is, "read access") to directories labeled with one of the types associated with the `domain` attributes. The wildcard operator in this rule means all types. A `neverallow` rule similar to this is commonly found in policies and is used to prevent inappropriate access to directories in `/proc/` that store process information (which will be labeled with the same type as processes).

We can see from the preceding example that the wildcard operator is needed in the source type lists for `neverallow` rules because we are referring to any and all types, including those not yet created. The wildcard operator allows us to prevent future mistakes.

Another common `neverallow` rule is this:

```
neverallow domain ~domain : process transition;
```

This `neverallow` rule reinforces the concept of the `domain` attribute described earlier in this chapter. This rule states that a process cannot transition to a type that does not have the `domain` attribute. This makes it impossible to create a valid policy with a type intended for a process that does not have the `domain` attribute.

---

### Loadable Module Dependency Handling

Loadable policy modules, which are a new feature in *Fedora Core 5* (FC5), contain language features for handling dependencies between modules. The dependency handling features ensure that the policy components (that is, identifiers) a module expects are present at module installation time. See Chapter 13, "Managing an SELinux System," for more information about how loadable policy modules are installed and managed. Possible policy component dependencies include object classes, permissions, users, roles, types or aliases, attributes, and Boolean identifiers.

The `require` statement states the policy components required for a loadable module. All policy components that are not declared in the module must be required in some form. For example, consider the following require statement:

```
require { type etc_t; }
```

The example above states that the loadable module in which it appears requires the type `etc_t` to be declared elsewhere in the policy (that is, in the base module or other loadable modules). This `require` statement allows the type `etc_t` to appear in policy rules within the module without being explicitly declared. Following is a more complete example showing a more `require` statement, type declaration, and an example `allow` rule:

---

```
require {
        attribute domain;
        type etc_t;
        class file { read getattr };
}
type httpd_t, domain;
allow httpd_t etc_t : file { read getattr };
```

---

As you can see, every policy component used in the example `allow` rule was either declared or required before it was used. For example, the `domain` attribute was required before it was used in the `httpd_t` type declaration. Obviously, many `require` statements would be needed for a loadable module of any complexity. In Chapter 12, "Reference Policy," we discuss how the reference policy automates the generation of `require` statements.

We use the `require` statement to state unconditional requirements that must be present in the policy for the loadable module to be installed. The `optional` statement is used to state requirements that may or may not be present. This allows the policy author to add rules based on whether policy components are present. For example, consider the following `optional` statement:

```
optional {
        require { type user_home_t; }
        allow httpd_t user_home_t : file read;
}
```

This statement allows processes with the type `httpd_t` to read files with the type `user_home_t` *if* that type is present. As you can see, the `optional` statement wraps standard policy statements, including `require` statements. Whenever modules are added or removed from the system, all the optional dependencies are checked and enabled or disabled as appropriate.

The full syntax of the `require` statement is as follows:

`require { ` *require_list* ` }`

*require_list*    One or more semicolon-separated require declarations. A require declaration consists of an identifier for the variety of policy component followed by the name of the policy component. Valid policy component variety identifiers are `class`, `user`, `role`, `type`, `attribute`, and `bool`. For users, roles, types, attributes, and Booleans, only a single name may be listed (for example, `type  httpd_t;`). For object classes, both the object classes and one or more permissions is listed (for example, `class file { read write };`).

`Require` statements not a part of an optional statement are valid only in non-base loadable modules. They are not valid in a base module or in any conditional statements.

The full syntax for the optional statement is as follows:

`optional { ` *rule_list* ` }`

*rule_list*    One or more policy statements that are enabled if all the required statements in the `optional` statement are satisfied. Valid policy statements are `user`, `role`, `type`, `attribute`, and `alias` declarations and TE and RBAC rules (including conditional statements).

`Optional` statements are valid only in base and non-base loadable policy modules. They are not valid in conditional statements.

## 5.4 Type Rules

Type rules specify default types for objects created or relabeled at runtime. We have already seen one example of this in Chapter 2 in the form of default domain transitions using the `type_transition` rule. There are two type rules defined in the policy language:

| | |
|---|---|
| `type_transition` | Specifies default type labeling behavior for domain transition and object creation |
| `type_change` | Specifies default types for relabeling performed by SELinux-aware applications |

We call these rules "type rules" because they are similar to AV rules except that the last field in the rule is a type name rather than a list of permissions.

### 5.4.1 Common Type Rule Syntax

As with AV rules, each of the type rules has a different purpose and semantics, but they all share common syntax. Each type rule has five elements:

- *Rule name*     `type_transition` or `type_change`
- *Source type(s)*     The type(s) of the creating or owning process
- *Target type(s)*     The type(s) of the object containing the new or relabeled object
- *Object class(es)*     The class(es) of object(s) being created or relabeled
- *Default type*     The single default type for the new or relabeled object

The full syntax for the type rules is in the sidebar on page 117.

Much of the type rule syntax is similar to AV rules, but there are important differences. First, there are no permissions. Unlike AV rules, type rules do not specify access or auditing, so there is no need for permissions. The second major difference is that the object class is *not* associated with the target types. Instead, the object class refers to the objects that will be labeled with the default type.

The simplest form of a type rule has one source, target, and default types, and one object class, as follows:

```
type_transition user_t passwd_exec_t : process passwd_t;
```

This rule, which you saw in Chapter 2, specifies that when a process of type user_t executes a file of type passwd_exec_t, the process type will attempt to transition, by default, to passwd_t unless otherwise requested. The target type is implicitly associated with the file object class when the stated object class is process. The stated object class (process) is associated with the source and default types. This subtle and implicit association is easy to overlook, even after you become an experienced policy writer.

As with AV rules, we can specify more than one object class by using a space-separated list enclosed in braces. Likewise, we can use attributes, and lists of types and attributes in type rules, as follows:

```
type_transition { user_t sysadm_t } passwd_exec_t : process passwd_t;
```

This type_transition rule includes two types, user_t and sysadm_t, in the source list. As with AV rules, this rule would be expanded into two rules. The preceding rule has the exact same meaning as the following two rules:

```
# These two rules...
type_transition user_t passwd_exec_t : process passwd_t;
type_transition sysadm_t passwd_exec_t : process passwd_t;

# are equivalent to this single rule.
type_transition { user_t sysadm_t } passwd_exec_t : process passwd_t;
```

The use of attributes also works the same as in AV rules.

Unlike source and target type fields, *attributes and/or multiple types cannot be used for the default type.* The reason for this restriction is clear when you understand the purpose of this rule (that is, to specify a single default type). If we could list more than one default type, the rule would be ambiguous and it would be impossible for the kernel to determine which default type to use.

The restriction for a single default type also means that we cannot have two separate type rules that have the same source, target, and object class, as this would be semantically equivalent to two default types. For example, the following two rules would conflict:

```
# These two rules conflict and will cause a compile-time problem
type_transition user_t passwd_exec_t : process passwd_t;
type_transition user_t passwd_exec_t : process user_passwd_t;
```

The policy compiler generates an error if both of these rules are present in a policy. These conflicting `type_transition` rules also make the reason for the restriction clear. If both rules were present, which type, `passwd_t` or `user_passwd_t`, would be used for the default type?

---

### Common Type Rule Syntax

The full common syntax for type rules is as follows:

*rule_name*    *type_set*    *type_set* : *class_set*    *default_type*;

*rule_name*    The name of the type rule. Valid rule names are `type_transition`, `type_change`, and `type_member`.

*type_set*    One or more types or attributes. There is a separate *type_set* for each of the source and target types of the rules. Multiple types and attributes are specified using a space-separated list enclosed in braces (`{ }`)—for example, `{ bin_t sbin_t }`. Types can be excluded from the list by prepending `-` to the type name (for example, `{ exec_type -sbin_t }`).

*class_set*    One or more object classes. Multiple object classes must be enclosed in braces (`{ }`)—for example, `{ file lnk_file }`.

*default_type* A single type that is the default for the newly created or relabeled object. Attributes or multiple types cannot be used.

All type rules are valid in monolithic policies, base loadable modules, non-base loadable modules, and conditional statements.

---

## 5.4.2 Type Transition Rules

We use `type_transition` rules to specify default type labeling rules for certain events. Currently, there are two forms of the `type_transition` rule. The first supports *default domain transition* events, which is the form of `type_transition` rule introduced in Chapter 2. The second form of this rule supports *object transitions,* which allow us to specify default object labeling.

Both forms of the `type_transition` rule help make the enhanced security of SELinux transparent to the Linux user. In SELinux, by default, newly created objects receive the type of their containing object (for example, directory), and processes inherit the type of their parent process. The `type_transition` rule enables us to override these defaults. This is useful, for example, to ensure that when the password program creates a file in the `/tmp/` directory, that its file is given a different type than those of ordinary users.

The `type_transition` rule does not allow access; it provides only a new type labeling default. A successful type transition always requires the associated set of allow rules that permit the process type the ability to create the object and label the object as specified. In addition, the default labeling specified in `type_transition` rules takes effect only if the creating process does not explicitly override the default labeling behavior.

### 5.4.2.1 Default Domain Transitions

Let's examine the domain transition form of this rule in more detail. Domain transitions change the type of a process when executing a file. For example, look at this rule:

```
type_transition init_t apache_exec_t : process apache_t;
```

This `type_transition` rule states that when processes of type `init_t` execute a file of type `apache_exec_t` the process type should be changed to `apache_t`. The object class `process` is the only indication that this is a domain transition form of the rule. Figure 5-1 shows a domain transition. Domain transitions actually change the type of an existing process instead of labeling a newly created process. This is because in Linux a new process is created by first making a copy of an existing process using the `fork()` system call. If the process type were changed on fork, it would allow the calling domain to execute arbitrary code in the new domain. It is much safer for the domain transition to happen when executing a new program via the `execve()` system call.

> WARNING    Recent versions of SELinux introduced the `process` object class permission `dyntransition`. This permission, which was added primarily for compatibility with other systems, allows a process to change its domain type at request instead of just on execute. This type of process transition is not safe because it allows the calling domain to execute arbitrary code in the new domain, destroying the separation between the two domains. In addition, the same functionality can often be achieved using other, safer mechanisms. We recommend that you *never* use this permission in your policies unless you are building a userspace object manager or if you are absolutely sure it is required.

As mentioned previously, a type transition can occur only if the policy allows the associated access. For a domain transition to succeed, the policy must allow at least three accesses:

- *execute*   The source type (`init_t`) must have `execute` permission for files with the target type (`apache_exec_t`).

- *transition*   The source domain (`init_t`) must have `transition` permission to the default type (`apache_t`).

- *entrypoint*   The new (default) type (`apache_t`) must have `entrypoint` permission to files with the target type (`apache_exec_t`).

The domain transition above would require at least the following `allow` rules to succeed:

```
# This domain transition rule...
type_transition init_t apache_exec_t : process apache_t;

# would require at least the following 3 allow rules to succeed
allow init_t apache_exec_t : file execute;
allow init_t apache_t : process transition;
allow apache_t apache_exec_t : file entrypoint;
```

In practice, we will likely want to allow additional access beside the above minimum. For example, it is common to allow the default type to signal the source type upon exit (that is, `sigchld` permission), inherit file descriptors, and communicate using pipes.

The key concept with domain transitions is that there is a clearly defined *entry point*—that is, the file labeled with the type (`apache_exec_t`) for which the new (default) type (`apache_exec_t`) has `entrypoint` permission. The entry point file allows us to strictly control which programs may execute in which domains (arguably the security trait that makes type enforcement so strong). We know that the only program that can be used to enter a given domain is that program whose executable file is labeled with a type to which the domain has `entrypoint` access. Thus we can know and control which programs have which privileges.

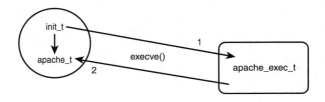

type_transition init_t apache_exec_t : process apache_t

**FIGURE 5-1**
A depiction of a default domain transition

## 5.4.2.2 Default Object Transitions

Object transition rules specify a default type for newly created objects. In practice, we commonly use this form of the `type_transition` rule primarily for filesystem-related objects (for example, `file`, `dir`, `lnk_file`). Like domain transitions, these rules cause only a default object labeling to be attempted; the attempt can succeed only if the policy allows the associated access.

Object transition rules are identified by object class, as follows:

```
type_transition passwd_t tmp_t : file passwd_tmp_t;
```

This `type_transition` rule states that when a process of type `passwd_t` creates an ordinary file (`file` object class) in a directory of type `tmp_t` the file, by default, should have the type `passwd_tmp_t` if allowed by the policy. Notice that the object class refers not to the target type (`tmp_t`) but to the default type (`passwd_tmp_t`). In this example, `tmp_t` is implicitly associated with the `dir` object class because that is the only object class that can contain files. Also, as before, the policy must allow the access for the default labeling to occur. Access required for the preceding example includes `add_name`, `write`, and `search` for directories of type `tmp_t`, and `write` and `create` for files of type `passwd_tmp_t`.

This example is typical and shows one technique for solving the security problems inherent in a directory shared by many applications such as a temporary directory. Object transition rules are useful for any objects that will be created at runtime and need to have types other than that of the containing object.

Some circumstances cannot be handled with object transition rules. Whenever a process needs to create objects with multiple different types in the same container object, a `type_transition` rule is not sufficient. For example, consider a process that creates two UNIX domain sockets in `/tmp/` that will be used by other domains for communication. If we want to give each `sock` file a different type, object transition rules would not suffice. We would end up with two rules with the same source, target, and object class and a different default type, which would result in a compiler error. The possible solutions to this problem are to create the `sock` files at installation time and explicitly label them, place the `sock` files in separate directories with different directory types, or have the process explicitly request types on creation.

### 5.4.3 Type Change Rules

We use a `type_change` rule to specify default types for relabeling performed by SELinux-aware applications. Like `type_transition` rules, `type_change` rules specify labeling defaults but do not allow access. Unlike `type_transition` rules, the effects of `type_change` rules are not implemented in the kernel but rely on userspace applications, such as `login` or `sshd`, to relabel objects based on the policy. For example, consider this rule:

```
type_change sysadm_t tty_device_t : chr_file sysadm_tty_device_t;
```

This `type_change` rule states that when relabeling a character file of type `tty_device_t` on behalf of `sysadm_t`, the type `sysadm_tty_device_t` should be used.

This rule is an example of the most common use for `type_change` rules—that is, relabeling a terminal device on user login. The `login` program would query the policy via a kernel interface to the SELinux module, passing in the types `sysadm_t` and `tty_device_t` and receiving the type `sysadm_tty_device_t` as the type to use for the relabel change. This mechanism allows the login process to label the tty device on behalf of the user during a new login session while leaving the specifics of the types encapsulated in the policy instead of hard-coded in the application.

We will probably seldom, if ever, write `type_change` rules because they are usually used only by core operating system services.

---

### type_member Rule

The policy compiler also supports a third type rule, `type_member`. Currently, this rule has no semantic meaning and if used will have no effect. We mention it here because at the time of writing, work is ongoing that would create a need for it. A `type_member` rule is intended to support specifying the type for members of a *polyinstantiated object*. The `type_member` rule will be enabled with meaningful semantics. The syntax of this rule is the same as the other two type rules.

---

## 5.5 Exploring Type Enforcement Rules with Apol

We have already seen that examining a policy to understand all the type enforcement declarations and rules is difficult. Determining all the types that are part of an attribute, for example, requires examining all the `type` and `typeattribute` statements in a policy. In a large policy, that could be thousands of statements spread across dozens of files. This is a daunting task. Automating this kind of policy analysis was one of the primary motivations for creating the policy analysis and debug tool `apol`. Let's examine some of the ways we can use `apol` to explore a type enforcement policy.

When we first start `apol` and load a policy, as you can see in Figure 5-2, the Policy Component tab is visible with the Types tab selected. All the types and attributes are listed on the left and a search window is on the right. Selecting a type and clicking Show Type Info brings up a window that shows all the attributes and aliases for that type. Similarly, selecting an attribute and clicking Show Attribute Info brings up a window that shows all the types that are part of that attribute. Figure 5-3 shows the detailed information about the `domain` attribute for this policy. This is one of the simplest but most valuable functions of `apol`.

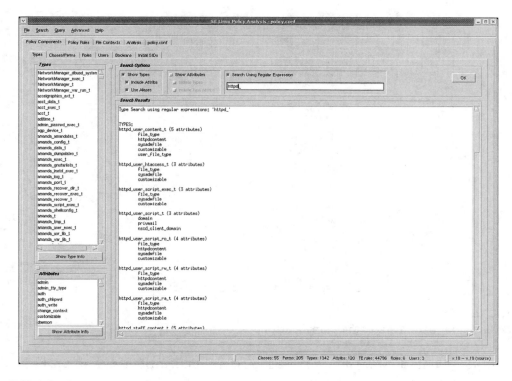

FIGURE 5-2
Examining types and attributes using apol

FIGURE 5-3
Detailed information about the domain attribute

In addition to showing information about types and attributes, apol enables us to search for types or attributes using regular expressions. Figure 5-4 shows a search for all types that contain the substring httpd_ with the attributes and aliases for those types displayed.

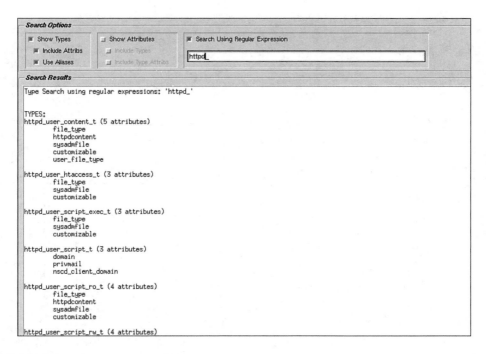

**FIGURE 5-4**
A regular expression search for types

Apol also enables us to search for policy rules, including searching for rules that indirectly include types via attributes. The rule searching functionality of apol is powerful, but we want to mention only some of that power here. Figure 5-5 shows a rule search for allow rules that contain shadow_t as the target type. Notice that the "Include indirect matches" button is selected, which means that rules that reference shadow_t indirectly through an attribute are included. Manually searching for rules and resolving attributes is an almost impossible task.

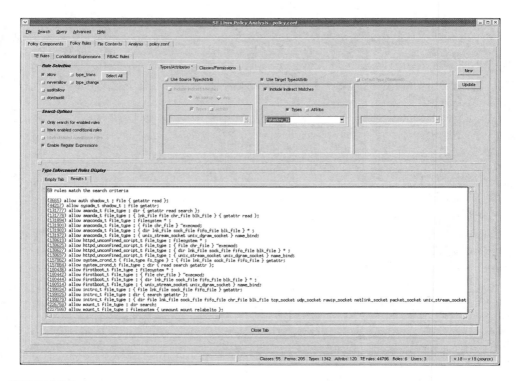

FIGURE 5-5
A rule search for allow rules with shadow_t as the target type

Apo1 is a valuable tool to use as you read through this book and try to under-stand an SELinux policy. It enables you to explore the content of a policy, perform sophisticated searches, and browse policy components such as types and object classes. In particular, you will find the TE Rules under the Policy Rules tab to be extremely valuable to answer the ubiquitous question, "What's going on with this type?" As you get familiar with the tool and with SELinux policy, you should explore the tools under the Analysis tab. These tools perform complex analyses of the policy.

## 5.6 Summary

- Types are the primary basis for access control in SELinux. They serve as access control attributes for all objects (process, file, dir, socket, and so on). Types are declared using the `type` statement.

- Attributes are groups of types. We can use them in place of types in most policy statements. We must declare attributes before using them. We can add types to attributes as part of a `type` declaration or using the `typeattribute` statement.

- Aliases are alternate names for types, most often used to provide backward compatibility when renaming types. We declare aliases as part of a type declaration or using the `typealias` statement.

- There are four AV rules that share common syntax: `allow`, `neverallow`, `auditallow`, and `dontaudit`.

- We use an `allow` rule to specify what access a domain type may have to an object type. We specify access in terms of object classes and permissions.

- Audit messages are, by default, not generated when access is allowed, but are generated when access is denied. We use `dontaudit` rules to specify denied accesses that *should not* generate an audit message. We use `auditallow` rules to specify allowed accesses that *should* generate an audit message.

- AV rules (for example, `allow`) are cumulative, and the access that will be allowed or audited at runtime for a given source type, target type, and object class key is the union of all the rules that refer to that key.

- We use `neverallow` rules to state invariant properties about access that should never be allowed by an `allow` rule. If an `allow` rule violates an invariant, the `checkpolicy` compiler will generate a compile error.

- Two type rules share a common syntax: `type_transition` and `type_change`. Type rules do not allow access; instead, they specify desired default labeling policy for object creation and relabel events.

- We use `type_transition` rules to label new objects upon creation (object transition) or to change process types on execution of new applications (domain transition).

- We use `type_change` rules to specify default types for relabeling objects. They are used by SELinux aware software such as `login` or `sshd`.

- The policy analysis tool `apol` is valuable for understanding and analyzing complex SELinux policies.

## Exercises

1.  Declare a type named `samba_t` with the attribute `domain` and the alias `smbd_t`.

2.  Create an `allow` rule that gives a process with the type `samba_t` read, write, and `getattr` access to files of type `user_home_t`.

3.  Convert these `allow` rules into as few rules as possible:

    ```
    allow samba_t self : process *;
    allow samba_t user_homedir_t : dir { read getattr search };
    allow samba_t user_homedir_t : dir { write add_name };
    allow samba_t user_homedir_t : file { read getattr };
    allow samba_t user_home_t : file { write };
    ```

4.  Write an access vector rule that will cause an audit message to be generated whenever a user's SSH key file, represented by the type `user_ssh_key_t`, is written.

5.  Write a `type_transition` rule that will cause files of type `sysadm_tmp_t` to be created by default when processes of type `sysadm_t` create files in directories of type `tmp_t`.

6.  Write a `type_transition` rule that will cause a domain transition to `games_t` to occur when processes of type `user_t` execute files of type `games_exec_t`.

7.  Write the minimum `allow` rules required that will allow the `type_transition` rule from Exercise 6 to succeed.

# Chapter 6

## Roles and Users

**In this chapter**

SELinux provides a form of *role-based access control* (RBAC) that builds upon *type enforcement* (TE). Roles are used to group domain types and to restrict relationships between domain types and users. Users in SELinux associate one or more roles with a Linux user. Using roles and users, the RBAC features allow for the efficient definition and management of the privileges ultimately granted to Linux users.

## 6.1 Role-Based Access Control in SELinux

Roles and users exist in SELinux as the basis for its RBAC feature. It may be surprising that we have not discussed roles or users in any significant way until this point. The security features of most other mainstream operating systems are mostly centered on granting access to users, either directly or through some form of group or role mechanism. This is not the case in SELinux, where access is *not* granted directly to users or roles. Instead, as discussed in Chapter 5, "Type Enforcement," access is granted to types via TE `allow` rules. Roles act as a supporting feature to type enforcement, and together with users provide a means to bind type-based access control with Linux users and the programs they are allowed to run. RBAC in SELinux further constrains type enforcement by defining the relationship between domain types and users to control Linux users' privileges and access permissions. RBAC does not allow access. As always in SELinux, allowed access is the providence of type enforcement.

> WARNING The fact that Linux and SELinux have distinct user identifiers (that are sometimes related) can be confusing. To help avoid this confusion, we write "Linux user" when meaning the user account as defined in `/etc/passwd`. Anytime we discuss "user" or "user identifier" without a qualifier, we mean the user identifier in security contexts as defined in the SELinux policy.

### 6.1.1 Overview of RBAC in SELinux

As stated, in SELinux, RBAC features build upon and support the TE features. We grant privileges to a user indirectly by associating domain types with one or more roles. The RBAC policy statements do not grant access. Instead, RBAC further constrains the TE policy by controlling the associations of domain types, roles, and users in a security context. In this way, the domain transitions available to a user's domain type are restricted based on the user's role, ultimately restricting the total privileges of the user.

To illustrate, consider the example from Chapter 2, "Concepts," which we elaborate further in Figure 6-1. This example illustrates a domain transition from a bash shell process with the domain type `user_t` to a process running the password program with the domain type `passwd_t`. Notice that we added the user and role portions of the security contexts for the process security contexts (`joe:user_r:user_t` and `joe:user_r:passwd_t`). Let's also assume that the policy includes the necessary TE rules to permit the domain transition (which are not shown).

This example demonstrates two kinds of RBAC policy statements: a *user declaration statement* (`user`) and two *role declaration statements* (`role`). These statements create associations between the user, role, and type identifiers in the policy. You will see the full syntax of these statements later in the chapter. For now, understand their effect on domain transitions.

The `user` statement shown in Figure 6-1 associates the SELinux user `joe` with the role `user_r`. This statement tells SELinux that the user `joe` and the role `user_r` are allowed to coexists in a security context. Without this statement, the user `joe` and role `user_r` process security contexts in Figure 6-1 would be invalid and SELinux would refuse to create them, resulting in a denial of the domain transition attempt.

The two `role` statements associate the role `user_r` with the domain types `user_t` and `passwd_t`. Like the `user` statement, the `role` statements are required for the process security contexts to be valid. In particular, without the `role` statement associating the type `passwd_t`, this domain transition would fail even though the TE policy allows it. If we did not want the `user_r` role to run the password program, we could simply remove this `role` statement and the security context would never be created by the kernel, even if the TE rules allowed the access.

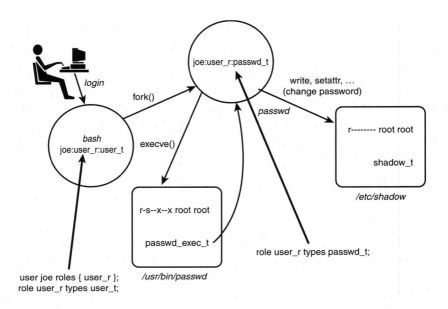

**FIGURE 6-1**
Relationship of users, roles, and types, and the SELinux RBAC statements

## 6.1.2 Managing User Privileges with Roles

As the example in Figure 6-1 illustrates, we do not directly associate domain types with users. Instead, we associate roles with domain types, which are in turn associated with SELinux users. This additional layer of indirection serves two purposes. First, it makes the management of the overall policy less complex. A system may only have three or four roles, but could have many hundreds of users and domain types. Directly associating domain types with users would be difficult to manage. Assigning the domain types to a handful of roles that characterize the privileges of the set of types (for example, ordinary user domain types) and then assigning those roles to users is more manageable.

Roles in SELinux also allow us to limit the access of users based on their current privileges and responsibilities as represented by the active role. For any given process, one role is "active" at a time (that is, the role in the process security context) and, because the domain types are associated with roles, the available domain transitions are limited to those domain types associated with the active role.

Limiting domain transitions to only the currently active role allows a user to be associated with more than one role without gaining the union of the access rights for all the roles. For example, we could associate a user with both a system administration role and a more restrictive ordinary user role, the latter being used for normal interactive, nonadministrative activities. In this scenario, the more restrictive ordinary user role would be active during normal use, preventing access to powerful administrative domain types. The system administrator would "activate" (that is, change via a domain transition) the more privileged administrative role only when necessary to perform system administrative duties. This is similar to, but more fine-grained than, the common best practice for standard Linux of only switching to the root account for system administration and using a normal user account for all other activities.

The key point to remember about roles is that they are only a collection of domain types, which can be conveniently associated with a user. They are not a separate access control mechanism in SELinux.

> TIP   A number of utilities such as `newrole` and a modified `su` command provide a means by which a user (or user process) changes the current (that is, active) role by creating a new shell process with a different security context via a domain transition (see Chapter 13, "Managing an SELinux System"). (*Fedora Core 5* [FC5] removes the ability for `su` to change roles, instead requiring the use of `newrole`.) Changing roles is controlled by the associations of users and roles (that is, the `user` statement) and *role allow rules* (`allow`), which we discuss later in the chapter.

---

### Roles Versus User Domain Types

To date, most SELinux policies use roles only in limited ways. This is partly in recognition of the secondary purpose of roles with respect to type enforcement. The typical situation today is that one of the associated domain types for each role is a "user domain type," which is the type that shell processes for users of that role are assigned at initial login. For example, the ordinary, unprivileged user domain type user_t is associated with the role user_r. Likewise, the privileged user's untrusted domain type is staff_t, which is associated with the role staff_r.

These initial user domain types, and all the domain types to which they may transition, are truly what define the roles "user" and "staff." For example, the primary difference between these two "roles" is the ability of the staff role (and hence the staff_t domain type) to transition into the privileged administrator roles and user domain type (sysadm_t, which has an associated sysadm_r role).

One ramification of the practice of having one initial user domain type per role is that we tend to have *derived domain types* for some programs. For example, to keep downloaded data, including programs, separated by role (reducing the chance of co-opting administrative users), we could run a Web browser in different domain types for each role. To accomplish this goal, we would create different domain transition rules for the associated user domain types (user_t and staff_t). Upon executing the Web browser executable file, each user domain type would transition into separate domain types (that is, user_mozilla_t and staff_mozilla_t), rather than the same type (that is, mozilla_t) as we had with passwd_t. In this way, ordinary users (user_t) and administrative users (staff_t) would have domains for Web browsing protected from each other. We would associate each role only with the appropriate types. (For example, user_mozilla_t would be associated only with user_r.) To complete the separation, we would create separate file types for each Web browser domain and only allow the domains types "write" access to their respective file types. The result would be that the Web browser runs in a different domain depending on the role of the user and the downloaded data is separated based on the role.

---

### 6.1.3 Users and Roles in Object Security Contexts

In our password policy example (see Figure 6-1), we did not include the full security context for the file objects shown (that is, the executable file `/usr/bin/passwd` and the shadow password file `/etc/shadow`). This absence reflects the relatively low importance of the user and role portion of the security context for objects. Although objects must still have a full security context, the user field at most supports auditing, and roles have no purpose at all. If we examine the objects in Figure 6-1 on our example system, we see the following complete security contexts:

```
# ls --scontext /usr/bin/passwd /etc/shadow
system_u:object_r:shadow_t        /etc/shadow
system_u:object_r:passwd_exec_t   /usr/bin/passwd
```

As you can see, both objects have the special role `object_r`, which is typically the role for all objects. This role is hard-coded into SELinux, does not need to be declared, and is implicitly allowed for all types. You should never try to declare the role `object_r`.

The user portion of the security context for objects is usually set to the user portion of the creating process security context. This feature has some potential utility to track which user created the object but in general has no security enforcement purpose (other than possibly constraints, which we discuss in Chapter 9, "Conditional Policies"). In the preceding case, the user for both objects is `system_u`, which is a special user found in many policies representing system resources and processes.

## 6.2 Roles and Role Statements

SELinux does not have any built-in roles with the exception of `object_r`. Roles, like types, are declared in the policy and given meaning through consistent use. Four policy statements relate to roles: role declaration statements, role `allow` rules, role transition rules, and role dominance statements.

### 6.2.1 Role Declaration Statement

The *role declaration statement* (`role`) declares a role identifier, if it has not already been declared, and associates types with the role. The example in Figure 6-1 contains the following `role` statements:

```
role user_r types user_t;
role user_r types passwd_t;
```

These statements associate the domain types `user_t` and `passwd_t` with the role `user_r`. As you can see, `role` statements can be repeated for the same role identifier. The first `role` statement for a given role identifier will declare the role in addition to associating the listed types. All the subsequent `role` statements associate additional types. Multiple `role` statements for a single role are commonly used to place the role statements close to the declaration of the types with which they are associated (that is, in the same policy source module). The full syntax for the role declaration statement is provided in the sidebar on page 136.

---

### Role Declaration Statement Syntax

Role declaration statements declare role identifiers and associate types with the role. A type must be associated with a role to coexist in a security context with the role. The special role `object_r` is predefined and is implicitly associated with all types and used in the security context of all objects. There can be multiple `role` statements for the same role identifier. The first statement declares the role and associates one or more types; the subsequent statements only associate types. The full syntax for the role statement is as follows:

```
role role_name [types type_set];
```

*role_name*   An identifier for the role. If this is the first role statement for this identifier, the role is declared. The identifier can be any length and can contain ASCII characters, numbers, periods, and underscores (_). A period has a special meaning when used in a role identifier. A period is used to indicate restrictions on the set of types that may be assigned to a role. For example, the set of types for a role called `apache.cgi` must be a subset of the type set of a role called `apache`.

*type_set*   One or more type or attribute identifiers. Multiple identifiers are specified using a space-separated list enclosed in braces ({ })—for example, { `user_t passwd_t` }. Types can be excluded from the list by prepending - to the type name (for example, { `exec_type -sbin_t` }). If *type_set* is omitted (along with the `types` keyword), the role is declared without any type associations.

Role declarations are valid in monolithic policies, base loadable modules, and non-base loadable modules. They are not valid in conditional statements.

---

## 6.2.2 Role Allow Rules

SELinux provides a means to change roles during program execution via the `execve()` system call. This feature is similar in nature to domain transitions, which result in the domain type changing. *Role allow rule*s (`allow`) control role changes that can occur on program execution by specifying which roles are allowed to change to other roles. Successful role changes require that a user be authorized for the new role, a corresponding role `allow` rule permitting the transition from the old role to the new role, and the new role must be authorized for the new domain type. For example, consider the following role `allow` rule:

```
allow staff_r sysadm_r;
```

This example role `allow` rule allows a process with the role `staff_r` to change to the role `sysadm_r` during a domain transition. This change allows only transition from `staff_r` to `sysadm_r`; another role `allow` rule would be required to transition back from `sysadm_r` to `staff_r`. The full syntax for role `allow` rules is found in the sidebar on page 137.

> WARNING   Notice that the role `allow` rule and the vastly more common TE `allow` rule discussed in Chapter 5 both have the same keyword (that is, `allow`). Be careful not to confuse the two rules, whose syntax and semantics differ entirely. In general, when we refer to an "`allow` rule," we mean the *access vector* (AV) `allow` rule discussed in Chapter 5. We endeavor to always write "role `allow` rule" when we mean the role variety of this keyword.

---

### Role Allow Rule Syntax

Role `allow` rules authorize role changes on program execution. The full syntax for the role `allow` rule is as follows:

```
allow role_set role_set;
```

*role_set*   One or more role identifiers. Multiple identifiers are specified using a space-separated list enclosed in braces (`{ }`)—for example, `{ staff_r sysadm_r }`.

Role `allow` rules are valid in monolithic policies, base loadable modules, and non-base loadable modules. They are not valid in conditional statements.

---

## 6.2.3 Role Transition Rules

Because roles can change on program execution in a manner similar to types, we need a means to automate this transition within the policy language. For types, we used the `type_transition` rule to specify automatic, default type transitions. For roles, we have the *role transition rule* (`role_transition`). This rule is similar in purpose and syntax to the `type_transition` rule except that it specifies a default role change to occur when executing a file. For example, consider this rule:

```
role_transition sysadm_r http_exec_t system_r;
```

This rule states that, unless otherwise requested, when a process with the role `sysadm_r` executes a file with the type `http_exec_t`, SELinux should attempt to change the role to `system_r`. The full syntax for role transition rules is found on page 139.

As with `type_transition` rules, `role_transition` rules do not allow the access necessary to permit the role change. In this case, role `allow` rules must also be present for the role change to succeed. Role transition rules are commonly used to change the role of system daemons when directly executed by a system administrator rather than the initialization process (`init`). If role transition rules were not used in this situation, daemons would have a different role depending on how they were started. Other than this type of situation, we do not expect roles to change implicitly; instead, we expect users to explicitly change their role when necessary using programs designed for that purpose (for example, the `newrole` command).

## 6.2.4 Role Dominance Statement

A *role dominance statement* (`dominance`) declares a role in terms of other roles. We can use this statement to create a hierarchical relationship among roles. In this case, the "dominant role" would automatically inherit all the type associations of the roles it dominates. For example, consider the following statement:

```
dominance { role super_r {role sysadm_r; role secadm_r; }
```

This role `dominance` statement declares the role `super_r`, if it has not already been declared, and makes it dominate the roles `sysadm_r` and `secadm_r`. The role `super_r` will have all of the type associations of the roles `sysadm_r` and `secadm_r`. If the associations change for either of these "dominated roles," the association will change for `super_r`, too. Note that any types added to the dominated role after a dominance statement are not inherited by dominant role through the `dominance` statement. So, in the preceding example, if a type were added to the secadm_r role after the dominance statement, the super_r role would not inherit the new type. The role dominance statement has not yet been widely used in existing policies. The full syntax for the role dominance statement is in the sidebar on page 140.

---

### Role Transition Rule Syntax

Role transition rules specify a default role change to occur when executing a file of a given type. Role transition rules do not allow access. Role allow rules must also be present for the role change to succeed. The full syntax for role transition rules is as follows:

```
role_transition role_set type_set role;
```

*role_set*    One or more role identifiers. Multiple identifiers are specified using a space-separated list enclosed in braces ({ })—for example, { staff_r sysadm_r }.

*type_set*    One or more type or attribute identifiers. Multiple identifiers are specified using a space-separated list enclosed in braces ({ })—for example, { user_t passwd_t }. Types can be excluded from the list by prepending - to the type name (for example, {exec_type -sbin_t }).

*role*    The new role for the security context after the role transition.

Role transition rules are valid in monolithic policies, base loadable modules, and non-base loadable modules. They are not valid in conditional statements.

---

---

### Role Dominance Statement Syntax

The role dominance statement specifies a hierarchical relationship among roles. Roles inherit all the type associations of the roles they dominate. The basic syntax of the role dominance statement is as follows:

```
dominance { role role_name { role_set } }
```

*role_name*    An identifier for the role. The identifier can be any length and can contain ASCII characters, numbers, period, and underscore (_).

*role_set*    One or more roles specified in the form `role role_name ;`. Multiple roles are specified using a space-separated list (for example, `{ role staff_r; role sysadm_r; }`).

The policy language does support a much more complicated syntax where the *role_set* can contain embedded dominance relationship definitions that are indicated with braces. For example:

```
dominance { role a_r { role b_r; role c_r { role d_r; } } }
```

In this example, the roles would be defined as follows:

**d_r**    Only its own types

**c_r**    Its types and those of d_r

**b_r**    Only its own types

**a_r**    Its own types and all types in b_r, c_r, and d_r

Role dominance statements are valid in monolithic policies, base loadable modules, and non-base loadable modules. They are not valid in conditional statements.

---

## 6.3 Users and User Statements

Linux and SELinux user identifiers are distinct and are often unrelated. In SELinux, it is possible for the Linux user identifier and the SELinux user identifier of a given process to differ (for example, see the discussion of user_u that follows). The design decision for SELinux to have a distinct user identifier (rather than share that of Linux) is motivated by the desire to create an immutable SELinux user identifier. In standard Linux, the user identifier changes to reflect changes in privilege (for example, changing to root). In many cases, both the real and effective user identifiers change. This makes it difficult to track which user logged in for auditing, authentication, and other uses. Separating the Linux and SELinux user identifiers allows the Linux user identifier to change as needed without affecting SELinux.

> NOTE Many SELinux systems, including *Red Hat Enterprise Linux version 4* (RHEL4) and *Fedora Core 4* (FC4), can actually change the SELinux user identifier during a login session. In particular, the `su` program was modified to set the Linux and SELinux user identifier. This departure from the original design goal of an immutable SELinux user identifier was motivated by usability; it was thought that not changing the SELinux user identifier would confuse users and create a much more complicated process for adding user accounts. In addition, the Linux audit framework stores an immutable login user identifier for auditing purposes, somewhat reducing the need for the SELinux user identifier to remain constant. *Fedora Core 5* (FC5) reverts to the original behavior of not allowing SELinux user identifiers to change.

## 6.3.1 Declaring Users and Associating Roles

The *user declaration statement* (`user`) declares a user identifier in the policy and associates it with one or more roles. The `user` statement is the only policy statement relating to SELinux users. The example in Figure 6-1 includes the follow user declaration:

```
user joe roles { user_r };
```

This statement declares the user `joe`, if it has not already been declared in the policy, and associates the role `user_r` with the user. Unlike role statements that may be mixed among the TE statements, `user` statements must come *after* all the type and role statements and before constraints (see Figure 3-5 in Chapter 3, "Architecture").

Similar to the association between roles and types, the user association allows a role to be present in a security context with a specified user. The full syntax for the `user` statement is in the sidebar on page 142.

Note that there is no user transition or user `allow` rule. This reflects the initial design goal of immutable users. Changes to the user identifier are controlled only by constraints, which we discuss in Chapter 9.

---

### User Declaration Statement Syntax

The user declaration statement declares a user identifier, if it has not already been declared, and associates it with one or more roles. The full syntax for the statement is as follows:

```
user user_name roles role_set;
```

*user_name*   The identifier for the user. If this is the first user statement for this identifier, the user identifier is declared. The identifier can be any length and can contain ASCII characters, numbers, period, and underscore (_).

*role_set*   One or more role identifiers that must be previously defined in the policy. Multiple identifiers are specified using a space-separated list enclosed in braces (`{ }`)—for example, `{ staff_r sysadm_r }`.

User declarations are valid in monolithic policies, base loadable modules, and non-base loadable modules. They are not valid in conditional statements.

---

## 6.3.2 Mapping Linux Users to SELinux Users

The login programs (for example, `login`, `sshd`) are responsible for mapping Linux users to SELinux users. On login, if there is an SELinux user identifier that is exactly the same as the Linux user identifier, the matching SELinux user identifier becomes the user identifier in the security context for the initial shell process. In this way, if a Linux user identifier also exists as a user identifier in the SELinux policy, all login processes will set the initial shell process security context user identifier to that matching Linux identity.

In many cases, especially general-purpose configurations such the default policies in RHEL4 and FC4, it is not desirable to have to define each ordinary user in the policy. Ordinary users typically have the same privileges with respect to SELinux (that is, the `user_r` role and the `user_t` initial user domain type). To address this issue, SELinux has a special user identity, `user_u`, called the *generic user*. If the generic user `user_u` is defined in the policy, all Linux users will be mapped to it *if they do not have a matching SELinux user in the policy.*

For example, suppose we have the following `user` statement in our policy:

```
user user_u roles { user_r };
```

This statement defines the generic user user_u and authorizes it for the role user_r just as we did for joe earlier. The difference is that if user_u is defined in the policy, *all* Linux users that are not explicitly defined in the policy are mapped to user_u. So, for example, if jane is a Linux user identifier but there is no user jane defined in the SELinux policy, when the Linux user jane logs in, the user identifier in the initial shell process security context will be user_u. Because joe *is* defined in the policy, the initial SELinux user identifier for that user will be joe, even though user_u is also defined in the policy.

If the generic user user_u is not defined in the policy, any Linux user identifier not explicitly defined in the SELinux policy will be unable to log in, *even in permissive mode.* The reason for this is that on login the initial shell process must have a valid security context, including a user identifier. If neither user_u nor the Linux user identifier is defined in the policy, the login process cannot create a valid security context (because there is no user identifier for it to use). Therefore, if you do not include user_u in your policy (which for many configurations makes sense), you must explicitly add all Linux users to the SELinux policy.

> NOTE In FC5, the user-mapping mechanism is greatly enhanced to allow the explicit mapping of Linux users to SELinux users through a configuration file. This allows the creation of more than one generic user (for example, staff_u in addition to user_u). The existing mapping rules are retained as a fallback for backward compatibility. Chapter 13 includes additional information about new tools that can manage user mappings.

SELinux has a second special user, the *system user* system_u, which is typically used for all system processes such as init, and daemons started by init. Technically, the user system_u has no special meaning and is not treated exceptionally in any way within the policy language. However, most existing policies include this user, and systems are generally configured expecting that this SELinux user exists for system resources. It is generally a good idea to always include system_u in your policy.

> WARNING Never create a Linux user account with the identifier system_u. If you do, that Linux user will be able to log in with the system user identifier, which is usually highly privileged (though still much less privileged than root on an ordinary Linux system).

## 6.4 Exploring Roles and Users with Apol

Apol has features for searching and displaying roles and users. The Roles tab on the Policy Components tab, shown in Figure 6-2, displays all the roles and provides searching functions. In this example, we search for roles associated with the type user_ssh_t. The search results show that the role user_r is associated with this type. Because we have chosen to show all information about the roles in the search results, all the types associated with the matching roles are shown. As previously discussed, it is common for role declaration statements, which associate roles and types, to be distributed throughout the policy source. This feature of apol makes it easy to find the relationships between roles and type.

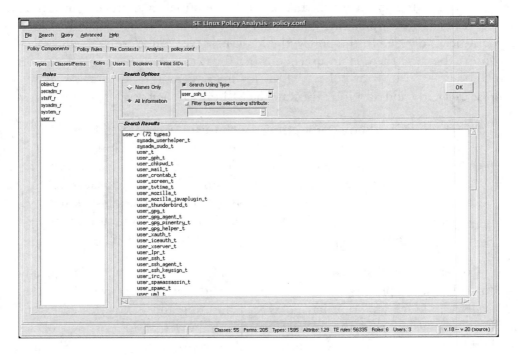

FIGURE 6-2
Apol displaying the types associated with the role user_r

The Users tab of the Policy Components tab offers similar features for users. Figure 6-3 shows all the SELinux users in this policy and the associated roles. Searching for SELinux users by associated roles is also possible.

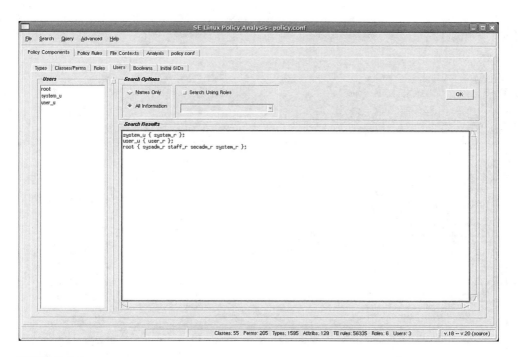

FIGURE 6-3
Apol displaying all the SELinux users and the associated roles

In addition to displaying roles and users, `apol` enables us to search for role `allow` and transition rules. This feature, which is located on the RBAC Rules tab of the Policy Rules tab, is similar to TE rule searching feature. Figure 6-4 shows a search for all the role `allow` and transition rules that have the role `sysadm_r` in the source field.

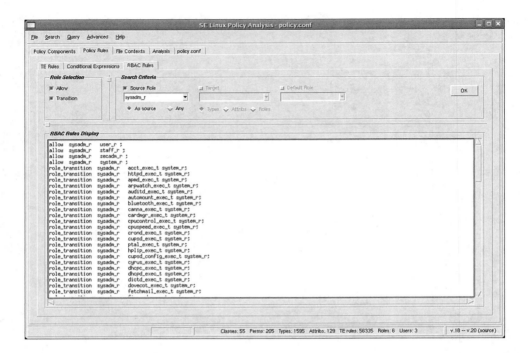

**FIGURE 6-4**
`Apol` displaying all the role `allow` and transition rules with the role `sysadm_r` as the source

## 6.5 Summary

- Within SELinux, roles and users provide for an RBAC feature. Unlike traditional RBAC mechanisms, in SELinux roles and users build upon the power of type enforcement rather than being an additional type of access control.

- Roles are a means of associating sets of domain types into a collection that represents "privileges" that we then assign to a user. Roles control domain transitions because SELinux will create a security context only if the new type is authorized for the role in the security context.

- The role declaration statement (`role`) defines a role identifier and associates it with one or more types. Multiple `role` statements for the same role can exist within a given policy; the definition of the role is cumulative. Roles can also be declared via the much less used role dominance statement (`dominance`).

- Role allow rules (`allow`) control whether the role in a security context may change on an `execve()` system call. The role transition statement (`role_transition`) causes a role change to occur by default depending on the role of the calling process and the type of the file executed.

- SELinux users and Linux users are distinct identifiers. Any association between the two is the result of login process conventions. The general behavior is if the Linux and SELinux user identifier match, the initial user process security context will have the matching user identifier. Otherwise, if the special user `user_u` is defined in the policy, all nonmatching Linux users will have `user_u` as the user in their initial process security context. If there is no matching user and `user_u` is not defined, the user account cannot log in, even in permissive mode.

- In SELinux, users provide the means to associate a Linux user with an SELinux role (and by extension with the set of domain types authorized for that role). The user declaration statement (`user`) specifies this association. SELinux will not create a security context unless the role is associated with the user via a `user` statement.

## Exercises

1. Declare an SELinux user with the name `tom` associated with the roles `staff_r` and `sysadm_r`.

2. Associate the role `sysadm_r` with the type `sysadm_mozilla_t`.

3. Write a role transition statement that causes a change to the role `system_r` when a process with the role `sysadm_r` executes a file with the type `initrc_exec_t`.

# Chapter 7

## Constraints

**In this chapter**

$\mathbf{S}$ELinux provides a constraint mechanism to further restrict the access allowed by the policy regardless of the policy `allow` rules. In this chapter, we explore the constraint feature in SELinux.

## 7.1 A Closer Look at the Access Decision Algorithm

To understand the purpose of constraints, let's revisit the SELinux *Linux Security Module* (LSM). Recall the SELinux kernel architecture discussed in Chapter 3, "Architecture," the salient portion of which is depicted again in Figure 7-1.

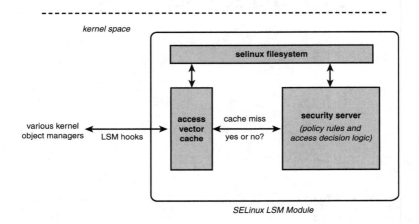

FIGURE 7-1
Review of the SELinux LSM module

We want to take a closer look at how the access decision logic works within the security server. The *access vector cache* (AVC)[1] is keyed by a triple of source *security identifier* (SID), target SID, and object class. SIDs are internal references to security contexts (see the sidebar on page 151).

---

1   See linux-2.6/security/selinux/avc.c.

---

### Security Contexts and SIDs

SELinux implements the Flask security architecture, which provides a framework for implementing enhanced access control but remains security policy neutral. This means that the AVC and its interfaces with the LSM hooks are not specifically tied to *type enforcement* (TE) and the other security policies SELinux implements. As far as the AVC is concerned, a security identifier is an opaque unique reference to a set of security credentials. The AVC caches access decision results indexed by source and target SIDs as well as object class identifier.

The SELinux security server applies semantic meaning to SIDs by internally associating security contexts with SIDs. Thus, SELinux can use SIDs to find type, user, and role identifiers while the AVC and the LSM hook interfaces can remain ignorant of these details.

---

In the source code, you can see the policy-neutral portions of the SELinux LSM module, including the AVC, in `linux-2.6/security/selinux/*.c` and the policy-specific portions (that is, the security server) in `linux-2.6/security/selinux/ss/*`.

When the SELinux LSM hooks[2] ask for an access decision, they provide the SIDs of the subject (source) and object (target) and the object class. The AVC uses the SID-SID-class triple to look up allowed access, which is stored as a bit mask.

When a cache miss occurs, the AVC calls the security server function `security_compute_av()`[3] to determine allowed access. This function has two basic steps in its access decision logic: 1) create a mask representing the object permissions allowed according to the TE allow rules for the type-type-class triple, and 2) remove from the allowed mask those permissions disallowed by any constraint. This second step allows a constraint to be a means to restrict permissions that otherwise would be allowed by the policy.

---

2   See linux-2.6/security/selinux/hooks.c.

3   See linux-2.6/security/selinux/ss/services.c.

The primary purpose of constraints is to enforce global restrictions for certain permissions regardless of the `allow` rules in the policy. All constraints are checked each time the `security_compute_av()` function is called before returning the allowed access mask to the AVC. So, as you can see, constraints further limit the access allowed in an SELinux policy.

SELinux has two types of constraints. The `constrain` statement is the most common constraint and enables you to further restrict access based on the user, role, and/or type of the source and target security contexts. The `validatetrans` statement is a more recent addition to SELinux and enables you to further restrict access for security context change events based on the old, new, and process security context.

> NOTE At the time of this writing, the `apol` tool does not support constraints. Therefore, you cannot view these statements with that tool. Support for constraints is planned and should be available in the future.

## 7.2 Constrain Statement

The `constrain` statement has three elements: a set of object classes to which the constraint applies, a set of permissions for those classes that are being constrained, and a Boolean expression of the constraint. Constraints are organized and stored within the policy by object class. You can see the full syntax for the `constrain` statement in the sidebar on page 152.

---

### Constrain Statement Syntax

The `constrain` statement enables you to restrict specified permissions for specified object classes by defining constraints based on relationships between source and target security contexts. The full syntax for the `constrain` statement is as follows:

`constrain class_set perm_set expression ;`

`class_set`   One or more object classes. Multiple object classes must be separated by spaces and enclosed in braces ({  })—for example, {file lnk_file}. The special operators *, ~, and – are not allowed in class sets for this statement.

| | |
|---|---|
| *perm_set* | One or more permissions. All permissions must be valid for all object classes in the *class_set*. Multiple permissions must be separated by spaces and enclosed in braces ({ })—for example, {read create}. The special operators *, ~, and – are not allowed in permission sets for this statement. |
| *expression* | A Boolean expression of the constraint. |

The Boolean expression syntax supports the following keywords:

| | |
|---|---|
| t1, r1, u1 | Source type, role, and user, respectively |
| t2, r2, u2 | Target type, role, and user, respectively |

Constraint expression syntax also support the following operators:

| | |
|---|---|
| == | Set member of or equivalent |
| != | Set not member of or not equivalent |
| eq | (Roles keyword only) equivalent |
| dom | (Roles keyword only) dominates |
| domby | (Role keyword only) dominated by |
| incomp | (Role keyword only) incomparable |

The complete semantic meaning and allowed parameters for each operator is described in Table 7-1.

Constrain statements are valid only in monolithic policies and base loadable modules. They are not valid in conditional statements or non-base loadable modules.

---

The constrain statement lets you express constraints on any combination of the three elements of a security context (user, role, and type). Constraint expressions compare the contexts of the source (subject) process and the target (object) with each other and/or with explicit names (such as type or role identifiers).

Constraint expressions can be complex, but in practice are usually small and specifically targeted. Here is an example constraint:

```
constrain process transition (u1 == u2) ;
```

Let's take a closer look at this constraint. First, note that it applies to the process object class only, and only constrains the transition permission for processes. Recall that the transition permission is required to allow a domain transition; in effect, this constraint further restricts domain transitions.

Now let's look at the constraint expression (u1 == u2). The keywords u1 and u2 indicate, respectively, the source and target user identifiers for the security contexts. So, this expression resolves to true when the source and target user identifiers are the same. In the case of domain transitions, the source is the "current" security context, and the target is the "new" security context for the process.

Looking at the preceding constraint in its entirety, we see that it requires that the source and target user identifiers remain the same for all domain transitions. How? Recall the description of the access algorithm earlier. When a process requests transition permission, and the AVC calls the security server to determine allowed access for the triple source-target-class, the preceding constraint would become effective (for the process object class) and would check the user identifier in the source and target security contexts. If the user identifiers are not the same, the bit in the mask indicating transition permission is removed before the granted access mask is returned to the AVC.

Let's look at another example:

```
constrain process transition (r1 == r2) ;
```

This constraint is similar to the previous statement except that it constrains role identifiers rather than user identifiers. The keywords r1 and r2 indicate source and target role identifiers, respectively. This constraint requires that role identifiers not change on a domain transition in much the same way that the previous constraint requires user identifiers not to change.

Because these two constraints relate to the same object class and permission, the constrain expression syntax allows us to combine them into a single Boolean expression:

```
constrain process transition (u1 == u2 and r1 == r2) ;
```

This single statement is equivalent to the two previous statements. Either form will have the same effect of restricting user and role identifier changes relating to domain transitions.

Let's take our example a little further. In some situations, we want to allow the user and/or role identifier to change on a domain transition. For example, the login process needs to change the user and role identifiers to those of the user logging in. Another example is a program that allows you to change your role, which must be able to change the role identifier during a domain transition. In general, such programs are trusted processes, and we need a way to allow them to change user/role identifiers while ensuring that the constraint is active for all other programs.

To achieve this goal, let's first define a way to recognize those domain types that are trusted to change user and role identifiers. We do this via a type attribute. In particular, let's assume that there are two attributes defined in the policy: `privuser` and `privrole`. The former is associated with all types allowed to change user identifiers, and the latter with those allowed to change role identifiers. With these attributes, we can change our constraint as follows:

```
constrain process transition (u1 == u2 or t1 == privuser) ;
constrain process transition (r1 == r2 or t1 == privrole) ;
```

In both statements, `t1` refers to the source type (just as `t2`, if used, refers to the target type). The first statement allows the user identifier to be changed in a domain transition only if the source type has the `privuser` attribute. Likewise, the role can be changed if the source type has the `privrole` attribute.

Let's make sure you understand how attributes affect these constraints. Recall that the kernel expands attributes into the list of types that contain the attribute. So, to the kernel, the constraint really is a list of types rather than a single attribute. In the case of a list of types (or an attribute) on the right side of the operator, the `==` operator really means "is a member of" the set of types listed. Likewise the `!=` means "is not a member of" the set of types. So, in our preceding example, the partial statement `t1 == privuser` really means "if the source type is in the list of types that have the `privuser` attribute."

> NOTE For constraint expressions, the left side of all operators must be one of the allowed keywords (for example, u1 or u2) and may never be a type, attribute, role, or user identifier (or list of identifiers). The right side of an operator may be a key word or one or more identifier names.

If the left and right sides of the operator are the role keywords `r1` and `r2`, you have a few more role operators to choose from; specifically `eq`, `dom`, `domby`, and `incomp`, although these are rarely used. Table 7-1 summarizes the operators allowed for expressions in `constrain` statements.

TABLE 7-1
Allowed Arguments and Semantic Meaning for Constrain Expressions

| Operator | Left Side | Right Side | Semantic Meaning |
|---|---|---|---|
| == | t1 | t2 | Source type <u>equals</u> target type. |
| | t1 (t2) | type and/or attribute *name(s)* | Source (target) type <u>is a member of</u> the set of types indicated by *names*. |
| | r1 | r2 | Source role <u>equals</u> target role. |
| | r1 (r2) | role *name(s)* | Source (target) role <u>is a member of</u> the set of roles indicated by *names*. |
| | u1 | u2 | Source user <u>equals</u> target user. |
| | u1 (u2) | user *name(s)* | Source (target) user <u>is a member of</u> the set of users indicated by *names*. |
| != | t1 | t2 | Source type <u>does not equal</u> target type. |
| | t1 (t2) | type and/or attribute *name(s)* | Source (target) type <u>is not a member of</u> the set of types indicated by *names*. |
| | r1 | r2 | Source role <u>does not equal</u> `target` role. |
| | r1 (r2) | role *name(s)* | Source (target) role <u>is not a member of</u> the set of roles indicated by *names*. |
| | u1 | u2 | Source user <u>does not equal</u> target user. |
| | u1 (u2) | user *name(s)* | Source (target) user <u>is not a member of</u> the set of users indicated by *names*. |
| eq | r1 | r2 | Source role <u>equals</u> target role (exactly same semantics as `r1 == r2`). |
| dom | r1 | r2 | Source role <u>was defined to dominate</u> target role using role `dominates` statement. |
| domby | r1 | r2 | Target role <u>was defined to dominate</u> source role using role `dominates` statement. |
| incomp | r1 | r2 | Neither source nor target role dominates the other. |

## 7.3 Label Transition Constraints

SELinux supports a second constraint statement, `validatetrans`. This statement was added as part of the modified multilevel security features we discuss in the next chapter. With the `validatetrans` statement, we can further control the ability to change the security context of *supported objects*. As of this writing, the only supported objects for this constraint are the filesystem objects (file, directory, device files, and so on).

Unlike the `constrain` statement, the `validatetrans` statement allows you to relate the new and old security context of an object with each other and/or with a third security context, that of the process attempting to relabel the object. Thus, new keywords are added for this statement, specifically `t3`, `r3`, and `u3`, respectively representing the type, role, and user of the process security context. The `*1` keywords represent the old security context, and the `*2` keywords represent the new security context. The full syntax for this statement is available in the sidebar on page 157.

> WARNING Be careful not to confuse the keyword associations between the `constrain` and `validatetrans` statements. For the `constrain` statement, `t1` represents the source (or calling process) type, and `t2` represents the target (object) type. However, in the `validatetrans` statement, `t3` is now the source process type, `t1` is the "old" type, and `t2` is the "new" type.

---

### Validatetrans Statement Syntax

The `validatetrans` statement restricts the ability to change the security context of specified supported objects by defining constraints-based relationships with old and new security contexts and the security context of the process. The full syntax for the `validatetrans` statement is as follows:

`validatetrans` *class_set expression* `;`

*class_set*    One or more supported object classes. Multiple object classes must be enclosed in braces (`{   }`)—for example, `{file lnk_file}`. Currently, only filesystem object classes are supported.

*expression* A Boolean expression of the constraint.

The Boolean express syntax supports the following keywords:

| `t1, r1, u1` | Old type, role, and user respectively |
| `t2, r2, u2` | New type, role, and user respectively |
| `t3, r3, u3` | Process type, role, and user respectively |

Constraint expression syntax also supports the following operators:

| `==` | Set member of or equivalent |
| `!=` | Set not member of or not equivalent |
| `eq` | (Roles keyword only) equivalent |
| `dom` | (Roles keyword only) dominates |
| `domby` | (Role keyword only) not dominated by |
| `incomp` | (Role keyword only) incomparable |

The complete semantic meaning and allowed parameters for each operator is described in Table 7-2.

---

`Validatetrans` statements are valid only in monolithic policies and base loadable modules. They are not valid in conditional statements and non-base loadable modules.

To date, we have seen no example use of the `validatetrans` constraint. This statement was added as the cousin to the *multilevel security* (MLS) variant described in Chapter 8, "Multilevel Security," on the future possibility of it being useful. To help understand how one might use this statement, let's look at example. The key feature of the `validatetrans` statement is that it enables us to associate old and new security contexts on a label change for file objects.

Suppose that we have a type `user_tmp_t` that in our policy we use as the type for ordinary untrusted user programs' temporary files. We might, for example, want to ensure that a domain with privilege to change all file labels (for example, a label maintenance program an administrator might run) does not accidentally relabel a file with `user_tmp_t` as its type to certain highly critical types (say `shadow_t` type, which is the type of the `/etc/shadow` file). Here's our constraint that would provide this restriction:

```
validatetrans {file lnk_file} ( t2 != shadow_t or t1 != user_tmp_t );
```

Notice several features of this constraint. First, notice that we included both ordinary files and symbolic links (`lnk_file`) because we do not want someone to use a link in place of a file. Now examine the constraint expressions. In simple language, the constraint says that for a security context change to be allowed for file and symbolic link objects, the new type may only be shadow_t if the old type is *not* user_tmp_t. In other words, no domain type may be authorized to relabel a user temporary file into the type of the shadow password file.

To expand this example, assume there are a subset of domain types that we do want to allow to relabel user_tmp_t to shadow_t. (It is hard to imagine a situation where this would be advisable, but you never know.) So, now we create an attribute relabel_any and assign it to those domain types we want to grant this privilege. We then expand this constraint as follows:

```
validatetrans {file lnk_file}
        ( ( t3 == relabel_any) or
          ( t2 != shadow_t or t1 != user_tmp_t ) );
```

Now we have a set of domain types (those with the relabel_any attribute) that this constraint will not restrict in any way.

TABLE 7-2
Allowed Arguments and Semantic Meaning for Validatetrans Expressions

| Operator | Left Side | Right Side | Semantic Meaning |
|---|---|---|---|
| == | t1 | t2 | Old type equals new type. |
| | t1 (t2) | type and/or attribute *name(s)* | Old (new) type is a member of the set of types indicated by *names*. |
| | t3 | type and/or attribute *name(s)* | Process type is a member of the set of types indicated by *names*. |
| | r1 | r2 | Old role equals new role. |
| | r1 (r2) | role *name(s)* | Old (new) role is a member of the set of roles indicated by *names*. |
| | r3 | role *name(s)* | Process role is a member of the set of roles indicated by *names*. |
| | u1 | u2 | Old user equals new user. |
| | u1 (u2) | user *name(s)* | Old (new) user is a member of the set of users indicated by *names*. |

TABLE 7-2
Allowed Arguments and Semantic Meaning for Validatetrans Expressions

| Operator | Left Side | Right Side | Semantic Meaning |
|---|---|---|---|
| | u3 | user *name(s)* | Process user <u>is a member of</u> the set of users indicated by *names*. |
| != | t1 | t2 | Old type <u>does not equal</u> new type. |
| | t1 (t2) | type and/or attribute *name(s)* | Old (new) type <u>is not a member of</u> the set of types indicated by *names*. |
| | t3 | type and/or attribute *name(s)* | Process type <u>is not a member of</u> the set of types indicated by *names*. |
| | r1 | r2 | Old role <u>does not equal</u> new role. |
| | r1 (r2) | role *name(s)* | Old (new) role <u>is not a member of</u> the set of roles indicated by *names*. |
| | r3 | role *name(s)* | Process role <u>is not a member of</u> the set of roles indicated by *names*. |
| | u1 | u2 | Old user <u>does not equal</u> new user. |
| | u1 (u2) | user *name(s)* | Old (new) user <u>is not a member of</u> the set of users indicated by *names*. |
| | u3 | user *name(s)* | Process user <u>is not a member of</u> the set of users indicated by *name*. |
| eq | r1 | r2 | Exactly the same semantics as ==. |
| | r1 (r2) | role *name(s)* | Exactly the same semantics as == . |
| dom | r1 | r2 | Source role was <u>defined to dominate</u> target role using role `dominates` statement. |
| domby | r1 | r2 | Target role was <u>defined to dominate</u> source role using role `dominates` statement. |
| incomp | r1 | r2 | Neither source nor target role dominates the other. |

## 7.4 Summary

- Constraints provide global restrictions for certain permissions regardless of the `allow` rules contained in the policy.

- The `constrain` statement enables us to restrict permissions granted based on relationships between source and target types, roles, and user identifiers.

- The `validatetrans` statement enables us to restrict the ability to change object security contexts based on relationships between the old, new, and process type, role, and user identifiers. This statement is supported only for filesystem objects.

## Exercises

1. Take the two constraints listed together on page 96 and write them as a single constraint statement.

2. A common `neverallow` invariant rule is this:
   ```
   neverallow domain ~domain : process transition ;
   ```
   Write a constraint that is as close as possible to the equivalent meaning of this invariant.

3. Recall the example `validatetrans` statement from page 93:
   ```
   validatetrans {file lnk_file}
   ( ( t3 == relabel_any) or
     ( t2 != shadow_t or t1 != user_tmp_t ) );
   ```
   Let's suppose that you want to add a number of other types to the list of those you do not to be relabeled from `user_tmp_t`. How would you change this constraint to achieve this goal?

# Chapter 8

# Multilevel Security

## In this chapter

In recent enhancements to SELinux, the constraint feature has been extended to implement an optional *multilevel security* (MLS) policy. MLS is another form of mandatory access control, which is built upon *type enforcement* (TE). In this chapter, we explore the optional MLS policy features.

## 8.1 Multilevel Security Constraints

MLS is another form of mandatory access control that is applicable to some security problems, especially those associated with government-classified data control. Much of the early computer security research was driven by the goal of implementing MLS access controls within operating systems. SELinux provides optional support for MLS. Although type enforcement remains the fundamental access control mechanism of SELinux, we can also enable the optional MLS features to provide additional MLS-style mandatory access controls. In SELinux, MLS is an optional extension to type enforcement; you cannot have MLS features without it.

> NOTE *Fedora Core 5* (FC5) enabled the optional MLS features by default. In FC5, the MLS features are used to implement so-called *multicategory security* (MCS) policy rather than a traditional MLS policy modeled after government-classified systems. These two uses of the MLS features alone show the flexibility of SELinux. In any case, all uses of MLS are built upon the underlying TE security.

We enable MLS in SELinux by creating a binary kernel policy file that indicates that it is an MLS policy. The primary method to create such a kernel policy is to compile the policy using the -M option to the checkpolicy program. With this option, checkpolicy will create an MLS-enabled kernel policy, and when loaded into the kernel, the kernel will enforce additional MLS constraints. You will find available policy source build trees (for example and reference policies, see Chapters 11, "Original Example Policy," and 12, "Reference Policy") manage whether the optional MLS features are available via a Makefile or configuration file.

> NOTE As this book was preparing to be published, Tresys released a new version of the apol tool (SeTools, release 2.4) that now supports examining MLS security contexts and rules. We do not describe those features in this chapter, but they are simple to use after you become familiar with apol.

## 8.2 Security Contexts with MLS

As discussed in Chapter 2, "Concepts," when MLS is enabled, the security context is extended with two additional fields: a low and high *security level*. A security level itself has two fields: a *sensitivity* and a set of *categories*. Sensitivities are strictly hierarchical reflecting an ordered data sensitivity model, such as Top Secret, Secret, and Unclassified in government classification controls. Categories are unordered, reflecting the need for data compartmentalization. The basic idea is that you need both a high enough sensitivity clearance and the right categories to access data.

> WARNING Do not confuse *security level* with *sensitivity*. A security level is a combination of a single sensitivity and a set (zero or more) of categories. Sensitivities are strictly hierarchical and can be compared using equivalence relationships (<, =, >). Security levels are not hierarchical and are compared using a dominance relationship (dom, domby, eq, incomp), which we briefly discuss in Chapter 2.

### 8.2.1 Defining Security Levels

In an SELinux policy, you define sensitivities using the sensitivity statement, as follows:

```
sensitivity s0;
sensitivity s1;
sensitivity s2;
sensitivity s3;
```

These statements define four sensitivities called s0, s1, s2, and s3. These names are a typical generic sensitivity naming convention in SELinux. We could use any name you want here. The `sensitivity` statement also supports the ability to associate additional alias names with a sensitivity that will be treated the same as the core sensitivity name. For example:

```
sensitivity s1 alias unclassified;
```

> NOTE Recent improvement to SELinux, included in FC5, has added the utility `semanage`, which among other features enables you to assign human-readable (and printable) names to the policy sensitivities and categories. These human-readable names are translated by an SELinux library and are not part of the kernel policy enforcement language. The file that contains the printable mappings is `/etc/selinux/[policy]/setrans.conf`, where [policy] is an installed policy.

Because sensitivities must be hierarchically related, we must specify in the policy the hierarchy of sensitivities using the `dominance` statement, as follows:

```
dominance { s0 s1 s2 s3 }   # s0 is "low" and s3 "high"
```

The `dominance` statement lists the sensitivity names in order from lower to highest. Thus, in our example, s0 is lower than s1, which is lower than s2, and so forth.

> WARNING The absence of an ending semicolon in the `dominance` statement is the correct syntax (even though most other policy statements end with a semicolon). In this case, the closing curly brace unambiguously denotes the end of the statement. It is one of those legacy-language design decisions that you have to keep in mind.

Categories are defined in a similar manner as sensitivities using the `category` statement. As with sensitivities, categories may also have alias names. Unlike sensitivities, categories are not hierarchically related (or related at all). So, there is no need to define any explicit relationship between categories. The following statements are examples of the `category` statement:

```
category c0 alias blue;
category c1 alias red;
category c2 alias green;
category c3 alias orange;
category c4 alias white;
```

The final step in defining security levels in the policy language is to define allowed security level combinations using the `level` statement. The `level` statement dictates how you may associate categories with sensitivities. Remember that a combination of a single sensitivity and a set of categories constitute a security level. Here are some examples of the `level` statement:

```
level s0:c0.c4;
level s1:c0.c4;
level s2:c0.c4;
level s3:c0.c4;
```

These statements enable you to combine any of the defined categories with all the defined sensitivities from our earlier examples. You would generally have a single `level` statement for each defined sensitivity that identifies the categories that may be associated with each sensitivity in a valid security level.

In the preceding example, we associated all five defined categories (`c0.c4`) with all four defined sensitivities. You can be more restrictive in this association:

```
level s0:c0.c2;
level s1:c0.c2,c4;
```

In this example, `s0` may be associated only with categories `c0`, `c1`, and `c2`; and `s1` with categories `c0`, `c1`, `c2` and `c4` (but not `c3`). By now, you should have noticed that a dot (`.`) indicates an inclusive range of categories, and a comma (`,`) indicates a noncontiguous list of categories.

> WARNING Just because ranges of categories are specified using the range operator (`.`), this does not mean that categories are hierarchically related. Instead, the range operator is just a convenient way to refer to a set of categories. The ordering of the categories for the range operator is just the order in which they are declared and has nothing to do with any intrinsic ordering implied by their names.

So, for example, if you declare that categories in the order c1, c0, and c2, the expressions c0.c2 would mean c0 and c2, and not c1.

The level statement defines what combinations of sensitivities and categories constitute an acceptable security level for the MLS portion of the SELinux policy.

---

### Security Level Statements Syntaxes

There are four statements that together enable you to define security levels in an SELinux policy. The full syntax of each are listed in this sidebar.

**Sensitivity statement**

This statement defines the policy sensitivity identifiers and optional alias identifiers.

sensitivity *identifier* [ alias *alias_id* [*alias_id(s)*] ] ;

*identifier*   String identifier for sensitivity.

*alias_id*   One or more additional string identifiers for sensitivity aliases.

The sensitivity identifier and associated alias identifiers can be used interchangeably within the policy.

**Dominance statement**

This statement defines the hierarchical relationship between all defined sensitivities:

dominance { *identifier*   *identifier* ...   *identifier* }

*identifier*   A sensitivity identifier defined by a sensitivity statement.

The ordering of sensitivities is from lower to highest. All defined sensitivities must be contained within the dominance statement in order to define the complete sensitivity hierarchy.

**Category statement**

This statement defines the policy category identifiers and optional alias identifiers:

category *identifier* [ alias *alias_id* [*alias_id(s)*] ] ;

*identifier*   String identifier for category.

*alias_id*   One or more additional string identifiers for category aliases.

The category identifier and associated alias identifiers can be used interchangeably within the policy.

### Level statement

This statement defines the allowed combinations of sensitivity and category sets:

```
level sensitivity[:category_set] ;
```

*sensitivity*     One of the defined sensitivity identifiers.

*category_set*    A set of defined category identifiers. Categories can be listed
                  as comma-separated lists and/or ranges of categories using
                  the . range operator. For example, the category set c0.c3,c5
                  means all defined categories from c0 to c3 inclusively, plus
                  c5. Note that there is *no* implicit ordering of categories
                  according to name (for example, alphanumeric ordering);
                  instead, the range operator uses the order in which the cate-
                  gory identifiers are defined.

You may use only one `level` statement for each defined sensitivity. The category set is optional; an unspecified category set means the "empty" category set. (That is, that sensitivity may have no categories associated with it.) A valid security context may associate only a sensitivity with the categories defined in the `level` statement for that sensitivity.

Security `level` statements are valid only in monolithic policies and base loadable modules. They are not valid in conditional statements and non-base loadable modules.

---

## MLS Extensions to Security Contexts

For MLS SELinux systems, the security context is extended to include two security levels: a *low* or *current* security level and a *high* or *clearance* security level. In general, the low level reflects the *current security level* of a process or the sensitivity of data contained within an object. The high level reflects the *clearance level* of the user identifier in the context (thereby determining the highest possible security level allowed for the current level of any security context) or the maximum range of data allowed for some so-called multilevel objects. When MLS is enabled, the extended security context has the following format:

```
user:role:type:sensitivity[:category,...][-sensitivity[:category,...]]
```

Notice that the security levels require a single sensitivity and zero or more categories (that is, categories are optional). In addition, when you specify a security context you need not specify the high level. If unspecified, the high level will be equal to the low level, which is a common case for objects.

For a security context to be valid, the high level must always dominate[1] the low level. In addition, the categories associated with the sensitivities must be valid per the `level` statements in the policy. So, for example, if we have the previous `level` statements:

```
level s0:c0.c2;
level s1:c0.c2,c4;
```

and `user_u`, `user_r`, and `user_t` are valid user, role, and type identifiers, the following security contexts are invalid:

```
user_u:user_r:user_t:s0-s0:c2,c4 (c4 is invalid for s0)
user_u:user_r:user_t:s0:c0-s0:c2 (high does not dominate the low)
```

## 8.3 MLS Constraints

SELinux supports two MLS constraint statements, `mlsconstrain` and `mlsvalidatetrans`, which together enable us to specify the optional MLS access enforcement rules. These two statements are identical to their non-MLS counterparts except that they allow you to also express constraints based on the security levels of a security context. You may only use the MLS constraints in policies that have the optional MLS features enabled. You may use the non-MLS constraint statements from Chapter 7, "Constraints," in either type of policy.

### 8.3.1 mlsconstrain Statement

The `mlsconstrain` statement is based on the `constrain` statement. We can use any of the syntax discussed for the `constrain` statement in Chapter 7. The `mlsconstrain` statement adds new keywords for stating constraints based on the low and high security levels of the source (`l1` and `h1`) and target (`l2` and `h2`). The sidebar on page 171 contains the full syntax for the `mlsconstrain` statement.

---

1  Recall from Chapter 2 that security levels are related using the "dominance" relationship. We discuss this relationship later in this chapter.

---

### mlsconstrain Statement Syntax

The `mlsconstrain` statement allows you to restrict specified permissions for specified object classes by defining constraints based on relationships between source and target security contexts that include the optional MLS features (that is, high and low security levels). The full syntax for the `mlsconstrain` statement is as follows:

`mlsconstrain` *class_set perm_set expression* ;

*class_set*    One or more object classes. Multiple object classes must be separated by spaces and enclosed in braces (`{  }`)—for example, `{file lnk_file}`. The special operators `*`, `~`, and `-` are not allowed in class sets for this statement.

*perm_set*    One or more permissions. All permissions must be valid for all object classes in the *class_set*. Multiple permissions must be separated by spaces and enclosed in braces (`{  }`)—for example, `{read create}`. The special operators `*`, `~`, and `-` are not allowed in class sets for this statement.

*expression*    A Boolean expression of the constraint.

The Boolean expression syntax supports the following keywords:

  `t1, r1, u1, l1, h1`    Source type, role, user, low level, and high level, respectively

  `t2, r2, u2, l2, h2`    Target type, role, user, low level, and high level, respectively

Constraint expression syntax also supports the following operators:

`==`      Set member of or equivalent.

`!=`      Set not member of or not equivalent.

`eq`      (Roles and security level keywords only) equivalent.

`dom`      (Roles and security level keywords only) dominates.

`domby`      (Role and security level keywords only) not dominated by.

`incomp`    (Role and security level keywords only) incomparable.

The complete semantic meaning and allowed parameters for each operator is described in Table 8-1—along with those defined for the `constrain` statement—Chapter 7 (Table 7-1).

The `mlsconstrain` statement is supported only for optional MLS policies.

The `mlsconstrain` statement is valid only in monolithic policies and base loadable modules. It is not valid in conditional statements and non-base loadable modules.

---

To illustrate the `mlsconstrain` statement, let's look at applying MLS to ordinary filesystem objects. As a simple constraint suppose that we want to ensure that file objects may have only a single level. (That is, the high and low levels must be the same.) We can accomplish this restriction with a constraint such as this:

```
mlsconstrain file { create relabelto }
      ( l2 eq h2 );
```

Assuming that `create` and `relabelto` are the `file` permissions required to set the security level of a file object, this constraint is sufficient to require that all files have high and low security levels that are the same.

Let's now look at more central MLS policy restrictions. Recall the basic premise of MLS from Chapter 2, namely to prevent information from flowing "downward" from higher security levels to lower or incomparable security levels. We do this by enforcing the "no read up, no write down" rules on all objects. In SELinux, the low security level generally represents the current security level of processes and objects. Thus, we have the following MLS constraint for files:

```
mlsconstrain file write ( l1 domby l2 );
```

In this statement we constrain `write` permissions for the `file` object class requiring the source security level (`l1`) to be dominated by ("lower than") the object security level (`l2`). In other words, a process can write files only at or "above" its current security level ("no write down").

This constraint is unfortunately too simple to ensure that MLS policy is enforced for file objects. First, let's consider file object class permissions. Many permissions other than `write` allow a process to "write" information to a file. For example, the `append` permission also allows information to flow from the process to the file. Likewise, less obvious permissions, such as `rename`, also allow some form of information to flow to the file (in this case, the name of the file). To be comprehensive, we need to expand our constraint to cover all "write-capable" file permissions:

```
mlsconstrain file { write create setattr relabelfrom append
                    unlink link rename mounton }
      ( l1 domby l2 );
```

We now include a list of several permissions besides the standard `write` permission, all of which allow some form of information to flow from the source to the object. The constraint expression remains the same.

This constraint is still too simple. We need to address the situation where we have a trusted domain type that we need to give special permission to violate the "no write down" rule. Although you should avoid such trusted domains, nearly all applications of MLS systems have had a need for them. To accommodate this concept, we need to expand the constraint to allow for these trusted domains.

To implement trusted downgrading domains, we can create a type attribute, say `mlsfilewritedown`, which identifies any such trusted domain. So now our constraint is this:

```
mlsconstrain file { write create setattr relabelfrom append
                                 unlink link rename mounton }
        ( ( l1 domby l2 ) or
        ( t1 == mlsfilewritedown ) );
```

Now the constraint allows an exception for any source domain (`t1`) that has the `mlsfilewritedown` attribute (that is, trusted domains).

For a complete MLS policy, we also need to also restrict read access (that is, "no read up"). As with write access, a number of permissions allow "read" access besides the `read` permission. For example `execute` permissions essentially allows a process to "read" the contents of an executable file. Here is a possible MLS read constraint for file objects:

```
mlsconstrain  file  { read getattr execute }
        ( ( l1 dom l2 ) or
         ( t1 == mlsfilewritedown ) );
```

As with the write restriction we have an attribute, `mlsfilereadup`, that allows for "read up" privilege for those few privileged domain types that have the attribute.

In writing a complete MLS policy, you need to examine all object classes and their associated permissions to ensure read and write restrictions are properly constrained. For example, in the preceding "read" constraint, we might want to address all filesystem objects in a single statement, as follows:

```
mlsconstrain { dir file lnk_file chr_file blk_file sock_file fifo_file }
           { read getattr execute }
     ( ( l1 dom l2 ) or
       ( t1 == mlsfilereadup ) );
```

You will typically find the MLS constraints for a given SELinux policy stated in a single source policy file, typically called `mls`. We do not extensively cover MLS features of SELinux outside of this chapter; if you are interested in additional information, find this file and examine it.

TABLE 8-1
Allowed Arguments and Semantic Meaning for `Mlsconstrain` Expressions (Plus Those Defined for the Contrain Statement in Table 7-1 [Chapter 7])

| Operator | Left Side | Right Side | Semantic Meaning |
|---|---|---|---|
| == | l1 | l2, h1, h2 | Source's low (current) security level <u>equals</u> the target's low (l2), source's high (h1), or target's high (h2) security level. |
| | l2 | h2 | Target's low (current) security level <u>equals</u> the target's high security level. |
| | h1 | l2, h2 | Source's high (clearance) security level <u>equals</u> the target's low (l2) or high (h2) security level. |
| != | l1 | l2, h1, h2 | Source's low (current) security level <u>does not equal</u> the target's low (l2), source's high (h1), or target's high (h2) security level. |
| | l2 | h2 | Target's low (current) security level <u>does not equal</u> the target's high security level. |
| | h1 | l2, h2 | Source's high (clearance) security level does not equal the target's low (l2) or high (h2) security level. |
| eq | l1 | l2, h1, h2 | Exactly the same semantics as ==. |
| | l2 | h2 | Exactly the same semantics as ==. |
| | h1 | l2, h2 | Exactly the same semantics as ==. |

| Operator | Left Side | Right Side | Semantic Meaning |
|----------|-----------|------------|------------------|
| dom | l1 | l2, h1, h2 | Source's low (current) security level <u>dominates</u> the target's low (l2), source's high (h1), or target's high (h2) security level. |
| | l2 | h2 | Target's low (current) security level <u>dominates</u> the target's high security level. |
| | h1 | l2, h2 | Source's high (clearance) security level <u>dominates</u> the target's low (l2) or high (h2) security level. |
| domby | l1 | l2, h1, h2 | Source's low (current) security level <u>is dominated by</u> the target's low (l2), source's high (h1), or target's high (h2) security level. |
| | l2 | h2 | Target's low (current) security level <u>is dominated by</u> the target's high security level. |
| | h1 | l2, h2 | Source's high (clearance) security level <u>is dominated by</u> the target's low (l2) or high (h2) security level. |
| incomp | l1 | l2, h1, h2 | Neither the source's low (current) security level nor the target's low (l2), source's high (h1), or target's high (h2) security level dominate the other. |
| | l2 | h2 | Neither the target's low (current) security level nor the target's high security level dominate the other. |
| | h1 | l2, h2 | Neither the source's high (clearance) security level nor the target's low (l2) or high (h2) security level dominate the other. |

## 8.3.2 mlsvalidatetrans Statement

We have one more MLS constraint we need to examine, the MLS variant of the validatetrans constraint discussed in Chapter 7, namely mlsvalidatetrans. This statement is similar to the validatetrans statement except that it introduces the six keywords l1 and h1, l2 and h2, and l3 and h3, meaning old low and high security levels, new low and high security levels, and the source process low and high security levels, respectively. The other difference between the two statements is that the mlsvalidatetrans statement is more commonly used to support an MLS policy than the `validatetrans` statement is in a typical TE policy. The full syntax of the `mlsvalidatetrans` statement is in the sidebar on page 176.

---

### mlsvalidatetrans Statement Syntax

The `mlsvalidatetrans` statement restricts the ability to change the security context of specified supported objects by defining constraints-based relationships with old and new security contexts and the security context of the source process. The full syntax for the `mlsvalidatetrans` statement is as follows:

`mlsvalidatetrans class_set expression ;`

`class_set`     One or more object supported classes. Multiple object classes must be enclosed in braces (`{  }`)—for example, `{file lnk_file}`. Currently, only permanent filesystem object classes are supported.

`expression`   A Boolean expression of the constraint.

The Boolean expression syntax supports the following keywords:

| | |
|---|---|
| `t1, r1, u1, l1, h1` | Old type, role, user, low level, and high level, respectively |
| `t2, r2, u2, l2, h2` | New type, role, and user, low level, and high level, respectively |
| `t3, r3, u3, l3, h3` | Process type, role, user, low level, and high level, respectively |

The constraint expression syntax also supports the following operators:

| | |
|---|---|
| `==` | Set member of or equivalent |
| `!=` | Set not member of or not equivalent |
| `eq` | (Roles and security level keywords only) equivalent |
| `dom` | (Roles and security level keywords only) dominates |
| `domby` | (Role and security level keywords only) not dominated by |
| `incomp` | (Role and security level keywords only) incomparable |

The complete semantic meaning and allowed parameters for each operator is described in Table 8-2 in addition to those defined for the `validatetrans` statement in Chapter 7 (Table 7-2).

The `mlsvalidatetrans` statement is supported only for optional MLS policies.

The `mlsvalidatetrans` statement are valid only in monolithic policies and base loadable modules. They are not valid in conditional statements and non-base loadable modules.

---

As an example, for MLS we generally do not want file security levels to change; over the years of experimentation with operational MLS systems, however, we have learned that some MLS applications have evolved the need for a trustworthy application to change the security levels of existing objects such as files. So, to enforce this restriction while allowing for those trusted applications, we can use the `mlsvalidatetrans` constraint:

```
mlsvalidatetrans file
    ( ( l1 eq l2 ) or
      (( t3 == mlsfileupgrade ) and ( l1 domby l2 )) or
      (( t3 == mlsfiledowngrade ) and ( l1 dom l2 or l1 incomp l2 )) );
```

This constraint has a number of features. First, it has the basic requirement that when a file object security context changes, its current (low) security level must be the same (`l1 eq l2`). However, it provides for upgrading (`mlsfileupgrade` attribute) and downgrading (`mlsfiledowngrade` attribute) privileges. Upgrading (that is, the old level `l1` is dominated by the new level `l2`) is allowed if the process domain type has the `mlsfileupgrade` attribute. Likewise, downgrading (that is, the old level dominates or is incomparable to the new level) is allowed if the process domain type has the `mlsfiledowngrade` attribute.

TABLE 8-2

Allowed Arguments and Semantic Meaning for `Mlsvalidatetrans` Expressions (Plus Those Defined for the Validatetrans Statement in Table 7-2 [Chapter 7])

| Operator | Left Side | Right Side | Semantic Meaning |
|---|---|---|---|
| == | l1 | l2, h1, h2 | Old low (current) security level equals the new low (l2), old high (h1), or new high (h2) security level. |
| | l2 | h2 | New low (current) security level equals the new high security level. |
| | h1 | l2, h2 | Old high (clearance) security level equals the new low (l2) or new high (h2) security level. |
| != | l1 | l2, h1, h2 | Old low (current) security level does not equal the new low (l2), old high (h1), or new high (h2) security level. |

*continues*

TABLE 8-2 (continued)
Allowed Arguments and Semantic Meaning for `Mlsvalidatetrans` Expressions (Plus Those Defined for the Validatetrans Statement in Table 7-2 [Chapter 7])

| Operator | Left Side | Right Side | Semantic Meaning |
|---|---|---|---|
| != | 12 | h2 | New the old low (current) security level <u>does not equal</u> the new high security level. |
| | h1 | 12, h2 | Old high (clearance) security level <u>does not equal</u> the new low (12) or new high (h2) security level. |
| eq | 11 | 12, h1, h2 | Exactly the same semantics as ==. |
| | 12 | h2 | Exactly the same semantics as ==. |
| | h1 | 12, h2 | Exactly the same semantics as ==. |
| dom | 11 | 12, h1, h2 | Old low (current) security level <u>dominates</u> the new low (12), old high (h1), or new high (h2) security level. |
| | 12 | h2 | New low (current) security level <u>dominates</u> the new high security level. |
| | h1 | 12, h2 | Old high (clearance) security level <u>dominates</u> the new low (12) or new high (h2) security level. |
| domby | 11 | 12, h1, h2 | Old low (current) security level <u>is dominated by</u> the new low (12), old high (h1), or new high (h2) security level. |
| | 12 | h2 | The new low (current) security level <u>is dominated by</u> the new high security level. |
| | h1 | 12, h2 | The old high (clearance) security level <u>is dominated by</u> the new low (12) or new high (h2) security level. |
| incomp | 11 | 12, h1, h2 | Neither the old low (current) security level nor the new low (12), old high (h1), or new high (h2) security level dominate the other. |
| | 12 | h2 | Neither the new low (current) security level nor the new high security level dominate the other. |
| | h1 | 12, h2 | Neither the old high (clearance) security level nor the new low (12) or new high (h2) security level dominate the other. |

> NOTE Remember that, as of this writing, `validatetrans` and
> `mlsvalidatetrans` constraint statements support only filesystem
> objects, specifically, `dir`, `file`, `lnk_file`, `chr_file`, `blk_file`,
> `sock_file`, and `fifo_file` object classes.

## 8.4 Other Impacts of MLS

This chapter describes the basic mechanisms that enable you to define an MLS policy in SELinux; however, it does not describe a full policy for MLS. Unlike type enforcement, which is flexible and adaptable, MLS is intended to strictly and inflexibly enforce a single security invariant ("no write down, no read up"). This singular, inflexible focus is important for the protection of strictly hierarchically related sensitive data (such as national secrets). However, it presents many challenges that you must address as a secure system designer that are beyond the scope of this book.[2]

Because in SELinux the MLS feature extends the security context, everywhere you specify a security context you must now include security level information. One statement this impacts is the `user` statement described in Chapter 6. For MLS systems, all users must have a defined clearance security level, which represents the highest-level process users may run on their behalf. For MLS, the syntax of the `user` statement changes to this:

```
user username roles role_set  level default_level range allowed_range ;
```

The `username` and `role_set` arguments are the same as before. However, we add two new keywords that define the user's default login security level (`level`) and the range of security levels that a user is allowed to run processes or log in (`range`). The default level is a single valid security level, and the allowed range is a range of security levels from low to high. For example:

```
user joe roles user_r level s0 range s0 - s3:c0.c4;
```

---

2  For additional information on the challenges of building MLS trusted systems, see *Building a Secure Computer System* by Morrie Gasser and Van Nostran Reinhold, New York, 1988, which is out of print but freely available at http://nucia.ist.unomaha.edu/library/gasserbook.pdf.

This statement assigns the user `joe` with the default login level of `s0` (the lowest sensitivity we defined earlier, with no categories) and allows the user to log in at any level ranging from `s0` with no categories to `s3` with all the categories we defined earlier (`c0.c4`). For example, the user is allowed to log in with a security level of `s1:c1.c2` but would not be allowed to log in with a security level `s4:c0` because this latter level is not in the user's allowed range.

The other major area of impact of MLS is everywhere you label an object with a security context. In Chapter 10, "Object Labeling," we discuss object labeling in more detail for non-MLS systems. Just remember that in an MLS system you must extend the object security context to include low and high security levels according to the syntax listed on page 105. You will find that the real challenge with MLS systems is determining the appropriate security level to assign to each object.

## 8.5 Summary

- The SELinux policy language provides optional support for MLS through the use of additional constraint statements and extensions to the security context.

- For an MLS policy, you must define hierarchical sensitivities and nonhierarchical categories. A valid security level is a combination of a single sensitivity and a set of categories (including the empty set).

- For MLS, the security context is extended with a low (current) and high (clearance) security levels. A hard-coded invariant requires that the high security levels always dominate the low.

  The primary purpose of an MLS policy is to implement the "no read down, no write up" invariant for all objects. We can implement this invariant using the `mlsconstrain` statement, which is exactly like the `constrain` statement except that it allows restrictions to also be based on relationships between the source and target security levels.

  The `mlsvalidatetrans` statement is exactly the same as the `validatetrans` statement except that it also allows us to restrict security context changes based on the old, new, and process security levels. This allows us to control the ability to change filesystem object security levels.

- For a complete MLS security policy, you must implement MLS constraints on all relevant object class permissions and extend the security context labeling everywhere a security context is applied to an object.

## Exercises

1.  Assume the following sensitivity and category definitions:

    ```
    sensitivity s0;
    sensitivity s1;
    sensitivity s2;

    category c0;
    category c1;
    category c2;
    category c3;
    category c4;

    level s0;
    level s1:c0.c2;
    level s2:c0.c4;
    ```

    Also assume `user_u`, `user_r`, and `user_t` are valid user, role, and type identifiers. Determine which of the following security contexts are valid and explain why or why not:

    a. `user_u:user_r:user_t:s0-s0:c0`

    b. `user_u:user_r:user_t:s0-s1`

    c. `user_u:user_r:user_t:s0-s1:c0.c4`

    d. `user_u:user_r:user_t:s1:c0.c2-s2:c0.c1`

    e. `user_u:user_r:user_t:s1-s2:c0,c4`

2.  Look again at the following MLS constraint:

    ```
    mlsconstrain file { write create setattr relabelfrom append
          unlink link rename mounton }
          ( ( l1 domby l2 ) or
            ( t1 == mlsfilewritedown ) );
    ```

    This constraint restricts the ability to "write down," but allows any domain to "write up." Indeed, there is no MLS-related reason to restrict "write up" because it does not constitute a downgrading of information, and there are valid uses of this capability to build MLS-aware security applications. Nonetheless, some MLS system developers like to provide a privilege to control "write up" just like "write down." As an exercise, change the preceding constraint to control writing up and down.

# Chapter 9

# Conditional Policies

## In this chapter

In this chapter, we explore conditional policies, created via policy statements and which enable us to define rules enabled or disabled based on circumstances. In this chapter, we discuss the SELinux policy language statements that support conditional policies and explore the use of conditional policies.

## 9.1 Overview of Conditional Policies

Support for conditional policies was one of the first major functional enhancements to the SELinux policy language after its initial release. Conditional policy statements enable us to define sets of policy rules that are enabled only under the circumstances defined by a conditional expression, which is a logical expression constructed using defined variables and logical operators.

Let's look at a contrived example. Suppose we have a mobile computer and want to define policy rules that enable access for a particular program's domain type (for example, `myprog_t`) such that it may access only the wired Ethernet network interface when the computer is docked and the wireless network interface when the computer is undocked. To achieve this goal, we might write a conditional, such as this:

```
bool docked true;
if (docked) {
      # rules to allow my_prog_t access to wired Ethernet device
} else {
      # rules to allow my_prog_t access to wireless device
}
```

In this example, we first declare a single *Boolean variable*, `docked`. We use this Boolean to indicate to SELinux whether the device is docked. As part of the declaration, we give the Boolean `docked` a default value of "true." We then create a *conditional statement* (`if`), which includes a *conditional expression* (`docked`) and a true and optional false list of rules. This statement allows us to write the `allow` rules for each case (that is, when the device is docked and when it is not docked). All we have to do is change the value of the Boolean when we dock/undock the device (for example, a running service might monitor this state and set the Boolean accordingly) to enable the appropriate set of policy rules.

This simple example illustrates the main features of conditional policies. In the rest of this section, we discuss how to define and change Boolean variables, list the syntax of conditional statements, and show example uses of conditional policies.

## 9.2 Boolean Variables

What makes conditional policies "conditional" is the effect of conditional expressions. Conditional expressions are formed by using one or more Boolean variables in conjunction with logical operators and then changing the Boolean values to effect the value of the conditional expression, thereby changing which set of rules in the conditional statement are in effect. Therefore, the first step in writing conditional policies is creating the Boolean variables.

### 9.2.1 Defining Boolean Variables

We use the `bool` statement to define Boolean variables. For example, suppose we want to configure the policy such that the ability for ordinary users to use the ping program can be turned on and off. For this example, we need to define a Boolean variable, say `user_ping`, that we will use in a conditional expression. To define this variable, we write the following statement:

```
bool user_ping false; # controls whether users may use ping program
```

The `bool` statement has two arguments, the name of the Boolean (`user_ping`) and its *default value,* which can be true or false. In this case, the default value (`false`) means that ordinary users, by default, cannot use ping (assuming our conditional statement is written correctly). You can see the full syntax for the `bool` statement in the sidebar on page 186.

---

### Bool Statement Syntax

The `bool` statement defines conditional booleans and their default value. The full syntax for the `bool` statement is as follows:

bool *bool_name default_value* ;

*bool_name*      An identifier for the Boolean variable. The identifier can be any length and can contain ASCII characters, numbers, or an underscore (_). It must begin with an ASCII character.

*default_value* The default Boolean value of the variable, either `true` or `false`.

The `bool` statement is valid in monolithic policies, base loadable modules, and non-base loadable modules. It is not valid in conditional statements.

---

## 9.2.2 Managing Booleans in a Running System

The ability to change Boolean variable values in a running system is what enables us to vary the value of conditional expressions, and hence gives us conditional policies. Therefore, it is necessary for the SELinux kernel to make Boolean variables available to running processes for changes. This is different from any other component of the policy, which once loaded into the kernel is static until a new entire policy is loaded. Booleans are individually accessible and changeable on the running system.

The kernel exposes the Booleans via the `selinux` pseudo filesystem. This pseudo filesystem is the primary interface between user space and the SELinux *Linux Security Module* (LSM) in the kernel. The filesystem is typically mounted on `/selinux/`. All Boolean variables defined in the current policy will show up as files in the `booleans` directory of this pseudo filesystem. So, for example, you would be able to see the Boolean defined above as a file with a path name of `/selinux/booleans/user_ping`.

We use the Boolean files in the `selinux` filesystem to query and set the current values of Boolean variables. If you view the contents of a Boolean file, you will always see a pair of numbers (either 0 or 1 for false or true), as follows:

---

```
# cat /selinux/booleans/user_ping
1 1
```

This first number indicates the *current value* of the Boolean variable; in this case, 1 for true. The second number represents the *pending value* of the Boolean variable. The current value is the actual value being used by the kernel for the Boolean and for determining the value of conditional expressions. The pending is the value to which the Boolean's current value will be changed when Booleans changes are committed.

We change the current value of a Boolean by changing the Boolean's pending value and then committing the changes to the kernel. We change the pending value by writing a 1 or 0 to the Boolean file, as follows:

```
# cat /selinux/booleans/user_ping    # current & pending values same (1)
1 1
# echo 0 > /selinux/booleans/user_ping # write a '0' to the file
# cat /selinux/booleans/user_ping      # pending value is changed (0)
1 0
```

As you can see, the pending value has now changed to 0, meaning false. The current value remains the same. This means that the value of the Boolean `user_ping` is still true (1) even though you changed its pending value to false (0). The reason is that changing Booleans requires a two-step commit process. First, you change the pending value for those Booleans you want to change (the default pending value is always the current value), and then you commit the pending values to the current value. This allows you to change more than one Boolean and then commit all changes in one step.

The file `/selinux/commit_pending_bools` is the interface for committing the pending values of all Booleans as the current values. You cause the commit to occur by writing a 1 to this file, as follows:

```
# echo 1 > /selinux/commit_pending_bools # commit all pending values
# cat /selinux/booleans/user_ping
0 0
```

The first command writes the `commit_pending_bools` file, which causes the kernel to change the current value for all Booleans to their pending value. As you can see by examining the `user_ping` Boolean, the change we made earlier is now committed. The current value of this Boolean is now false (0) as is the pending value. (Recall that the default pending value is always the current value.)

To reset the Boolean back to true, we just do the reverse:

```
# echo 1 > /selinux/booleans/user_ping      # set pending value true
# cat /selinux/booleans/user_ping           # see pending value changed
0 1
# echo 1 > /selinux/commit_pending_bools    # commit pending value
# cat /selinux/booleans/user_ping           # see current value changed
1 1
```

SELinux provides convenient commands for querying and changing Booleans without having to remember their file locations. The `getsebool` command displays the state of a Boolean as `active` (true) or `inactive` (false). For example:

```
# getsebool user_ping
user_ping -> active
```

> NOTE  Recent improvements in SELinux, available in *Fedora Core 5* (FC5), have changed the displayed values from the command `getsebool` to the more intuitive `on` and `off` rather than `active` and `inactive`.

To see all Booleans defined in the running system and their state, you would use the `-a` option, as follows:

```
# getsebool -a
docked -> inactive
user_ping -> active
...
```

We can also change the value of Booleans using the `setsebool` command:

```
# getsebool user_ping                # show current state
user_ping -> active
# setsebool user_ping false          # change and commit current state
# getsebool user_ping                # show changed stated
user_ping -> inactive
```

Notice that the `setsebool` command changes both the pending state and commits the change as the current state. We do not need to run the two separate commands as you saw earlier when using the `setsebool` command, nor do we need to know the full path name of the Boolean file.

We can also use the `setsebool` command to change multiple Booleans in a single transaction using an alternative format for the arguments, such as this:

```
# getsebool user_ping docked          # show current state
user_ping -> active
docked -> inactive
# setsebool user_ping=0 docked=1      # change state of both
# getsebool user_ping docked          # show current state
user_ping -> inactive
docked -> active
```

> WARNING  The Booleans defined on your system depend on the policy loaded into the running kernel. You will likely see different Booleans than those used here in our contrived examples. Do not be confused by this. If you want, add these Booleans as an exercise, or play with the Booleans defined in your policy.

### 9.2.3 Persistent Changes to Boolean Values

As previously discussed, Boolean variables are defined in the policy file along with their default state. After the inclusion of Booleans into the SELinux policy language, a problem arose of how to change the default state of a Boolean without having to re-create the policy. (The policy once written should be a fairly static entity.) Thus the idea of a *persistent value* was introduced. A standard library used by SELinux utilities provides a means for making persistent changes to Booleans by maintaining a file with Boolean persistent values. The `init` process uses this file to override the policy defaults during system initialization. In this way, we can make changes to the current values of Booleans that persist across a reboot, without having to modify the static SELinux policy.

In *Fedora Core 4* (FC4) and *Red Hat Enterprise Linux version 4* (RHEL4) systems, loadable SELinux policies are conventionally stored in the directory `/etc/selinux/[pol_name/]`, where `pol_name` is a the name of a subdirectory containing an SELinux policy and related files. In RHEL4, the file in a policy subdirectory we want to discuss here is named `booleans`. This file contains names of Booleans and their default override values. The `init` process reads this file for the active policy after loading the policy into the kernel and then changes the current value for all Booleans listed in the file. If we look inside this file, we would see contents something such as the following, depending on the associated policy:

```
# cat booleans      # run in policy subdir, for example, /etc/selinux/strict/
ftpd_is_daemon=1
ftp_home_dir=1
ssh_sysadm_login=1
staff_read_sysadm_file=1
user_ping=1
```

We can see our `user_ping` Boolean here and other Booleans that require examining the policy to understand their intended use. Therefore, to make a change to a Boolean current value consistent, we would change the current value as previously discussed and edit the `booleans` file for the active policy. Doing so will ensure that the change to the current value will persist across a reboot, if that is the desired effect.

> NOTE When the policy is reloaded on a running system, the currently active state of the Booleans is maintained instead of being reset to the default or persistent state. This ensures that nonpersistent Boolean changes are preserved while a system is running.

In FC4, a new file was introduced named `booleans.local`, which is used in the same way as the `booleans` file is used on RHEL4. The `booleans` file remains, but its purpose was changed to store distribution-defined default Boolean values defined as part of the policy package. The `booleans.local` file contains locally defined override values for Booleans that take precedence over the `booleans` file. This change allows the default state in the `booleans` file to be easily changed when upgrading the policy without impacting local customizations.

FC5 includes the loadable module infrastructure, which no longer has user-editable files for storing persistent Boolean values. The tools for managing the policy, including the persistent mode of `setsebool` (discussed below), interact directly with the module infrastructure to store the persistent Boolean values. Therefore, in FC5, you should always use the `setsebool` or other system command to change Boolean values.

The `setsebool` command provides a convenient option, `-P`, to make Boolean changes persistent. This option works across RHEL4, FC4, and FC5. When this option is used with `setsebool`, all changes are reflected in the active policy as a local override of the policy default values. (Otherwise, the change affects only the running policy and will be reset to the default value at the next boot.) For example, on an RHEL4 system, we have the following:

```
# getsebool user_ping              # show current running state
user_ping -> active
# cat booleans | grep user_ping    # and persistent state
user_ping=1
# setsebool user_ping false         # change current state
# getsebool user_ping              # current stated changed
user_ping -> inactive
# cat booleans | grep user_ping    # but persistent state did not
user_ping=1
# setsebool -P user_ping false      # persistent change with -P
# getsebool user_ping              # current state still false
user_ping -> inactive
# cat booleans | grep user_ping    # now persistent changed too
user_ping=0
```

> NOTE You do not necessarily want to make a change to a Boolean current value persistent. It all depends on your use of the Boolean. In some cases, you want to change, or toggle, the Boolean, perhaps several times, on a running system but reset to its default value on a reboot. In this case, you do not want to make the change persistent.

## 9.3 Conditional Statements

The reason we have Boolean variables in an SELinux policy is to allow us to write rules that are conditionally enabled using the conditional statement (if). The conditional statement has a conditional expression that is formed using Booleans and a true and optional false list of rules. If the conditional expression resolves to true, the true list of rules is enabled, and the false list of rules is disabled. If the conditional expression resolves to false, the opposite case prevails. We can change the value of a conditional expression on a running system by changing the current values of the Boolean variables the expression uses.

## 9.3.1 Conditional Expressions and Rule Lists

The simplest and most common form of a conditional statement has a single Boolean variable as its conditional expression and a true list (but no false list) of rules. For example, continuing with our ping example, we can write rules that allow user domains to use ping when the Boolean `user_ping` is enabled with a conditional statement similar to the following:

```
# Example: controlling user ping via a Boolean
#    Assumptions (defined elsewhere in policy):
#       unpriv_userdomain: attribute for all ordinary user domains
#       ping_t: domain type for the ping process (which has necessary
#                network interface access for ping to work)
#       ping_exec_t: entrypoint file type of the ping executable

if ( user_ping ) {
    # domain transition access to allow user access
    allow unpriv_userdomain ping_t : process transition;
    allow unpriv_userdomain ping_exec_t : file { read getattr execute };
    # entrypoint might be redundant since ping_t should already have it
    # but adding it again is not harmful
    allow ping_t ping_exec_t : file entrypoint;

    # cause the transition to happen by default
    type_transition unpriv_userdomain ping_exec_t: process ping_t;
}
```

In this example, we see that all we have to do to enable access is give all ordinary user domain types (all of which are assumed to be associated with the `unpriv_userdomain` attribute elsewhere in the policy) domain transition access to the ping program domain type (`ping_t`). Elsewhere in the policy, we would write the rules that provide the ping domain type the network access necessary for ping to work. In the conditional policy, all we have to do is control the ability of user domain type to transition to `ping_t`. We also need to ensure that the user's role is also authorized for the `ping_t` domain type (see Chapter 6, "Roles and Users"). In this case, it is typical to unconditionally authorized the `ping_t` domain type for the intended user role, and control whether this authorization can be utilized via type transition permission as we illustrated previously.

---

### Conditional (if) Statement Syntax

The conditional statement (if) specifies policy statements that are enabled/disabled (that is, enforced or not enforced by the kernel) depending on the value of a conditional expression. The full syntax of the conditional statement is as follows:

```
if (cond_expression) { true_list } [ else { false_list } ]
```

*cond_expression*   A conditional expression made up of one or more Boolean variables with logical operators. Supported logical operators are listed in Table 9-1. Boolean variables must be defined using the `bool` statement.

*true_list,*
*false_list*   A list of rules that are conditionally enabled or disabled depending on the value of the conditional expression. When the conditional list is true, the true list of rules is enabled (and the false disabled). When false, the opposite is the case. The false list is optional. The kernel will enforce only conditional rules that are enabled. The supported rules for these lists are `allow`, `auditallow`, `dontaudit`, `type_transition`, and `type_change`.

The conditional statement is valid in monolithic policies, base loadable modules, and non-base loadable modules.

At the time of this writing, conditional expressions may not be nested.

---

Let's look at another example that uses both the true and false list of rules. Suppose that we want to control the `ping_t` domain such that the `docked` Boolean introduced earlier determines what access the ping program has (that is, access to wireless Ethernet devices only when "not docked"). The following policy statements are a partial solution to this objective:

```
# Example: restricting ping's access based on docked state
#   Assumptions (defined elsewhere in policy):
#       docked: Boolean indicating docked state
#       ping_t: domain type for the ping process
#       wired_netif: attrib for all wired netif types
#       wireless_netif: attrib for all wireless netif types
```

```
# Allowed wired access when docked, wireless otherwise
if ( docked ) {
    allow ping_t wired_netif:netif { tcp_send tcp_recv udp_send
            udp_recv rawip_send rawip_recv };
} else {
    allow ping_t wireless_netif:netif { tcp_send tcp_recv udp_send
            udp_recv rawip_send rawip_recv };
}

# Remaining network and other access needed regardless of interface
allow ping_t self:capability { net_raw setuid };

# etc., remaining rules not listed for simplicity
```

In this example, we control access to the two kinds of network interfaces, including raw access (`rawip_send` and `rawip_recv`), using the conditional statement. We provide other access needed by ping regardless of network interface using *unconditional rules* (that is, rules not within a conditional statement, which are always enabled regardless of the value of any Boolean).

> WARNING  In SELinux, *type enforcement* (TE) rules are always additive; that is, they always add permissions for a source-target-class triple. There is no way to remove permissions from a policy using conditional statements. Because no permissions are allowed by default, this means that you must be careful when writing `allow` rules not to add a permission in one place in the policy and then try to make it conditional in another. The unconditional rules (that is, those not within a conditional statement) will always take precedence. Therefore, if you try to control a permission in a conditional rule that is already allowed by an unconditional rule, the conditional rule will have no effect. Whereas the conditional rule will be enabled/disabled according to the conditional expressions, the nonconditional rule will always allow the permission.

Finally, let's examine one additional example where we use a more complex conditional expression. Suppose we want to expand the notion of user_ping above to control whether ping is allowed for any user domain and not just for ordinary user domains. So, instead of a Boolean named user_ping, we will use a Boolean named `allow_ping` to better represent our intent. Further, we want ping accessible only when the computer is docked. Therefore, we create the following partial solution:

```
# Example: restricting ping based on docked state and allow Boolean
#   Assumptions (defined elsewhere in policy):
#       docked: Boolean indicating docked state
#       allow_ping: Boolean indicating whether ping is allowed
#       ping_t: domain type for the ping process
#       ping_exec_t: entrypoint file type of the ping executable
#       wired_netif: attrib for all wired netif types
#       userdomain: attrib for all user domains (priv & unpriv)

# Allowed wired access when docked if allowed
if ( allow_ping && docked ) {
    # domain transition permission
    allow userdomain ping_t : process transition;
    allow userdomain ping_exec_t : file { read getattr execute };
    allow ping_t ping_exec_t : file entrypoint;
    type_transition userdomain ping_exec_t: process ping_t;

    # wired netif access for ping
    allow ping_t wired_netif:netif { tcp_send tcp_recv udp_send
            udp_recv rawip_send rawip_recv };
}
```

This example shows the use of a two Booleans and a logical operator (`&&`) in a conditional expression. In this case, the values of both Booleans control whether this condition is true and the associated allow rules are enabled. Conditional expressions support a common set of C-like logical operators and typical parentheses rules for precedence. The logical operators supported for conditional expressions are listed in Table 9-1.

TABLE 9-1
Supported Operators for Conditional Expressions

| Operator | Syntax | Semantic |
|----------|--------|----------|
| `&&` | `bool_1 && bool_2` | Logical and |
| `\|\|` | `bool_1 \|\| bool_2` | Logical or |
| `^` | `bool_1 ^ bool_2` | Logical exclusive or |
| `!` | `!bool_1` | Logical not |
| `==` | `bool_1 == bool_2` | Are equivalent |
| `!=` | `bool_1 != bool_2` | Are not equivalent |

## 9.3.2 Conditional Statement Limitations

The conditional policy language extensions have several significant limitations that were known at the time the extensions were developed. In reality, these limitations have not, as yet, resulted in any practical limitations. Nonetheless, you should be aware of the limitations. Some of these limitations will likely be removed or improved as greater use of conditional policy comes into being.

### 9.3.2.1 Supported Statements

As of now, the only policy statements allowed within a true or false list of a conditional are the following:

`allow` (type allow rules, and not role allow rules)

`auditallow`

`dontaudit`

`type_transition`

`type_change`

These are the TE policy rule statements. The reason for this limitation is that conditional policies were really developed to support *conditional TE policies*. Therefore, the TE rules were supported. This makes sense because what we are talking about is enabling and disabling rules that allow access, audit access, and setup access defaults.

In particular, we do not allow you to define types or other policy identifiers within a conditional expression. It is difficult to imagine good policy design where policy components are defined based on runtime conditions (as controlled by Booleans). Instead, policy component identifiers such as types are either defined or not in a given policy. They are not "conditional." This reasoning also explains why user and role declarations, and indeed Boolean declarations, are not supported within conditional statements.

Some unsupported statements would be valuable within conditional statements. For example, we are finding that the `typeattribute` statement, which associates a previously defined attribute with a previously defined type, is a useful statement to allow within conditional true/false list. Because adding an attribute to a type is essentially adding rules that allow access to/from that type, it makes sense that one might want to include this in a runtime conditional. The reason why the `typeat-tribute` statement was not supported in the initial conditional policy implementation is simply that the `typeattribute` statement itself was not supported in the policy language at the time. We expect this and other statements will eventually be supported by the policy compiler.

> WARNING Do not confuse policy *build-time options* with *runtime conditionals*. It is common to use a scripting/macro language (for example, `m4`) to provide build-time options (see Chapters 11, "Original Example Policy," and 12, "Reference Policy"). For example, you can control whether certain domain types and their associated rules are included in a given policy (for example, because our intended system does not use the programs for which those domain types were designed). In this case, we would exclude all the rules and the associated type declarations from the compiled policy. This is a compile-time customization, which is entirely different from a runtime conditional. In the latter case, we include all the rules and types we want, but allow some *rules* (but not types) to be toggled on/off based on conditions as controlled by Booleans.

### 9.3.2.2 Nesting Conditional Statements

Currently, the conditional statement syntax does not support nesting. So, for example, the following policy statements would cause a compiler error:

```
# These statements would currently fail due to nonsupport for nesting
if (docked) {
     # docked statements
     if (allow_ping) {
          # docked and allow statements
     }
} else {
     # undocked statements
}
```

Instead, we would have to write this as more verbose separate statements, such as the following:

```
# This workaround with no nesting works!
if (docked && allow_ping) {
      # docked and allow statements
}

if (docked) {
      # docked statements
} else {
      # undocked statements
}
```

We expect support for nesting conditional statements to be added to the language soon, possibly by the time this book is published.

## 9.4 Examining Booleans and Conditional Policies with Apol

We can use `apol` to more easily examine conditional policy statements and the associated Booleans. `Apol` proves particularly useful when trying to understand the effects of conditional policy statements and when the same condition is repeated several places within the policy.

Figure 9-1, we show how to use `apol` to examine defined Booleans within a policy. The Booleans tab under the Policy Components tab shows all Booleans and their default and current values. `Apol` also enables you to change the current value of a Boolean, which proves useful when exploring conditional policy rules, as you will see shortly.

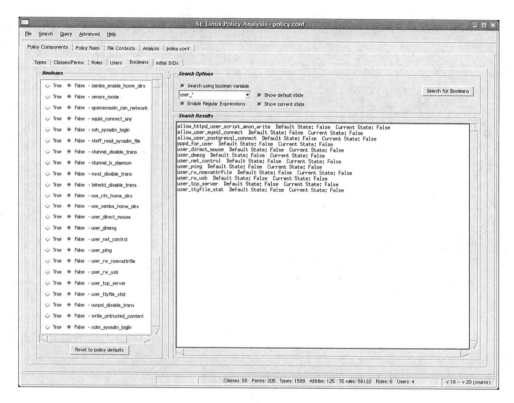

FIGURE 9-1
Examining Boolean variables using apol

More interesting is when you are searching the policy rules. In the TE Rules tab under the Policy Rules tab, you can configure `apol` to show all rules, whether enabled or disabled, and show their current state, as shown in Figure 9-2. Most rules are not in conditional statements and will not show a current state. However, those that are in conditional statements will have their current state (enabled/disabled) so indicated, as shown in Figure 9-2.

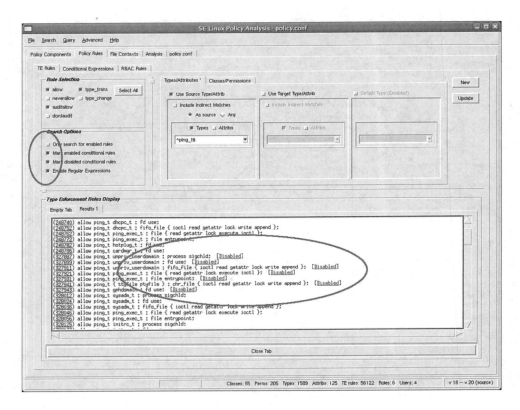

FIGURE 9-2
Viewing disabled conditional rules in apol

You can use the Booleans tab to change the current value of a Boolean to experiment with the effects within `apol`. For example, in Figure 9-3, we changed the current value of `user_ping` from its default value of false to a current value of true. This will then effect what rules are enabled or disabled, as shown in Figure 9-4, where rules that were previously disabled now become enabled.

**FIGURE 9-3**
Changing current state of Boolean value in apol

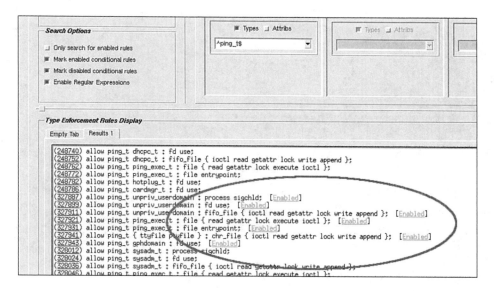

**FIGURE 9-4**
Changing current Boolean values in apol changes the enabled/disabled state of rules

Finally, by using the Conditional Expression tab under the Policy Rules tab, you can search for entire conditional statements by searching for Booleans, as illustrated in Figure 9-5. Apol will show you all conditional expressions that use the provided Boolean variable and their true and false list of rules. Further, the tool will collapse like conditionals (for example, if there are five conditionals all with the same conditional expression, apol will show them as one combined conditional), making it easier to understand the entire set of related conditional rules. As with the rule search shown in Figure 9-4, the current state of the Boolean variables will affect the result of this search.

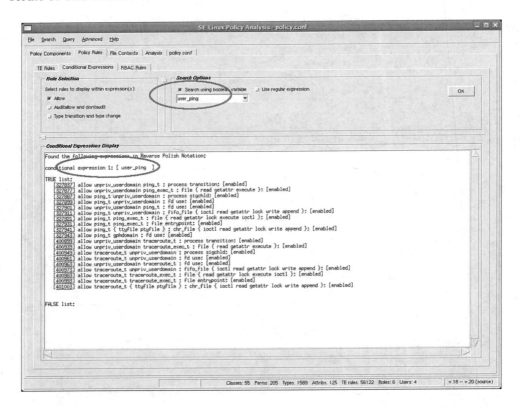

FIGURE 9-5
Searching conditional expressions by Boolean name within apol

## 9.5 Summary

- Conditional statements allow you to create policy rules that can be enabled or disabled by changing Boolean variable values on a running system. Rules that are not within a conditional statement (typically the vast majority of rules in a system) are unconditional and always enabled.

- Boolean variables are defined in the policy using the `bool` statement, along with the default value for each Boolean.

- All defined Booleans in the running policy also have filenames in the `selinux` filesystem, usually mounted at `/selinux/booleans/`. These files indicate the current and pending value for each Boolean. To change the current value of a Boolean, you would write the new value (`1` or `0`) into this file and then make the change effective by writing a `1` to the file `/selinux/commit_pending_bools`. The commands `getsebool` and `setsebool` provide a convenient and stable way for changing these values without remembering the various filenames.

- Booleans support a persistent value that will override the default value in the policy on a reboot. The persistent value allows you to change the effective default value without having to modifying the policy itself. The easiest way to make a persistent change to a Boolean value is to use the `setsebool -P` command.

- The conditional statement (`if`) allows you to express a logical conditional expression using a defined Boolean variable and a true and optional false list of rules. These rules will be enabled/disabled by the kernel depending on the value of the conditional expression, which in turn depends on the current values of the Booleans the expression contains.

- The only statements currently supported in a conditional statement true/false list are `allow`, `auditallow`, `dontaudit`, `type_transition`, and `type_change`.

- At present, you cannot nest conditional statements. This limitation is likely to change in the near future.

## Exercises

1.  Explain the differences between the default, current, pending, and persistent values of a Boolean variable.

2. Suppose that our policy has three Booleans defined: `booll`, `bool2`, and `bool3`. Now take a look at the following commands:

```
# cd /selinux/booleans
# cat booll
0 1
# cat bool2
1 1
# cat bool3
1 0
```

What are the current values of all three Booleans?

3. Take the set of comments from the previous question, and add the following command:

```
# echo 1 > /selinux/commit_pending_bools
```

Now what are the current values of the three Booleans?

4. One use of conditional policies is to control the level of auditing performed by SELinux by enabling and disabling packages of audit rules. Suppose we want to create a Boolean (`enhanced_audit`) to control auditing of access attempts (success and denial events). Further, suppose that there are two kinds of events, among others, we want to capture for enhanced auditing: transitions into any domain type and any use of the ping program to access the network. Write a partial policy to achieve these goals. Assume that there are two attributes in your policy: `domain`, which is associated with all domain types; and `netif_type`, which is associated with all the types used for network interface objects.

# Chapter 10

# Object Labeling

**In this chapter**

For the SELinux policy to work, all object instances must be labeled with a security context. In this chapter, we discuss the various means of applying security contexts to object instances, including how security contexts are assigned when objects are created and the later modification of those labels (called relabeling).

## 10.1 Introduction to Object Labeling

All objects in SELinux have an associated security context from the time they are created until they are destroyed. This property is central to the ability of SELinux to enforce access control. For example, let's look at the security context of a file we first discussed in Chapter 2, "Concepts:"

```
# ls -Z /etc/shadow
-r--------  root   root   system_u:object_r:shadow_t   shadow
```

This example demonstrates the program `ls` displaying the security context for the file `/etc/shadow`. The security context associated with an object, in this case `system_u:object_r:shadow_t`, is the only attribute SELinux uses in access control decisions. Therefore, it is fundamentally important that this and all objects have the correct security context assigned to them.

Until this point, we have generally discussed objects with the assumption that they have a security context, with little or no mention of how that security context was determined and applied. This reflects the goal that labeling should not be a normal concern when *using* an SELinux system. Users and administrators can use SELinux systems in much the same way they use standard Linux systems without having to be concerned with security contexts. In addition, this goal allows nearly all programs to run unmodified on SELinux.

The SELinux policy language includes features, such as `type_transition` rules for file and domain transitions, that make labeling decisions automatic and largely transparent. However, sometimes, like during system administration, policy development, and system installation, labeling becomes an issue with which we need to concern ourselves. As policy writers, we must carefully craft labeling policy statements to ease label management at runtime.

An object is labeled on an SELinux system in four basic ways:

- **Policy statements**   The SELinux policy language includes features, such as `type_transition` rules, that specify behavior for object labeling decisions.

- **Hard-coded defaults**   Most object classes have some type of default labeling behavior encoded within the object managers. For example, by default when a process creates a new socket, the new socket has the same security context as its creating process.

- **Program-requested labeling**   For some object classes, SELinux provides a variety of *application programming interfaces* (APIs) that allow programs to explicitly request a label, both for new and existing object instances. For file-related objects that are stored on filesystems that support labeling, these APIs are used by SELinux utilities that initialize and repair file labels (for example, by the `rpm` package manager when installing the system).

- **Initial SIDs**   SELinux has a set of initial *security identifiers* (initial SIDs) used to label a few objects and as a failsafe label when an object would otherwise have a missing or invalid label.

For many objects, a combination of all these behavior types may be used to determine the label of a new object. Labeling decisions also use information from the execution environment (for example, the security context for the process and related object instances) to compute a security context for new objects. In all cases, the policy must allow the appropriate access for the labeling to occur. Object labeling behavior usually controls only how object labeling is attempted and not whether it is allowed.

We have already discussed some of the policy rules (that is, type and role transition rules) that support labeling decisions in Chapter 2, Chapter 5, "Type Enforcement," and Chapter 6, "Roles and Users." In this chapter, we discuss additional policy statements for labeling network-related object classes. As you will see, these statements are object class-specific and do not apply to all object classes.

The default labeling behaviors for each object class are hard-coded into the object managers that implement the classes. These defaults are used in the absence of relevant policy labeling rules and for those object classes that have no associated policy labeling rules. The default for most object classes is to inherit the security context of the creating process and/or containing object. For example, file-related objects inherit the type of the containing directory, a hard-coded role (object_r), and the SELinux user of the creating process.

In the remainder of this chapter, we discuss the many ways that a policy writer must address object labeling.

## 10.2 File-Related Object Labeling

In SELinux, labeling most often refers to the labeling of file-related objects because this is the only form of label management that a normal user or administrator is likely to encounter. Much of the challenge with file labeling comes from the sheer number of files present on a normal system combined with the customization of how those files will be stored in the directory structure. The variety of filesystems available for Linux also contributes to the complexity. Common filesystems include traditional, native filesystems intended to store data on hard disks and removable media (for example, ext3 and XFS); non-native filesystems present for compatibility with other systems (for example, iso9660 and vfat); and in-memory, pseudo filesystems used for communication between the kernel and userspace (for example, proc and sysfs).

How file-related objects are labeled varies according to the intended purpose of the filesystem and the specific semantics of how the objects are created, stored, and used. For example, files stored persistently to hard disk using the ext3 filesystem are labeled when created and the security context stored with the file. In contrast, files in the proc filesystem exist only at runtime and must have their labels generated at runtime instead of stored persistently.

---

### SELinux Mount Options

The context mount option (filesystems mounted with this option are often referred to in documentation as "mountpoint labeled") overrides the labeling behavior of any filesystem and applies a single security context to all of the file-related objects it contains. For example, consider the following mount command:

```
mount -t nfs -o context=user_u:object_r:user_home_t
      gotham:/shares/homes/ /home/
```

In this example, the mount option `context=` `user_u:object_r:user_`
`home_t` instructs SELinux to apply the specified security context to all file-
related objects in the `nfs` filesystem mounted on the `/home/` directory. The
security context specified in the option, `user_u:object_r:user_home_t` in
this example, will be applied to both existing and new files.

The context mount option works for all filesystems regardless of what labeling
behavior they support or is specified in the policy. For example, filesystems that
would normally use extended attribute labeling, such as `ext3`, can be mounted
using the `context` option. (Although when mounted with the context option,
new inodes do not receive any SELinux attributes on disk and existing on-disk
inodes are not changed.) This is useful for removable media transferred from
non-SELinux systems.

There are two related filesystem mount options, `fscontext` and `defcontext`,
that may be used together or separately instead of the `context` option. The
`fscontext` option is used to set or override the filesystem object instance security context (for example, to set the filesystem security context for an `ext3`
filesystem to something other than the default set for ext3 filesystems in the policy). The `defcontext` option is used to override the default file security context
for a given filesystem. (The default file security context for filesystems is normally the file initial SID, which is explained later in this chapter.)

The standard `nosuid` mount option, besides negating standard Linux
`setuid/setgid` behavior, also changes the behavior of SELinux for files on a
filesystem. The `nosuid` option disables SELinux security context transitions for
files labeled with `entrypoint` types on the filesystem. It is possible to use the
`context` mount option to achieve the same effect (that is, force all files to be
labeled with an untrusted type), but the `nosuid` option is another good choice.

---

SELinux supports four kinds of labeling for file-related objects to address the various types of filesystems: extended attribute, task-based, transition-based, and generalized security contexts. The primary difference between these mechanisms is how
SELinux determines the initial label of inodes for the filesystem. Security-extended
attribute labeling also stores security contexts persistently to disk. Table 10-1 lists
the filesystem labeling mechanisms and the filesystems that use each labeling mechanism on a *Fedora Core 4* (FC4) system.

TABLE 10-1
Kinds of Filesystem Labeling Mechanisms and Associated Filesystems

| Labeling Mechanism | Filesystems |
|---|---|
| Extended attributes | `ext2, ext3, xfs, jfs, reiserfs` |
| Task-based | `pipefs, sockfs` |
| Transition-based | `devpts, tmpfs, shm, mqueue` |
| Generalized | `proc, rootfs, sysfs, selinuxfs, autofs, auto-mount, usbdevfs, iso9660, udf, romfs, cramfs, ramfs, vfat, msdos, fat, ntfs, cifs, smbfs, nfs, nfs4, afs, debugfs, inotifyfs, hugetlbfs, capifs, eventpollfs, futexfs, bdev, usbfs, nfsd, rpc_pipefs, binfmt_misc` |

The kind of labeling is specified per filesystem in the policy using either the *filesystem use statements* or the *generalized filesystem labeling support statement,* normally called the *genfscon statement.* The SELinux policy language supports three filesystem use statements: `fs_use_xattr`, `fs_use_task`, and `fs_use_trans`, which specify extended attribute, task-based, and transition-based labeling behaviors, respectively.

The syntax for the all three filesystem use statements is identical (see the sidebar on page 211). As an example, consider the following `fs_use_xattr` statement:

```
fs_use_xattr ext3 system_u:object_r:fs_t;
```

This statement indicates that the `ext3` filesystem (that is, all instances of `ext3` on the system) will be labeled using security-extended attributes, and the filesystem object instance associated with all `ext3` filesystems will be labeled with the security context `system_u:object_r:fs_t`. The filesystem name, `ext3` in this example, is the same as that understood by the kernel and the `mount(8)` command. These names are listed in the file `/proc/filesystems`.

The *generalized filesystem labeling support statement* (`genfscon`) specifies both that the filesystem will use generalized filesystem security context labeling and how the individual file-related objects in that filesystem are labeled. The `genfscon` syntax is more complicated; we describe it later in this section.

---

### Filesystem Use Statements Syntax

The *filesystem use statements* specify the labeling mechanism to be used for a kind of filesystem. The *filesystem use statements* begin with one of three keywords, which are marked in brackets. There can be only one *filesystem use statement* for each filesystem. The full syntax of the statements are as follows:

```
[fs_use_xattr | fs_use_task | fs_use_trans] fs_name fs_context
```

*fs_name*      The name of the filesystem that will use the specified labeling mechanism (for example, ext3). The filesystem names are the same as those understood by the kernel and mount(8) command and are listed in /proc/filesystems.

*fs_context*    The security context for the filesystem object instance associated with this filesystem.

The fs_use_xattr statement indicates that the filesystem will provide security context information (through its getxattr(2) method) using extended attributes. The fs_use_task statement indicates that the filesystem will use task-based labeling behavior, and the fs_use_trans statement indicates that the filesystem will use transition-based labeling behavior. The filesystem implementation must support the labeling behavior when using fs_use_xattr. (In the other cases, SELinux handles the labeling.)

The filesystem use statements are valid only in monolithic policies and base loadable modules. They are not valid in conditional statements or non-base loadable modules.

---

## 10.2.1 Extended Attribute Filesystems (fs_use_xattr)

Most native, disk-based Linux filesystems use extended attribute labeling. This labeling mechanism extends the standard extended attribute mechanisms to support setting, retrieving, and storing the security contexts associated with all file-related objects. (See the sidebar on page 212 for more details.) Filesystems that use this labeling mechanism support program-requested labeling and, when stored to persistent media, preserve the security contexts across reboots.

---

### More on Security Contexts Using Extended Attributes

File-related resources stored in native Linux filesystems typically have important information about the resource, such as ownership and access mode, stored in a special data structure called an inode. In recent versions of Linux, additional information is associated with inodes in the form of extended attributes. Extended attributes, which store the additional information as name/value pairs, are used for storing system information, such as *access control lists* (ACLs), or other data required by some application or service. SELinux uses extended attributes to store the security context of all file-related objects.

The name portion of extended attributes is divided into multiple namespaces to allow different kinds of data to easily coexist. SELinux uses the security namespace, denoted by the prefix `security.`, to store security contexts. This namespace is intended to be shared by all *Linux Security Module* (LSM) modules, so SELinux uses the name `selinux` to store the security contexts in the security namespace. To illustrate, let's directly examine the extended attributes of a file on SELinux:

```
# getfattr -n security.selinux /etc/shadow
# file: etc/shadow
security.selinux="system_u:object_r:shadow_t\000"
```

As you can see, the security context is stored directly as a string. Indeed, examining the extended attribute is how the `ls -Z` command displays security contexts for file-related objects. We recommend always using the `libselinux` API (for example, `getfilecon(3)`) instead of using the extended attribute API directly because the storage of the security context may change over time.

---

## 10.2.1.1 Labeling Behavior for Extended Attribute Filesystems

Labeling decisions for extended attribute filesystems use a combination of policy rules and security context inheritance. By default, all new file-related objects inherit the type of the containing directory and the user of the creating process. The role is always set to the special object role `object_r`. If a `type_transition` rule matches the type of the creating process and the type of the directory that will contain the new object, the default type specified in that rule will be used for the type of the new file-related object. The rest of the security context is set in the same way as if there were no `type_transition` rule.

Program-requested labeling allows processes to request a specific security context for a new file using the `setfscreatecon(3)` library call. In this situation, the object will be created with the requested security context unless the process lacks the required access. Normally, only applications that extend SELinux or are an SELinux utility (that is, so-called *SELinux-aware* applications) use this feature; files created by standard applications receive the correct security context through the automatic labeling decision described previously.

In addition to setting security contexts on creation, file-related objects can be relabeled for extended attribute labeled filesystems. This is done with the `setfilecon(3)`, `lsetfilecon(3)`, and `fsetfilecon(3)` library calls. Explicitly changing the label of an object requires appropriate `relabelfrom` and `relabelto` permissions, which should be tightly controlled by the policy. (See the sidebar on page 213 for more information.)

---

### Policy Control of Object Labeling

The ability to change the security context of an object is a powerful privilege. Recall from Chapter 4, "Object Classes and Permissions," that the policy controls changing of types on file-related objects with `relabelfrom` and `relabelto` permissions for most object classes. The `relabelfrom` permission controls the starting type for the object, and the `relabelto` permission controls the resulting type; a domain must have both permissions to successfully relabel an object. For example, consider the following `allow` rules:

```
allow user_t user_home_t : file { relabelfrom };
allow user_t httpd_user_content_t : file { relabelto };
```

These `allow` rules state that a process with the type `user_t` is allowed to relabel files from the type `user_home_t` to the type `httpd_user_content_t`.

The `relabelto` and `relabelfrom` permissions control only changes to the type of the object. We saw in Chapter 7, "Constraints," that changing the user and role portions of security contexts can be controlled by constraints. For example, consider the following constraint:

```
constrain file { create relabelto relabelfrom }
( u1 == u2 or t1 == privowner );
```

This constraint states that when a process requests `create`, `relabelto`, or `relabelfrom` permission on a file, the user portion of the security context must match that of the process or the process type must have the `privowner` attribute.

---

## 10.2.1.2 Managing Security Contexts in Extended Attribute Filesystems (File Contexts)

The labeling of file-related objects using extended attributes differs from the other filesystem and most other nonfile object classes. The security contexts using extended attributes are initialized, normally during installation with a package manager such as rpm, using runtime labeling requests. The runtime labeling requests are directed by one or more configuration files, called *file context* files, which list paths, or partial paths, and security contexts. The file context files are not included directly within the policy but are stored with it on the filesystem in a standard location (see Chapter 13, "Managing an SELinux System"). By using the appropriate file context files for a policy, the file-related object security contexts can be correctly initialized based on path name. Initialization puts the system in a known, secure state. After initialization, the automatic labeling decisions take over and ensure that any files created subsequently are correctly labeled and a secure state is always maintained.

This label management strategy is used to separate the policy, which deals primarily with types and security contexts, from path names and filenames. This strategy has several advantages. First, the layout of filesystems can vary greatly because of differences between distributions or user customization. By removing this aspect of variability from the policy, a single policy can be more easily adapted to multiple systems.

More important, in native Linux filesystems, file-related objects are not uniquely identified by a single path name. Hard links, chroot environments, and per-process filesystem namespaces all mean that a single file-related object could be identified by several path names. If the policy were enforced within the kernel using path names directly, there would be no way to determine which of these names was the correct one to use, possibly leading to a process having different access to the same object depending on how the access was attempted. For this reason, SELinux associates the security context directly with the object and uses only paths to initialize the security context. Only if initialization occurs when the system is in a protected, known-secure state (for example, during installation) is it safe from this ambiguity.

The format of a line in the file context files is a regular expression representing one or more file-related object paths, an optional object class specification, and a security context. For example, consider the following portion of a file context file:

```
1   /bin(/.*)?                          system_u:object_r:bin_t
2   /bin/tcsh               --          system_u:object_r:shell_exec_t
3   /bin/bash               --          system_u:object_r:shell_exec_t
4   /bin/bash2              --          system_u:object_r:shell_exec_t
5   /bin/sash               --          system_u:object_r:shell_exec_t
6   /bin/d?ash              --          system_u:object_r:shell_exec_t
7   /bin/zsh.*              --          system_u:object_r:shell_exec_t
8   /usr/sbin/sesh          --          system_u:object_r:shell_exec_t
9   /bin/ls                 --          system_u:object_r:ls_exec_t
10  /boot(/.*)?                         system_u:object_r:boot_t
11  /boot/System\.map(-.*)?             system_u:object_r:system_map_t
12  /dev(/.*)?                          system_u:object_r:device_t
13  /dev/pts(/.*)?                      <<none>>
14  /dev/cpu/.*             -c          system_u:object_r:cpu_device_t
15  /dev/microcode          -c          system_u:object_r:cpu_device_t
16  /dev/MAKEDEV            --          system_u:object_r:sbin_t
17  /dev/null               -c          system_u:object_r:null_device_t
18  /dev/full               -c          system_u:object_r:null_device_t
19  /dev/zero               -c          system_u:object_r:zero_device_t
```

This example specifies how the files in the /bin/, /boot/, and part of /dev/ directories should be labeled. For example, line 3 is a simple entry that matches the filename /bin/bash and specifies that it should be labeled with the security context system_u:object_r:shell_exec_t. The *object class specification* is – in this case, which means a regular file. The object class specifications are the same as those understood by the command find(1).

When processes query the file contexts, files using the matchpathcon(3) library call to match the name of a file-related object, the most specific entry is always used. For example, line 1 has a regular expression that will match all files in the /bin/ directory. If there is no object class specifier, as is the case in line 1, it will match all file-related objects. Lines 2 through 9, however, have regular expressions that are more specific and will match some files in the /bin/ directory. When the match for /bin/bash is requested, line 3 will match because it is an exact match. The file /bin/dd, however, has no more specific match than line 1.

Line 13 uses the special <<none>> syntax to specify that file-related objects that match this entry should not be labeled. This is used for files that must be labeled at runtime. Entries with <<none>> are used to prevent other, more general regular expressions from matching and causing the file-related objects to be labeled.

Many different utilities and applications use file contexts files, often during policy development and system administration. Chapter 13 describes these tools and their intended use.

## 10.2.2 Task-Based Filesystems (fs_use_task)

With task-based labeling, new file-related objects inherit their security context from the creating process. Filesystems that use task-based labeling do not support program-requested labeling. This type of labeling behavior is useful for simple pseudo filesystems that are not truly intended to store user data but rather are designed to support certain kinds of kernel resources such as unnamed pipes. For example, consider the following `fs_use_task` statement:

```
fs_use_task pipefs system_u:object_r:fs_t;
```

This statement specifies that the `pipefs` filesystem uses task-based labeling and that the security context for the filesystem object for `pipfs` is `system_u:object_r:fs_t`.

The `pipefs` filesystem is a good example of a filesystem that uses task-based labeling. This filesystem is a pseudo filesystem used to implement unnamed pipes. Unnamed pipes, created with the `pipe(2)` system call, are by their very nature not associated with a file in a user-space visible filesystem. Despite this, communications over pipes is done using standard read and write system calls on file descriptors. The Linux implementation, therefore, uses a special-purpose filesystem called `pipefs` that is not visible to userspace. The filesystem is mounted and used by the kernel internally and labeled using task labeling.

## 10.2.3 Transition-Based Filesystems (fs_use_trans)

Transition-based filesystem labeling is similar to task-based labeling. Both are normally used for simple pseudo filesystems. However, instead of using the security context from the creating process, transition-based labeling sets the security context of file-related objects based on type transition (`type_transition`) rules.

Type transition rules for transition-based labeling are subtly different from those for the more common extended attribute mechanism. On extended attribute labeled filesystems, labeling decisions use the security context of the creating process and the containing directory. For transition-based labeled filesystems, the `type_transition` rules use the security context of the creating process and the security context of the associated `filesystem` object instance for the filesystem. No provision exists for basing the security context of a new object on the context of the containing directory; the security context is always based on the type of the associated `filesystem` object. If there is not a relevant `type_transition` rule, the security context defaults to that of the `filesystem` object.

Consider the following filesystem use statement:

```
fs_use_trans devpts system_u:object_r:devpts_t;
```

This statement specifies that the `devpts` filesystem uses transition-based labeling. The security context for the `devpts` filesystem object is specified as `system_u:object_r:devpts_t`.

As mentioned previously, transition-based labeled filesystems use `type_transition` rules to derive the type for file-related objects. For example, consider the following type transition rule:

```
type_transition sysadm_t devpts_t : chr_file sysadm_devpts_t;
```

This rule states that when processes with the type `sysadm_t` create objects of `chr_file` class in filesystems labeled `devpts_t`, the resulting object should be labeled `sysadm_devpts_t`. The implied object class for the target of this type transition is `filesystem` rather than `dir` because this type transition will apply to the creation of objects in a transition-based filesystem regardless of the directory type. If there is no appropriate `type_transition` rule, any objects created on this filesystem will have the filesystem security context.

## 10.2.4 Generalized Security Context Labeling (genfscon)

The generalized security context statement (`genfscon`) is used for runtime labeling of pseudo filesystems, such as `proc` or `sysfs`, and legacy filesystems that do not support extended attributes. Unlike the other filesystem labeling mechanisms discussed so far, which require modification of the kernel filesystem code, `genfscon` labeling, at least in a limited form, can be used with unmodified filesystems.

The `genfscon` statement specifies both the labeling mechanism for the filesystem and the labeling for the file-related objects stored in the filesystem. There are two forms of `genfscon` statements: a full form that specifies fine-grained labeling for file-related objects and a limited form useful for legacy filesystems.

### 10.2.4.1 Fine-Grained Labeling with genfscon Statement

Consider the following example of the full-feature `genfscon` statements for the `proc` filesystem:

```
1  genfscon proc /               system_u:object_r:proc_t
2  genfscon proc /kmsg           system_u:object_r:proc_kmsg_t
3  genfscon proc /kcore          system_u:object_r:proc_kcore_t
4  genfscon proc /mdstat         system_u:object_r:proc_mdstat_t
5  genfscon proc /mtrr           system_u:object_r:mtrr_device_t
6  genfscon proc /net            system_u:object_r:proc_net_t
7  genfscon proc /sysvipc        system_u:object_r:proc_t
8  genfscon proc /sys            system_u:object_r:sysctl_t
9  genfscon proc /sys/kernel     system_u:object_r:sysctl_kernel_t
10 genfscon proc /sys/net        system_u:object_r:sysctl_net_t
11 genfscon proc /sys/vm         system_u:object_r:sysctl_vm_t
12 genfscon proc /sys/dev        system_u:object_r:sysctl_dev_t
13 genfscon proc /net/rpc        system_u:object_r:sysctl_rpc_t
14 genfscon proc /irq            system_u:object_r:sysctl_irq_t
```

As these example statements show, the `genfscon` statement syntax requires the name of the filesystem, a full or partial path name (relative to the root of the filesystem), and a security context. The full syntax for the `genfscon` statement can be found on page 220.

These example `genfscon` statements show that there can be multiple `genfscon` statements for the same filesystem. For filesystems that support this full form of the `genfscon` statement, the multiple statements are used to specify fine-grained labels for file-related objects. When multiple `genfscon` statements are present, the security context for file-related objects is determined by matching the `genfscon` statement with the most specific partial path name and using the security context from that statement.

For example, assume that the `proc` filesystem is mounted at `/proc` (the standard location). Using these example `genfscon` statements, the file `/proc/filesystems` would match the statement on line 1 and receive the security context `system_u:object_r:proc_t`. Similarly, the directory `/proc/sys/kernel/` would match the `genfscon` statement on line 9 (with the partial path `/sys/kernel`) and be labeled `system_u:object_r:sysctl_kernel_t`.

All filesystems that use `genfscon` labeling include at least one `genfscon` statement with / as the partial path. The security context in this `genfscon` statement is used to label the filesystem object associated with the filesystem in addition to being the default security context for all file-related objects stored in the filesystem. In the preceding example, the filesystem object for `proc` would receive the security context `system_u:object_r:proc_t`.

---

### Labeling PID Files in Proc

The `proc` filesystem contains files and directories representing every active process on the system. These files and directories, which are contained in a directory named with the *process ID* (PID) of the process, can be used to get or set properties of the process preferably through `libselinux` calls (for example, `getcon(3)`, `setcon(3)`). The PID directory and all the files and directories that it contains receive the same security context as the process that they represent.

For this reason, it is not uncommon to see rules such as the following:

```
allow apache_t self : dir { read getattr search };
allow apache_t self : file { read getattr write };
```

Rules such as these allow a domain, `apache_t` in this example, access to the files and directories representing it.

---

## 10.2.4.2 Legacy Filesystem Labeling with the genfscon Statement

As mentioned previously, `genfscon` can be used in two ways. Before examining the more limited form of this statement intended for legacy filesystems, let's examine some properties of the `proc` filesystem that make it work well with the full `genfscon` statement. This will help you understand why other filesystems cannot use the features. These properties concern how file-related object naming is handled on a Linux system.

First, the names of all the files and directories that can appear in the `proc` filesystem are well known and consistent across systems, with the exception of the files and directories representing active processes. For example, `/proc/sys/kernel/hostname` is *always* a file that is used to get or set the host name. Although the location of important files is often known for other filesystems (for example, `/etc/shadow`), the location is seldom known relative to the filesystem mount point and, more important, it is seldom the case that the security properties of all of the file-related objects can be determined by the path.

Second, file-related objects are uniquely identified by path name in the `proc` filesystem, and the kernel can easily determine this absolute path in all circumstances. The `proc` filesystem does not support the concept of hard links. This means, for example, the object identified by the path `/proc/sys/kernel/hostname` is never identified by any other path.

Together these properties make the `proc` filesystem suitable for labeling based on path name, as is done by `genfscon` labeling. Very few filesystems exhibit these properties, making labeling by path name not only difficult but potentially dangerous, as discussed previously.

We use the limited form of `genfscon` for labeling many legacy filesystems, including many that do not exhibit the same properties as `proc`. To handle filesystems that cannot be safely labeled by path name, we set a default label using the `genfscon` statement for the filesystem and *all* the file-related objects in that filesystem. We do this with a single `genfscon` statement for the entire filesystem. For example, consider the following `genfscon` statements:

```
genfscon vfat /          system_u:object_r:dosfs_t
genfscon msdos /         system_u:object_r:dosfs_t
genfscon fat /           system_u:object_r:dosfs_t
genfscon ntfs /          system_u:object_r:dosfs_t
```

These `genfscon` statements for the `vfat`, `msdos`, `fat`, and `ntfs` filesystems set the security context for the associated `filesystem` objects and all the file-related objects stored in the filesystems to `system_u:object_r:dosfs_t`.

---

### Generalized Security Context Statement (genfscon)

The generalized security context statement (`genfscon`) specifies the labeling mechanism to be used for a filesystem and the labeling for file-related objects stored in the filesystem. There can be multiple `genfscon` statements for each filesystem. The full syntax of the statement is as follows:

`genfscon` *fs_name partial_path context;*

*fs_name*         The name of the filesystem that will use `genfscon` labeling (for example, `proc`). The filesystem names are the same as those understood by the kernel and `mount(8)` command and are listed in `/proc/filesystems`.

*partial_path*   A partial path relative to the mount point of the filesystem. (For example, for a filesystem mounted at /proc, the partial path / translates to /proc at runtime.) If multiple genfscon statements are specified for a filesystem, file-related objects are labeled using the security context from the statement that includes the partial path that most closely matches the path to the file-related object.

*context*   A security context used to label file-related objects that most closely match this genfscon statement. For genfscon statements with the partial path of /, this security context is also used to label the filesystem object associated with the filesystem.

The genfscon statement is valid only in monolithic policies and base loadable modules. They are not valid in conditional statements and non-base loadable modules.

## 10.3 Network and Socket Object Labeling

Network and socket objects are labeled using policy statements and initial SIDs; there is no mechanism for program-requested labeling. We use several policy labeling statements to label network and socket objects. Table 10-2 lists all the network and socket-specific labeling statements and the relevant object classes.

TABLE 10-2
Network and Socket-Related Object Labeling Mechanisms

| SELinux Policy Statement | Linux Resources and SELinux Object Classes |
|---|---|
| netifcon | Network interfaces: netif |
| nodecon | IP addresses representing network hosts: node |
| portcon | Network sockets: tcp_socket (name_bind, recv_msg, and send_msg only), udp_socket (name_bind, recv_msg, and send_msg only), and rawip_socket (recv_msg and send_msg only) |

### 10.3.1 Network Interface Labeling (netifcon)

Network interfaces are labeled with the *network interface security context statement* (netifcon) or with the netif initial SID. For example, consider the following statement:

```
netifcon eth0 system_u:object_r:netif_t
 system_u:object_r:packet_t
```

This statement provides the security context for the network device eth0 as system_u:object_r:netif_t (that is, the first security context) and the default label for packets received on this interface as system_u:object_r:packet_t (that is, the second security context). The default packet label is not currently used and is awaiting support for per-packet labeling. The full syntax for the netifcon statement is shown in the sidebar on page 146. The network interface name, eth0 in this example, is the same interface as understood by the ifconfig(8) command.

> NOTE Per-packet labeling, which allows finer-grained control over networking, was part of the initial implementation of SELinux but was not included when SELinux was merged into the Linux kernel as an LSM module. There was concern over the invasiveness and performance impact of many of the fine-grained network controls, particularly those that would result in additional access checks on the processing of every packet. As a result, some SELinux network controls, such as per-packet labeling, were not included. Work is ongoing to re-create these features in a way acceptable to the Linux kernel community leveraging other technologies such as Netfilter and IPsec.

Any network interface that is not labeled with a netifcon statement is labeled with the netif initial SID security context.

---

### Network Interface Security Context (netifcon) Statement

The network interface security context statement is used to label `netif` object instances. The full syntax for the statement is as follows:

```
netifcon interface if_context packet_context
```

| | |
|---|---|
| *interface* | The name of the network interface to label (for example, eth0). The interface names are the same as those understood by the `ifconfig(8)` command. |
| *if_context* | The security context for the `netif` object instance associated with the specified network interface. |
| *packet_context* | The default security context for packets received on the specified network interface. This is currently unused. |

The `netifcon` statement is valid only in monolithic policies and base loadable modules. They are not valid in conditional statements and non-base loadable modules.

---

## 10.3.2 Network Node Labeling (nodecon)

Node objects are labeled with the *node security context statement* (`nodecon`) or the `node` initial SID. The `nodecon` statement labels node objects by subnet and network mask. Recall from Chapter 4 that the `node` object class represents network nodes by IP address. For example, consider the following statement:

```
nodecon 127.0.0.1 255.255.255.255 system_u:object_r:node_lo_t
```

This statement indicates that all nodes with the IPv4 address 127.0.0.1 and the subnet mask 255.255.255.255 (that is, exactly one host, 127.0.0.1 or localhost) are labeled with the security context system_u:object_r:node_lo_t. The full syntax for the `nodecon` statement can be seen in the sidebar on page 148.

The `nodecon` statement supports IPv4 addresses, like the example above, and IPv6 addresses. For example, consider the following statement:

```
nodecon ::1 ffff:ffff:ffff:ffff:ffff:ffff:ffff:ffff system_u:object_r:node_lo_t
```

This `nodecon` statement is the IPv6 equivalent of the previous IPv4 example for specifying localhost.

The nodecon statement supports inexact matches in addition to exact matches. For example, the following statement matches an entire subnet:

```
nodecon 192.168.0.0 255.255.255.0 system_u:object_r:node_intranet_t
```

The example statement above would match all hosts on the 192.168.0.0 subnet for a Class C network.

Node security context statements are automatically ordered by the policy compiler so that more specific statements are matched first, similarly to how genfscon statements work. This convention allows the policy to contain nodecon statements with overlapping IP address ranges and resolve the conflicts naturally. For example, consider a policy with the following statements:

```
nodecon 192.168.0.0 255.255.0.0 system_u:object_r:node_intranet_t
nodecon 192.168.1.0 255.255.255.0 system_u:object_r:node_webserver_t
```

In this example, the nodecon statement with the partial IP address 192.168.0.0 is more general than a statement with the partial IP address 192.168.1.0. The automatic node security context statement ordering ensures that all addresses in the 192.168.1.0 subnet (for example, 192.168.1.100) will match the second statement and receive the type webserver_t while all other addresses in the 192.168.0.0 subnet (for example, 192.168.2.1) will match the first statement.

The currently available policies do not make extensive use of node labeling, generally labeling only localhost and all other nodes. For example, these statements are representative of the IPv4 nodecon statements for most general-purpose policies:

```
nodecon 127.0.0.1    255.255.255.255 system_u:object_r:node_lo_t
nodecon 0.0.0.0 255.255.255.255 system_u:object_r:node_inaddr_any_t
```

This strategy is used to remove the need for customizing the policy based on local network settings. Many custom-built policies for specific applications tend to reengineer the network policy to afford better control of the network.

All nodes without a matching nodecon statement are labeled with the node initial SID security context.

---

### Node Security Context Statement (nodecon)

The node security context (`nodecon`) statement labels `node` object instances. The full syntax for the statement is as follows:

`nodecon` *subnet netmask context*

*subnet*   An IP address or subnet (for example, `127.0.0.1` or `192.168.0.0`). This can be an IPV4 or IPv6 address.

*netmask*   The network mask for the subnet. The network mask must match the protocol version of the subnet.

*context*   The security context for the node object instance that represents the specified subnet and netmask.

The `nodecon` statement is valid only in monolithic policies and base loadable modules. They are not valid in conditional statements and non-base loadable modules.

---

## 10.3.3 Network Port Labeling (portcon)

Socket objects representing ports are labeled with the *port security context statement* (`portcon`) or the `port` initial SID. The `portcon` statement labels ports based on protocol and port number or range. For example, consider the following statement:

```
portcon tcp 80   system_u:object_r:http_port_t
```

This statement shows that the `portcon` statement syntax requires the protocol (`tcp` or `upd`), the port number or range, and a security context. Notice that the statement does not end in a semicolon. The full syntax for the port security context statement is in the sidebar on page 150. The above statement labels the TCP port 80 with the security context `system_u:object_r:http_port_t`.

It is common for `portcon` statements to overlap when using port ranges. For example, consider the following statements:

---

```
portcon tcp 80           system_u:object_r:http_port_t
portcon tcp 1-1023       system_u:object_:reserved_port_t
```

---

Both of these `portcon` statements match TCP port 80. In the case of overlap, the first matching statement is used. In this example, TCP socket objects associated with network port 80 would receive the security context `system_u:object_r:http_port_t`, whereas any other port between 1 and 1023 would receive the security context `system_u:object_:reserved_port_t`. This method of resolution makes policy maintenance simpler by allowing the insertion of a broad labeling statement that can be overridden over time by inserting more specific statements. When a new, specific statement is inserted the original initial statement does not need to be changed.

Unlike the `nodecon` statements, which are ordered by specificity, the `portcon` statements are matched in the order specified in the policy. This means that it is possible to order `portcon` statements in a way that a statement would never be matched. In this case, the policy compiler issues a warning.

Network ports that do not match any `portcon` statements are labeled with the `port` initial SID.

What may not be clear from our discussion of the `portcon` statement so far is what objects are actually being labeled. You might have noticed from Chapter 4 that there is no object class specifically for ports. Permissions relating to ports are access checks against socket objects labeled with the port type. The socket object instance used to check port permissions is distinct from the socket object instance used for communication by the process, which is labeled with the type of the creating process.

For example, assume that TCP port 80, which is normally used for HTTP traffic, is labeled `http_port_t`. Allowing a process of type `httpd_t` to receive TCP data on this port would require permission on a TCP socket labeled with the process type *and* permission on a TCP socket with the type `http_port_t`. To illustrate, the rules to allow only the receipt of the TCP data (via the `recv_msg` permission on the `tcp_socket` object class), would look like the following:

```
allow httpd_t self : tcp_socket recv_msg;
allow httpd_t http_port_t : tcp_socket recv_msg;
```

These rules clearly show the two `tcp_socket` object instances. Table 10-2 shows which permissions on which socket object classes are checked on objects labeled with the port type.

---

### Port Security Context Statement (portcon) Syntax

The port security context statement (`portcon`) labels network ports based on protocol and port number or range. The full syntax for the statement is as follows:

`portcon` `protocol port_num context`

`protocol`  The network protocol (`tcp` or `udp`).

`port_num`  A port number or range (for example, 80 or 1–1023). If multiple statements overlap, the first matching statement is used to label the port.

`context`  The security context for the socket object instances associated with the port.

The `portcon` statement is valid only in monolithic policies and base loadable modules. They are not valid in conditional statements and nonbase loadable modules.

---

## 10.3.4 Socket Labeling

Sockets created by processes using the `socket(2)` system call inherit their security context from the creating process. Sockets used to check the permissions associated with ports are discussed above with the `portcon` statement.

For example, a process with the security context `system_u:system_r:httpd_t` would create sockets with the same security context. This means that to allow this domain type to send and receive using a TCP socket, an `allow` rule similar to the following would be required:

```
allow httpd_t self : tcp_socket { read write send_msg recv_msg };
```

This example illustrates how the TCP socket object is labeled; additional permissions are required for realistic usage of sockets. The labeling of all socket objects created by userspace processes, including local sockets such as Netlink and UNIX domain sockets, are labeled in this way. Sockets created by the kernel are labeled with the security context of the `kernel` initial SID.

## 10.4 System V IPC

The System V *interprocess communication* (IPC) objects are, with the exception of the msg objects, labeled with the security context of the creating process. For example, if a process with the security context user_u:object_r:user_xserver_t creates a shared memory segment, the associated shm object would have the same security context, user_u:object_r:user_xserver_t. This labeling behavior is the same for the shm, sem, and msgq object classes.

The msg objects are labeled using type_transition rules (see Chapter 5). The rule uses the type of the sending process and the type of the message queue. For example, the type of the messages sent on that message queue could be specified with a type_transition rule, as follows:

```
type_transition user_t user_xserver_t : msg user_msg_t;
```

This type_transition rule states that when processes with the type user_t send messages on a message queue of type user_xserver_t, the message type should be user_msg_t. Unlike other type_transition rules previously discussed, no provision exists for a process to explicitly request the type of the message and override the rule. If there is no matching type_transition rule, the message receives the same type as the sending process.

Regardless of whether the message receives the type through inheritance or a type_transition rule, the process must have permission to send messages of that type. For example, the following allow rule would be required for the example type_transition rule above:

```
allow user_t user_msg_t : msg send;
```

This allow rule states that processes of type user_t are allowed to send messages of type user_msg_t. Notice that there is no access needed to label the message, only the ability to send the message. There is no provision for creating messages without sending. These conditions are all based on the implementation of System V messages and message queues.

## 10.5 Miscellaneous Object Labeling

The labeling mechanisms for the remaining object classes (capability, process, security, and system) are listed in Table 10-3.

TABLE 10-3
Miscellaneous Object Classes Associated Labeling Mechanisms

| Object Class | Labeling Mechanism(s) |
|---|---|
| `capability` | Inherited from the associated `process` object |
| `process` | Inherited from parent process, or set by domain transition, or dynamic context transition |
| `security` | `SECURITY` initial SID |
| `system` | `SYSTEM` initial SID |

## 10.5.1 Capability Object Labeling

The capability object class is closely related to the process object class. Not surprisingly, capability objects have the same security context as the process with which they are associated. For example, consider the following rule:

```
allow user_t self : capability dac_override;
```

This `allow` rule states that processes of type `user_t` are allowed to retain the `dac_override` capability. The type of the `capability` object is, by virtue of the `self` keyword, the same as the process. There is no policy statement or mechanism for setting or changing the security context of capability objects.

## 10.5.2 Process Object Labeling

The labeling of process objects is central to SELinux, because it is the mechanism for associating the correct access with an application. Chapter 2 contains a lengthy description of the mechanics and concepts of domain transitions, which are the most important aspect of process labeling. Here we discuss the other aspects of process labeling.

In Linux, process objects are not created when applications are executed with the `execve(2)` system call. Instead, new processes are created by copying another process using `fork(2)` or `clone(2)`. New process objects, therefore, inherit the security context of the creating process to reflect that they have the same security properties. There is no provision for overriding this labeling decision; both domain transitions and dynamic security context transitions, which are the only means to change the security context of a process, can change only the security context of an existing process.

A domain transition is a change of the process security context on an `execve(2)` system call. The security context change can happen automatically as the result of a `type_transition` rule or program request through the use of the `setexeccon(3)` library call. As always, a change of the security context for a process must be explicitly allowed by the policy.

We normally focus on changing the process type during domain transition via the `execve(2)` system call, but it is also possible to change the user or the role. Role changes can be automatic, through role transition statements, and both user and role changes can be program requested explicitly through `setexeccon(3)`. Changing the user or role of a process is controlled by constraints and role allow rules, which are covered in Chapters 6 and 7.

A dynamic security context transition is program requested labeling that changes the security context of an existing process. The change, which is accomplished with the `setcon(3)` library call, must be allowed by the policy through the `dyntransition` permission. Chapter 5 has more information on dynamic security context transition, including a discussion of its dangers and our advice not to use it.

### 10.5.3 System and Security Object Labeling

The `system` and `security` object classes are unique in that there is only ever one instance for each. The `kernel` and `security` initial SIDs are used to label the `system` and `security` object instances, respectively. There is no mechanism for changing the security context of these objects.

## 10.6 Initial Security Identifiers

A special kind of default labeling behavior is provided by initial SIDs. Initial SIDs are used in two circumstances: early in system initialization before the policy is loaded, and when an object would otherwise have an invalid or missing security context (that is, as a failsafe label).

Chapter 7 introduced SIDs, which are opaque references to security contexts used internally by SELinux. Initial SIDs are a set of reserved SIDs used during system initialization or for predefined objects. Unlike most SIDs, which are created on demand at runtime when a security context is used for the first time, initial SIDs are always present in the system. (That is, they are hard-coded in the SELinux LSM module.) Table 10-4 lists the initial SIDs used in a FC4 system.

Some objects are labeled via an initial SID early in system initialization, even before the policy is loaded. This labeling behavior is needed, for example, to label objects such as the kernel security server and the root filesystem, which are present in the system before the first policy load. When the policy is eventually loaded, the initial SIDs are then associated with the appropriate security context.

Initial SIDs are also used to prevent objects from having a missing or invalid security context, which would make it impossible for SELinux to correctly enforce access. Instead, SELinux associates these objects with the special `unlabeled` initial SID. The `unlabeled` initial SID should have a security context that allows only limited access, thereby preventing inappropriate access until the objects can be relabeled by the administrator or destroyed.

Invalid security contexts most commonly result from loading a new policy that removes users, roles, or types, or changes role or type authorizations. In this situation, the SIDs representing security contexts that use these invalid names or associations will become invalid and are mapped to the `unlabeled` SID at policy load. Invalid security contexts can also arise when transferring object instances between systems (for example, using removable media). Further, if the objects are created on a non-SELinux system, they will have no associated security context. Regardless of whether the security context is invalid or missing, SELinux will use the `unlabeled` initial SID on first access to the object as the security context.

**TABLE 10-4**
Example Initial SIDs in FC4

| Initial SID | Description |
| --- | --- |
| `kernel` | Applied to all objects created by the kernel (for example, threads and sockets created by the kernel), the `system` object instance, and is used as a default for kernel resources. |
| `security` | Applied to the `security` object instance. |
| `unlabeled` | Applied to all objects with an invalid security context. |
| `file` | Default security context for file-related objects that do not otherwise have a security context. This is for file-related objects without security contexts; file-related objects with invalid security contexts receive the `unlabeled` SID. |
| `port` | Default security context for socket objects associated with ports that do not have a matching port security context statement. |

TABLE 10-4 (continued)
Example Initial SIDs in FC4

| Initial SID | Description |
|---|---|
| netif | Default security context for `netif` objects associated with network interfaces that do not have a matching network interface security context statement. |
| node | Default security context for `node` objects associated with nodes that do not have a matching node security context statement. |
| sysctl | Default security context for `proc` filesystem system objects. These objects are normally labeled via generalized filesystem security context statements rather than via this initial SID. |

Like object classes, initial SIDs are defined by the kernel and other object managers in addition to being declared in the policy. The *initial SID declaration statement* declares an initial SID for use in the policy. We will not normally change initial SID statements as a part of policy writing. To illustrate the syntax, consider the following statement:

```
sid kernel
```

This statement declares the initial SID `kernel`. This statement does nothing more than reserve the name. Initial SID names are in their own namespace and can overlap with type, object class, or other policy component names. The full syntax for the initial SID statement is in the sidebar on page 232.

---

### Initial SID Declaration Statement Syntax (sid)

The initial SID statement (`sid`) reserves a name for an initial SID. Initial SIDs are defined by the kernel and other object managers; this statement makes them available to the policy. The full syntax is as follows:

```
sid sid_name
```

*sid_name*   The name of the initial SID. The name may contain letters or numbers.

The initial SID declaration statement is valid only in monolithic policies and base loadable modules. They are not valid in conditional statements and non-base loadable modules.

---

The *initial SID security context statement* associates a security context with a previously declared initial SID. For example, consider the following statement:

```
sid kernel     system_u:system_r:kernel_t
```

The statement above states that the security context for the initial SID `kernel` is `system_u:system_r:kernel_t`. As you can see, both statements have the same keyword name (`sid`), so be careful with the differing syntax. The effect of the initial SID *security context* statement is to associate the security context `system_u:system_r:kernel_t` with the initial SID `kernel`, which must be previously declared with the initial SID *declaration* statement. The full syntax for the initial SID security context statement is in the sidebar on page 233.

---

### Initial SID Security Context Statement Syntax (sid)

The initial SID security context statement (`sid`) associates a security context with a previously declared initial SID. The full syntax is as follows:

```
sid sid_name context;
```

*sid_name*   The name of a previously declared initial SID.

*context*    The security context to associate with this initial SID.

The initial SID security context statement is valid only in monolithic policies and base loadable modules. They are not valid in conditional statements and non-base loadable modules.

---

## 10.7 Exploring Object Labeling with Apol

`Apol` currently has two primary features for understanding object labeling: rule searching and file security context indexing and searching. We have explored rule searching in Chapters 5 and 6. Figure 10-1 shows the File Contexts tab of `apol`, which is used to create and search indexes of the security contexts for file-related objects. This allows us to examine how the file-related objects on a system are *actually* labeled as opposed to examining the file contexts specifications, which show how the file-related objects *should* be labeled. When trying to understand how a policy will be enforced on a particular system, information about how file-related objects are actually labeled is essential.

A file contexts index is a snapshot of the security contexts of all of the file-related objects on a system. This index can be created from `apol`, using the Create and

Load button, or with the `indexcon` command (included in the Setools package). Both tools recursively walk all mounted filesystems, recording the name, object class, and security context of all file-related objects. After the index is created (the data is stored in a file), it can be searched using `apol` or the `searchcon` command (also in Setools). The index is stored so that it can be searched efficiently, unlike searching the actual filesystem. For example, Figure 10-1 shows the result of searching for all file-related objects with the type `user_home_t`. Searching the file context index to find *all* files with this type was fast, whereas searching the filesystem would have taken several minutes. In addition, searching the file context index can be done on a different system than the one on which it was created.

Searches can be performed on any combination of name, user, object class, or type. Searching based on role is not supported because all file-related objects will normally have the special `object_r` role.

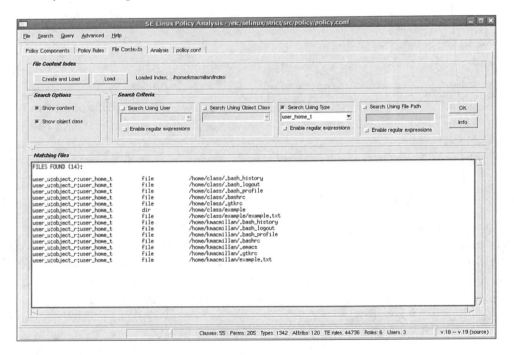

FIGURE 10-1
File context indexing and searching

## 10.8 Summary

- An object is labeled in one of four ways: policy statements (for example, type transition rules), hard-coded object manager defaults, program-requested labeling, and initial SIDs.

- The policy must always contain the appropriate access in addition to any relevant labeling statements for an object to be successfully labeled.

- Labeling decisions often use information from the execution environment (for example, security context for the process and related object instances).

- File-related labeling behavior is specified per-filesystem using the filesystem use statements or the generalized security context statement.

- Extended attribute labeling is used for most native Linux filesystems and supports program-requested labeling and persistent storage of security contexts.

- Labels on extended attribute labeled filesystems are managed using file context files and utilities that read those files.

- Task-based and transition-based labeling are used primarily for pseudo filesystems.

- Generalized security context labeling is used primarily for labeling `proc` and legacy filesystems.

- Network interfaces are labeled by interface name (for example, `eth0`) using the `netifcon` statement.

- Network nodes are labeled by IP address and netmask using the `nodecon` statement.

- Ports are labeled by number using the `portcon` statement.

- Successfully sending or receiving network data often requires permissions on several socket objects in addition to permission on the relevant `node` and `netif` objects.

- System V IPC objects, with the exception of `msg` objects, receive the security context of the creating process. `Msg` objects are labeled based on `type_transition` rules or the security context of the creating process.

- Processes receive the same security context as their parent. This security context can be changed through a domain or dynamic context transition.

- The capability object has the same security context as the associated process.

- The `security` and `system` objects receive the security context of the `kernel` and `security` initial SIDs, respectively.

- Initial SIDs are used to label some objects and are a failsafe default to prevent objects from having a missing or invalid security context.

## Exercises

1. Given a file context file with the following entries, what security context would the files /etc/passwd, /etc/shadow, and /etc/mtab receive?

   ```
   /etc(/.*)?                    system_u:object_r:etc_t
   /var/db/.*\.db         --     system_u:object_r:etc_t
   /etc/\.pwd\.lock   --   system_u:object_r:shadow_t
   /etc/passwd\.lock  --   system_u:object_r:shadow_t
   /etc/group\.lock   --   system_u:object_r:shadow_t
   /etc/shadow.*      --   system_u:object_r:shadow_t
   /etc/gshadow.*     --   system_u:object_r:shadow_t
   /var/db/shadow.*   --   system_u:object_r:shadow_t
   /etc/blkid\.tab.*  --   system_u:object_r:etc_runtime_t
   /etc/fstab\.REVOKE     --      system_u:object_r:etc_runtime_t
   /etc/\.fstab\.hal\..+ --      system_u:object_r:etc_runtime_t
   /etc/HOSTNAME          --      system_u:object_r:etc_runtime_t
   /etc/ioctl\.save   --   system_u:object_r:etc_runtime_t
   /etc/mtab          --   system_u:object_r:etc_runtime_t
   /etc/motd          --   system_u:object_r:etc_runtime_t
   ```

2. What is unique about file-related object labeling on filesystems that use extended attribute labeling?

3. Write a `portcon` statement that would label port 22 with the security context `system_u:object_r:sshd_t` for TCP. What is the object class that is labeled by this statement?

4. Write a `nodecon` statement that would label the system `192.168.1.128` with the security context `system_u:object_r:webserver_t`. What object class is labeled by this statement?

# Part III

## Creating and Writing SELinux Security Policies

# Chapter 11

## Original Example Policy

### In this chapter

The job of taking all the elements of an SELinux policy and composing a complete and comprehensive security policy that meets all your security goals can be difficult if you work with just the raw policy language described in Part II. In this chapter, we discuss one of the two principal methods (derived from the original *National Security Agency* [NSA] example policy) that have evolved the past several years to allow policy developers to manage the policy build process.

## 11.1 Methods for Managing the Build Process

If you have read through Part II, by now you might have concerns about the practicality of building a complete, comprehensive, and secure SELinux policy. Certainly an SELinux policy is rich and complex; necessarily so because SELinux provides fine-grained access control for the rich and complex Linux kernel and its interactions with the multitude of userspace applications.[1] Fear not. In this chapter, we discuss ways to manage the entire policy build process, and methods that the SELinux community has evolved to aide in this process.

The methods for building policies are changing and evolving at a rapid pace. In this chapter, we overview one prevalent means of building policies using the basic policy language tools and compilers. This kind of low-level policy development is currently the predominant method for creating and modifying SELinux policies. Higher-level development methods are being developed, but none are in practice yet.

---

1   When you hear criticism that SELinux is complex, you should view this comment with skepticism. Those who make this remark are usually implying that Linux is fine, but SELinux *adds* too much complexity. The reality is that SELinux simply exposes the complexity that is inherent to Linux. It *does not add any.* If you truly want to have comprehensive, strong security for Linux, there is no better option than SELinux. If you are content with partial solutions that provide incomplete (but simple) security solutions for this complex operating system, perhaps SELinux may not be to your taste. In any case, as we discuss later in this book, tools and methods are being developed to manage the complexities of Linux that SELinux exposes, so that you can have comprehensive security with increasing ease of use.

The method for building policies we discuss in this chapter, the *example policy*, is based on the original example policy released by NSA with the original SELinux. We discuss another method called the reference policy in Chapter 12, "Reference Policy." Both of these methods have common low-level characteristics (for example, a tree of source modules), an organization and build process, and macros used to provide basic abstractions over the core language.

The example policy has been evolved through years of community development far beyond what was originally released by NSA. One of the principal enhancements has the ability to build both strict and targeted policies with two different variations of the policy source tree. Both of these example policy variations share common characteristics and are related to each other. The *strict policy* is based on an example policy that is most directly descended from the original NSA example policy. As its name implies, the strict policy attempts to provide a domain type for every program that reasonably requires a private domain. The strict policy has evolved through years of open source community development and reflects the most extensive collective knowledge of policy statements.

A challenge with the strict policy is that by trying to be strict, it inevitably causes breakage with existing Linux applications, which expect looser security controls. For many users, these annoying application breakages are an unacceptable tradeoff for increased security. To address this concern, the concept of a *targeted policy* was created. A version of a targeted policy is the default policy released with *Red Hat Enterprise Linux version 4* (RHEL4) and *Fedora Core* (FC) systems. The purpose of the targeted policy is to allow most programs to run as if they were *not* running on an SELinux system. These programs are called *unconfined,* and the concept is achieved by creating an *unconfined domain* that essentially has access to all types in the SELinux policy.

In the targeted policy, the more confining rules are focused on a small set of critical, likely-to-be-attacked programs such as network-facing daemons. These programs run in restricted domains as in the strict policy. In this way, the targeted policy has less chance of causing problems with legacy applications by having fewer programs that have tighter security. With targeted policy, we do a have less strict security enhancements; for many system solutions, however, the targeted policy is adequate and a great improvement over current security practice. The targeted policy is also a nice way to start using the features of SELinux without having to immediately use them everywhere.

In the remainder of this chapter, we provide an overview of the key features and capabilities of the strict and targeted example policy source trees.

> WARNING The one area where change is rapid is policies. All the policy build methods we discuss (strict and targeted example policies in this chapter and the reference policy equivalents in Chapter 12) are constantly under development and change. Be aware that the specific conventions and organization of a policy source tree may have changed since the time of this book's writing.

## 11.2 Strict Example Policy

The strict example policy is the longest-lived version of the example policy. It is largely maintained and updated via the NSA and FC mail lists, but with contributions from other distributions, too. Both NSA and Red Hat maintain versions of the strict example policy, which are essentially the same source tree. You can obtain a version of this policy both from the NSA SELinux project page (http://selinux.sourceforge.net) or from Red Hat for FC. If your system has strict example policy sources installed (see Appendix A, "Obtaining SELinux Sample Policies"), you should be able to see the sources in `/etc/selinux/strict/src/policy/`. The examples from earlier in this book are from a version of the strict example policy. Our overview is based on the FC4 version of the strict example policy; we encourage you to download the latest versions and use that as a baseline if you choose to use this policy version.

The strict example policy builds a complete policy source file (`policy.conf`) using the source module method described in Chapter 3, "Architecture." Recall that source modules use a combination of scripts and macros to create higher-level constructs and produces a single, monolithic policy file (see Figure 11-1). Source modules make extensive use of macros using `m4`, which is a flexible and powerful macro tool.

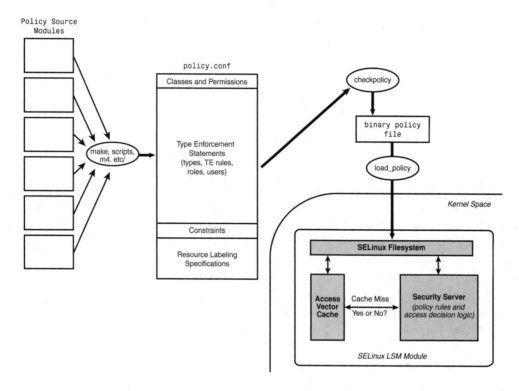

**FIGURE 11-1**
Build and load process for SELinux policy using the example policy

The strict policy Makefile supports a number of build targets. The command make policy compiles the entire policy and builds a binary policy file (for example, ./policy.19). This target is useful for building a policy for testing or for installation on another system. The command make policy.conf constructs a complete policy source file (./policy.conf) but will not compile the policy source. This is useful if we want to construct a complete policy source for analysis (for example, using apol). The command make install builds the binary policy and installs it and all supporting policy management files. In the case of strict policy, the default installation directory is in /etc/selinux/strict/. This command installs the new policy but does not load it into the kernel. You would need to reboot the machine or use the make load command.

Finally, the make relabel command applies the security contexts to all files in the system. In general, we would relabel only the entire system during initial install and/or after we load an entirely new policy.

> NOTE The primary method for relabeling an entire filesystem is no longer using `make relabel` from the policy source tree. Instead, the current methods of relabeling the entire system are to use either the `fixfiles relabel` command or the `touch /.autorelabel` command and reboot the systems. These two methods can be done with only the file contexts configuration installed and not the entire policy source.

## 11.2.1 Overview of Policy Source File Structure

For this chapter, we examine the strict example policy sources from FC4; depending on the version of the system you are using, there may be some differences. All filenames are from the policy source root directory (for example, `/etc/selinux/strict/src/policy`). You will find various levels of comments within each file *and* the `./README` file at the top-level for additional information. In this section, we give you a guided tour of the key files and directories, along with insights to their purposes and uses. Our goal is to give you a head start in understanding the file structure; only experience will allow you to fully understand them.

### 11.2.1.1 Object Class and Permission Definitions

As discussed in Chapter 4, "Object Classes and Permissions," object classes and their associated permission sets are defined in the policy language. For the example policy, the directory `./flask/` contains these definitions. The Flask definitions are essentially static for all policies and should not be changed. Kernel source header files are automatically generated from these files, because the kernel and the policy must both agree on the set of object classes and associated permissions. The principal files in this directory are as follows:

| | |
|---|---|
| `./flask/security_classes` | Declarations of object classes. See Chapter 4. |
| `./flask/access_vectors` | Declarations of common permissions, and association of common and unique permissions with each object class. See Chapter 4 and Appendix C, "Object Classes and Permissions." |
| `./flask/initial_sids` | Declarations of initial SID identifiers, which are used to manage default security context labeling. See `./initial_sid_contexts` *and* Chapter 10, "Object Labeling." |

In addition, this directory also contains several shell scripts that are used to construct the kernel header files.

> WARNING In general, you would *not* edit any of the files in the `./flask/` directory. These files must correspond with kernel header files. Unless you are positive you know what you are doing, which would imply familiarity with the kernel SELinux *Linux Security Module* (LSM) source code, leave this directory alone.

### 11.2.1.2 Domain Types and Policy Rules

The primary policy modules for an example policy are kept in the `./domains/` directory. There are two files and two subdirectories in this directory:

`./domains/admin.te`

`./domains/user.te`

These two files (the `.te` is for type enforcement) define domain types of user login sessions. These "user domains" are unlike most other domain types in that they are not associated with a specific program, but rather are the default domain types for classes of users. The file `admin.te` defines the domain type `sysadm_t`, which is the most powerful user domain type. Although `sysadm_t` has nowhere near the level of privilege, this domain type is the SELinux analogue to root. The file `user.te` defines less-privileged user domain types, `user_t` and `staff_t`. Both of these types have limited privileges and are intended for "ordinary users." The primary difference between the two is that `staff_t` is able to transition its role and domain type to the more privileged `sysadm_t`.

These files also define a number of *Boolean*s that are used to provide runtime policy configuration options.

`./domains/program/`

`./domains/misc/`

These two directories contain the policy source modules for the strict example policy. The `program/` directory is where most of the modules are located, typically one file per domain type (or set of related domain types). Each policy module is contained in a `.te` file. Each module has a separate file contexts file that identifies how file-related objects should be labeled with security context for those objects associated with the module's types. We discuss file contexts later in this chapter.

The `misc/` directory contains a small number of modules that are not the typical domain types (for example, the type for the kernel: `kernel_t`) and do not have related `.fc` (file context) files. There is little difference between the two directories in terms of functionality; in general, you should add any new module to the `program/` directory.

The `./domains/` directory is organized to support a coarse level of policy customization. Both policy module directories have an `unused/` directory (for example, `./domains/program/unused` for the primary module directory). The `.te` module files in those unused directories will not be included in the policy build, nor will the associated file contexts. Therefore, we can exclude unneeded policy statements from the policy we build by moving unnecessary policy modules to the `unused/` directory. We examine a policy module later in this chapter.

> WARNING Dependencies are not well managed in the example policy. Therefore, as you move policy modules in and out of the unused directory, you might find other policy modules that depend upon the newly used/unused module resulting in build errors.

## 11.2.1.3 Unaffiliated Resource Types

Besides the policy modules described previously, most of the rest of the type declarations for a strict example policy are contained in the `./types/` directory. The files in this directory generally (but not always) just define types and not rules to access the types. These types are primarily passive objects of the kernel and key user-space services and are not active domain types. You may need to change these files, especially if you want to change the policy associated with certain kernel resources (for example, networking). The files in this directory are as follows:

`./types/device.te`   This file defines types for many device special files, including the default device file type `device_t`. Many of the types applied to objects in the `/dev/` directory are defined in this file.

| | |
|---|---|
| `./types/devpts.te` | This file defines the types for the devpts filesystem and its root directory (that is, the filesystem for pseudo terminal devices in Linux). |
| `./types/file.te` | This file defines general file-related types, including `unlabeled_t`, which is used when the type of a file-related object is invalid for the loaded policy and `file_t`, which is the type used for a file-related object that has no associated context. (Both situations indicate a problem with the policy and/or filesystem labeling.) This file declares other standard filesystem types, such as the default types for the /etc/ (`etc_t`) and /tmp/ (`tmp_t`) directories. |
| `./types/network.te` | This file defines the types for all the network-related objects (node, network interfaces, ports, *and so on*). Many of the reserved network ports have their own type (`ssh_port_t`, `dns_port_t`, `smtp_port_t`, and so on). However, in general, you will find the network policy architecture for the strict example policy (and most other generic policies) is designed to allow either most or all networking, or no networking at all for a given domain type. You might need to rework this file if you want to provide greater control of the network (for example, have types for ranges of nodes and control access based on IP ranges) or if you want a multi-interface network configuration (for example, a router). |
| `./types/nfs.te` | *Network File System* (NFS) is not well supported in SELinux yet. For example, network contexts are not passed between SELinux kernels for NFS-mounted filesystems. This file defines basic NFS support by defining the `nfs_t` type, which is used for all NFS files. In general, NFS does not currently provide proper support of types and *type enforcement* (TE). |

`./types/procfs.te`    This file provides the types for the proc filesystem (`/proc/`) including the default type `proc_t` and many special purpose `proc_*_t` types.

`./types/security.te`    This file defines various types relating to SELinux and its policy files. The type `security_t` is the type of the security object class. Several other types are defined that are used to protect installed policy files, and related configuration and source files.

### 11.2.1.4 Miscellaneous Top-level Files and Directories

At the top-level directory, a number of files capture some of the less-frequently changed and used policy components. Here we list these files and the conventions expected for each file:

`./assert.te`    This file is where all `neverallow` rules (that is, invariant assertions) are located for the policy. See Chapter 5, "Type Enforcement," for more on assertions.

`./attrib.te`    This file is where almost all attributes are declared. Associating attributes with types happens throughout the policy files, but the convention is that all attributes are first declared in this file using the `attribute` statement. All attributes should be declared in this file, with appropriate comments explaining their purposes. Throughout the rest of the policy files, these attributes are associated with types and used in policy rules. See Chapter 5 for more about attributes.

`./constraints`    This file is where all non-*multilevel-security* (MLS) constraints are defined. See Chapter 7, "Constraints," on policy constraints.

`./macros/`    This directory contains a number of files that have the m4 macros used throughout the policy modules. These macros provide a level of abstraction for writing policies. Just about every policy module uses and calls several of these macros.

| | |
|---|---|
| `./mls` | This file is where all MLS constraints are defined for a traditional MLS policy *and* all declaration of MLS sensitivities, categories, and levels. This file is included only if you decide to build the optional MLS features into your policy. See Chapter 8, "Multilevel Security," for more on the optional MLS features. |
| `./mcs` | This file is an alternative MLS configuration that primarily uses just the categories, and not the sensitivities. This file, like the standard MLS configuration (`./mls`), is optionally built in to a policy. As with the MLS configurations, see Chapter 8 for more information. |
| `./rbac` | This file originally contained all role `allow` rules. Over time, these rules have migrated throughout the other policy files. There are usually few such rules in most policies to date. See Chapter 6, "Roles and Users," on role declarations and rules. |
| `./users` | This file contains all policy-wide user declarations for the policy. These are generic user declarations that are always expected in the policy. Typically, this file will declare the special users, `system_u` and `user_u`, *and* `root` and possibly other system default users. See Chapter 6 for more information on users in the policy. |
| `./local.users` | This file is a recent enhancement to SELinux policy management that enables system administrators to add local users to the policy without having the policy source files available. This file will be installed in `/etc/selinux/ strict/users/local.users`. You can hand-edit the installed version of this file, and every time the policy is reloaded, the local user definitions will be added to the kernel policy. |

These files are fairly simple and straightforward in their purpose. You will find that you will likely change them little if you are just trying to use and adapt the policy for your application.

## 11.2.1.5 Security Context Labeling

One of the great challenges with using SELinux, besides writing a good TE policy, is ensuring that all the various object instances (files, directories, ports, network interfaces, and so on) are labeled with the correct type for the current policy. After you have a properly compiled TE policy, many of your debugging problems will be related to improperly labeled objects. We discussed the mechanisms and issues for object labeling in Chapter 10. Next we discuss how object labeling is managed in the strict example policy source files.

Several files in the policy source root directory address some of the security context labeling for a system, in particular those context labeling statements that are part of the policy language proper:

| | |
|---|---|
| `./initial_sid_contexts` | As discussed previously, initial SIDs are defined as part of the flask definitions in the `./flask/initial_sids` file. That file simply declares the initial SIDs available in the policy (which generally you should not change). The `initial_sid_contexts` file assigns a security context to each initial SID. For example, the initial SID `security` is used to assign a security context to the single instance of the security object class (the type of which should be `security_t`). Most of the initial SIDs define default cases in case there is no explicit labeling statement. For example, the initial SID `port` assigns the default context for port objects (for example, with the type `port_t` by default) for those ports that do not have an explicit `portcon` statement in the policy. See Chapter 10 for more information on initial SIDs. |
| | You could edit this file *to* change the security contexts associated with each initial SID. However, more likely you would enhance other parts of the policy to have explicit statements to address your need (for example, by adding more `portcon` statements to label additional ports). |

./net_contexts       This file contains all the network-related security context
                     statements (for example, `portcon` and `nodecon`). For
                     example, we saw that the file `./types/network.te`
                     declared various types for specific reserved ports. This file
                     is where you would assign these types to the ports (for
                     example, associating a security context with the type
                     `ssh_port_t` to TCP port 22).

./genfs_contexts     This file contains all the `genfscon` statements for the
                     policy (that is, all the security context labeling for filesys-
                     tems that do not support extended attributes such as
                     `proc`). For example, this file would contain the `genfs-`
                     `con` statement that labels the `procfs` filesystem root
                     directory with a security context containing the type
                     `proc_t` defined in the `./types/procfs.te` file.

./fs_use             This file contains the various `fs_use_*` statements that
                     define how object labeling is handled for each filesystem
                     type (see Chapter 10).

These files address all object labeling concerns except the most complex issue (that
is, labeling of all the file-related objects for the various disk-based filesystems). Disk-
based object labeling is called file context labeling, as we discussed in Chapter 10.

To create an initial file context labeling policy, we have the directory
`./file_contexts/`. This directory contains a number of files that together with
the files in `./file_contexts/misc/` are used to create a complete file contexts file
useable to label and relabel all disk-based filesystems. One directory, `./file_con-`
`texts/program/`, is directly related to the similarly named module directory in the
`./domains/program/` directory. This directory contains `.fc` files (`fc` for file contexts) that have the file context statements associated with the like named module
file from the `./domains/program/` directory. When building a complete file contexts file, only those `.fc` files whose associated policy module `.te` file are currently
"used" (that is, not in the `unused` directory under `./domains/program/`) are
included. In this way, you can manage both the TE file (`.te`) and the associated
security context file (`.fc`) using the same method.

The file `./file_contexts/types.fc` defines labeling statements not specific to a program module (for example, how to label file in `/etc/`). This file is always included in a strict example policy build. The file `./file_contexts/distro.fc` is similar to `types.fc` except that it contains configuration options specific to a particular distribution.

The file `./file_contexts/home_dir_template` contains file labeling instructions for files and directories in a user home directory. This file is a template so that users' home directories can be labeled depending on users' roles. This file is also installed and used when managing the policy in an operational system (see Chapter 13, "Managing an SELinux System"). These files, along with the "used" `.fc` files, are concatenated during the build process to make a single `file_contexts` file. This file is what the `setfiles` program (and other related programs that use the `matchpathcon(3)` library) uses to set and fix disk-based object labels as discussed in Chapter 10.

### 11.2.1.6 Application Configuration Files

The directory `./appconfig/` contains a set of files that specify security context information that various services and applications use in running systems. These files are installed in the operational policy directory (for example, `/etc/selinux/strict/contexts`). We discuss the purpose of these files in Chapter 13.

## 11.2.2 Examining an Example Policy Module

To help understand the strict example policy and how it manages the process of building a policy, let's examine an example policy module. In particular, let's look at the policy module for the `ping` program. A partial listing of this module is shown in Listing 11-1. You should find a similar module in `./domains/program/ping.te` or `./domains/program/unused/ping.te`.

**LISTING 11-1**
**Policy Module for Ping from the Strict Example Policy (ping.te)**

```
 1 type ping_t, domain, privlog, nscd_client_domain;
 2 role sysadm_r types ping_t;
 3 role system_r types ping_t;
 4 in_user_role(ping_t)
 5 type ping_exec_t, file_type, sysadmfile, exec_type;
 6
 7 # Transition into this domain when you run this program.
 8 domain_auto_trans(sysadm_t, ping_exec_t, ping_t)
 9 domain_auto_trans(initrc_t, ping_exec_t, ping_t)
10 bool user_ping false;
11 if (user_ping) {
12     domain_auto_trans(unpriv_userdomain, ping_exec_t, ping_t)
13     # allow access to the terminal
14     allow ping_t { ttyfile ptyfile }:chr_file rw_file_perms;
15     ifdef(`gnome-pty-helper.te', `allow ping_t gphdomain:fd use;')
16 }
17
18 uses_shlib(ping_t)
19 can_network_client(ping_t)
20 can_resolve(ping_t)
21 allow ping_t dns_port_t:tcp_socket name_connect;
22 can_ypbind(ping_t)
23 allow ping_t etc_t:file { getattr read };
24 allow ping_t self:unix_stream_socket create_socket_perms;
25
26 # Let ping create raw ICMP packets.
27 allow ping_t self:rawip_socket {create ioctl read write bind getopt
setopt };
28
29 # Use capabilities.
30 allow ping_t self:capability { net_raw setuid };
31
32 # Access the terminal.
33 allow ping_t admin_tty_type:chr_file rw_file_perms;
34 allow ping_t privfd:fd use;
35 dontaudit ping_t fs_t:filesystem getattr;
36
37 # it tries to access /var/run
38 dontaudit ping_t var_t:dir search;
39 ifdef(`hide_broken_symptoms', `
40     dontaudit ping_t init_t:fd use;
41 ')
```

Notice that lines 4, 8 and 9, 12, 18 through 20, and 22 contain macros rather than policy language statements. Macros using the m4 macro processor are common in example policy source files. These macros, some of which we examine in this chapter, cause several lines of policy language to be included into the module source file during the policy compile process.

### 11.2.2.1 Defining Types for a Domain

Lines 1 and 5 define two types, `ping_t` and `ping_exec_t`. The type `ping_t` is the domain type for the `ping` program, and the type `ping_exec_t` is the type associated with the `ping` executable file on disk. Having a domain type and associated file executable type appended with `_exec_t` is a common convention. As you can see, several attributes are associated with each type. For example, the attribute `domain` is associated with the type `ping_t`; all domain types have this attribute in the strict example policy.

Lines 2 and 3 associate the ping domain type with two roles: `sysadm_r`, which is the privileged user role; and `system_r`, which is the role for system processes. Line 4 also associates the ping domain type with a role, but this time using a macro `in_user_role()`. We can find this macro defined in `./macros/user_macros.te`, as in the following:

```
define(`in_user_role', `
role user_r types $1;
role staff_r types $1;
')
```

As you can see, this macro associates the domain type with two additional roles: `user_r`, which is the role for ordinary users; and `staff_r`, which is the unprivileged role for users authorized to change roles to the privileged `sysadm_r` role.

> **NOTE** `M4` macros use string substitution for argument. So, for example, `$1` in the macro definition refers to the first supplied argument, `$2` to the second, and so on. As we see in line 4 of the `ping` module, the `in_user_role` macro is invoked with this line:
>
> `in_user_role(ping_t)`
>
> This invocation provides a single argument `ping_t`, which is substituted for `$1`.

---

### User Roles and Domain Type

In the strict example policy, the three standard user roles (sysadm_r, staff_r, and user_r) have an associated domain type that defines the privileges of programs that are executed without a domain transition (which would mean they would continue with the security context and therefore the domain type of the calling user process). For example, the standard domain type of the role user_r is user_t. Likewise, for the privileged domain sysadm_r, there is a domain type sysadm_t, which is a fairly powerful domain type (although nowhere near the power of root in a standard Linux system).

You can examine the policy rules for the unprivileged user domain types (user_t and staff_t) in ./domains/user.te and for the privileged user domain type (sysadm_t) in ./domains/admin.te.

---

## 11.2.2.2 Specifying Domain Transition Rules

Now look at lines 8 and 9, where we have two invocations of the domain_auto_trans() macro. This macro is probably the most common macro in the strict example policy as it defines the standard rules to allow a domain transition as we discussed in Chapter 2, "Concepts." You can find the definition of this macro in ./macros/core_macros.te. The actual macro is quite short as it calls another macro, domain_trans(), which is defined in the same file:

```
# $1 is original domain, $2 is executable file type, $3 is new domain
define(`domain_auto_trans',`
domain_trans($1,$2,$3)
type_transition $1 $2:process $3;
')
```

The domain_auto_trans() macro grants the necessary permissions to allow a domain transition (by calling the domain_trans() macro) and makes the transition happen automatically by default via a type_transition rule.

If we further examine the domain_trans() macro, we see many more rules that mostly address permissions necessary for *interprocess communication* (IPC) between the parent and child process types that results from a domain transition. However, this macro also contains the three minimally required `allow` rules required for a domain transition as discussed in Chapter 2, specifically the following:

```
# key rules from domain_trans macro
# $1 is original domain, $2 is executable file type, $3 is new domain
define(`domain_trans',`
allow $1 $3:process transition;   # old domain can trans to new domain
allow $1 $2:file { read x_file_perms }; # # old domain execute file type
allow $3 $2:file entrypoint;   # new domain can be entered from file type

# remaining domain_trans rules not shown...
`)
```

Notice that the second rule has `read` and `x_file_perms` in the permission field. Although `read` is a permission for the `file` object class, `x_file_perms` is not. Instead, it is a another type of `m4` macro that is replaced with a set of permissions that generally represent "file execute" permissions. We find this macro defined in `./macros/core_macros.te` as follows:

```
define(`x_file_perms', `{ getattr execute }')
```

So looking back at lines 8 and 9 from the `ping` module, we see that the privileged administrator domain type `sysadm_t` and the init process script domain `initrc_t` both are given access to transition into the `ping_t` domain, which in effect means they can run the `ping` program. These two macros each result in many policy statements via macro processing as we have illustrated.

### 11.2.2.3 Conditional Policy Example

Starting on line 10, we see an example of a conditional policy block. Line 10 defines the *Boolean* `user_ping`, and lines 11 through 16 contain the conditional clause that uses this *Boolean*. In this case, the conditional policy statements use a *Boolean* variable to control whether unprivileged user domains are allowed to use the `ping` program. This is accomplished primarily via the conditional call to the `domain_auto_trans()` macro on line 12. Notice that the originating domain for the transition is an attribute (`unpriv_userdomain`) rather than a type as in lines 8 and 9. This means that all types with that attribute are given the set of permissions that grant a domain transition into `ping_t`. There is no easy way to determine what those types are in the policy source files; generally, we are expected to know what that attribute represents and expect that none of the policy source files violate this expectation. The only practical way to determine the types associated with an attribute is to use the `apol` tool discussed earlier in this book.

### 11.2.2.4 Network and Other Access for Ping

Looking again at the `ping` module, line 18 invokes a macro that grants the `ping_t` domain permissions needed to use and link with shared libraries. Lines 19 through 24 provide various other access the ping domain will need to network and system resources. Many of these lines invoke macros that you should explore further at your leisure. For example, take a closer look at line 19 and the `can_network_client()` macro, which is defined in `./macros/network_macros.te`. Notice that this macro gives nearly all access to do most types of client networking over all available network interfaces. This is a coarse level of permission, and SELinux will allow you to be much more explicit in network control. However, this type of macro is common in general-purpose policies such as the example policy (although later versions of the example policy have attempted to improve this). As you can see lines 20 through 22 and line 27 provide additional network access over and above what `can_network_client()` provides. Take some time to further explore all of these macros.

> TIP To examine what a macro does, you must first find it. The easiest way to do this is to use `grep` from the policy macro directory `./macros`. For example, to find the definition of the `uses_shlib` macro from line 18 of the `ping` module, do the following:
>
> ```
> # cd /etc/selinux/strict/src/policy/macros
> # grep -r uses_shlib * | grep define
> global_macros.te:define('uses_shlib','
> ```

Let's look at line 30 of the `ping` module. Here we see the `ping_t` domain type is given access to itself using the `self` keyword for the `capability` object class. This object class controls the Linux capabilities; it only ever makes sense to give domains permissions to itself for this object class. In this case, we are giving `ping_t` permission to use the privileged capabilities necessary to perform raw networking and to use the `setuid` kernel call to change user IDs (that is, in this case to change to root).

The remaining `allow` rules in lines 33 and 34 give the `ping_t` domain permission to interact with terminal devices for display of output. Neglecting to provide access for terminal devices is a common mistake.

### 11.2.2.5 Audit Rules

Finally, we have a couple examples of `dontaudit` rules. These rules are used to mask out access denials we expect that do not prevent `ping` from functioning. It is not uncommon for Linux applications to attempt to use more permission than they need. Rather than grant them this excessive access, it is better to let the access denial occur, but filter out the resulting audit message using `dontaudit` rules so that the audit log is not polluted.

### 11.2.2.6 File Security Contexts Labeling

The final component of the `ping` module is the file context statements used to correctly label the `ping`-related files and directories. You can find the `ping` file contexts in `./policy/file_contexts/program/ping.fc`. For example:

```
/bin/ping.*              --      system_u:object_r:ping_exec_t
```

This file contexts specification causes the `setfiles` utility to label any file in `/bin/` that starts with `ping` (on our system that includes `ping` and `ping6`, both versions of the standard `ping` program) with the specified security context which includes the file executable type `ping_exec_t`.

## 11.2.3 Build Options for Strict Example Policy

The strict example policy source tree provides a few basic configuration options that enable us to control the contents of the kernel policy. These configuration options allow some control over the content of the resulting policy without having to write policy statements.

### 11.2.3.1 Configuring Policy Modules

We can control which policy modules are included in the policy by using the `unused/` directories discussed previously. So, for example, if we did not want the `ping` policy module included in our policy, we would move the file `ping.te` from `./domains/program/` to `./domains/program/unused/`. This will prevent `ping.te` (and the associated `ping.fc`) file from being included in the policy build.

You may find yourself removing many modules to customize the policy for your particular installation. Although extraneous policy modules (that is, for programs that are not installed) will generally not impact the operation of the system, it will add memory usage inside the kernel. In some cases (for example, a Web browser), the absence of a policy is less desirable because the application would run in the user's domain with more access than it would in a more restrictive browser domain.

Including unwanted policy modules also creates the risk that software may accidentally be installed and then have the privilege to run. For example, suppose we did not want any user to run the `ping` program, so we did not install the software, but we forgot to remove the `ping` policy module. If, at some later date, we installed a software package that installed its own version of `ping` (because it needed it and its installation script saw that it was not installed), all of a sudden our users have access to `ping`! If we had removed the `ping` policy module in our original policy, when the software package installed its `ping` program, users would not be able to use the program because there would be no domain `ping_t` defined. (That is, it would likely get a common utility label like `bin_t` that would allow users to execute it in their domain, but not in the more privileged `ping_t` domain.)

### 11.2.3.2 Enabling Optional MLS Features

We have mentioned throughout this book the optional capabilities for MLS policies and the related *multicategory security* (MCS) configuration that uses the MLS optional features. By default, the strict example policy configuration does not enable either of these configurations for the MLS features. To use the MLS features, the policy must be compiled with a special option to tell the kernel that MLS is being used. More important, *all* security contexts must be extended with the required MLS sensitivities, as discussed in Chapter 8.

The strict example policy `Makefile` has configuration options to automate these steps. If you look near the top of the `Makefile` (`./Makefile`), you will see the following:

```
# Set to y if MLS is enabled in the policy.
MLS=n
# Set to y if MCS is enabled in the policy
MCS=n
```

Setting either of these flags tells the `checkpolicy` compiler to build a policy that has the optional MLS features enabled. When this policy is loaded into the kernel, this will in turn tell the kernel to use the optional MLS features for access enforcement. You should not enable both of these options as they are mutually exclusive.

Enabling either the MLS or the MCS option only builds a policy file that has MLS enabled. It will *not* ensure that all the various security context specifications are extended to include the extended MLS security context information. The strict example policy comes with `make` targets that perform a basic reconfiguration of all security contexts: `make mlsconvert` and `make mcsconvert`. These targets will change all security contexts throughout the policy; however, the MLS portion of the security context will generally be inadequate for a real MLS system. More than likely, you will have to build your own file contexts that label all files, directories, ports, network interfaces, and so on as appropriate for your MLS applications. For example, `make mls` will change `ping.te` to this:

```
/bin/ping.*              --       system_u:object_r:ping_exec_t:s0
```

See Chapter 8 for more information on MLS security contexts.

> WARNING Using either `make mlsconvert` or `make mcsconvert` will permanently change the security context specifications throughout the example policy source files. There is no mechanism for returning to the original state. Therefore, you are advised to make a copy of the source tree before trying this feature.
>
> Both of these configuration options will set the corresponding `MLS=y` or `MCS=y` option in the `Makefile`. You do not need to manually set these options if you use these `make` targets.

### 11.2.3.3 Build-Time Tunables

In the directory `./tunables/` are two files, `distro.tun` and `tunable.tun`, that allow us to enable/disable configuration options that are built in to the various policy modules of the strict example policy. The `distro.tun` file is used for distribution-specific configuration options. For example, on our FC4 system, the file contains the following:

```
define('distro_redhat')
dnl define('distro_suse')
dnl define('distro_gentoo')
dnl define('distro_debian')
```

This file indicates that the `distro_redhat` options are enabled and not the various other distributions. (`dnl` is a `m4` command meaning "discard up to newline.") The `tunables.tun` file has similar options that we can configure to be on or off controlling more general (that is, nondistribution specific) options.

Throughout the policy modules, statements are included within `m4 ifdef` clauses that will or will not be included in the policy depending on whether a tunable is enabled or disabled. For example, in lines 39 through 41 of the `ping` module in Listing 11-1, we have a `dontaudit` rule included within `ifdef('hide_broken_symptoms')`, which is an `m4 ifdef` statement. If you look in `./tunables/tunable.tun`, you see will see this option and whether it is enabled.

## 11.3 Targeted Example Policy

The target example policy is derived from the strict example policy, and its structure and organization are nearly identical. Whereas the strict policy attempts to make maximum use of all the SELinux power to provide strong security for most programs, the targeted policy has a goal to isolate high-risk programs and otherwise make SELinux neutral. The benefit of the targeted policy is that significant security can be added to a Linux system while reducing the risk of causing problems with existing user programs. The targeted policy primarily focuses on network-facing system services (that is, those components most likely to be attacked by outsiders) and generally enforces no additional restrictions on local programs and ordinary users. The targeted policy is the standard policy for RHEL and FC systems because it strikes a good balance between enhanced security while reducing the risk of excessive application breakage.

If installed (see Appendix A), we should be able to see the targeted example policy sources in `/etc/selinux/targeted/src/policy/`. In most respects, the targeted example policy source looks exactly like the strict example policy sources so we do not provide a detailed overview of the targeted file structure. We instead highlight the differences.

The primary difference between strict and targeted example policies is the use of the unconfined domain type (`unconfined_t`) and removal of any other user domain type (for example, `sysadm_t`, `user_t`). This also means the basic role structure of the strict example policy is removed (all users run as `system_r`) and that nearly all user-run programs execute with the `unconfined_t` domain type.

We can find the unconfined domain defined in `./domain/unconfined.te`. Notice that in the targeted example policy, the strict policy files `admin.te` and `user.te` are no longer present in `./domains/`. These files define the various user domains for the strict example policy, each of which has limited privilege. In targeted example policy, all programs run with `unconfined_t` domain type unless they are specifically "targeted" (hence the name). The unconfined domain essentially has access to all SELinux types, making it largely exempt from the SELinux security controls (hence "unconfined").

This leads to the next major difference between strict and targeted policies (that is, the targets themselves). In the strict example policy, `./domains/program/` contains many policy modules, each of which represents one or more domain types and associated types and rules for specific programs. In the targeted example policy, this directory contains a smaller set of files; these are the targets.

The target example policy modules are similar to the policy modules in strict policy. For example, we should find the strict `ping` module and the targeted `ping` module to be identical. However some of the targeted modules simply define types but then make the domain unconfined (rather than targeted). For example, if we look at the targeted policy for `crond` (`crond.te`), we will find the line `unconfined_domain(crond_t)`. This macro, which is defined in `./policy/macros/global_macros.te` for the targeted example policy, effectively gives the `crond` domain type all SELinux access, making it unconfined. If we compare this with the strict version of the `crond` module (`/etc/selinux/strict/src/policy/domains/program/crond.te`), we will see a significant difference. In targeted policy, `crond` is considered an unconfined domain, whereas `ping` remains a strict domain in both policies.

The remaining differences between strict and targeted example polices are subtle and outside the scope of this book. You will find that the make targets and build options are all similar to strict.

## 11.4 Summary

- The goal of strict policy is to make maximum use of SELinux to provide separate domain types for each program that reasonably needs one. The strict example policy is most directly reflective of the original NSA example policy that has evolved through many years of community development.

- Targeted example policy is derived from the strict example policy. The goal of the targeted policy is to use SELinux to isolate high-risk system services from the rest of the system. Targeted policy runs most programs in an unconfined domain that essentially neutralizes the enhanced security of SELinux. Only the targeted services have enhanced restrictions.

- Both strict and targeted example policy source trees are similar in nature. They have evolved over time, and contain a large set of files and directories.

- The build conventions for strict example policy use a loose modular construct that allows the policy source file to be structured on a per-domain basis. In this way, we can decide which program domains we want to include and which we do not. The m4 macro processor is used to provide abstract concepts in the policy sources.

- The primary difference between the strict and targeted policies is that the targeted policy limits the permission sets of a few outwardly vulnerable services while providing no extra limits for local users and programs; whereas the strict policy defines permission sets for all users and most applications and services.

- FC4 and RHEL4 systems use the targeted example policy as their default supported policy.

## Exercises

1. Describe the differences and uses between a policy binary file (for example, `policy.19`) and a complete policy source file (`policy.conf`).

2. Describe the primary differences between a strict and targeted policy.

3. Describe the difference between the policy source modules in `./domains/program/` and the file context modules in `./file_contexts/program/`. What is in each and why?

4. In the policy module for `ping` shown in Listing 11-1, examine the statements at lines 11 and 39. What is the difference between these two forms of "if"?

5. Examine lines 19 and 20 in Listing 11-1. Locate where both of these macros are defined.

6.  Examine lines 19 and 20 in Listing 11-1. Locate where both of these macros are defined.

7.  Examine the usage and implementation of two network macros from Question 5. Notice that the implementation of the `can_resolve` macro that we use in line 20 calls the `can_network_client` macro. In line 19, we also separately invoke the `can_network_client` macro. Now examine the implementations of both of these macros. Is the invocation of `can_network_client` on line 19 redundant given that the `can_resolve` macros also invokes it? Explain your conclusion.

# Chapter 12

# Reference Policy

**In this chapter**

The reference policy is a newer method for building SELinux policies with the goal of making the policy easier to understand, modify, maintain, and validate. These goals are largely achieved through greater application of modern software engineering principles, such as modularity and encapsulation. The reference policy also allows strict and targeted policy variants to be built from the same source tree and incorporates support for emerging SELinux technologies, such as loadable modules.

## 12.1 Goals of the Reference Policy

The reference policy project is an effort to reengineer the existing policies derived from the *National Security Agency* (NSA) example policy into an easier to use, understand, and maintain policy. The primary goals are to create a strong design philosophy in policy development by applying well-understood software design principles, while retaining the years of experience learned by community effort in developing the existing policies. In other words, keep the good and fix the bad.

Chief among the "bad" with the existing example policy is its lack of strong modularity and the tight coupling of the policy source modules that results. Although macros add abstraction to the example policy, all policy identifiers (types, roles, attributes, and so on) are, in reality, global. Editing one policy module might require knowledge of many others and interdependency among modules is pervasive and poorly documented. Likewise, creating a new policy module requires detailed understanding of the implementation details of other policy modules.

Some of the key characteristics of the reference policy that make policy development easier and more understandable are as follows:

- A single source tree that supports (without destructive modification) strict and targeted policies, optional *multilevel security/multicategory security* (MLS/MCS) extensions, a single kernel policy file (called a *monolithic policy*), and the new loadable module infrastructure.

- Application of strong design principles, chiefly in the area of loosely coupled modules, with well-defined interfaces and no global use of type and other identifiers. (So, for example, all changes relating to a type are made entirely within a single module.)

- Integrated documentation support, capturing descriptions of module interfaces so that, for example, a policy module developer can use an interface without having to understand how the interface is implemented in the module.

- Simplify and standardize policy configuration and build options, so in general policy module writing and customization is easier and requires less expertise.

Besides making policy development easier, the reference policy also intends to make verifying the security properties of a policy easier to achieve (for example, for security certifications) and to increase support for high-level developments tools, such as graphical integrated development environments and sophisticated policy debuggers.

The reference policy is new, but we expect it to gain popularity as the definitive "reference" for building SELinux systems. At the time of this writing, *Fedora Core 5* (FC5) has changed its supported policy from the older targeted example policy to a targeted policy based on the reference policy.

> WARNING The reference policy is new at the time of this writing, with its initial development just nearing completion. Therefore, it is likely that some details of the reference policy have changed since this book was published.

For more information on the reference policy project and the latest policy sources, see the project's Web site at http://serefpolicy.sourceforge.net. If you are using an FC5 system, your default targeted policy is likely based on a reference policy build. If you have a reference policy installed on your system according to our instructions in Appendix A, "Obtaining SELinux Sample Policies," you can find the reference policy source files in `/etc/selinux/refpolicy/src/policy`. If you obtained a reference policy source tree from your distribution, the source files may be in a different directory under the `/etc/selinux/` directory. (FC5 installs its version of the targeted reference policy in `/etc/selinux/targeted/`.) All path names we use in this chapter are relative to the policy source root directory.

## 12.2 Overview of Policy Source File Structure

The file structure for the reference policy differs from the example policy. Before we describe the key implementation details of the reference policy, let's overview the layout of the reference policy source files to familiarize ourselves with its file structure.

### 12.2.1 Build and Support Files

The following files and directories are used for building or otherwise supporting the building of a reference policy:

`build.conf`
This file defines the set of build options that we can change and set to control the build process. This file is included within the `Makefile` during the `make` process. We will discuss some of these build options later in this chapter.

`Rules.modular`
This file contains the `make` rules for building a policy that supports loadable modules (see Chapter 3, "Architecture"). It supports building both the base policy module and loadable policy modules. Which modules are built as part of the base module, and which are built as loadable modules, is defined in `policy/modules.conf` (see below). The build option `MONOLITHIC` in `build.conf` controls whether a modular or monolithic policy is built.

`Rules.monolithic`
If a monolithic policy is being built, this file (rather than `Rules.modular`) is included in the `Makefile` to define the rules for building a monolithic policy.

`config/`
This directory contains subdirectories for the application configuration files for every variety of policy that can be built with the reference policy. These configuration files are exactly the same as the files in the `appconfig/` directory for the example policy. These are files installed in the operational policy directory (for example, `/etc/selinux/refpolicy`) to support various services and applications (see Chapter 13, "Managing an SELinux System").

doc/ This directory contains files that support integrated documentation generation that is part of the reference policy. To see the resulting documentation generation, view the reference policy Web site (http://serefpolicy.source forge.net/) or run the command `make html` and look in the `doc/html/` directory.

support/ This directory contains source code and scripts for the tools used to support the build process.

## 12.2.2 Core Policy Files

In the reference policy, the primary files used to create a policy (or loadable modules) are contained in the `policy/` directory. These are the files that we, as policy writers, will most commonly modify and examine:

policy/constraints This file is where all non-MLS constraints are defined. It is essentially identical to the same file in the example policy. See Chapter 7, "Constraints," for more on policy constraints.

policy/flask/ This directory contains the Flask definitions identical with the example policy. See the description for the example policy in Chapter 11, "Original Example Policy," for this directory and its files.

policy/mls and policy/mcs These two files define two configurations for the optional MLS features in SELinux. They are identical in intent to the same files in the example policy; see the description in Chapter 11.

policy/global_booleans and policy/global_tunables These two files currently store defined Booleans and their default values. They are combined and installed in `/etc/selinux/refpolicy/ booleans` and enable an administrator to change the default values of Booleans as we discussed in Chapter 9, "Conditional Policies." The reason for two files is one of a philosophy that may eventually lead to a difference in implementation. The `global_booleans` file contains Booleans intended to support truly conditional policies that an administrator may want to toggle on and off in a production system. The `global_tunables` contains Booleans that are build/runtime configuration options that are likely changed once during installation and never changed again. Some of these latter Booleans (that is, the tunables) may be implemented using features of loadable modules in the future.

`policy/modules.conf`       This file configures which modules are to be included in a build process and in what form. A module can be built in to a monolithic policy or the base module for a loadable policy, built as a loadable module, or not built at all. The `modules.conf` file is created with the `make conf` command. We discuss module configuration options later in this chapter.

`policy/modules/`           This directory contains all the policy modules divided into subdirectories by layer. Most of the files that we would examine, edit, and change will be in this directory. We discuss modules and layers in the next section.

`policy/support/`           This directory contains macros used throughout the policy modules to aide in policy writing. For example, the file `policy/support/obj_perm _sets.spt` defines macros that define sets of permissions. We use these macros to simplify some of the policy writing steps and to create easier to read policy.

`policy/users`              This file is the same as the `users` file in the example policy though it uses an interface (that is, a macro), `gen_user()`, to create the user statements; see the description in Chapter 11.

## 12.3 Design Principles

The reference policy is structured around several design principles. These principles are focused on achieving the goals of the project. Currently, most of these principles are enforced only through convention; as high-level development environments and tools evolve on top of the reference policy, we expect to see these principles start to be more strictly enforced by the build tools themselves.

### 12.3.1 Layering

As discussed in the next section, the reference project achieves most of its design goals through strong modularity. A weak, although still important, design principle of the reference policy is the *layering* of its modules. The layers provide a loose organizational structure for the modules that reflects the overall system architecture. Figure 12-1 depicts the layers currently defined for reference policy.

In general, the reference policy tries to keep dependencies between modules within a layer or to a layer "below" the module's layer. We can find the layer directories, which contain the modules for each layer, in `policy/modules/`. The reference policy currently defines the following layers:

- *Kernel*   This layer contains policy modules that directly relate to the Linux kernel. This is the lowest layer of modules. Modules at this layer include policy statements for the kernel, devices, filesystems, and basic networking. Most of these modules will always be included in any type of policy.

- *System*   These are policy modules that are also usually included in a policy but do not directly support the kernel. Modules at this layer include policy for common libraries, login processes, and network management.

- *Services*   This layer contains policy modules for all services and daemons not part of the system layer. These modules range from `cron`, to `sshd`, to `apache`.

- *Admin*   This layer contains policy modules for administrative tools and commands that have their own domain type.

- *Apps*   This layer contains policy modules for all other programs that have their own domain type and policy module.

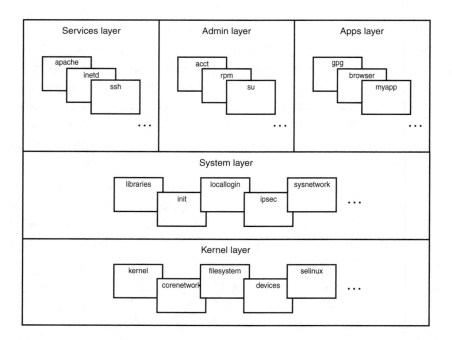

FIGURE 12-1
Reference policy layers and sample modules within a layer

Again, the layering is not strictly enforced and is primarily useful as a way to organize the collection of modules. As you can see from Figure 12-1, some of the layers are really peer groupings rather than "layered" (that is, services, admin, and apps).

## 12.3.2 Modularity

Modularity is the strongest design principle of the reference policy. Although the example policy discussed in Chapter 11 has a notion of modules, these modules have loose conventions resulting in tightly coupled modules (primarily due to the use of global type and attribute names). In the reference policy, modules are required to be loosely coupled. This loose coupling is achieved through the enforcement of two strong design conventions: encapsulation and abstraction.

### 12.3.2.1 Encapsulation

*Encapsulation* is a reference policy modularity convention that requires that type and attribute names may only be used within a single module. In effect, type and attribute names may not be used as global names. Only the module that defines the type/attribute may reference the name directly. Any other module that would require the use of the type/attribute must do so through well-defined *interfaces* that the owning module defines.

For example, in the example policy, all types that are domain types are given the `domain` attribute. Every policy module simply has this knowledge built in and explicitly adds `domain` to the list of attributes for all domain types they define. If we decided to change how the concept of a domain was implemented in the policy (say by granting each type explicit rules or even by renaming the attribute), we would have to change every module that defines a domain type.

In the reference policy, a module called "domain" in the kernel layer defines the concept of a domain. It just so happens that this concept is implemented using the `domain` attribute as with the example policy. However, this implementation detail is private to the domain module and could be changed (for example, renamed) without impacting any other module source. Any module that wants to make one of its types a domain type would call an interface defined in the domain module:

```
domain_type(my_type)    # interface to make a type a domain type
```

The domain module interfaces in `policy/modules/kernel/domain.if`; we discuss this interface in more detail later in this chapter.

Encapsulation enables us to make the reference policy modules' implementation details private to the module resulting in loosely coupled modules.

### 12.3.2.2 Abstraction

*Abstraction* is a design goal where interfaces describe *what* abstract access they provide and not *how* they do it. The intent of reference policy interfaces is to describe what abstract access is given or system capability is being enabled with the interface. The policy statements required to enable that access should not be a concern of the interface caller. For example, the macro we discussed previously to make a type a domain type is called `domain_type()` and not `add_domain_attribute()`. The intent of the interface is to make a type a domain type; doing this by adding the `domain` attribute is just the private implementation detail of the `domain_type()` interface. This interface could have instead simply added explicit rules for each individual type provided with the interface, and we can still change that implementation if we choose without impacting other modules that use this interface.

As another example, to allow a directory to be used as a mount point we would call the `file_mountpoint()` macro in the "files" module. We do not need to know that the implementation of this interface applies the attribute `mountpoint` to all directory types called with this interface and then defines rules for the attribute to allow the type to be used as a mount point. As a policy writer, all we need to know is that the `file_mountpoint()` interface is how we allow a directory type to be a mount point.

Currently, the reference policy has a low-level of interfaces implemented within each module. Eventually higher-level abstractions will be developed through additional interfaces that combine the lower-level interfaces.

### 12.3.2.3 Module Files

As discussed earlier, within the reference policy source tree all modules are kept in `policy/modules/[layer]/` where the layer is a directory whose name coincides with one of the layers discussed previously. Each module *must* consist of three related files, all of which have the same root name (that is, module name):

- *Private policy file (.te)*   This file contains the module private declarations and rules. In general, all module type and attribute declarations are contained in the `.te` file and the rules that give these types and attributes their core access.

- *External interface file (.if)*   This file contains the module interfaces. These interfaces are the means by which other modules access the types and attributes of this module.

- *Labeling policy file (.fc)*   This file contains the file context labeling statements relating to this module (see Chapter 10, "Object Labeling").

Because a strong requirement is that no type or attribute be global, only the `.te` and `.if` file for a given module may use the module's type/attribute names explicitly. All other references to a module's types and attributes must be via the module's interfaces.

## 12.3.2.4 Interfaces

As discussed previously, one of the most significant improvements implemented in the reference policy is the use of interface macros for gaining access to a type outside of the module in which the type is defined. Interfaces provide access to a module's policy resources (for example, to its privately declared types and attributes). All other modules needing a particular access use the same interface; therefore, the policy rules required for the access will be consistent across all users of the interface. Therefore, policy changes for access to a type require only a change in one place, rather than requiring changes to all the modules that use the type as is common in the example policy.

As noted above, interfaces are kept in a module's .if file and are implemented as macros. Currently, reference policy supports two kinds of interfaces: access interfaces and template interfaces.

The name we give each interface follows the convention of modname_purpose. So, for example, we can tell that the domain_type() interface is defined in the "domain" module and its purpose is to make a provided type a domain type. (We avoid the verbose name such as domain_domain_type() when the module name is also part of the purpose.)

### 12.3.2.4.1 Access Interfaces

The most common kind of interface is called an *access interface*. As its name implies, the purpose of an access interface is to provide some type of access that requires use of the module's private types and attributes. Access interfaces are implemented using the interface() macro. The domain_type() interface is an example of an access interface. Let's examine this interface more closely (see Listing 12-1).

LISTING 12-1
Partial Interface Listing for domain_type Access Interface (domain.if)

```
 1 ##########################################
 2 ## <summary>
 3 ## Make the specified type usable as a domain.
 4 ## </summary>
 5 ## <param name="type">
 6 ## Type to be used as a domain type.
 7 ## </param>
 8 interface('domain_type','
 9    domain_base_type($1)
10
```

```
11      # Use trusted objects in /dev
12      dev_rw_null_dev($1)
13      dev_rw_zero_dev($1)
14      term_use_controlling_term($1)
15
16      # read the root directory
17      files_list_root($1)
18
19      # send init a sigchld and signull
20      init_sigchld($1)
21      init_signull($1)
22
23      ifdef('targeted_policy','
24           unconfined_use_fd($1)
25           unconfined_sigchld($1)
26      ')
27
28      tunable_policy('allow_ptrace','
29           userdom_sigchld_sysadm($1)
30      ')
31
32      # allow any domain to connect to the LDAP server
33      optional_policy('ldap','
34           ldap_use($1)
35      ')
36 ')
```

In line 8 of Listing 12-1, we see the interface() macro, which is implemented as an m4 macro, as are all macros in reference policy. The interface() macro is what we use to define an access interface. This and other macros that support the conventions and build process of reference policy (collectively called *support macros*) are located in one of the files in policy/support/ directory. The interface() macro handles the details of defining an interface and a central spot where debugging and other build information can be inserted into the results. Therefore, we must always use the interface() macro to define an access interface.

The purpose of the domain_type() interface is to allow the provided type (the only argument for this macro, $1) to be used as a domain type in the policy. We see a description of the interface and its arguments in lines 1 through 7. Reference policy uses XML to capture information about interfaces and other aspects of the policy for generation of documentation. In this case, we have a summary of the interface purpose and a list of its parameters, all of which will be included in a list of interfaces when the documentation is generated.

Lines 9, 12 through 14, 17, 20, and 21 are all calls to other interfaces. The name of an interface give us a hint of the module where the interface is defined. As noted, by convention, the first component of all interface names is the name (or partial name) of the module in which the interface is defined. For example, the interfaces `dev_rw_null_dev()` and `dev_rw_zero_dev()` are defined in the "devices" module (`policy/modules/kernel/devices.if`) and the interface `files_list_root()` in the "files" modules (`policy/modules/kernel/files.if`). We can examine each of these interfaces to see how they are implemented or we can examine the interface documentation if all we want is a description of each interface.

> NOTE The command `make html` creates the reference policy documentation including the interface descriptions; open `doc/html/index.html` with a browser to see the documentation.

Lines 23 through 26 show a use of the `m4 ifdef` statement. Although `ifdef` was commonly used in the example policy, for reference policy the use of `ifdef` is greatly limited by convention (see the sidebar on page 184 for more information). In this case, we call additional interfaces (from the targeted policy-specific "unconfined" module) if we are building a targeted policy. The symbol `targeted_policy` is defined as part of the build process based on the options in `build.conf`, which we discuss later in this chapter.

Lines 28 through 30 show another support macro, `tunable_policy()`. The purpose of this macro is to allow conditional behavior based on the value of a defined tunable. As noted previously, tunables, which are intended as build/install time policy options, are defined in `policy/global_tunables`. Currently, tunables are implemented using Booleans, but eventually with loadable modules we expect the implementation of tunables to differ from conditional policy Booleans. In this case, we have a tunable `allow_ptrace`, which when true allows the administrative user domain(s) to debug any other user domain type.

Finally, let's examine lines 33 through 35 of Listing 12-1, where we have an example of the `optional_policy()` support macro. This macro enables us to optionally call an interface depending on whether a module is included in the policy. This support macro implements this capability differently depending on whether a monolithic policy, base module, or loadable module is being built. Nonetheless, the concept from a policy writer's perspective is the same. If the module is being included in the build process (in this case, the `ldap` module), the interface `ldap_use()` is also called.

---

### Allowed Uses of ifdef

In the reference policy, the m4 `ifdef` statement may only be used, by convention, for a limited set of defined conditions. These become hard-coded implementation variations within the policy build process. All other forms of policy options must use either the native conditional policy statements (if) based on Booleans defined in `policy/global_booleans` or one of the reference policy support macros such as `tunable_policy()` for tunables defined in `policy/global_tunables` or `optional_policy()` for optional policy statements based on the name of a module. These support macros allow us to change the implementation of these concepts to better support the build process and development tools in the future.

The only allowed use of `ifdef` in reference policy is with the following defines:

| | |
|---|---|
| `targeted_policy` | This is defined when a targeted policy is being built. |
| `strict_policy` | This is defined when a strict policy is being built. |
| `enable_mls` | This is defined when the optional MLS policy is being built. |
| `enable_mcs` | This is defined when the optional MLS features are being used to build an MCS policy. |
| `hide_broken _symptoms` | This is used to control `dontaudit` rules; we place all such rules that mask expected denial audit messages (that is, due to access we intentionally did not allow but we expect the program to attempt even though it is not needed). These `dontaudit` rules help remove benign "false positive" audit messages we expect to see during normal operation. |
| `direct_sysadm _daemon` | This enables us to determine whether the policy permits the system administrator user domains to directly control daemons that otherwise are started and controlled by `init`. Note that if this is disabled, the administrator may still control daemons with the `run_init` tool. |
| `distro_tunable` | One of several distribution tunables can be set for policy variations specific to a particular distribution of Linux. For example, `redhat` is the tunable for *Fedora Core* (FC) and *Red Hat Enterprise Linux* (RHEL) systems, and `gentoo` is the tunable for Gentoo systems. |

### 12.3.2.4.2 Template Interfaces

The second type of interface is a *template interface,* which is far less common than an access interface. A template interface is necessary when two modules share responsibility for one or more types. We call this kind of a type a *derived type.* A derived type name is derived from the calling module's type. From a logical perspective, the derived type is considered a private type of the calling module. However, the definition of the derived type and the core set of rules that define access for that type are implemented in a template interface in another module (that is, the called module). This is necessary because the called module is creating access rules for policy permissions only it understands, but on behalf of the calling module. In all cases, the derived type name is partly based on a name provided by the calling module and a name provided by the called module. Neither fully knows the name; this keeps our abstraction intact and allows us to change the template interface without impacting the calling module.

An example of a derived type and a template interface can be found in the `ssh` module, which implements the client and server policy rules for the Secure Shell service (`sshd`). We should find this module in `policy/modules/services/ssh.*`. In particular, we want to examine the template interface `ssh_per_user-domain_template()`, a partial listing of which is shown in Listing 12-2.

LISTING 12-2
Partial Interface Listing for ssh_per_userdomain_template Interface (ssh.if)

```
 1 #########################################
 2 ## <summary>
 3 ## The per user domain template for the ssh module.
 4 ## </summary>
 5 ## <desc>
 6 ## <p>
 7 ## This template creates a derived domains which are used
 8 ## for ssh client sessions and user ssh agents.  A derived
 9 ## type is also created to protect the user ssh keys.
10 ## </p>
11 ## <p>
12 ## This template is invoked automatically for each user and
13 ## generally does not need to be invoked directly
14 ## by policy writers.
15 ## </p>
16 ## </desc>
17 ## <param name="userdomain_prefix">
18 ## The prefix of the user domain (for example, user
19 ## is the prefix for user_t).
20 ## </param>
```

```
21 ## <param name="user_domain">
22 ## The type of the user domain.
23 ## </param>
24 ## <param name="user_role">
25 ## The role associated with the user domain.
26 ## </param>
27 template('ssh_per_userdomain_template','
28     ##############################
29     # Declarations
30
31     type $1_home_ssh_t;
32     userdom_home_file($1,$1_home_ssh_t)
33     role $3 types $1_ssh_t;
34
35     type $1_ssh_t;
36     domain_type($1_ssh_t)
37     domain_entry_file($1_ssh_t,ssh_exec_t)
38
39     type $1_ssh_agent_t;
40     domain_type($1_ssh_agent_t)
41     domain_entry_file($1_ssh_agent_t,ssh_agent_exec_t)
42     role $3 types $1_ssh_agent_t;
43
44     type $1_ssh_keysign_t; #, nscd_client_domain;
45     domain_type($1_ssh_keysign_t)
46     domain_entry_file($1_ssh_keysign_t,ssh_keysign_exec_t)
47     role $3 types $1_ssh_keysign_t;
48
49     # Private policy for each derived types not shown
50     #      see policy/modules/ssh.if
51
52     # remainder not shown...
53 ')
```

The `ssh_per_userdomain_template()` interface creates a per-domain set of derived types that allow each domain to have private types for their ssh sessions and cryptographic keys. Because the ssh module cannot (and should not for modularity reasons) know all the possible domain types that need a per-domain ssh type, it cannot possible directly create the rules necessary in its .te file. Likewise, any given module that wants an ssh private type for its domains cannot (and again should not) possibly know how to implement ssh private session and key types. Thus the need for a template interface.

As you can see from Listing 12-2, this interface takes three arguments: the base type name prefix (for example, for the domain type user_t we would provide the prefix user), the user domain type (for example, user_t), and the primary role associated with the user domain. A template interface has two primary sections. The first section is where the derived types are created (using the provided type name prefix). We can see these declarations in lines 31 through 47 of Listing 12-2. For example, line 35 defines the main derived domain type. If the prefix were user, the derived domain type would be user_ssh_t and that would be the domain type for the ssh client when the domain user_t runs it (as implemented by this interface). As you can see, three other derived types are also created for various aspects of an ssh session.

The second part of a template interface is the private rules for the derived type. This is where rules are defined for all derived types of this kind, and it is the one place we need to change them. We do not examine these rules in this book, but you are encouraged to do so on your own. Although template interfaces are uncommon, they are valuable to simplify certain types of policy writing.

## 12.4 Examining a Reference Policy Module

To help further understand how the reference policy works, let's examine all aspects of the policy for the ping program as we did with the example policy. Whereas in the example policy the ping program had its own module, in the reference policy ping is included in a module that addresses all administrative network utilities (netutils). We can find this module in policy/modules/admin/netutils.*.

> NOTE In the reference policy, we try to package policy pieces in ways that make sense for installation with software packages. Reference policy is mostly influenced by the packaging conventions for FC. This allows us to define modules that can be built as loadable modules and installed as part of the package installation (the real benefit of loadable modules). This is the reason that ping is coupled with a number of other network utilities; these utilities are all part of the same software package in FC (specifically the iputils package).

Listing 12-3 shows a partial listing of the netutils.te module file, focusing on those components related to ping. Recall that the .te file is the file that contains the module's private declarations and rules. This is the file in which we would generally expect to find type and attribute declarations. First notice the use of the policy_module() support macro on line 1. All modules must use the policy_module() as their first line in their .te file. This macro requires two arguments: the name of the module and the version of the module. Currently, the `policy_module()` support macro effects only the build process when the module is being built as a loadable module. Nonetheless, its use is mandatory for all modules, and its function will likely evolve over time (for example, better debugging support).

LISTING 12-3
Partial Listing for netutils (ping) Private Module File (netutils.te)

```
 1 policy_module(netutils,1.0)
 2 ########################################
 3 # Declarations
 4 type ping_t;
 5 type ping_exec_t;
 6 init_system_domain(ping_t,ping_exec_t)
 7 role system_r types ping_t;
 8
 9 ########################################
10 # Ping local policy
11 allow ping_t self:capability { setuid net_raw };
12 dontaudit ping_t self:capability sys_tty_config;
13
14 allow ping_t self:tcp_socket create_socket_perms;
15 allow ping_t self:udp_socket create_socket_perms;
16 allow ping_t self:rawip_socket { create ioctl read write bind
   getopt setopt };
17
18 corenet_tcp_sendrecv_all_if(ping_t)
19 corenet_udp_sendrecv_all_if(ping_t)
20 corenet_raw_sendrecv_all_if(ping_t)
21 corenet_raw_sendrecv_all_nodes(ping_t)
22 corenet_tcp_sendrecv_all_nodes(ping_t)
23 corenet_udp_sendrecv_all_nodes(ping_t)
24 corenet_tcp_sendrecv_all_ports(ping_t)
25 corenet_udp_sendrecv_all_ports(ping_t)
26 corenet_udp_bind_all_nodes(ping_t)
27 corenet_tcp_bind_all_nodes(ping_t)
28
29 fs_dontaudit_getattr_xattr_fs(ping_t)
30
31 domain_use_wide_inherit_fd(ping_t)
32
33 files_read_etc_files(ping_t)
34 files_dontaudit_search_var(ping_t)
35
36 libs_use_ld_so(ping_t)
37 libs_use_shared_libs(ping_t)
38
```

```
39 sysnet_read_config(ping_t)
40 sysnet_dns_name_resolve(ping_t)
41
42 logging_send_syslog_msg(ping_t)
43
44 ifdef('hide_broken_symptoms','
45     init_dontaudit_use_fd(ping_t)
46 ')
47
48 ifdef('targeted_policy','
49     term_use_unallocated_tty(ping_t)
50     term_use_generic_pty(ping_t)
51     term_use_all_user_ttys(ping_t)
52     term_use_all_user_ptys(ping_t)
53 ','
54     tunable_policy('user_ping','
55             term_use_all_user_ttys(ping_t)
56             term_use_all_user_ptys(ping_t)
57     ')
58 ')
```

On lines 4 through 7, we define our domain type (ping_t) and entrypoint type (ping_exec_t). These two types serve exactly the same purpose as with the example policy. Indeed, the goal of the reference policy implementation of the ping domain type is to be the functional equivalent to the policy rules in the example policy (but implemented in an entirely different manner). Notice on line 6 that we call an interface from the init module that allows the ping domain to be used in system initialization scripts. As a point of comparison, this interface performs nearly the exact same purpose as the macro called on line 9 of the example policy ping module in Listing 11-1.

All the remaining lines in Listing 12-3 implement the rules that allow the ping domain type access necessary to perform its function. For example, the interface calls in lines 18 through 27 provide the necessary network access by using interfaces from the core network (corenetwork) module. Much of the access is provided via interfaces; this is the expected form of a module implementation so that access is defined only in one place and interfaces are called elsewhere to use that access. Again, we can examine the purpose of each of these interfaces by examining their implementation or more easily by reading through the interface documentation that is generated. As you read through this listing, you will also notice uses of the target_policy conditional on line 48 to define targeted-only policy rules.

Now let's look at the interfaces for ping, which will be defined in the netutils interface file (netutils.if), a partial list of which is shown in Listing 12-4. In addition to defining the interfaces themselves, the .if file also contains the XML statements that are used to generate documentation. As you see on line 1 in Listing 12-4, all module interface files must start with a summary statement that provides a concise statement of the module's purpose. Because ping is part of a larger network utilities module, we see a statement that summarizes the whole purpose of the module (although in Listing 12-4 we show only those parts of the module that relate to ping).

**LISTING 12-4**
**Partial Listing for netutils (ping) Interface Module File (netutils.if)**

```
 1 ## <summary>Network analysis utilities</summary>
 2
 3 #########################################
 4 ## <summary>
 5 ## Execute ping in the ping domain.
 6 ## </summary>
 7 ## <param name="domain">
 8 ## The type of the process performing this action.
 9 ## </param>
10 interface('netutils_domtrans_ping','
11     gen_require('
12             type ping_t, ping_exec_t;
13             class process sigchld;
14             class fd use;
15             class fifo_file rw_file_perms;
16     ')
17
18     domain_auto_trans($1,ping_exec_t,ping_t)
19
20     allow $1 ping_t:fd use;
21     allow ping_t $1:fd use;
22     allow ping_t $1:fifo_file rw_file_perms;
23     allow ping_t $1:process sigchld;
24 ')
25
26 #########################################
27 ## <summary>
28 ## Execute ping in the ping domain, and
29 ## allow the specified role the ping domain.
30 ## </summary>
31 ## <param name="domain">
32 ## The type of the process performing this action.
33 ## </param>
34 ## <param name="role">
```

```
35 ## The role to be allowed the ping domain.
36 ## </param>
37 ## <param name="terminal">
38 ## The type of the terminal allow the ping domain to use.
39 ## </param>
40 interface('netutils_run_ping','
41     gen_require('
42             type ping_t;
43     ')
44
45     netutils_domtrans_ping($1)
46     role $2 types ping_t;
47     allow ping_t $3:chr_file rw_term_perms;
48 ')
49
50 ########################################
51 ## <summary>
52 ## Conditionally execute ping in the ping domain, and
53 ## allow the specified role the ping domain.
54 ## </summary>
55 ## <param name="domain">
56 ## The type of the process performing this action.
57 ## </param>
58 ## <param name="role">
59 ## The role to be allowed the ping domain.
60 ## </param>
61 ## <param name="terminal">
62 ## The type of the terminal allow the ping domain to use.
63 ## </param>
64 interface('netutils_run_ping_cond','
65     gen_require('
66             type ping_t;
67             bool user_ping;
68     ')
69
70     role $2 types ping_t;
71
72     if ( user_ping ) {
73             netutils_domtrans_ping($1)
74             allow ping_t $3:chr_file rw_term_perms;
75     }
76 ')
77
78 ########################################
79 ## <summary>
80 ## Execute ping in the caller domain.
81 ## </summary>
82 ## <param name="domain">
83 ## The type of the process performing this action.
84 ## </param>
85 interface('netutils_exec_ping','
86     gen_require('
```

```
87          type ping_exec_t;
88    ')
89
90    can_exec($1,ping_exec_t)
91 ')
```

In lines 11 through 16, 41 and 43, 65 through 68, and 86 through 88, we see the use of another support macro, gen_require(). This macro is key to supporting the loadable module infrastructure and eventually for supporting development tools that need module and interface dependency information. Each module interface file must have a gen_require() macro that lists the policy identifiers (names of types, attributes, roles, Booleans, and so on) that this interface uses. For types and attributes, these identifiers must be types and attributes private to the module (because only private types and attributes may be explicitly named within a module). The gen_require() macro will generate the appropriate dependency information to support various types of policy builds. This allows, for example, the ability to link a loadable module without the entire policy source being available.

The rest of the partial .if file in Listing 12-4 defines four ping-related interfaces in much the same way we already discussed. All these interfaces are access interfaces using the interface() macro. The first interface, netutils_domtrans_ping(), which is defined in lines 3 through 24, supplies all the rules to allow a provided domain type permission to cause a domain transition into the ping domain type. The two interfaces, netutils_run_ping(), defined in lines 26 through 48, and netutils_run_ping_cond(), defined in lines 50 through 76, call the netutils_domtrans_ping() interface but also require a role to ensure that the role is authorized for the ping domain. The latter of these two interfaces support the use of a conditional expression based on the user_ping Boolean (lines 72 through 75) much as we discussed for the example policy in Chapter 11.

The final interface, netutils_exec_ping(), defined in lines 78 through 91, simply allows the provided domain type the ability to execute the ping program *without* a domain transition. In this case, the provided domain type must have the necessary network access itself, which is the case of some system utilities and daemons.

Finally, let's look at the file labeling policy, which we can find in the netutils.fc file. In that file, there should be a line such as this

```
/bin/ping.*  --   gen_context(system_u:object_r:ping_exec_t,s0)
```

This line is similar to `ping`'s file context file we saw in the example policy with one significant difference: The file context is provided within another support macro, `gen_context()`. This macro contains a full security context, including any optional MLS portion. The `gen_context()` macro generates security contexts with or without the MLS portion based on the build type. In this way, we can write a policy with or without the optional MLS features without having to change the contents of the file or cause irreversible changes to the sources as with the example policy.

## 12.5 Build Options for Reference Policy

The reference policy was designed to be customizable without having to understand all the details of the policy. The primary build targets for reference policy are all identical in name and function to the example policy. For example, the `Makefile` targets, `policy`, `policy.conf`, `relabel`, and `load` all produce the same results as we discussed in Chapter 11 for the example policy.

Two policy build configuration files that are unique to reference policy are the `build.conf` and the `modules.conf`.

### 12.5.1 The build.conf File

We discussed some of the options controlled by the `build.conf` earlier in this chapter. The first option we want to discuss in this file is the *policy type*. One of the goals of the reference policy is the ability to create differing types of policies from the same source tree. This build option controls what type of policy is built. It is specified with the `TYPE` option in `build.conf`. As noted throughout this chapter, we can build either a targeted or a strict policy. For example, if we wanted to build a strict policy, we would use the following value for this option:

```
TYPE = strict
```

For a targeted policy, we would set the option to `targeted` instead. In addition, we can enable the optional MLS features in one of two ways, as a typical MLS policy (`strict-mls` or `targeted-mls`) or as the MCS configuration (`strict-mcs` or `targeted-mcs`). These six values (`strict`, `targeted`, `strict-mls`, `targeted-mls`, `strict-mcs`, and `targeted-mcs`) are the only currently supported policy types for reference policy.

Another option in `build.conf` is the *policy name,* which is specified with the `NAME` option. This is a nice feature in reference policy that allows us to name the policy something other than its policy type. The name is used to determine the install directory for the policy in `/etc/selinux/`. For example, take the policy name as provided by default from the reference policy project:

```
NAME = refpolicy
```

In this case, when we install the policy, the install directory for the policy is `/etc/selinux/refpolicy/`. If no value is provided, the policy type name will be used. For example, assume our build.conf file has these two lines:

```
TYPE = targeted
NAME =
```

Our install directory would then be `/etc/selinux/targeted/`. This is fine if you want to use the reference policy in place of your default targeted policy. If you are trying to experiment with the reference policy, however, you do not necessarily want to overwrite your current, system-provided targeted policy.

Another option of interest is the distribution tunable, `DISTRO`. As discussed in the sidebar on page 184, the reference policy supports a distribution-specific tunable for distribution-specific policy variations. For example, for FC and RHEL systems, this option would currently be set as follows:

```
DISTRO = redhat
```

The final `build.conf` option we want to discuss is whether the policy is a monolithic policy. This option is controlled by the `MONOLITHIC` option. If we are building a monolithic policy (that is, one entire kernel binary policy as is common today), we would set this option as follows:

```
MONOLITHIC=y
```

Otherwise, we would set this option like this:

```
MONOLITHIC=n
```

An n indicates that we want to support loadable modules and will be building both the base module and the loadable modules. Which modules are part of the base module, and which are loadable, is controlled by the `modules.conf`, which we discuss next.

## 12.5.2 The modules.conf File

The `modules.conf` file controls which modules we include in our policy build and in what form. We can find this file in `policy/modules.conf`. If the file is not present, you can create it with the `make conf` command from the policy root directory. This command creates a `modules.conf` file with an entry for all modules in the `policy/modules/` directory. If the `modules.conf` file already exists, `make conf` appends any new modules to the files (that is, those not already included in the file) without changing any settings for the existing modules. Thus, when we add new modules, we run `make conf` and then modify the settings for the new modules in `modules.conf`.

An entry in `modules.conf` looks like this:

```
# Layer: admin1
# Module: netutils
#
# Network analysis utilities
#
netutils = module
```

This is the entry that is generated from the `netutils` module discussed previously. The comment lines (proceeded by # ) are generated from the module for informational purposes. The layer comment comes from the name of the directory where the module files are located, the module name comment comes from the root names of the module files, and the description comment comes from the module summary description in the top of the module `.if` file.

The only effective line is the `netutils = module` line, which tells the policy build tools how to treat this module during the build process. A module can be set to one of three values. Depending on the type of build (monolithic or loadable module), these values determine how and if the module is built. Possible values for a module are as follows:

base    For a monolithic policy build, all modules marked as `base` will be included in the policy. For loadable module policy build, all modules marked as `base` will be included in the base module.

module  For a monolithic policy build, all modules marked as `module` will be treated the same as `base` and will be included in the policy. For a loadable module policy build, all modules marked as `module` will be built as loadable modules.

off        For both monolithic and loadable module builds, all modules marked
           as off will not be built in any fashion.

All modules that are in the policy/module/ directory that are not listed in the
modules.conf file, or which are listed but do not have a value, will not be built in
any fashion (as if they were marked as off).

When creating or updating the modules.conf file with the make conf command, all modules will be marked as module *unless* the module is marked as
required within the module interface (.if) file. For example, here is the header for
the kernel module .if file. The kernel module is always required:

```
## <summary>
##     Policy for kernel threads, proc filesystem, and
##     unlabeled processes and objects.
## </summary>
## <required val="true">
##     This module has initial SIDs.
## </required>
```

The block that starts with <required val="true"> indicates that this module is required along with a comment explaining why. For all such modules, the
default value from modules.conf will be base, ensuring that the module is always
included in a monolithic policy or as part as the base module for a loadable module policy. Thus, when we generate the modules.conf file, the kernel module
block looks something like this:

```
# Layer: kernel
# Module: kernel
# Required in base
#
# Policy for kernel threads, proc filesystem, and
# unlabeled processes and objects.
#
kernel = base
```

As you can see, in addition to setting the default value to base, there is also an
extra comment ("Required in base") that notes for future reference that this module should always be base.

## 12.6 Summary

- The reference policy project was started to reengineer the example policy derived from the original example policy for SELinux. The goals of this reengineering include the inclusion of modern software engineering design principles to make policy development and maintenance easier to perform, and to support emerging technology, such as loadable modules and sophisticated policy development tools.

- Layering is a weak design principle of reference policy. The layers organize policy modules in a manner that are generally reflective of our understanding of how the policy modules relate.

- Modularity is a strong design principle of reference policy. Although the example policy had a form of modularity, it was weakly defined and did not ensure that modules remained loosely coupled. Reference policy modules hide implementation details from other modules allowing easier maintenance of the overall policy and distributed policy development (that is, the ability to develop a policy module without detailed knowledge of other modules).

- Two properties of modularity primarily ensure that reference policy modules remain loosely coupled: encapsulation and abstraction.

- Encapsulation ensures that implementation details of a module are only required by the module itself. This goal is achieved primarily through requiring that type and attribute names always remain local identifiers that may only be explicitly used by the module that defines them. Other modules use these types and attributes via well-defined interfaces of the module.

- Abstraction ensures that policy module writers can think about policy development logically rather than focus on all the policy details. This is accomplished via module interfaces. Interfaces are designed and named to describe what the interface provides and not how it does it. The "how" can change over time without impacting the "what."

- A module consists of three files: the private policy file (.te), the external interface file (.if), and the labeling policy file (.fc). All three files must be present for each defined module even if empty.

- A reference policy module may have two types of interfaces: access and template. Access interfaces are by far the most common. These interfaces provide access to the module's private types and attributes. Template interfaces are less common and are used when we need to manage derived types between two modules.

- Reference policy introduces two configuration files that provide most of the policy build options we need to control. The `build.conf` file controls global policy build options, such as policy type and install location. The `modules.conf` file controls which policy modules are built and in what form.

- Currently, reference policy can build six types of policies from the same source tree: `strict`, `targeted`, `strict-mls`, `targeted-mls`, `strict-mcs`, and `targeted-mcs`.

- Two types of builds are supported by the reference policy. A monolithic build creates a single kernel binary policy. Monolithic policies are the only type of policy in general use at the time of this writing and are the type of policy we mostly discuss in this book. A loadable module build creates a base module and a number of loadable modules that make use of the new loadable module infrastructure. We expect loadable modules to become more common going forward.

## Exercises

1. Describe some of the key benefits of the reference policy over the example policy.

2. What is the primary goal of encapsulation within reference policy and how is it generally achieved?

3. What is the difference between a module's `.if` and `.te` files? How are they similar?

4. Which of the three kinds of module files are required or optional for a reference policy module?

5. Explain when you might need to use a template interface rather than the much more common access interface.

6.   Assume the following is a `modules.conf` file. Describe how each module is built for both a monolithic policy and a loadable module policy.

```
kernel = base
files = base
rpm = module
tftp = off
rpc = module
corenetwork = base
init = module
```

# Chapter 13

# Managing an SELinux System

An SELinux system looks and feels like any other Linux system in many ways. Indeed, *Red Hat Enterprise Linux* (RHEL) *is* an SELinux system whether you know it or not. However, with the enhanced security, "something" can break or not work for more reasons than before. Fixing problems may require additional administration procedures, and normal operations may now require additional steps. In this chapter, we discuss the way in which SELinux affects a Linux administrator and how to accomplish the most common important tasks.

## 13.1 SELinux Configuration and Policy Management Files

SELinux includes files that allow the management of SELinux specific additions, including the policy. This includes setting which policy to use when multiple policies are installed, label management files, and configuration files for SELinux applications and utilities.

> NOTE The files we describe in this chapter are based on a *Fedora Core 4* (FC4) system. There are subtle differences with a RHEL4 and more significant improvements in an FC5 system. We highlight these differences as appropriate throughout this chapter.

### 13.1.1 The SELinux Configuration File (/etc/selinux/config)

The SELinux configuration file, `/etc/selinux/config`, controls which policy will be loaded during the next system boot, and in what mode the system will run. We can determine the current SELinux system state using the `sestatus` command. Listing 13-1 shows an example of the `config` file.

**Listing 13-1**
Listing of /etc/selinux/conf File

```
1 # This file controls the state of SELinux on the system.
2 # SELINUX= can take one of these three values:
3 #       enforcing - SELinux security policy is enforced.
4 #       permissive - SELinux prints warnings instead of
                        enforcing.
5 #       disabled - SELinux is fully disabled.
6 SELINUX=enforcing
```

```
 7 # SELINUXTYPE= type of policy in use. Possible values are:
 8 #          targeted - Only targeted network daemons are
                         protected.
 9 #          strict - Full SELinux protection.
10 SELINUXTYPE=strict
```

This file controls two configuration settings: the *SELinux mode* and the *active policy*. The SELinux mode (determined by the SELINUX option on line 6) can be set to enforcing, permissive, or disabled. In *enforcing mode,* the policy is fully enforced. This is the primary mode of SELinux and should be used in all operational systems that require the enhanced security of SELinux. In *permissive mode,* the policy rules are *not* enforced. Instead, denials are audited, and otherwise SELinux generally does not impact the security of the system. This mode is useful for debugging and testing a policy.

In *disabled mode,* the SELinux kernel mechanism is completely turned off. A system may only be put into disabled mode when booting before the policy is loaded. This mode differs from permissive mode which has the SELinux kernel features operating but not denying any access (just auditing). In disabled mode, SELinux will not perform any action. This mode is only necessary in extreme circumstances (for example, when a policy error prevents you from even logging in, which can occur even in permissive mode) or if we truly do not want SELinux to operate.

> WARNING Be careful about switching between enforcing and permissive modes, or disabling and enabling SELinux (something you might commonly do in a development or test machine). Quite often, you can cause file labeling inconsistencies when you go back to enforcing mode. (Not to mention that you will have turned off your system's main security enhancement feature!) We discuss how to fix file labeling problems later in this chapter.

The mode set in the SELinux configuration file is used by init to configure SELinux before it loads the initial policy as part of the boot process.

The SELINUXTYPE option in the SELinux configuration file tells init which policy to load during system initialization. The string used for the setting must match the directory name where the binary version of the policy you want to use is stored. For example, throughout this book, we use a strict policy as an example. So, we set the option as SELINUXTYPE=strict and make sure that the policy we want the kernel to use is in `/etc/selinux/strict/policy/`. If we had created our own custom policy, called custom_policy, we would set the option as `SELINUX-TYPE=custom_policy` and make sure that our compiled policy is in `/etc/selinux/custom_policy/policy/`.

FC and RHEL systems provide a graphical tool (`system-config-securitylevel`) that enables us to set the options in the SELinux configuration file without having to edit the file directly (see Figure 13-1). The first two check boxes in this tool set the `SELINUX` option for us. The Policy Type drop-down box allows us to choose an active policy from the installed policies.

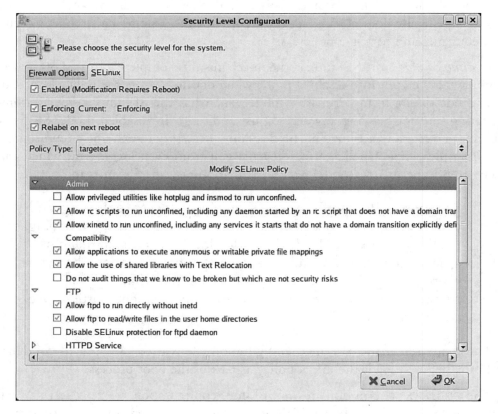

FIGURE 13-1
Red Hat security level configuration tool

## 13.1.2 The Policy Directories

As of FC3 (and RHEL4), every policy installed on a system has its own subdirectory under the `/etc/selinux/` directory. The subdirectory name corresponds to the name of the policy (for example, `strict`, `targeted`, `refpolicy`, and so on) and is used in the SELinux configuration file to tell the kernel which policy to load on boot. All path references in this section are relative to a policy directory path (that is, `/etc/selinux/[policy]/`). Here is a sample directory listing for `/etc/selinux/` from an FC4 machine:

```
# ls -lZ /etc/selinux
-rw-r--r--  root   root   system_u:object_r:selinux_config_t config
drwxr-xr-x  root   root   system_u:object_r:selinux_config_t strict
drwxr-xr-x  root   root   system_u:object_r:selinux_config_t targeted
```

As you can see, two policy directories are installed on our system: `strict` and `targeted`. Notice that the directory and the policy subdirectories are labeled with the type `selinux_config_t`. This is the type traditionally applied to binary policies and related support files. You can use `apol` to examine the rules for this type and get an idea of what programs and utilities may change policy files.

---

### Policy Directories in FC5

The layout of the policy subdirectories has changed significantly in FC5 with the introduction of the loadable policy module infrastructure (see Chapter 3, "Architecture"). The primary change is the introduction of libraries and tools to manage many of the policy files in a standardize way. This change make the installation and removal of loadable policy modules better and eases the management of many aspects of the policy. In general, it is not necessary to directly edit files in the policy subdirectories on an FC5 or other system that incorporates the loadable modules enhancements.

The commands `semodule` and `semanage` manage many aspects of the policy. The `semodule` command manages the installation, upgrading, and removing of loadable policy modules. It works on *loadable policy packages,* which include a loadable policy module and file context information. The `semanage` tool manages the addition, modification, and removal of users, roles, file contexts, *multilevel security / multicategory security* (MLS/MCS) translations, port labels, and interface labels. More information on these tools is available in their respective man pages.

---

Each policy subdirectory must follow a convention in the files they contain and how the files are labeled. This convention is used by various system utilities to help manage the policy. Generally, any well designed policy source tree will install the policy files correctly (as will properly constructed package installation scripts). Following is a listing of our `strict` policy directory, which is typical of any installed policy:

```
# ls -lZ /etc/selinux/strict
-rw-------   root root system_u:object_r:selinux_config_t   booleans
-rw-------   root root root:object_r:selinux_config_t        booleans.local
drwxr-xr-x   root root system_u:object_r:default_context_t  contexts
drwxr-xr-x   root root system_u:object_r:policy_config_t    policy
drwx------   root root system_u:object_r:policy_src_t       src
drwxr-xr-x   root root system_u:object_r:selinux_config_t   users
```

The `src/` directory is not required for a running system. It optionally contains the installed policy source tree (either the example policy or the reference policy source tree we discussed in Chapters 11, "Original Example Policy," and 12, "Reference Policy"). The actual monolithic binary policy file is stored in the `.policy/` directory, in a file named `policy.[ver]`, where `[ver]` is the version of the policy binary (for example, `policy.19`). This is the file that is loaded into the kernel during system boot.

We discuss the remaining files and directories in the following sections.

### 13.1.2.1 Installed Booleans Files

Chapter 9, "Conditional Policies," discussed how Booleans are managed in an SELinux system. An SELinux policy defines default values for all Booleans. The `booleans` file provides the distribution the ability to set persistent changes to these default values. The values in `booleans` override the policy defaults when the policy is loaded or the system is booted. The `booleans.local` file provides additional persistent values that override both the policy default values and the distribution persistent values. You should review Chapter 9 for how to set and control Boolean values. There is also a manual page, `man 8 booleans`, that provides a quick summary on the use of Booleans for FC and RHEL systems.

In FC5, where the `booleans` file is no longer present but the `booleans.local` file remains for local changes (although changes are made through `semanage/lib-semanage` and not from directly changing the file), distribution defaults are now managed in the policy itself. Red Hat sets their defaults in the policy sources, thereby removing the need to have a separate distribution file to override the policy defaults.

> NOTE In RHEL4 systems, the `booleans.local` file does not exist. Rather, the only ability to override policy default values (other than changing the policy itself) is the `booleans` file in the policy directory. The problem with a single file is that Red Hat uses this file to set distribution defaults, and utilities such as `rpm` may overwrite it destroying any local changes. In FC4, the `booleans.local` file was added to allow local changes that will not be effected by package managers.
>
> In Fedora Core 5, where the `booleans` file is no longer present but the `booleans.local` file remains for local changes (though changes are made through `semanage/libsemanage` and not from directly changing the file). Distribution defaults are now managed in the policy itself; Red Hat sets their defaults in the policy sources thereby removing the need to have a separate distribution file to override the policy defaults.

The `system-config-securitylevel` utility (see Figure 13-1) provides a graphical interface to change the local persistent values (that is, the `booleans.local` file). The items in the Modify SELinux Policy list box of this tool correspond to defined policy Booleans. The Boolean values can also be changed with the command-line tool `setsebool` and viewed with the `setatus` and `getsebool` commands (see Appendix D, "SELinux Commands and Utilities").

### 13.1.2.2 Application and File Security Contexts

The `contexts/` subdirectory, in an installed policy directory, contains various files that help system services and utilities manage file security context labeling. They also contain default security contexts for login processes. In general, these files would only be changed by a policy developer, but occasionally an administrator may have need to modify one of them. Here we summarize the purpose of some of these files:

`contexts/customizable_types`      Contains a list of types that by convention will *not* be relabeled when using the `restorecon` or `setfiles` utilities to fix file labeling issues (see later in this chapter). This feature is useful to help protect some file labels that change in intended ways from their installed defaults. Use the SELinux *application programming interface* (API) to check on whether or not a context is customizable is `is_context_customizable(3)`.

`contexts/default_contexts`  During initial login, a user may be authorized for more than one role/type pair for their login session (for example, an administrator who can log in as both an unprivileged user and a privileged user). This file provides the means by which a login process (`login`, `sshd`, and so on) determines the default role/type pair to use for initial login.

Each line in this file contains a role/type pair representing the security context of the login process followed by one or more role/type pairs that represent the default security context for the user's initial login process. For example, here are two typical lines for an SELinux system:

```
system_r:local_login_t  staff_r:staff_t user_r:user_t sysadm_r:sysadm_t
system_r:sshd_t  user_r:user_t sysadm_r:sysadm_t
```

The first line represents the local login process (login via its type `login_t`), and the second a Secure Shell login (`ssh` via its type `sshd_t`). The login process is determined by the first role/type pair on a line. For example, the assumption in this file is that the login process (for local logins) runs with a security context that has `system_r` as its role and `local_login_t` as its type. In that case, the subsequent list of role/type pairs on the same line will be used as the default security contexts (minus the user identifier) for a user login.

The first role/type pair in the list of default security context *that is authorized for the user* in the policy is used as the default security context. This file *does not authorize* a user for a role or a type; only the policy may do that (see Chapter 6, "Roles and Users"). So, for example, in the local login case for our example `default_contexts` file, if administrators log in locally (administrators are generally users authorized for both `staff_r:staff_t` and `sysadm_r:sysadm_t`), their default security context will be `staff_r:staff_t` even though they are authorized for `sysadm_r:system_t`. An administrator could later change their security context (for example, using the `newrole` command) because they are authorized for both, but the default is the "staff" set of privileges. Notice for an `ssh` login, the default is the "sysadm" set of privileges.

Note that these defaults may be overridden for a specific user if there is a `contexts/users/[USER]` file (see the following).

| | |
|---|---|
| `contexts/users/[USER]` | This file is exactly the same format as the `default_contexts` file except that it is for a particular user. If a file exists for a given user, default role/type pairs for that user are determined first from this file and then from the `default_contexts` file. |
| `contexts/failsafe_context` | If a login process cannot determine a default security context for a user, the user will not be able to log in to the system. This is most likely to be the case if the `default_contexts` file is corrupted or changed. This file provides a reasonable safe failsafe security context that allows at least the administrator to log in. It provides the last default security context that a login process attempts before failing the login attempt. It typically has a line like this: <br><br>`sysadm_r:sysadm_t` <br><br>This would at least allow administrator users to login (for example, to fix the corrupted `default_contexts` file). |
| `contexts/default_type` | This file contains a list of role/type pairs that are used by utilities, such as `newrole`. For example, if we use `newrole` to change our role but did not specify a type, the utility would consult this file to determine the default type for the role. For example, if we |

run the command `newrole -r sysadm_r`, and this file had a line such as `sysadm_r:sysadm_t`, the command would attempt to use `sysadm_t` as our default user domain type.

`contexts/files/file_contexts`

This file contains the file-related security context labeling information built as part of the policy build process and used to initialize the security context for file-related objects. It is installed here to help utilities that fix file label problems (see below).

`contexts/files/file_contexts.home_dirs`

This file is automatically generated using the `/usr/sbin/genhomedircon` script. Its format is the same as the `file_contexts` file, but it is specifically used to label user home directories.

`contexts/files/homedir_template`

This file contains a template that the `/usr/sbin/genhomedircon` script uses to generate blocks of label specifications in the `file_contexts.home_dirs` file discussed previously.

`contexts/files/media`

This file contains security contexts for storage devices mounted under the `/media/` directory. It is used by the `libselinux matchmediacon(3)` API.

`contexts/initrc_context`

This file contains the role/type pair that is used for the security context for `run_init` (that is, the program that an administrator runs to start system services in the same manner that `init` would) so that it can execute a script in `/etc/rc.d/` in a security context the same as if the script were started by `init`. This role/type pair is typically the same as `init` uses to start these services.

`contexts/removable_context` This file contains the default security context for removable media devices. This security context is used for devices not addressed by the `media` context file.

### 13.1.2.3 SELinux User Definitions

The two files in the `user/` directory were added to support better user management in an SELinux system without having to change the policy. Both files have the same format. Specifically, they list policy `user` statements as discussed in Chapter 6.

`users/system.users` This file provides the distribution provider with the ability to change role associations for users explicitly defined within the policy sources. Package managers will overwrite this file, so no local changes should be made in it. We should use the `local.user` files for locally defined users.

`users/local.users` This file is identical in function to `system.users` except that it will not be changed by the distributions. Thus, we can define local users in this file that will be added to the policy.

The `load_policy` utility reads these files and changes the binary policy before loading it into the kernel. (The change is only to the in-memory version of the policy; the on-disk binary policy does not change.) In general, for either file, if the user already exists in the policy file (that is, hard-coded in the original policy sources), the role associations are changed. Otherwise, the user is added to the policy before it is loaded into the kernel.

### 13.1.2.4 The SELinux Filesystem

The SELinux pseudo filesystem provides the primary control interface between the SELinux kernel-space *Linux Security Module* (LSM) and userspace programs (see Figure 3-2 in Chapter 3). This filesystem is usually mounted on `/selinux/`. Many SELinux utilities and APIs (provided by the `libselinux` library) use the SELinux filesystem to access the LSM module. In this section, we examine some of the files that may be of interest to an administrator. Most of the files in this filesystem exist to support APIs in `libselinux` and are not discussed here. The recommended way to use these files is through the more stable `libselinux` APIs and the tools that use that library, and not directly.

| | |
|---|---|
| `booleans/` | This directory contains a file for every Boolean defined in the policy. If the file is read, the current value of the Boolean and a pending value of the Boolean are returned. The pending value is the value the Boolean will be changed to when the Boolean values are committed (see `commit_pending_booleans`). The files have the same name as the Boolean names defined in the policy (see Chapter 9). |
| `commit_ pending_ bools` | This file signals the kernel-space security server that new policy Boolean values are ready to be activated. This feature allows multiple policy Boolean values to be changed in an atomic fashion (see Chapter 9). |
| `disable` | This file is the interface `init` uses to disable SELinux during initialization (see the SELinux configuration file above). When the initial SELinux policy is loaded or SELinux is disabled, this interface is no longer effective. Therefore, changes to the disable state always require a reboot. In general, the only way to enable/disable an SELinux system is to change `/etc/selinux/config` as discussed previously (or use the `system-config-securitylevel` shown in Figure 13-1) and reboot the system. Only `init` can use the direct interface via this file. |
| `enforce` | This file is the interface used to turn enforcing mode on and off. This is the interface that `init` uses during boot to set the mode to enforcing mode based on the settings in `/etc/selinux/config`. We can also directly use this interface to change mode by writing a `1` (enforcing mode) or `0` (permissive mode) to this file. The change in mode is effective immediately. The `setenforce` command does exactly this for us and is an easier way to change modes. |
| | It is also possible (and often desirable) to write a policy that does not allow any domain permission to toggle the mode to permissive from enforcing mode. |

load    This file is the interface used by the `load_policy` program to load a new binary policy.

mls    This file is used by the kernel to indicate whether or not MLS is activated on the system (see Chapter 8, "Multilevel Security").

policyvers    This file returns the maximum version of the policy that the kernel supports.

## 13.2 Impact of SELinux on System Administration

As with any Linux system, an administrator needs to understand numerous functions to manage an SELinux system. For the most part, SELinux is managed like an ordinary non-SELinux system. However, SELinux introduces additional requirements for several typical administrator actions. In this section, we discuss some of the areas of administration that commonly cause problems for administrators new to SELinux.

### 13.2.1 Managing Users

Adding, modifying, and deleting users has always been a challenge on SELinux systems. If not done correctly, it may appear that a user was added, but the user will not be able to log in (for example, due to problems with the `default_contexts` file). The generic SELinux user (`user_u`) resolved many of the user management difficulties for SELinux systems that do not require granular control over all Linux users. For example, when a user is added in FC4, it is automatically mapped to `user_u` simply because the new user was not defined in the policy. See Chapter 6 for more on `user_u`.

Another challenge with users is how to label files in a user's home directory, which raises several issues. One challenge is how to generalize labeling for different types of user domain types (for example, `sysadm_t` vs. `user_t`). Another is how to determine the proper labels for a user when they are added to an existing system. If a user's home directory and files are not initially labeled correctly the user may encounter a variety of problems, such as not being able to log in or not being allowed to write files in their home directory. Fortunately we have made significant progress in recent years in addressing user management in SELinux with the `./contexts/files/file_contexts.home_dirs` file discussed earlier.

### 13.2.1.1 Adding an Ordinary Unprivileged User

With the inclusion of the generic user, user_u, it is fairly straightforward to add a user to an SELinux system by just running useradd. For example, below we show the process of adding a user jimmy on a typical FC4 system:

```
# useradd jimmy
# ssh jimmy@localhost
jimmy@localhost password:
$ id
uid=502(jimmy) gid=502(jimmy) groups=502(jimmy) context=user_u:user_r:user_t
```

Notice that the user identifier in the security context is the generic user user_u. That is because we did not add jimmy as a specific SELinux user, so FC4 uses the generic user by default.

The generic user is adequate for most systems that do not need to define a large number of user roles. Most of the general purpose policies today have just a couple of roles (system, administrator, and user) and all new users are assigned to the user role (user_t domain type and user_r role) via the generic user as with jimmy. To add an ordinary unprivileged user to an SELinux system where user_u is defined, we do not have to do anything beyond the normal useradd command.

### User Management in FC5

In FC5, user management is improved by the introduction of the semanage tool. The semanage tool manages both SELinux users, their role authorizations, and the mapping of Linux users to SELinux users. (See Chapter 6 for more information on user mapping.) For instance, consider the following example:

```
# semanage user -a -R "sysadm_r user_r" staff_u
# semanage user -l

                MLS/         MLS/
SELinux User    MCS Level    MCS Range               SELinux Roles
root            s0           SystemLow-SystemHigh    sysadm_r user_r
system_r
staff_u         s0           s0                      sysadm_r user_r
system_u        s0           SystemLow-SystemHigh    system_r
user_u          s0           SystemLow-SystemHigh    sysadm_r user_r
system_r
# semanage login -a -s staff_u joe
# semanage login -l
```

| Login Name | SELinux User | MLS/MCS Range |
|---|---|---|
| __default__ | user_u | s0 |
| joe | staff_u | s0 |
| root | root | SystemLow-SystemHigh |

In this example, we add a new SELinux user named `staff_u` that is authorized for the roles `sysadm_r` and `user_r`, list all the SELinux users, add a new user mapping for the user `joe` to the SELinux user `staff_u`, and list all the user mappings.

Notice that because FC5 uses the optional MLS features by default (to implement the MCS policy), MLS ranges are shown for users.

### 13.2.1.2 Adding a Privileged User Account

For administrators, a `root` user is typically defined in the SELinux policy that corresponds to the root user account. The policy assigns this user a role (`sysadm_r`) and user domain (`sysadm_t`) that has sufficient privilege to manage a system. Although `root` in SELinux is not all-powerful as in a standard Linux system, it does have the authority to run all the programs that have the various privileges required. Users authorized to use the `root` user account (and its associated privileged user domain types) are generally given a different unprivileged user domain type (`staff_t`). This user domain type is exactly like the unprivileged domain type of ordinary users (`user_t`) except that it may transition into the privileged user domain type (`sysadm_t`).

To add a privileged user, we run the `useradd` command as we did with an ordinary user account. However, we also need to edit the active policy's `local.users` file discussed previously. In this file, we define the user to the policy. For example, if we want to create a Linux user called "admin" that has administrator privileges, we would do the following:

```
# useradd admin                                        # create ordinary user
# vi /etc/selinux/strict/users/local.users             # add admin as privileged
# load_policy /etc/selinux/strict/policy/policy.19      # reload policy
# genhomedircon                                         # fix homedir template
# restorecon -R /home/admin                             # fix admin's homedir
```

We used the same `useradd` command to create the account and home directory. However, this time we need to tell SELinux about the new user so that it does not treat it as a generic user. We do this by editing the `local.users` file and adding the following line:

```
user admin roles { staff_r sysadm_r };
```

This line lets the SELinux policy know of the user and defines the authorized roles for the user. To make this change effective, we need to run `load_policy` to reload the policy into the kernel. At this point, the user is defined in both the system and the SELinux policy. However, the user home directories are still labeled as if `admin` were a generic user. (This is the behavior of `useradd`.) So, next we need to run the `genhomedircon` utility that updates the home directory file security context file (`./contexts/files/file_contexts.home_dirs`) with the new user. We then use the `restorecon` program to update the new user's home directory based on its current roles.

At this point, the user account is now created and authorized for both the unprivileged administrator role (`staff_r`) and the privileged administrator role (`sysadm_r`). The behavior of most login processes is such that the default security context for a user authorized for both roles is `staff_r` so that an administrator logs in as an unprivileged user by default. For example, let's log in as our new administrator account:

```
# ssh admin@localhost
admin@localhost's password:
$ id
uid=506(admin) gid=506(admin) groups=506(admin) context=admin:staff_r:staff_t
```

Notice that our role and user domain type are `staff_r` and `staff_t`, respectively. As we said, these are the `unprivileged` role and type for administrative users. Choosing staff over sysadm as the default login role/type is a function of the default context for `sshd` as we discussed earlier. Processes with the `staff_t` domain type have essentially no more privilege than any other ordinary user, other than it is allowed to transition to the privileged domain type `sysadm_t`. For example, to perform administrator functions we could then do the following:

```
$ su
Password:
Your default context is root:sysadm_r:sysadm_t.
```

```
Do you want to choose a different one? [n]
# id
uid=0(root) gid=0(root)
groups=0(root),1(bin),2(daemon),3(sys),4(adm),6(disk),10(wheel)
context=root:sysadm_r:sysadm_t
```

The su program (which also acts like a login program) has its default context set up such that a user running with the staff role/type will default to the sysadm role/type. Notice that the su program also asks whether you want to provide a security context other than the defined default. You always have the option of trying something other than the defined default (if the policy permits it).

> NOTE In FC5, su does not change the security context. Instead, users must use the newrole command. For example, the command newrole -r sysadm_r -t sysadm_t makes the equivalent change to the security context as the FC4/RHEL 4 example above.

Remember that the default contexts for the various login programs define only defaults; they do not allow the necessary access. Only the policy may do that, as we discuss in Part II of this book.

### 13.2.1.3 Changing a User Role

Changing the role of an existing user is similar to adding a new administrator role. We just need to skip the useradd step because the user already exists. For example, to change the admin user we just defined back to an ordinary user we do the following:

```
# vi /etc/selinux/strict/users/local.users
# load_policy /etc/selinux/strict/policy/policy.19
# genhomedircon
# restorecon -R /home/admin
# ssh admin@localhost
admin@localhost's password:
id
uid=506(admin) gid=506(admin) groups=506(admin) context=user_u:user_r:user_t
```

To remove the administrator privileges, we remove the user from the local.users file, reload the policy, and fix the user home directory security contexts. As you can see, when we log in as this user now, our role/type is user and our user is now the generic user user_u.

## 13.2.2 Understanding Audit Messages

In Chapter 5, "Type Enforcement," we discuss the policy rules that control the generation of audit messages from SELinux. Here we discuss the format of the messages generated from these policy statements and how to examine and manage the audit messages on a production system.

On systems that utilize the kernel audit framework (including FC4 and 5), SELinux audit messages are stored in both the system log (that is, syslog) files and the audit daemon log files. By default, the audit daemon log is stored in `/var/log/audit/audit.log`, and the system log file is stored in `/var/log/messages`. The audit daemon log contains all the audit messages created by the audit framework including *access vector cache* (AVC) messages. AVC messages are the audit messages generated by SELinux as a result of access denials and `auditallow` rules. The system log contains more general SELinux audit messages.

> NOTE  The original version and first update of RHEL4 did not use the audit framework. This means that *all* SELinux audit message should be in the system log, typically `/var/log/messages`. Beginning with RHEL4 update 2, the audit framework is used and it should work just like FC4. Some SELinux messages are still sent to the system log because they are generated as kernel messages rather than audit messages (for example, policy load messages), and any SELinux audit messages generated before the audit daemon is started are also stored in the system log. In FC5, the audit daemon is optional, meaning that SELinux messages will appear in either system log or the audit log depending of the configuration of the system.

### 13.2.2.1 General SELinux Audit Messages

SELinux generates audit messages at system initialization, policy load, and when Boolean states are changed. The policy does not control the generation of these messages; they are hard-coded into SELinux. All the general SELinux audit messages are currently stored in the system audit logs.

At system initialization, SELinux generates audit messages that give information about the configuration of the SELinux LSM module. For example, here are the first audit messages from SELinux after booting the system:

```
1 Jul 22 11:44:25 milton kernel: Security Framework v1.0.0 initialized
2 Jul 22 11:44:25 milton kernel: SELinux:  Initializing.
3 Jul 22 11:44:25 milton kernel: SELinux:  Starting in permissive mode
4 Jul 22 11:44:25 milton kernel: selinux_register_security:  Registering
                secondary module capability
5 Jul 22 11:44:25 milton kernel: Capability LSM initialized as secondary
```

The initialization of the LSM framework generates line 1, and the subsequent initialization of SELinux generates line 2. This system was booted in permissive mode, which is reflected on line 3. Lines 4 and 5 show that the capability LSM module, which implements the standard Linux capability semantics, was registered as a secondary LSM module to SELinux.

Later in system initialization, the policy is loaded for the first time, generating audit messages similar to the following example:

```
 1 Jul 22 11:44:26 milton kernel: security:  3 users, 6 roles, 1341 types, 62
   bools
 2 Jul 22 11:44:26 milton kernel: security:  55 classes, 345260 rules
 3 Jul 22 11:44:26 milton kernel: SELinux:  Completing initialization.
 4 Jul 22 11:44:26 milton kernel: SELinux:  Setting up existing superblocks.
 5 Jul 22 11:44:26 milton kernel: SELinux: initialized (dev dm-0, type ext3),
   uses xattr
 6 Jul 22 11:44:26 milton kernel: SELinux: initialized (dev tmpfs, type tmpfs),
   uses transition SIDs
 7 Jul 22 11:44:26 milton kernel: SELinux: initialized (dev selinuxfs, type
   selinuxfs), uses genfs_contexts
 8 Jul 22 11:44:26 milton kernel: SELinux: initialized (dev mqueue, type
   mqueue), not configured for labeling
 9 Jul 22 11:44:26 milton kernel: SELinux: initialized (dev hugetlbfs, type
   hugetlbfs), not configured for labeling
10 Jul 22 11:44:26 milton kernel: SELinux: initialized (dev devpts, type
   devpts), uses transition SIDs
11 Jul 22 11:44:26 milton kernel: SELinux: initialized (dev eventpollfs, type
   eventpollfs), uses genfs_contexts
12 Jul 22 11:44:26 milton kernel: SELinux: initialized (dev tmpfs, type tmpfs),
   uses transition SIDs
13 Jul 22 11:44:26 milton kernel: SELinux: initialized (dev futexfs, type
   futexfs), uses genfs_contexts
14 Jul 22 11:44:26 milton kernel: SELinux: initialized (dev pipefs, type
   pipefs), uses task SIDs
15 Jul 22 11:44:26 milton kernel: SELinux: initialized (dev sockfs, type
   sockfs), uses task SIDs
```

```
16 Jul 22 11:44:26 milton kernel: SELinux: initialized (dev proc, type proc),
   uses genfs_contexts
17 Jul 22 11:44:26 milton kernel: SELinux: initialized (dev bdev, type bdev),
   uses genfs_contexts
18 Jul 22 11:44:26 milton kernel: SELinux: initialized (dev rootfs, type
   rootfs), uses genfs_contexts
19 Jul 22 11:44:26 milton kernel: SELinux: initialized (dev sysfs, type sysfs),
   uses genfs_contexts
20 Jul 22 11:44:26 milton kernel: SELinux: initialized (dev usbfs, type usbfs),
   uses genfs_contexts
```

The first two lines of this example show the audit message generated every time a policy is loaded. As you can see, this message shows statistics about the policy loaded. This example policy has 3 users, 6 roles, 1,341 types, 62 Booleans, 55 object classes, and 345,260 rules. Recall from Chapter 5 that rules are expanded in the kernel binary policy format (for policies before version 20). The number of rules shown in these audit messages are for the expanded rule format, which will be significantly higher than the number of rules present in the policy source files.

This example also shows the audit messages generated at the first policy load. Lines 3 and 4 show the completion of SELinux initialization, including the initialization of SELinux support for filesystem objects that were mounted before the first policy load. Lines 5 through 20 show the initialization of each filesystem object and the associated labeling behavior.

The final general SELinux audit message is generated when the state of Booleans is committed. For example, consider the following two audit messages:

```
Dec  2 14:07:41 book kernel: security: committed booleans { allow_write_xshm:1,
mozilla_read_content:0, mail_read_content:0, cdrecord_read_content:0,
allow_ptrace:0, read_untrusted_content:0, write_untrusted_content:0,
user_dmesg:0, use_nfs_home_dirs:0, allow_execmem:0, allow_execstack:0,
allow_execmod:0, use_samba_home_dirs:0, user_tcp_server:0, allow_ypbind:0,
allow_kerberos:1, user_rw_usb:1, user_net_control:0, user_direct_mouse:0,
user_rw_noexattrfile:1, read_default_t:1, staff_read_sysadm_file:1,
allow_httpd_user_script_anon_write:0, allow_httpd_staff_script_anon_write:0,
user_ttyfile_stat:0, httpd_unified:0, httpd_builtin_scripting:1,
httpd_enable_cgi:1, httpd_enable_homedirs:1, httpd_ssi_exec:1, httpd_tty_comm:0,
httpd_can_network_connect:0, allow_httpd_sys_script_anon_write:0,
allow_httpd_anon_write:0, httpd_suexec_disable_trans:0, comsat_disable_trans:0,
cron_can_relabel:0, cupsd_lpd_disable_trans:0, cvs_disable_trans:0,
dbskkd_disable_trans:0, disable_evolution_trans:0, ftpd_is_daemon:1, ftp_home_di
```

```
Dec  2 14:07:41 book kernel: :1, allow_ftpd_anon_write:0, disable_games_trans:0,
inetd_child_disable_trans:0, allow_java_execstack:0, ktalkd_disable_trans:0,
disable_mozilla_trans:0, allow_mplayer_execstack:0, allow_user_mysql_connect:0,
named_write_master_zones:0, secure_mode:0, user_ping:0,
allow_user_postgresql_connect:0, pppd_for_user:0, pppd_can_insmod:0,
rlogind_disable_trans:0, nfs_export_all_rw:0, nfs_export_all_ro:0,
allow_gssd_read_tmp:1, rsync_disable_trans:0, allow_rsync_anon_write:0,
allow_smbd_anon_write:0, samba_enable_home_dirs:0,
allow_saslauthd_read_shadow:0, spamassasin_can_network:0, squid_connect_any:0,
ssh_sysadm_login:1, allow_ssh_keysign:0, run_ssh_inetd:0,
stunnel_disable_trans:0, stunnel_is_daemon:0, swat_disable_trans:0,
telnetd_disable_trans:0, disable_thunderbird_trans:0, uucpd_disable_trans:0,
xdm_sysadm_login:0 }
```

Boolean commit messages show the current state of *all* Booleans in the current policy. As the preceding example shows, this can result in long audit messages that are split into two separate messages by the audit framework.

### 13.2.2.2 AVC Messages

AVC messages are the audit messages generated as a result of access denials that were not suppressed by `dontaudit` messages or permitted access that matches an `auditallow` rule. These messages contain valuable information that can be used for system monitoring, administration, and policy development. Chapter 14, "Writing Policy Modules," illustrates how these messages are used as part of policy development.

AVC messages are stored in the audit daemon log. The following is a representative example of an AVC message:

```
type=AVC msg=audit(1135098961.471:1770): avc:  denied  { read }  for  pid=19850
comm="cat" name="sysadm_tmp_file" dev=dm-0 ino=67482
scontext=kmacmillan:staff_r:staff_t tcontext=kmacmillan:object_r:sysadm_tmp_t
tclass=file
```

This AVC message shows that a process with the security context `kmacmillan:staff_r:staff_t` was denied read access to a file with the security context of `object_r:sysadm_tmp_t`. The process was executing the `cat` program on the file `/tmp/sysadm_tmp_file`.

As you can see, almost all the fields in AVC messages are in the form of name=value. For example, in the field `pid=19850`, the name of the field is `pid`, and the value, which is formatted according to the information in the field, is `19850`.

To understand the AVC messages, let's examine each of the fields. All AVC messages have the following six fields:

type     Messages generated by the audit daemon can be one of several types; the type of a message is identified by a prefix consisting of `type=` and the message type. The prefix in this message, `AVC`, identifies the message as an AVC message. Other message types (which are not SELinux specific) include `USER_AUTH`, `LOGIN`, `SYSCALL`, and `PATH`.

msg      The audit framework prepends a message header to all audit messages that includes a timestamp and serial number separated by colon. The timestamp, 1135098961.471 in this message, is the number of seconds and nanoseconds since the Epoch (the standard form for time on UNIX systems). The serial number, 1770 in this message, is used to identify multiple, related audit messages generated by the same event. For example, a single event might generate both a system call and AVC audit message; both of these messages would have the same serial number.

avc      This field, which is the only exception to the name/value format, identifies whether the audit message was generated from an allowed or denied access, and the permissions that were allowed or denied. There can be one or more permissions, all from a single object class, which is identified in a separate field. The keyword `denied` indicates this message is from an access denial. Allowed access is denoted by `granted`.

scontext The security context of the source, or subject.

tcontext The security context of the target, or object.

tclass   The object class of the target, or object. The allowed or denied permissions are from the access vector defined for this object class (see Chapter 4, "Object Classes and Permissions").

The rest of the fields in an AVC message provide additional detail about the access that was allowed or denied. The details are often object-class specific. For example, audit messages from file-related object classes often include the inode number of the object, and audit messages from network-related objects often include an IP address or port number. The preceding example has the following fields, which are typical for file-related object classes:

pid      The identifier of the process that attempted the access. This field is most useful to distinguish between multiple invocations of the same application or for servers that include multiple, long-running processes (for example, apache).

comm     The name of the executable file associated with the process. This field only includes the name of the file without a full path specification.

dev and ino   The device (dev) and inode number (ino) of the file-related object associated with the target. Together these can be used to identify the object if a full path is not available in the audit message.

name     The name of the file-related object. This field includes only the name of the file-related object without a full path.

> NOTE Under the new Linux audit framework, every AVC message is followed by a SYSCALL message with the same audit event ID. The SYSCALL message has the correct and full exe and path fields (corresponding to the comm and name fields, respectively) for the associated AVC message. This was done to supply the information that is not available at the time the AVC message is generated.

AVC messages generated as a result of allowed access are similar. Consider the following example:

```
type=AVC msg=audit(1135098723.344:1742): avc:   granted   { load_policy } for
pid=19618 comm="load_policy" scontext=root:sysadm_r:load_policy_t
tcontext=system_u:object_r:security_t tclass=security
```

This example AVC message shows the successful loading of a policy. The audit-allow rule that caused the generation of this AVC message is commonly included in policies because of the importance of loading a policy.

### 13.2.2.3 Using Seaudit to View Audit Logs

`Seaudit`, a tool included with the Setools package along with `apol`, parses and displays SELinux audit messages. Figure 13-2 shows a typical `seaudit` session.

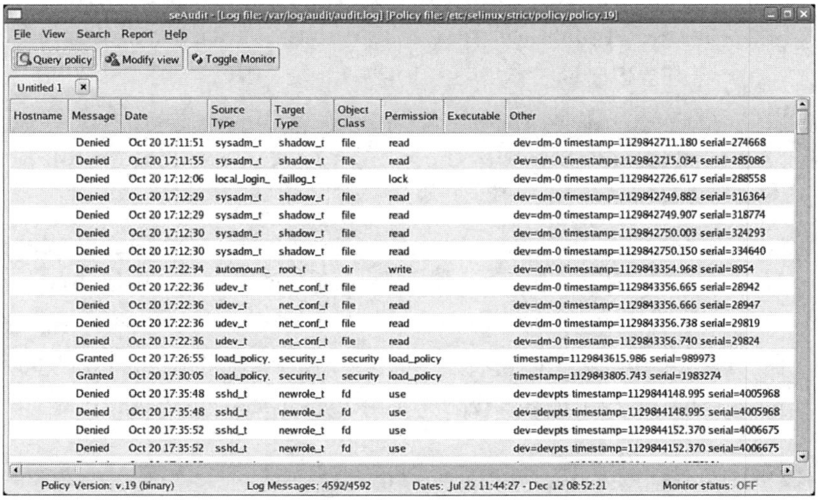

**FIGURE 13-2**
A typical seaudit session

This tool parses the log file and displays a list of all the messages. Sixteen customizable fields may be displayed for each message. The Modify view button allows you to create custom filters so that only "interesting" data displays. You may save the view as a report.

### 13.2.3 Fixing Problems: File-Related Object Labeling

During normal system use, file-related objects should not need labeling or relabeling. All of the files that are part of the operating system should be given a correct initial security context during installation, and the policy rules relating to labeling ensure that newly created files have the correct security context. However, during policy development, system setup, and system administration, files may need to be relabeled.

> WARNING  Relabeling objects has security risks, including poten-
> tial race conditions, inconsistent access control being applied to
> objects, malicious hard links, and the lack of full revocation sup-
> port. For the best security, relabeling should be avoided entirely
> on a production system. When it is unavoidable, however, the sys-
> tem should be in a known good state (for example, immediately
> after system installation or after verifying that the integrity of the
> system has not been compromised). For large labeling changes,
> such as would result from a large policy change, it is better for the
> system to be removed from production use.

### 13.2.3.1 File-Related Object Labeling Commands

Four main commands are used to relabel file-related objects: chcon(8),
restorecon(8), setfiles(8), and fixfiles(8). All these commands relabel
files, but they each have a specific use. Typically, chcon and restorecon are used
for small labeling changes, whereas setfiles and fixfiles are used for larger
changes.

The chcon command sets the same security context, or a portion of a security
context, for one or more files based on user input. It is the most basic labeling command and its use is analogous to chmod(1). For instance, consider the following
example:

```
$ mkdir public_html
$ ls -dZ public_html/
drwxrwxr-x   joe joe joe:object_r:user_home_dir_t public_html/
$ chcon -t httpd_user_content_t public_html/
$ ls -dZ public_html/
drwxrwxr-x   joe joe joe:object_r:httpd_user_content_t public_html/
```

In this example, we changed the security context of a newly created directory,
which was automatically assigned the security context joe:object_r:
user_home_dir_t, to joe:object_r:httpd_user_content_t. The -t option
alone specifies that the type of file should be changed while the rest of the security
context is retained.

The `restorecon` command is similar to `chcon` but sets the security context of file-related objects based on the default file context files for the current policy. The user, therefore, does not specify a security context. Instead, `restorecon` matches the filename with an entry in the file contexts files and applies the specified security context. In some sense, it is *restoring* the correct security context. For example, consider the following:

```
$ mkdir public_html
$ ls -Zd public_html/
drwxrwxr-x  joe joe joe:object_r:user_home_dir_t public_html/
$ /sbin/restorecon public_html/
$ ls -Zd public_html/
drwxrwxr-x  joe joe user_u:object_r:httpd_user_content_t public_html/
```

This example is functionally the same as the previous example using `chcon` but only because the file context files for this policy has the following entry:

```
/home/[^/]*/public_html(/.+)? user_u:object_r:httpd_user_content_t
```

The file context entry specifies that directories in user home directories named `public_html/` should be labeled `user_u:object_r:httpd_user_content_t`.

We can also use the `restorecon` command to check whether the labels on file-related objects match the specification in the file contexts files. For example:

```
$ mkdir public_html
$ /sbin/restorecon -nv public_html/
/sbin/restorecon reset /home/joe/public_html context
joe:object_r:user_home_dir_t->user_u:object_r:httpd_user_content_t
```

In this example, we specified the `-n` to prevent `restorecon` from actually performing the relabeling and the `-v` option, which causes `restorecon` to print in labeling changes performed. Together these options result in `restorecon` printing any differences between the on-disk labeling and the file contexts files.

Finally, the `restorecon` command can be used to recursively relabel a large number of files. The option `-R` directs `restorecon` to descend into directories, relabeling all the contained files and directories. For example, consider the following session:

```
$ mkdir public_html
$ scp -r gotham:public_html/*.html public_html/.
kmacmillan@gotham's password:
2005d10.html                    100%   28KB  28.3KB/s   00:00
2005d11.html                    100%   22KB  21.5KB/s   00:00
2005d12.html                    100% 8575    8.4KB/s   00:00
2005d7.html                     100%   15KB  14.9KB/s   00:00
calendar.html                   100% 2839    2.8KB/s   00:00
coding_style.html               100% 1040    1.0KB/s   00:00
$ ls —scontext public_html/*
joe:object_r:user_home_dir_t public_html/2005d10.html
joe:object_r:user_home_dir_t public_html/2005d11.html
joe:object_r:user_home_dir_t public_html/2005d12.html
joe:object_r:user_home_dir_t public_html/2005d7.html
joe:object_r:user_home_dir_t public_html/calendar.html
joe:object_r:user_home_dir_t public_html/coding_style.html
$ /sbin/restorecon -R public_html/
$ ls —scontext public_html/*
user_u:object_r:httpd_user_content_t public_html/2005d10.html
user_u:object_r:httpd_user_content_t public_html/2005d11.html
user_u:object_r:httpd_user_content_t public_html/2005d12.html
user_u:object_r:httpd_user_content_t public_html/2005d7.html
user_u:object_r:httpd_user_content_t public_html/calendar.html
user_u:object_r:httpd_user_content_t public_html/coding_style.html
```

In this example, we copied several Web pages from another system, which all automatically received the security context joe:object_r:user_home_dir_t. Running restorecon recursively on the entire directory relabeled all the files to user_u:object_r:httpd_user_content_t. Here all the files received the same security context because they matched the same file context specification, but it is equally possible that some files would have matched other specifications and received different labels.

Despite its ability to recursively relabel files and directories, restorecon is not normally used to make large labeling changes such as would result from switching policies. For this, we should use the fixfiles command. The fixfiles command is actually a shell script that uses either restorecon or setfiles depending on the requested use. Like restorecon, fixfiles uses the file contexts files for the current policy. Instead of requiring the user to specify which files or directories to relabel or check, `fixfiles` works on all mounted filesystems that support extended attribute labeling. The `fixfiles` command has three modes, one of which must be specified when running the command:

- `check`   Show any file-related objects whose security context does not match what is specified in the file context files.

- `restore`   Relabel any file-related objects whose security context does not match what is specified in the file context files.

- `relabel`   Like `restore`, but also optionally removes any files in the `/tmp` directory first.

For example, following is how to relabel all file-related objects on the system:

```
# /sbin/fixfiles relabel

    Files in the /tmp directory may be labeled incorrectly, this command
    can remove all files in /tmp.  If you choose to remove files from /tmp,
    a reboot will be required after completion.

    Do you wish to clean out the /tmp directory [N]? n
```

The final command, `setfiles`, requires that the user manually specify which file contexts files to use and the starting directory. In addition, `setfiles` does not traverse across mount points when descending into directories, meaning that it must be run once for each mounted filesystem that uses extended attribute labeling. It is more common to use `fixfiles` unless additional flexibility is needed.

### 13.2.3.2 Automatic Relabeling

In addition to using the file-related object labeling commands to relabel an entire system, a system can be automatically relabeled during boot. This is done by creating a file in the root of the filesystem called `/.autorelabel`. For example:

```
# touch /.autorelabel
```

If this file is present during boot, the entire system is relabeled and the file is removed. The kernel may also be booted with the `autorelabel` argument that causes a relabel upon boot without the `/.autorelabel` file. When an SELinux system is booted with SELinux disabled, the `/.autorelabel` file is automatically created.

### 13.2.4 Managing Multiple Policies

In general, a production system should not maintain multiple policies and switch between them. However, this is a common scenario for development systems and may be an issue for some types of deployments and policy updates.

The procedure for switching policies is as follows:

1. Install the policy under its name in `/etc/selinux/`. (For example, for a policy called `mypol`, install it in `/etc/selinux/mypol/`, the actual binary policy file should end up in `/etc/selinux/mypol/policy/policy.[ver]`).

2. Change the policy name in the SELinux configuration file (`/etc/selinux/config`). This can be done with a text editor or using the `system-config-securitylevel` command.

3. Set the system to automatically relabel the entire system on the next reboot by using the `/.autorelabel` file as discussed earlier.

4. Reboot the system.

On reboot, the system will load the new policy and relabel all of the file-related objects.

## 13.3 Summary

- The `/etc/selinux/config` file controls which policy is active (that is, will be loaded during boot and used by system utilities). This file also controls the default state of SELinux during boot: enforcing (normal), permissive, and disabled.

- Installed policies and their support files are stored in `/etc/selinux/[policyname]/`. For example, the default targeted policy in FC4 is stored in `/etc/selinux/targeted/`. Besides the actual binary policy file, this directory contains a number of files that are used by system utilities to manage portions of the policy (for example, users) or object labeling decisions. If installed, this directory also contains the policy sources.

- SELinux provides userspace interfaces to the SELinux LSM modules as a filesystem that is usually mounted on `/selinux/`. Most of the files in this filesystem support APIs in the `libselinux` library.

- The SELinux generic user, user_u, provides a means to add users to an SELinux system without having to add them to the policy. user_u defines permissions and role authorization for normal, unprivileged users. To add a privileged administrator user, you must add it to the policy by editing the active policy's local.users file and reloading the policy.

- SELinux produces two types of audit messages: general and AVC. General audit messages record events relating to system initialization, policy load, and Boolean value changes. AVC messages (by far the most common) record access denial and allowance events.

- In general, file security context labels should not require maintenance on a running production system. However, if the policy is updated or you are using a development/experimental system, you may need to manually fix or repair object labeling. SELinux provides four commands to aide in this task: chcon(8), restorecon(8), setfiles(8), and fixfiles(8). (See Appendix D for a description of these commands.)

## Exercises

1. Explain the differences between enforcing, permissive, and disabled mode.

2. How would you temporarily switch between enforcing and permissive mode?

3. Why don't we need to add ordinary unprivileged users to the policy via the local.users files?

4. Change a Boolean value. Make sure the change will be preserved.

5. Create a new user account system administrator named joe that may su into the privileged root account with administrator privilege.

6. Given the following audit message, write a corresponding allow rule that would allow the denied access in the future:

   ```
   type=AVC msg=audit(1129843356.666:28947): avc:  denied  { read } for
   pid=1730 comm="grep" name=ifcfg-lo dev=dm-0 ino=1243093 scontext
   =system_u:system_r:udev_t tcontext=system_u:object_r:net_conf_t
   tclass=file
   ```

7. Use restorecon to check the file labels for all files and directories in /etc/. How would you change the command to restore any labels that do not match the file context files?

# 14

# Writing Policy Modules

## In this chapter

This chapter brings together all we have learned throughout the book. It presents a guided tour of writing a policy module for both the example and reference policies.

## 14.1 Overview of Writing a Policy Module

In this chapter, we walk through the process of creating a policy module, bringing together all we have learned throughout the book. We discuss all the steps required to create a policy module for both the original example policy (Chapter 11, "Original Example Policy") and the newer reference policy (Chapter 12, "Reference Policy"). For most steps in the process, we present the general idea of the step and then show examples of that step from both kinds of policies. We think this "by example" procedure is the best way to understand both policies.

Our presentation is only an introduction to this topic; the only way to learn the techniques and strategies of an experienced policy writer is to attempt to write modules. The outline we present provides a starting point for your own policy development. The best guide in the future is the experience you gain through applying SELinux to solve your own security challenges.

The policy module that we create in this chapter is for the IRC daemon available as part of *Fedora Core 4* (FC4). We chose this example because it is a straightforward, yet representative example of a network-facing daemon.

In our experience, writing a policy module involves three basic steps: preparation and planning, initial policy module creation, and testing and analysis. In preparation and planning, we gather critical information, create a test environment, and specify the security goals for the policy module. In the initial policy creation step, we combine the gathered information and security goals to create a first version of the policy module. In the testing and analysis step, we determine the correctness of the policy module in terms of functionality and security.

In the remainder of this chapter, we present these steps in an idealized, linear fashion. In reality, policy writing is often an iterative process of writing, testing, and research. In particular, the testing and analysis step usually results in changes to the policy module.

## 14.2 Preparation and Planning

Before writing our policy module, we need to gather some information about the applications, create a test configuration, and specify our security goals. We also must choose our target platform and policies. For our example, we target an FC4 system and create policy modules for the example strict policy (see Chapter 11) and a strict reference policy (see Chapter 12).

### 14.2.1 Gathering Application Information

Like all policy modules, our IRC module is primarily about creating a domain for the IRC daemon. Writing the policy module will require as much information as possible about how this daemon is designed and functions. In general, the better we understand the target application, the better the security and functionality of the resulting policy. Of particular importance is the application architecture (for example, number and purpose of processes and resources), administration (for example, documentation of configuration files), and existing security information. Existing information about the security of the applications, including hardening guidelines, can prove helpful. Be warned, however, that security guidelines often do not give the full picture of the application security or necessarily meet your specific security needs.

Here is a sample of the information we collected about the Hybrid IRC daemon, which is standard for FC4:

- The daemon consists of a single process that listens for incoming IRC connections on port 6667.

- The IRC protocol (originally described in RFC 1459) is normally implemented on top of TCP, and there is a single connection per client.

- A number of configuration files are stored, by default, under `/etc/ircd/`.

- By default, the IRC daemon has private log files stored under `/var/log/ircd/`.

- The FC4 RPMs create a data directory for the IRC daemon under `/var/lib/`.

- Like most daemons configured for FC, the IRC daemon creates files in `/var/run/` storing the PID of the active daemon process while running.

- Other than the logs, PID, `/var/lib/`, and configuration files and directories, the IRC daemon does not require any other significant filesystem access.

## 14.2.2 Creating a Test Environment

Writing policy modules requires testing and (in many cases) experimentation. Therefore, we need a test installation of the service on a system configured for policy development. Like all testing, it is important that the test environment match the deployment environment as closely as possible. For our purposes, we create a basic example IRC daemon installation on FC4. We also need a test system with an IRC client on the same network.

We start with a basic workstation installation of FC4, to which we need to add the example and reference policy source files and the IRC daemon. Appendix A, "Obtaining SELinux Sample Policies," provides instructions on how to obtain and install the required strict example policy and reference policy. The IRC daemon is installed with the following `yum` command. (As `root` running with the security `root:sysadm_r:sysadm_t`, for example, log in and `su` to `root` on a standard FC4 system.)

```
# yum install ircd-hybrid
```

This installs the IRC daemon, startup scripts, and example configuration files. We are now ready to edit the configuration file `/etc/ircd/ircd.conf`. We start with the file `simple.conf` provided in the documentation (`/usr/share/doc/ircd-hybrid-7.2.0/simple.conf`) and modify it slightly (the `server info sid` and the `operator` password options), as shown in Listing 14-1 (changed options are bolded).

> TIP  For policy development, it is important to understand all the files and directories that are part of an application. The command `rpm -ql ircd-hybrid` will list the files and directories installed as part of the IRC daemon package.

**Listing 14-1**
**Modified IRC Daemon Configuration File (ircd.conf)**

```
1     # Hybrid 7 minimal example configuration file
2     #
3     # $Id: simple.conf 33 2005-10-02 20:50:00Z knight $
4     #
5     # This is a basic ircd.conf that will get your server running with
6     # little modification.  See the example.conf for more specific
7     # information.
8     #
9     # The serverinfo block sets your server's name.  Fields that may
10    # be set are the name, description, vhost, network_name,
11    # network_desc,  and hub.
12
13    serverinfo {
14        name = "irc.example.com";
15        sid = "1se";
16        description = "Test IRC Server";
17        hub = no;
18    };
19
20    # The administrator block sets up the server administrator
21    # information, that is shown when a user issues the /ADMIN
22    # command.  All three fields are required.
23
24    administrator {
25        description = "Example, Inc Test IRC Server";
26        name = "John Doe";
27        email = "jdoe@example.com";
28    };
29
30    # Class blocks define the "privileges" that clients and servers
31    # get when they connect.  Ping timing, sendQ size, and user
32    # limits are all controlled by classes.  See example.conf for
33    # more information
34
35    class {
36        name = "users";
37        ping_time = 90;
38        number_per_ip = 0;
39        max_number = 200;
40        sendq = 100000;
41    };
42
43    class {
44        name = "opers";
45        ping_time = 90;
46        number_per_ip = 0;
47        max_number = 10;
48        sendq = 500000;
49    };
50
```

Listing 14-1 (continued)
Modified IRC Daemon Configuration File (ircd.conf)

```
51   # Auth blocks define who can connect and what class they
52   # are put into.
53
54   auth {
55       user = "*@*";
56       class = "users";
57   };
58
59   # Operator blocks define who is able to use the OPER command
60   # and become IRC operators. The necessary fields are the
61   # user@host, oper nick name, and the password, encrypted with
62   # the mkpasswd program provided.
63
64   operator {
65       name = "JohnDoe";
66       user = "*@*.example.com";
67       # MD5 encrypted password - "selinux"
68       password = "$1$gv.dyLcq$wr2F.9AqZ/2EKxcsCexKm1";
69       encrypted = yes;
70       class = "opers";
71   };
72
73   # Listen blocks define what ports your server will listen to
74   # client and server connections on. ip is an optional field
75   # (Essential for virtual hosted machines.)
76
77   listen {
78       port = 6667;
79   };
80
81   # Quarantine blocks deny certain nicknames from being used.
82
83   quarantine {
84       nick = "dcc-*";
85       reason = "DCC bots are not permitted on this server";
86   };
87
88   quarantine {
89       nick = "LamestBot";
90       reason = "You have to be kidding me!";
91   };
92
93   quarantine {
94       nick = "NickServ";
```

```
95          reason = "There are no Nick Services on this Network";
96     };
97
98     # The general block contains most of the configurable options
99     # that were once in config.h. The most important ones are below.
100    # For the rest, please see example.conf. Note that variables not
101    # mentioned here are set to the ircd defaults, which are listed in
102    # src/s_conf.c:set_default_conf.
103
104    general {
105        hide_spoof_ips = yes;
106        # Identd is commonly disabled on modern systems
107        disable_auth = yes;
108        # Control nick flooding
109        anti_nick_flood = yes;
110        max_nick_time = 20;
111        max_nick_changes = 5;
112
113        # Show extra warnings when servers connections cannot succeed
114        # because of no "N" line (a misconfigured connect block)
115        warn_no_nline = yes;
116    };
```

The three changes that we make to this file are to change the unique identifier of the server (line 15), the administrative password (line 68), and disable the use of identd (line 107). After saving this file as /etc/ircd/ircd.conf, we start the server (for now, on a permissive mode SELinux FC4 system) with the following command:

```
# setenforce 0
# /etc/init.d/ircd start
Starting ircd: ircd: version hybrid-7.2.0
ircd: pid 9052
ircd: running in background mode from /usr/lib/ircd [  OK  ]
```

These commands show the ircd service starting successfully. Once started, the log file /var/log/ircd/ircd.log should contain the following entry (at or near the end):

```
[2006/2/3 04.25] Server Ready
```

Note that there may be some *access vector cache* (AVC) messages generated because we have not yet installed a specific policy for the server. We can ignore them for now.

### 14.2.3 Specifying Security Goals

The last preparation step is to specify the security goals for our IRC policy module. Without understanding what security means for this application, we have no basis for making security-critical decisions during the development of our policy module proverb. This is our chance to think about the overall security concerns before we become immersed in the many details of the policy language. (Or in the words of the proverbial saying, let's examine the "forest" before we are overwhelmed by the "trees.") We will revisit these security goals after creating our policy module to determine whether we meet our objectives (to determine whether our forest is what we expected after we spend all our time planting trees).

How to correctly determine and specify security goals is a large topic itself, beyond the scope of this book. It comes mostly with experience and the correct mind set. Following are some security goals for a basic policy module for our IRC daemon:

- **ircd service confinement**   Confine the ircd service to the minimum amount of access required to function properly. This will prevent an exploitable flaw in the service from being used to compromise the entire system.

- **System protection**   Protect the system from the IRC service to prevent privilege escalation through exploiting IRC.

- **Configuration file protection**   Protect the configuration files from modification by nonadministrative domains (for example, domains other than sysadm_t) and the service itself.

These security goals are just a starting point. Many other security goals are possible for an IRC daemon or similar applications.

## 14.3 Creating an Initial Policy Module

In the next steps, we create an initial policy based on the information we gathered and the security goals we specified. To create the most secure policy module possible, we want to create a policy that grants only the access that we expect the IRC daemon to require before testing begins.

### 14.3.1 Creating Policy Module Files

We begin our policy module development by creating all the policy module files for both the example and reference policies.

#### 14.3.1.1 Example Policy

As we discussed in Chapter 11, a policy module in the example policy consists of two files: the policy rules file (`.te`) and the file context files (`.fc`). Therefore, for the IRC daemon policy module we need to create the files `domains/programs/ircd.te` and `file_contexts/programs/ircd.fc`. Initially, these files can be empty.

> NOTE All path names are relative to the root of the policy source directory. For the example policy this is `/etc/selinux/strict/src/policy`, and for the reference policy this is `/etc/selinux/refpolicy/src/policy`. We also refer to just the filenames (for example `ircd.te`, meaning `/etc/selinux/strict/src/policy/domains/programs/ircd.te` for the example policy).

#### 14.3.1.2 Reference Policy

As discussed in Chapter 12, a reference policy module consists of three files: the private policy file (`.te`), an external interface file (`.if`), and the labeling policy file (`.fc`). Because the IRC daemon is a system service, we put its policy module files in the services layer (that is, `policy/modules/services/ircd.te`, `policy/modules/services/ircd.if`, and `policy/modules/services/ircd.fc`). The files `ircd.if` and `ircd.fc` can be empty initially, but the file `ircd.te` must minimally declare the module as follows:

```
# Ircd policy module declaration
policy_module(ircd, 1.0)
```

### 14.3.2 Declaring Types

The next step is to declare the appropriate domain and object types for our policy module. Remember, access can be allowed only between types, so we must identify and declare the correct set of types to represent our application architecture. In many ways, this is the most important step in policy module development. If we do not correctly identify the needed types, particularly domain types, the rest of the policy cannot be correct.

Policy modules typically declare types for the following:

- **Domains**   One or more domain types for the application processes

- **Entrypoints**   At least one entrypoint executable file type for each of the domains

- **Application resources**   One or more types for the resources controlled by the application (for example, temporary files, configuration files, log files, socket files, and so on)

The types we declare for our IRC daemon policy module closely match the high-level architecture of target application. Our IRC types are as follows:

- `ircd_t`   Domain type for the IRC daemon process

- `ircd_exec_t`   Entrypoint type for the IRC daemon executable file

- `ircd_var_run_t`   File type for PID files stored in the directory `/var/run`

- `ircd_conf_t`   File type for the IRC daemon configuration files

- `ircd_log_t`   File type for the IRC daemon logs

- `ircd_var_lib_t`   File type for files stored in `/var/lib/ircd`

This is a representative set of types for a simple daemon such as IRC. Notice that other than the first two types, which are the domain type and the entrypoint type (`ircd_t` and `ircd_exec_t`), all these types are for application resources controlled by `ircd`.

### 14.3.2.1 Example Policy

Recall that in the example policy, types are declared directly (including the list of associated attributes) or through macros. Listing 14-2 shows our type declarations for the example policy IRC daemon policy module. We have directly declared all the types in our policy module instead of using macros to make the policy module clearer. Notice that each of these types has a variety of attributes. For example, the log file type `ircd_log_t` has the attributes `file_type`, `sysadmfile`, and `log-file`. We determined the needed attributes based on the intended use for each type (that is, `ircd_log_t` is intended as a type for a log file that can be accessed by system administrators) and the available attributes.

Listing 14-2
Example Policy: IRC Daemon Type Declarations (ircd.te)

```
1     ##################################################
2     #
3     # Type declarations
4     #
5
6     # ircd domain
7     type ircd_t, domain;
8
9     # ircd entrypoint
10    type ircd_exec_t, file_type, exec_type;
11
12    # PID file /var/run/ircd.pid
13    type ircd_var_run_t, file_type;
14
15    # configuration files
16    type ircd_conf_t, file_type, sysadmfile;
17
18    # log files
19    type ircd_log_t, file_type, sysadmfile, logfile;
20
21    # files and directories under /var/lib/ircd
22    type ircd_var_lib_t, file_type, sysadmfile;
```

> TIP Recall that the file `attrib.te` in the root directory of the example policy source contains all the attribute declarations and documentation about their use.

## 14.3.2.2 Reference Policy

In the reference policy, types are always directly declared and do not include attributes. Listing 14-3 shows our type declarations for the IRC reference policy private policy module (`ircd.te`). Notice that each of the type declarations is paired with an interface call (to another, existing policy module) that is functionally equivalent to the attribute assignments in the example policy module in Listing 14-2. For instance, line 24 declares the type `ircd_conf_t`, and line 25 marks it as a configuration file by calling the interface `files_config_file()`. Determining which interface to call for each type declaration is similar to determining which attributes

are required, although the reference policy has better documentation and is easier
to understand and use.

Listing 14-3
Reference Policy:  IRC Daemon Private Type Declarations (ircd.te)

```
1       # Ircd policy module declaration
2       policy_module(ircd, 1.0)
3
4       #########################################
5       #
6       # Type declarations
7       #
8
9       # ircd domain
10      type ircd_t;
11
12      # ircd entrypoint
13      type ircd_exec_t;
14
15      # mark ircd_t as a domain and ircd_exec_t
16      # as an entrypoint into that domain
17      init_daemon_domain(ircd_t, ircd_exec_t)
18
19      # PID file /var/run/ircd.pid
20      type ircd_var_run_t;
21      files_pid_file(ircd_var_run_t)
22
23      # configuration files
24      type ircd_conf_t;
25      files_config_file(ircd_conf_t)
26
27      # log files
28      type ircd_log_t;
29      logging_log_file(ircd_log_t)
30
31      # files and directories under /var/lib/ircd
32      type ircd_var_lib_t;
33      files_type(ircd_var_lib_t)
```

> TIP Remember that the reference policy includes a significant
> amount of documentation generated from the source. The docu-
> mentation is the best way to find appropriate interfaces like those
> used above in the type declarations. You can view the documen-
> tation at the reference policy Web site or locally after running the
> command make html in the reference policy source directory. In
> FC5, the HTML documentation is available under /usr/share/
> doc/selinux-policy-x.y.z/html/.

### 14.3.3 Allowing Initial Restrictive Access

The next step is to grant permissions based on our best understanding of the initial, restrictive access needed for the IRC domain type (`ircd_t`). The access allowed should reflect both our security goals and the functional needs of the IRC daemon. In our experience, it is helpful to first plan the access required in an abstract way because writing raw SELinux policy rules requires significant attention to detail. By creating a higher-level plan first, it is easier to keep the larger security goals in mind. For example, we expect the `ircd_t` domain to have the following access consistent with our security goals:

- **Log files**   Create, read, and append (`ircd_log_t`)

- **Configuration files**   Read (`ircd_conf_t`)

- **PID files**   Create, read, and write (`ircd_var_run_t`)

- **var files**   Create, read, and write (`ircd_var_lib_t`)

- **Network access**

  - Network interfaces. TCP send and receive on all

  - Nodes. TCP send and receive to all

  - Ports. TCP `name_bind` on IRC ports and send and receive to all others

  - Resolve DNS names

- **Use shared libraries**

- **Read localization resources**

- **Read directories and files commonly needed by network applications**
  include the device `/dev/null` and sysctl configuration data under the `/proc/` directory

  > NOTE We have chosen to give fairly broad network access initially. We are not, for example, restricting the network interfaces and hosts with which the IRC daemon can communicate. This is a common practice that removes the need to customize the policy based on local network settings and topology. It is possible (and often desirable), however, to add these restrictions if customizing the policy for each server because local adjustments are feasible.

### 14.3.3.1 Example Policy

In the example policy, we allow access using a combination of direct `allow` rules and example policy macros. For example, consider Listing 14-4. (This policy section is added after the type declarations that were discussed in Listing 14-2.)

Listing 14-4
Example Policy: IRC Daemon Initial Allowed Access (ircd.te)

```
1     ###################################################
2     #
3     # Ircd - core access
4     #
5
6     # Log files - create, read, and append
7     append_logdir_domain(ircd)
8
9     # Configuration files - read
10    allow ircd_t ircd_conf_t : dir r_dir_perms;
11    allow ircd_t ircd_conf_t : file r_file_perms;
12    allow ircd_t ircd_conf_t : lnk_file { getattr read };
13
14    # PID file - create, read, and write
15    file_type_auto_trans(ircd_t, var_run_t, ircd_var_run_t, file)
16    allow ircd_t var_t : dir search;
17
18    # /var/lib/ircd files/dirs - create, read, write
19    file_type_auto_trans(ircd_t, var_lib_t, ircd_var_lib_t, file)
20    allow ircd_t ircd_var_lib_t : dir rw_dir_perms;
21
22    # Network access - the ircd daemon is allowed to send
23    # and receive network data to all nodes and ports over
24    # all network interfaces (through the can_network_server
25    # macro). Additionally, it can name_bind to the ircd
26    # port (ircd_port_t).
27    allow ircd_t ircd_port_t:tcp_socket name_bind;
28    can_network_server(ircd_t)
29
30    # use shared libraries
31    uses_shlib(ircd_t)
32
33    # read localization data
34    read_locale(ircd_t)
35
36    # read common directories / files including
37    #       * proc
38    #       * /dev/null
39    #       * system variables
40    allow ircd_t { self proc_t }:dir r_dir_perms;
```

```
41    allow ircd_t { self proc_t }:lnk_file { getattr read };
42    allow ircd_t null_device_t:chr_file rw_file_perms;
43    allow ircd_t sysctl_type:dir r_dir_perms;
44    allow ircd_t sysctl_type:file r_file_perms;
45    allow ircd_t sysctl_t:dir search;
46    allow ircd_t sysctl_kernel_t:dir search;
47    allow ircd_t sysctl_kernel_t:file { getattr read };
```

Notice that each commented block of rules corresponds to one of the items in our list of initial accesses specified. To allow access between types declared in our module, we primarily use `allow` rules directly. For example, lines 10–12 permit the domain type `ircd_t` to read configuration files (that is, files and directories with the type `ircd_conf_t`). There are exceptions, however, where policy rules between our IRC types are added to our policy through macros. For example, the `file_type_auto_trans()` macro on line 19 allows the domain type `ircd_t` to create, read, and write files with the type `ircd_var_run_t` (that is, `/var/run/ircd.pid`).

Access to types declared outside of our policy module is also allowed using a combination of direct `allow` rules and macros. For example, line 42 allows the `ircd_t` domain to read and write character device files with the type `null_device_t` (that is, `/dev/null`) using an `allow` rule that directly references both types. This is an example of one of the example policy's biggest weakness of the example (that is, closely coupled policy modules). Because our IRC module must have explicit knowledge of types declared in other modules (`null_device_t`), the implementation of the two modules are intertwined. By contrast, the access required to use shared libraries is allowed entirely by the `uses_shlib()` macro, as shown on line 31.

In the example policy, the choice of whether to use direct access or macros is primarily one of style and whether an appropriate macro is available. There are no strong conventions as in the reference policy.

The network access for the IRC daemon is allowed through the `can_network()` macro. Unfortunately, this macro allows more access than our (or nearly any) application needs, although it has been improved from its original implementation. In particular, it allows sending and receiving raw and UDP packets in addition to TCP. We used the macro despite the additional access it allows to reflect common practice for the example policy. There is no convenient way, other than direct allow rules, to allow a smaller subset of network access and most policy modules use the `can_network()` macro to allow network access.

> TIP Most of the macros used in our policy module reflect common practice for the example policy. Reading existing policy modules is the best way to familiarize yourself with the common macros and how they are used. Reading the macros in the `macros/*.te` files is also helpful.

### 14.3.3.2 Reference Policy

Access in the reference policy is allowed by a combination of `allow` rules and call to interfaces defined in other modules. Recall from Chapter 12 that access to any type not declared in our policy module is allowed only through an interface. So, unlike our example policy module, the IRC daemon private policy file will never reference types from other modules directly. Listing 14-5 is the reference policy version of our initial restrictive access for the IRC daemon (which would be in the `ircd.te` file following the rules in Listing 14-3).

**Listing 14-5**
**Reference Policy: IRC Daemon Private Allowed Access (ircd.te)**

```
1    ###########################################
2    #
3    # Ircd - core access
4    #
5
6    # Log files - create, read, and append
7    allow ircd_t ircd_log_t : dir ra_dir_perms;
8    allow ircd_t ircd_log_t : file { create ra_file_perms };
9    logging_filetrans_log(ircd_t, ircd_log_t, file)
10   logging_search_logs(ircd_t)
11
12   # Configuration files - read
13   allow ircd_t ircd_conf_t : dir r_dir_perms;
14   allow ircd_t ircd_conf_t : file r_file_perms;
15   allow ircd_t ircd_conf_t : lnk_file { getattr read };
16
17   # PID file - create, read, and write
18   allow ircd_t ircd_var_run_t : dir rw_dir_perms;
19   allow ircd_t ircd_var_run_t : file create_file_perms;
20   files_filetrans_pid(ircd_t, ircd_var_run_t, file)
21
22   # /var/lib/ircd files/dirs - create, read, write
23   allow ircd_t ircd_var_lib_t : dir create_dir_perms;
24   allow ircd_t ircd_var_lib_t : file create_file_perms;
25   files_filetrans_var_lib(ircd_t, ircd_var_lib_t, { file, dir })
26
```

```
27      # Network access - the ircd daemon is allowed to send
28      # and receive network data to all nodes and ports over
29      # all network interfaces. Additionally, it can name_bind
30      # to the ircd port (ircd_port_t)
31      allow ircd_t self : tcp_socket create_stream_socket_perms;
32      corenet_tcp_sendrecv_all_if(ircd_t)
33      corenet_tcp_sendrecv_all_nodes(ircd_t)
34      corenet_tcp_sendrecv_all_ports(ircd_t)
35      corenet_non_ipsec_sendrecv(ircd_t)
36      corenet_tcp_bind_all_nodes(ircd_t)
37      corenet_tcp_bind_ircd_port(ircd_t)
38      sysnet_dns_name_resolve(ircd_t)
39
40      # use shared libraries
41      libs_use_ld_so(ircd_t)
42      libs_use_shared_libs(ircd_t)
43
44      # read localization data
45      miscfiles_read_localization(ircd_t)
46
47      # read common directories / files including
48      #         * /etc (search)
49      # * system variables
50      files_search_etc(ircd_t)
51      kernel_read_kernel_sysctl(ircd_t)
52      kernel_read_system_state(ircd_t)
53      kernel_read_all_sysctl(ircd_t)
```

Again, each commented block represents where we have allowed all of the initial access listed. The choice of using direct `allow` rules versus interfaces in the reference policy follows a strong convention. It is more straightforward than the choice of using direct `allow` rules versus macros in the example policy because of the clear encapsulation of types in the reference policy.

Notice that the interfaces used in the reference policy are clearer and more explicit than the macros in the example policy. The explicit nature of interfaces sometimes makes a reference policy module more verbose, as is the case in allowing the use of shared libraries on lines 41 and 42. However, this verbosity also allows for more choice and better granularity of access. For example, the network access that we allow in the reference policy version of our policy module exactly matches the initial restrictive access that we intended. This is possible because the network access is broken down into many interfaces, each allowing a small portion of the access, rather than one broad macro in the example policy (that is, the `can_network()` macro).

## 14.3.4 Allowing Domain Transitions and Authorizing Roles

For our new domain to be effective, we must permit other domains to transition to our new domain. To do this, we must create `type_transition` rules, allow the domain transition, and authorize our domain type for the appropriate roles.

As a general practice, the number of domains that may transition to a daemon domain should be limited. The IRC daemon package that comes with FC4 includes `init` scripts to allow starting from `init` during boot or directly by the system administrator. To permit both of these startup methods, we must ensure our policy does the following:

- Allow `initrc_t` to automatically transition to `ircd_t` through `ircd_exec_t` (allow `init` to start the daemon).

- Allow `sysadm_t` to automatically transition to `ircd_t` through `ircd_exec_t` (allow system administrator to start the daemon).

- Authorize `ircd_t` for the `system_r` role (authorize for `init`'s role).

- Automatically role transition from `sysadm_r` to `system_r` on execution of `ircd_exec_t` (authorize for system administrator's role).

> NOTE Using a role transition rule to run the IRC daemon in the `system_r` role is not required. We could have authorized `ircd_t` for `sysadm_r` instead. The use of the role transition is standard practice for `system_r`, however, because it results in more similar security contexts regardless of whether the daemon as started by `init` or the system administrator. The tradeoff is that the user, presumably `root`, must be authorized for both roles.

### 14.3.4.1 Example Policy

We accomplish the domain transitions and role authorizations in the example policy as shown in Listing 14-6.

Listing 14-6
Example Policy: IRC Daemon Domain and Role Authorizations (ircd.te)

```
1    ##################################################
2    #
3    # Domain Transitions and Role Authorizations
4    #
5
6    role system_r types ircd_t;
7
8    # allow init to start ircd
9    domain_auto_trans(initrc_t, ircd_exec_t, ircd_t)
10
11   # allow sysadm_t to start ircd_t
12   domain_auto_trans(sysadm_t, ircd_exec_t, ircd_t)
13   role_transition sysadm_r ircd_exec_t system_r;
```

The `domain_auto_trans()` macro both allows the domain transition and adds the necessary type transition rule required for an automatic domain transition.

### 14.3.4.2 Reference Policy

We have already accomplished this step in the reference policy by using the interface `init_daemon_domain()` on line 17 in Listing 14-3. This interface allows all the domain and role transitions described previously in a consistent, configurable manner.

## 14.3.5 Integrating into the System Policy

Our initial restrictive access is primarily concerned with allowing the access needed by the IRC daemon. We also have to allow other domain types access to the resource types in our policy module. For example, log files are useful only if an administrator tool can read them. This is what we mean by integrating into the system policy.

Much of the more common additional access is handled automatically through attributes in the example policy and interfaces in the reference policy. For example, adding the `file_type` attribute (example policy) or calling the `files_type()` interface (reference policy) allows a variety of domains, including `sysadm_t`, to read files with the associated file type.

We often need to allow module-specific access for certain types of policy resources that we can grant to other domains. To demonstrate, let's expand our modules to allow other domains to read files with the type `ircd_log_t`.

### 14.3.5.1 Example Policy

There is no defined way to allow access from other policy modules in the example policy. The rules can simply be placed either in our policy module or in the other policy, with types from both policy modules being directly referenced. For instance, the policy statements in Listing 14-7 allow `logrotate_t` to read the IRC daemon log files. In an example policy, we could have just as easily put these rules in the logrotate module.

Listing 14-7
Example Policy: IRC Daemon, Allowing Access for logratate Domain (ircd.te)

```
1     ##################################################
2     #
3     # Integrate Into System Policy
4     #
5
6     ifdef('logrotate.te', `
7     allow logrotate_t ircd_log_t:dir search;
8     allow logrotate_t ircd_log_t:file { getattr read };
9     ')
```

Notice that we wrap these rules in an `m4` `ifdef` statement that prevents the inclusion of the rules if the `logrotate` policy module is not present during policy compilation. The challenge with this approach of course, is that it is difficult to know where all the rules for a given type are located in the policy. This is another example of one of the motivations for the improvements in reference policy (that is, strong modularity and encapsulation).

### 14.3.5.2 Reference Policy

Allowing access from other policy modules is more structured in the reference policy through the use of interfaces. Listing 14-8 shows the external interface file (`ircd.if`) for our IRC policy module that declares an interface for reading the IRC daemon log files. As discussed in Chapter 12, in the reference policy, the only way for other modules to access a private type is to use an interface.

Listing 14-8
Reference Policy: IRC Daemon External Interface Example (ircd.if)

```
1     ## <summary>IRC daemon</summary>
2
3     #########################################
4     ## <summary>
5     ##        Read IRC daemon log files.
6     ## </summary>
7     ## <param name="domain">
8     ##        Domain allowed access.
9     ## </param>
10    #
11    interface(`irc_read_log',`
12        gen_require(`
13            type ircd_log_t;
14        ')
15
16        logging_search_logs($1)
17        allow $1 ircd_log_t:dir search_dir_perms;
18        allow $1 ircd_log_t:file r_file_perms;
19    ')
```

Allowing access by other domains is a simple matter of calling this interface in the other policy modules. For example, to allow `logrotate` to read the IRC log files, the following interface call would be added to the `logrotate` policy module:

```
irc_read_log(logrotate_t)
```

> NOTE Notice that the interface file also includes the module summary documentation and summaries for each interface. This allows us to generate detailed interface documentation from reference policy source files.

## 14.3.6 Creating the Labeling Policy

The next step, which completes our initial policy module, is to create and apply the labeling policy in the form of file contexts statements, as discussed in Chapter 10, "Object Labeling." The labeling policy assigns the types intended for filesystem objects to files and directories. We use the information we gathered about the location of files and directories installed with the IRC daemon to derive statements.

### 14.3.6.1 Example Policy

Listing 14-9 shows the file context file (`ircd.fc`) for the example policy. Notice that this file is a straightforward, hard-coded listing of files and directories for the IRC daemon in a syntax understandable by the `setfiles` program (see Chapter 10).

**Listing 14-9**
**Example Policy: IRC Daemon File Contexts File (ircd.fc)**

```
1      # ircd labeling policy
2      # file: ircd.fc
3      /usr/bin/ircd           --        system_u:object_r:ircd_exec_t
4      /etc/ircd(/.*)?                   system_u:object_r:ircd_conf_t
5      /var/log/ircd(/.*)?              system_u:object_r:ircd_log_t
6      /var/lib/ircd(/.*)?              system_u:object_r:ircd_var_lib_t
7      /var/run/ircd(/.*)?              system_u:object_r:ircd_var_run_t
```

### 14.3.6.2 Reference Policy

Listing 14-10 shows the labeling policy file (`ircd.fc`) for our reference policy module.

**Listing 14-10**
**Reference Policy: IRC Daemon Labeling Policy File (ircd.fc)**

```
1      # ircd labeling policy
2      # file: ircd.fc
3      /usr/bin/ircd  --      gen_context(system_u:object_r:ircd_exec_t, s0)
4      /etc/ircd(/.*)?        gen_context(system_u:object_r:ircd_conf_t, s0)
5      /var/log/ircd(/.*)?    gen_context(system_u:object_r:ircd_log_t, s0)
6      /var/lib/ircd(/.*)?    gen_context(system_u:object_r:ircd_var_lib_t, s0)
7      /var/run/ircd(/.*)?    gen_context(system_u:object_r:ircd_var_run_t, s0)
```

The reference policy `ircd.fc` is essentially identical to the equivalent file in the example policy, except for the use of the `gen_context()` template interface macro. This template interface allows the reference policy to transparently handle *multi-level security / multicategory security* (MLS/MCS) and non-MLS/MCS policies from the same policy source. All security contexts must be specified using `gen_context()` in the reference policy.

## 14.3.7 Applying the Policy

The final step before testing is to compile, install, load, and apply the policy. This is done in the same way for both the example and reference policies. First, compile, install, and load the policy using the following commands:

```
# make && make install && make load
```

If this is successful you should not see any errors and the build system will show a successful policy load. For example, for the example policy, the end output for a successful compile will be similar to the following. The reference policy output will be different but equally obscure to the uninitiated.

```
Building file contexts fliles...
/usr/bin/checkpolicy  -o policy.20 policy.conf
/usr/bin/checkpolicy:  loading policy configuration from policy.conf
/usr/bin/checkpolicy:  policy configuration loaded
/usr/bin/checkpolicy:  writing binary representation (version 20) to policy.20
Compiling policy ...
/usr/bin/checkpolicy  -o /etc/selinux/strict/policy/policy.20 policy.conf
/usr/bin/checkpolicy:  loading policy configuration from policy.conf
/usr/bin/checkpolicy:  policy configuration loaded
/usr/bin/checkpolicy:  writing binary representation (version 20) to
/etc/selinux/strict/policy/policy.20
/usr/bin/checkpolicy  -c 19 -o /etc/selinux/strict/policy/policy.19 policy.conf
/usr/bin/checkpolicy:  loading policy configuration from policy.conf
/usr/bin/checkpolicy:  policy configuration loaded
/usr/bin/checkpolicy:  writing binary representation (version 19) to
/etc/selinux/strict/policy/policy.19
install -m 644 tmp/system.users /etc/selinux/strict/users/system.users
install -m 644 tmp/customizable_types
/etc/selinux/strict/contexts/customizable_types
install -m 644 tmp/port_types /etc/selinux/strict/contexts/port_types
Installing file contexts files...
install -m 644 file_contexts/homedir_template
/etc/selinux/strict/contexts/files/homedir_template
install -m 644 file_contexts/file_contexts
/etc/selinux/strict/contexts/files/file_contexts
Loading Policy ...
/usr/sbin/load_policy /etc/selinux/strict/policy/policy.19
touch tmp/load
```

In addition, the policy load can be seen in the audit log. For example, here is an audit message generated from a load policy event:

```
Feb 13 23:07:48 kernel: audit(1139890068.158:15709654): avc:  granted  {
load_policy } for  pid=1173 comm="load_policy"
scontext=root:sysadm_r:load_policy_t tcontext=system_u:object_r:security_
t tclass=security
```

---

### Building and Installing Policy Modules on FC5

Building and installing policy modules is greatly simplified in FC5 through the use of loadable policy modules and the development environment installed with the policy rpm. To build our reference policy IRC module as a loadable module, we need to 1) create a new directory, 2) copy our IRC source files to the new directory (that is, `ircd.te`, `ircd.fc`, and `ircd.if`), and 3) copy the example loadable module `Makefile` from `/usr/share/selinux/devel/Makefile` to the new directory. After these steps, we will have a directory that looks like the following:

```
$ ls
ircd.fc   ircd.if   ircd.te   Makefile
```

Running the `make` command should now build a loadable policy module package. For example:

```
$ make

Compiling targeted ircd module

/usr/bin/checkmodule:   loading policy configuration from
tmp/ircd.tmp

/usr/bin/checkmodule:   policy configuration loaded

/usr/bin/checkmodule:   writing binary representation (version
5) to tmp/ircd.mod
Creating targeted ircd.pp policy package

rm tmp/ircd.mod tmp/ircd.mod.fc
```

This creates the policy package `ircd.pp`. The example `Makefile` builds the policy against the current active policy using the reference policy interfaces installed in `/usr/share/selinux/devel/include`. The policy package can be installed with the following command (as the system administrator):

```
# /usr/sbin/semodule -i ircd.pp
```

If there are no errors our loadable policy module is installed. The `semodule` command will show the loadable modules installed with the following command:

```
# /usr/sbin/semodule -l
ircd    1.0
```

As you can see, we have successfully installed our IRC policy package, and it is now active as part of the running policy.

---

After the policy is successfully installed and loaded, we can relabel the filesystem to ensure that our new file contexts file is effective. Again, this procedure is the same for the example and reference policy. Below, we use the restorecon command to relabel all the files and directories specified in the file context file for our module:

```
# restorecon /usr/bin/ircd
# restorecon -R /etc/ircd/ /var/log/ircd/ /var/lib/ircd/
```

We can verify that the labeling occurred correctly using the ls command (note you can also use ls -z), as follows:

```
# ls -scontext /usr/bin/ircd /var/log/ircd/
system_u:object_r:ircd_exec_t    /usr/bin/ircd

/var/log/ircd/:
system_u:object_r:ircd_log_t      ircd.log
```

> TIP Labeling a filesystem with newly defined types can only occur after loading the new policy because the kernel must be aware of the new types.

After these steps, our initial policy module for the IRC daemon is now complete and ready for testing.

## 14.4 Testing and Analyzing the Policy

In the testing and policy analysis step, we verify that our policy module is functionally correct and meets our security goals.

### 14.4.1 Testing the Policy Module

Assuming that we were able to compile, install, and load our new policy, and that we successfully labeled the filesystem, we are ready to begin functional testing of the IRC daemon and policy module. We perform only basic functional tests in this step. More extensive testing should be performed before using this policy module in a production environment.

First, we verify that the system is in permissive mode and the daemon is stopped. Running in permissive mode allows the IRC daemon to function properly so that we can see all of the requested access that our policy module did not allow. (Recall that in permissive mode, access denials are audited but not enforced.) The commands to switch to permissive mode and stop the IRC daemon are as follows:

```
# setenforce 0
# /etc/init.d/ircd stop
Stopping ircd:                                              [  OK  ]
```

Next, we need to use the `seaudit` utility from the setools package, which should be installed on FC4 systems (see Appendix D, "SELinux Commands and Utilities," for an overview of setools, the open source package which, among other tools, includes `apol`). With `seaudit`, open the audit log and turn on monitoring using the Toggle Monitor button, ensure the status is On on the status bar. (see Figure 14-1). We use `seaudit` to view the audit log to determine whether the IRC daemon requests additional access not allowed by our policy module. We can also view the log files using the `tail` utility with the command `tail -f /var/log/audit/audit.log`.

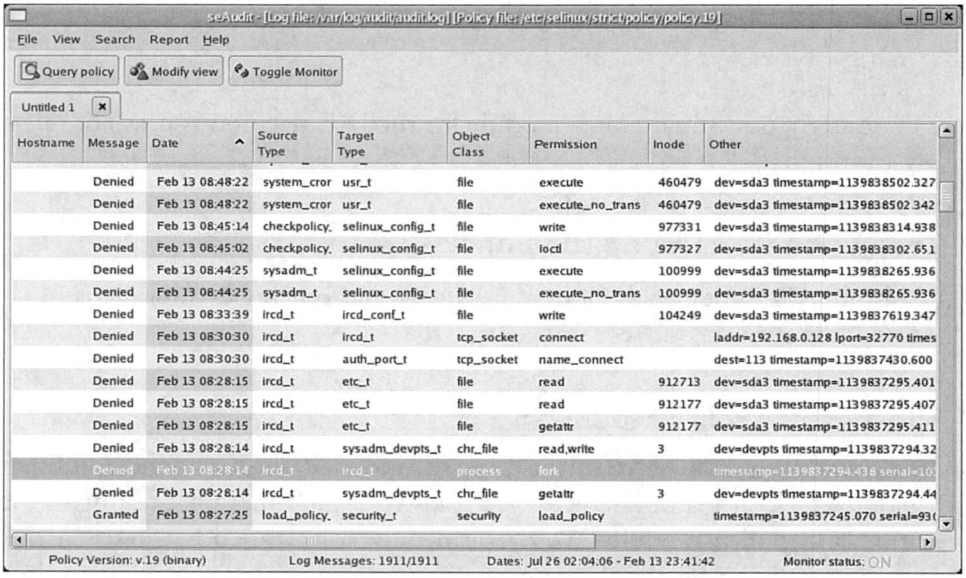

FIGURE 14-1
Seaudit displaying audit messages generated while testing the IRC daemon

After starting `seaudit`, we start the IRC daemon with the following command:

```
# setenforce 0
# /etc/init.d/ircd start
Starting ircd: ircd: version hybrid-7.2.0
ircd: pid 9052
ircd: running in background mode from /usr/lib/ircd [  OK  ]
```

If everything is configured correctly, we should be able to display the IRC daemon process with the correct type using the `ps` command, as follows:

```
# ps axZ | grep ircd
root:system_r:ircd_t            1519 ?        00:00:00 ircd
```

We see that the IRC daemon is running with the correct security context.

Next, we connect to the IRC daemon using an IRC client. For example, Figure 14-2 shows the `xchat` client successfully connecting to the IRC daemon.

> TIP Make certain that the firewall settings for the test system allow IRC traffic if you are using an IRC client on a separate machine.

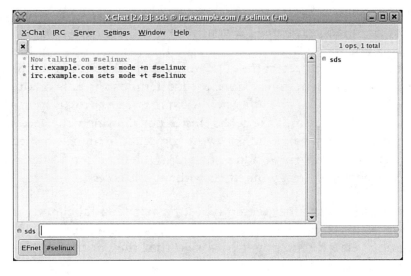

FIGURE 14-2
Connecting to the IRC daemon using `xchat`

### 14.4.1.1 Evaluating Audit Messages and Allowing Additional Access

After exercising the IRC daemon with simple tests, such as joining and talking on a channel, we can examine the audit logs for denials related to our policy module. Figure 14-1 shows the relevant audit messages generated during our testing of the IRC daemon. These messages show the IRC daemon requesting five additional accesses, which we did not allow in our initial policy:

- Read configuration files in /etc/ (etc_t).

- Fork another process.

- Read and write to pseudo terminals owned by the system administrator (sysadm_devpts_t).

- Write access to the configuration file (ircd_conf_t).

We must consider each of the access requests to determine whether additional access should be added to our policy module. It is important to not allow additional access simply because the IRC daemon attempted the access. When evaluating audit messages, the goal is not to just add allow rules until the denial messages disappear. Instead, each requested access should be carefully considered and, if it conflicts with our security goals, not permitted if the application can continue to function properly.

For example, in the audit messages listed previously, we see that the IRC daemon attempts to access its configuration file (ircd_conf_t) for writing. Allowing this access violates our security goal to protect the configuration file. Also, allowing the daemon to read and write system administrators' pseudo terminals is unnecessary and opens a potential attack vector. The other access requests appear to be appropriate, so we add allow rules to permit the access. Instead of allowing write access to the configuration files and allowing read and write to pseudo terminals owned by the system administrator, however, we add dontaudit rules and test to determine whether the IRC daemon correctly functions without this access.

> TIP Audit messages with unexpected types may signal a labeling problem. For example, a denial message for sysadm_t accessing an IRC daemon related type might be a sign that the entrypoint (/usr/bin/ircd) is not labeled correctly (ircd_exec_t), preventing the domain transition.

### 14.4.1.2 Adding Additional Access in the Example Policy

The additional access is allowed in the example policy with the following new policy statements in the `ircd.te` file:

```
allow ircd_t self : process fork;
allow ircd_t etc_t : file r_file_perms;
```

Audit messages related to the access that we are not permitting are suppressed with the following `dontaudit` rules:

```
dontaudit ircd_t ircd_conf_t : file write;
dontaudit ircd_t sysadm_devpts_t : chr_file { getattr read write };
```

### 14.4.1.3 Adding Additional Access in the Reference Policy

To add the other additional accesses, we add the following policy statements in the `ircd.te` file:

```
allow ircd_t self : process fork;
files_read_etc_files(ircd_t)
```

As before, audit messages related to the access that we are not permitting are suppressed with the following `dontaudit` rule and interface call:

```
dontaudit ircd_t ircd_conf_t : file write;
userdom_dontaudit_use_sysadm_ptys(ircd_t)
```

### 14.4.1.4 Testing the Additional Access

After compiling, installing, and reloading the modified policy, we must test the IRC daemon again. This time we will test in enforcing mode. Enforcing mode can be set and the IRC daemon restarted using the following commands:

```
# setenforce 1
# /etc/init.d/ircd restart
Stopping ircd:                                        [  OK  ]
Starting ircd: ircd: version hybrid-7.2.0
ircd: pid 2075
ircd: running in background mode from /usr/lib/ircd    [  OK  ]
```

Performing the same functional tests shows that the IRC daemon functions correctly despite the denial of write access to the configuration file and read/write access to system administrators' pseudo-terminals. Additional testing is likely required, but otherwise we have demonstrated that our policy module is functionally correct.

## 14.4.2 Policy Analysis

The final step in developing our policy module is to perform policy analysis to verify that we met our security goals. Functional testing is not sufficient as our goal is to add security, not functions. After all, we had a functioning IRC daemon before creating our policy module. Policy analysis, particularly using automated tools such as apol, enables us to verify that we added security with our policy module.

For example, Figure 14-3 shows a search in apol for all access that ircd_t has to ircd_conf_t, including indirect access through attributes. This allows us to verify that the IRC daemon (ircd_t) does not have write access to its configuration files (ircd_conf_t).

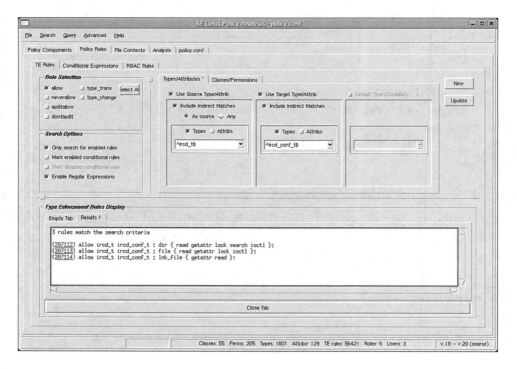

FIGURE 14-3
An apol rules search showing no write access by ircd_t to ircd_conf_t

## 14.5 Emerging Policy Development Tools

Many different development tools are emerging that simplify the policy module development process. These range from integrated development environments such as SLIDE (shown in Figure 14-4) to automated policy generation tools such as Polgen. More information about these tools is provided in Appendix D.

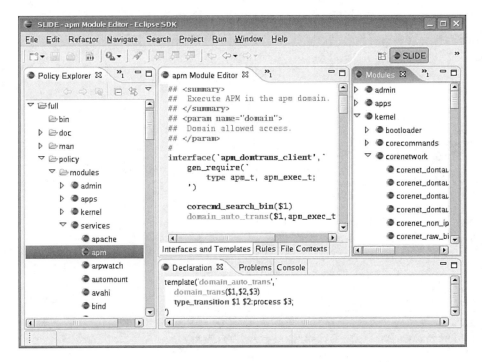

FIGURE 14-4
SLIDE integrated policy development environment

## 14.6 Complete IRC Daemon Module Listings

For completeness, we conclude this chapter with complete listings of the IRC daemon modules for both the example and reference policy.

Listing 14-11
Example Policy: IRC Daemon Policy Module File (ircd.te)

```
1     ##################################################
2     #
3     # ircd policy module
4     #
5     # file: ircd.te
6     #
7
8     ##################################################
9     #
10    # Type declarations
11    #
12
13    # ircd domain
14    type ircd_t, domain;
15
16    # ircd entrypoint
17    type ircd_exec_t, file_type, exec_type;
18
19    # PID file /var/run/ircd.pid
20    type ircd_var_run_t, file_type;
21
22    # configuration files
23    type ircd_conf_t, file_type, sysadmfile;
24
25    # log files
26    type ircd_log_t, file_type, sysadmfile, logfile;
27
28    # files and directories under /var/lib/ircd
29    type ircd_var_lib_t, file_type, sysadmfile;
30
31    ##################################################
32    #
33    # Ircd - core access
34    #
35
36    # allow ircd_t to fork copies of itself
37    allow ircd_t self : process fork;
38    # Log files - create, read, and append
39    allow ircd_t var_log_t : dir ra_dir_perms;
40    allow ircd_t ircd_log_t : dir ra_dir_perms;
41    allow ircd_t ircd_log_t : file { create ra_file_perms };
42    type_transition ircd_t var_log_t : { file dir } ircd_log_t;
43
44    # Configuration files - read
45    allow ircd_t ircd_conf_t : dir r_dir_perms;
46    allow ircd_t ircd_conf_t : file r_file_perms;
47    allow ircd_t ircd_conf_t : lnk_file { getattr read };
48    dontaudit ircd_t ircd_conf_t : file write;
```

```
49
50     # PID file - create, read, and write
51     file_type_auto_trans(ircd_t, var_run_t, ircd_var_run_t, file)
52     allow ircd_t var_t : dir search;
53
54     # /var/lib/ircd files/dirs - create, read, write
55     file_type_auto_trans(ircd_t, var_lib_t, ircd_var_lib_t, file)
56     allow ircd_t ircd_var_lib_t : dir rw_dir_perms;
57
58     # Network access - the ircd daemon is allowed to send
59     # and receive network data to all nodes and ports over
60     # all network interfaces (through the can_network_server
61     # macro). Additionally, it can name_bind to the ircd
62     # port (ircd_port_t).
63     allow ircd_t ircd_port_t:tcp_socket name_bind;
64     can_network_server(ircd_t)
65
66     # use shared libraries
67     uses_shlib(ircd_t)
68
69     # read localization data
70     read_locale(ircd_t)
71
72     # read common directories / files including
73     #     * /etc/resolv.conf (etc_t)
74     #     * proc
75     #     * /dev/null
76     #     * system variables
77     allow ircd_t etc_t : file r_file_perms;
78     allow ircd_t { self proc_t }:dir r_dir_perms;
79     allow ircd_t { self proc_t }:lnk_file { getattr read };
80     allow ircd_t null_device_t:chr_file rw_file_perms;
81     allow ircd_t sysctl_type:dir r_dir_perms;
82     allow ircd_t sysctl_type:file r_file_perms;
83     allow ircd_t sysctl_t:dir search;
84     allow ircd_t sysctl_kernel_t:dir search;
85     allow ircd_t sysctl_kernel_t:file { getattr read };
86
87     ##################################################
88     #
89     # Domain Transitions and Role Authorizations
90     #
91
92     role system_r types ircd_t;
93
94     # allow init to start ircd
95     domain_auto_trans(initrc_t, ircd_exec_t, ircd_t)
96
97     # allow sysadm_t to start ircd_t
98     domain_auto_trans(sysadm_t, ircd_exec_t, ircd_t)
99     role_transition sysadm_r ircd_exec_t system_r;
```

## Listing 14-11 (continued)
## Example Policy: IRC Daemon Policy Module File (ircd.te)

```
100    # dontaudit use of the sysadm_r terminal
101    dontaudit ircd_t sysadm_devpts_t : chr_file { getattr read write };
102
103    ##################################################
104    #
105    # Integrate Into System Policy
106    #
107
108    ifdef(`logrotate.te', `
109        allow logrotate_t ircd_var_run_t:dir search;
110        allow logrotate_t ircd_var_run_t:file { getattr read };
111    ')
```

## Listing 14-12
## Example Policy: IRC Daemon File Contexts File (ircd.fc)

```
1    # ircd labeling policy
2    # file: ircd.fc
3    /usr/bin/ircd          --          system_u:object_r:ircd_exec_t
4    /etc/ircd(/.*)?                     system_u:object_r:ircd_conf_t
5    /var/log/ircd(/.*)?                system_u:object_r:ircd_log_t
6    /var/lib/ircd(/.*)?                system_u:object_r:ircd_var_lib_t
7    /var/run/ircd(/.*)?                system_u:object_r:ircd_var_run_t
```

## Listing 14-13
## Reference Policy: IRC Daemon Private Policy File (ircd.te)

```
1     ########################################
2     #
3     # Reference Policy ircd policy module
4     #
5     # file: ircd.te
6     #
7
8     # Ircd policy module declaration
9     policy_module(ircd, 1.0)
10
11    ########################################
12    #
13    # Type declarations
14    #
15
16    # ircd domain
17    type ircd_t;
```

```
18
19    # ircd entrypoint
20    type ircd_exec_t;
21
22    # mark ircd_t as a domain and ircd_exec_t
23    # as an entrypoint into that domain
24    init_daemon_domain(ircd_t, ircd_exec_t)
25
26    # PID file /var/run/ircd.pid
27    type ircd_var_run_t;
28    files_pid_file(ircd_var_run_t)
29
30    # configuration files
31    type ircd_conf_t;
32    files_config_file(ircd_conf_t)
33
34    # log files
35    type ircd_log_t;
36    logging_log_file(ircd_log_t)
37
38    # files and directories under /var/lib/ircd
39    type ircd_var_lib_t;
40    files_type(ircd_var_lib_t)
41
42    ###########################################
43    #
44    # Ircd - core access
45    #
46
47    # allow ircd_t to fork copies of itself
48    allow ircd_t self : process fork;
49
50    # Log files - create, read, and append
51    allow ircd_t ircd_log_t : dir ra_dir_perms;
52    allow ircd_t ircd_log_t : file { create ra_file_perms };
53    logging_log_filetrans(ircd_t, ircd_log_t, file)
54    logging_search_logs(ircd_t)
55
56    # Configuration files - read
57    allow ircd_t ircd_conf_t : dir r_dir_perms;
58    allow ircd_t ircd_conf_t : file r_file_perms;
59    allow ircd_t ircd_conf_t : lnk_file { getattr read };
60    dontaudit ircd_t ircd_conf_t : file write;
61
62    # PID file - create, read, and write
63    allow ircd_t ircd_var_run_t : dir rw_dir_perms;
64    allow ircd_t ircd_var_run_t : file create_file_perms;
65    files_pid_filetrans(ircd_t, ircd_var_run_t, file)
66
67    # /var/lib/ircd files/dirs - create, read, write
68    allow ircd_t ircd_var_lib_t : dir create_dir_perms;
```

Listing 14-13 (continued)
Reference Policy: IRC Daemon Private Policy File (ircd.te)

```
69    allow ircd_t ircd_var_lib_t : file create_file_perms;
70    files_var_lib_filetrans(ircd_t, ircd_var_lib_t, { file dir })
71
72    # Network access - the ircd daemon is allowed to send
73    # and receive network data to all nodes and ports over
74    # all network interfaces. Additionally, it can name_bind
75    # to the ircd port (ircd_port_t)
76    allow ircd_t self : tcp_socket create_stream_socket_perms;
77    corenet_tcp_sendrecv_all_if(ircd_t)
78    corenet_tcp_sendrecv_all_nodes(ircd_t)
79    corenet_tcp_sendrecv_all_ports(ircd_t)
80    corenet_non_ipsec_sendrecv(ircd_t)
81    corenet_tcp_bind_all_nodes(ircd_t)
82    corenet_tcp_bind_ircd_port(ircd_t)
83    sysnet_dns_name_resolve(ircd_t)
84
85    # use shared libraries
86    libs_use_ld_so(ircd_t)
87    libs_use_shared_libs(ircd_t)
88
89    # read localization data
90    miscfiles_read_localization(ircd_t)
91
92    # dontaudit use of the sysadm_r terminal
93    userdom_dontaudit_use_sysadm_ptys(ircd_t)
94
95    # read common directories / files including
96    #    * /etc (search and read)
97    #    * system variables
98    files_search_etc(ircd_t)
99    files_read_etc_files(ircd_t)
100   kernel_read_kernel_sysctls(ircd_t)
101   kernel_read_system_state(ircd_t)
102   kernel_read_all_sysctls(ircd_t)
```

## Listing 14-14
## Reference Policy: IRC Daemon Labeling Policy File (ircd.fc)

```
1     # ircd labeling policy
2     # file: ircd.fc
3     /usr/bin/ircd      --      gen_context(system_u:object_r:ircd_exec_t, s0)
4     /etc/ircd(/.*)?            gen_context(system_u:object_r:ircd_conf_t, s0)
5     /var/log/ircd(/.*)?        gen_context(system_u:object_r:ircd_log_t, s0)
6     /var/lib/ircd(/.*)?        gen_context(system_u:object_r:ircd_var_lib_t, s0)
7     /var/run/ircd(/.*)?        gen_context(system_u:object_r:ircd_var_run_t, s0)
```

## Listing 14-15
## Reference Policy: IRC Daemon External Interface File (ircd.if)

```
1     ## <summary>IRC daemon</summary>
2
3     #########################################
4     ## <summary>
5     ##      Read IRC daemon log files.
6     ## </summary>
7     ## <param name="domain">
8     ##      Domain allowed access.
9     ## </param>
10    #
11    interface(`irc_read_log',`
12       gen_require(`
13          type ircd_log_t;
14       ')
15
16       files_search_var($1)
17       logging_search_logs($1)
18       allow $1 ircd_log_t:dir search_dir_perms;
19       allow $1 ircd_log_t:file r_file_perms;
20    ')
```

## 14.7 Summary

- As in all modern enterprises, writing policy modules is a skill best learned through practice.

- The basic steps for writing a new policy module, whether it be for the example policy or the reference policy, are as follows:

  1. Prepare and plan:

       Gather information about the application.

       Create a test configuration.

       Specify security goals.

  2. Create an initial policy module:

       Create the basic module files.

       Declare our module's types.

       Allow initial restrictive access.

       Allow domain transitions and role access.

       Integrate into system policy.

       Create labeling policy.

       Apply the policy.

  3. Test and analyze the policy:

       Functional test the policy module.

       Analyze the policy modules against our security goals.

- In general, we iterate among the steps until we achieve the policy module we desire.

# A

# Obtaining SELinux Sample Policies

**In this chapter**

This appendix provides instructions about how to obtain the sample policy source files discussed in this book. All the policies are freely available for use. Community support is available from many places, but the easiest methods are the SELinux mailing lists (see Appendix B, "Participation and Further Information").

## A.1 Example Policy

The example policy (both strict and targeted) we discuss in Chapter 11, "Original Example Policy," is available from several sources. At the time of this writing, a version of the example policy was still available from the upstream SELinux source tree, but the *National Security Agency* (NSA) has announced it is planning to drop support soon in favor of the reference policy. Red Hat supports the example policy in both the *Fedora Core 4* (FC4) and the *Red Hat Enterprise Linux version 4* (RHEL4). (*Fedora Core 5* [FC5] is moving to the reference policy.)

> NOTE The examples throughout the book are based on the Fedora Core strict policy, specifically version 1.27.1-2.6. For the purposes of the examples and exercises, however, any version of the FC4 strict policy should work.

### A.1.1 Example Policy from Upstream SELinux Sites

The NSA example policy is the ancestor of just about every policy that has been developed. The Red Hat/Fedora policies and the reference policy all trace their origins to the NSA policy. It was meant to provide an example of a full system policy that developers could use as a starting point when writing their own policies. NSA has recently stopped supporting the example policy on their Web site (in favor of the reference policy). Historical versions are available at the following site:

```
www.nsa.gov/selinux/code/download0.cfm
```

These historical policies most likely require some tweaking. We recommend installing the packages for the specific Fedora or RHEL releases.

The NSA SELinux project tree, including the NSA example policy, are also available via cvs from the SELinux open source site. To browse the tree or download the package, access the following site:

```
http://selinux.sourceforge.net/
```

Several other Linux distributions support SELinux. At one time, they all had policies based on the NSA example. They have been at least minimally tweaked to conform to the specific distributions. The best place to find pointers to different Linux distributions that support SELinux is at the SELinux open source site previously mentioned.

## A.1.2 Strict and Targeted Policies for Fedora Core 4

For most of this book, we used examples from the strict example policy for FC4. However, the targeted policy is installed as the default policy for a FC4 system. Only the prebuilt policy (without the policy source) is installed in most cases. The targeted policy is installed in /etc/selinux/targeted/. During installation if you choose the "complete" install option when deciding on which packages to install, both the strict and targeted policies are installed with their respective policy source files.

If you install only the targeted policy, you have several simple options for installing the targeted source and the strict policy and its source files. The most straightforward way is to use the yum utility as the system administrator as follows. First find out the exact package you have on your system and what is available:

```
# yum list | grep -i selinux-policy
selinux-policy-targeted.noarch         1.27.1-2.6      installed
selinux-policy-strict.noarch           1.27.1-2.16     updates-released
selinux-policy-strict-sources.noarch 1.27.1-2.16     updates-released
selinux-policy-targeted.noarch         1.27.1-2.16     updates-released
selinux-policy-targeted-sources.noarch  1.27.1-2.16 updates-released
```

On our system, we have the targeted policy installed without the source. To install the source and the strict policy with source, we run the following:

```
# yum install selinux-policy-targeted-sources
```

and

```
# yum install selinux-policy-strict-sources
```

Note that when we installed the strict source files, the prebuilt policy was installed, too, because `yum` recognizes that the `sources` package is dependent on the `policy` package. All these policies are installed into the standard Fedora policy location, `/etc/selinux/`. To switch over to the strict policy, you can use the administrative tool mentioned in Chapter 13, "Managing an SELinux System," or you can perform the switch to the strict policy by hand if you change the `SELIN-UXTYPE` line in `/etc/selinux/config` to `strict` and `touch /.autorelabel`. In either case, you must then reboot the system to ensure all processes and files are labeled correctly.

You can also obtain and install the policy packages from the Fedora installation CDs. Disc 1 contains the packages for the prebuilt policies (that is, all the policy files except the policy source files) for both the targeted and strict policies. If you put Disc 1 in your drive, you should see it under `/media/cdrecorder` or `/media/cdrom`, or `mount` it as `root` with something like `mount /dev/cdrom /media/cdrom` (depending on your hardware configuration). The package files are under the following:

```
./Fedora/RPMS/
selinux-policy-strict-1.23.16-6.noarch.rpm
selinux-policy-targeted-1.23.16-6.noarch.rpm
```

The policy source RPMs are on Disc 4:

```
/Fedora/RPMS/
selinux-policy-strict-sources-1.23.16-6.noarch.rpm
selinux-policy-targeted-sources-1.23.16-6.noarch.rpm
```

You install them with the standard `rpm` command. (Remember, however, that the `sources` packages depend on the policy packages, so you must install the policy packages before you install the respective sources packages.) For example, you can install the strict policy with source (`rpm` output removed for brevity) as follows:

```
# rpm -ivh selinux-policy-strict-1.23.16-6.noarch.rpm
# rpm -ivh selinux-policy-targeted-sources-1.23.16-6.noarch.rpm
```

After you install the policies with `rpm`, if you want to switch to the strict policy, you still need to "activate" it in the same way as described previously for `yum`.

## A.1.3 Red Hat Enterprise Linux 4 (RHEL4)

The RHEL4 default policy, for all flavors (that is, AS, ES, and WS), is the targeted policy based on the example policy. The strict policy is not included or supported. The prebuilt targeted policy is on Disc 2 of the installation CDs. You can find it by mounting Disc 2 under the following:

```
./RedHat/RPMS/selinux-policy-targeted-1.17.30-2.52.1.noarch.rpm
```

The source package for the targeted policy is on Disc 4:

```
./RedHat/RPMS/selinux-policy-targeted-sources-1.17.30-2.52.1.noarch.rpm
```

You can install the packages by using the `rpm -ivh package-name.rpm` command. You can install the strict policy using the strict packages from Fedora Core (see above). You switch the system over to the strict policy in the same manner as described for FC4. Note that because the strict policy is not supported for RHEL4, you might need to tweak the policy to get it to work properly in your configuration. We recommend initially setting the `SELINUX` line to `permissive` in `/etc/selinux/config` until you ensure a clean boot.

### A.1.4 Fedora Core Experimental and Test Policies

You can find the most recently patched policies and test and other experimental policies (for example, *multilevel security* [MLS] and *multicategory security* [MCS]) at Dan Walsh's Red Hat site:

```
ftp://people.redhat.com/dwalsh/SELinux/
```

These tend to be new and minimally tested.

## A.2 Reference Policy

Chapter 12, "Reference Policy," discussed the reference policy, which we expect to be the primary policy source for the future. At the time of this writing, Red Hat used reference policy for FC5. You can use the reference policy to build strict or targeted policies, with or without the optional MLS features. Reference policy supports RHEL4.

Instructions for installing and using reference policy on RHEL4 are complicated because they involve upgrading several packages and libraries to support the latest policy language. You can find instructions on how to do this and where to find prebuilt RPMs for the required packages and libraries in the `INSTALL` file in the top-level directory of the reference policy tree.

## A.2.1 Primary Reference Policy

The reference policy is primarily developed by Tresys Technology as an open source project. It is available via its open source project site:

```
http://serefpolicy.sourceforge.net/
```

The reference policy supports loadable modules and the traditional monolithic policy build (all from the same source tree). At this time, loadable modules are still in development, but you can find up-to-date information and instructions on the policy server project open source site:

```
http://sepolicy-server.sourceforge.net/
```

## A.2.2 Red Hat's Fedora Core 5 Reference Policy

Several versions of reference policy are available for FC5, including a targeted, strict, and MLS policy package. All of these are based on the primary reference policy tree. You can find the prebuilt policy RPMs at the following site:

```
http://download.fedora.redhat.com/pub/fedora/linux/core/5/i386/os/Fedora/RPMS/
```

At the time of this writing, the relevant files were called `selinux-policy-*`.

The previous RPMs install as policy modules. You will find the policy packages (that is, the .pp files) under `/usr/share/selinux/`, in the associated policy directory (targeted, strict, and so on).

There is no "sources" RPM (that is, a package that automatically installs the policy source files), but you can find an src RPM (that is, a package that contains the sources to build the policy but does not automatically install the sources). You can find the `src` RPM at the following site:

```
http://download.fedora.redhat.com/pub/fedora/linux/core/5/source/SRPMS/
```

At the time of this writing, the package name was `selinux-policy-2.2.23-15.src.rpm`. The `src` RPM contains a reference policy source tree and a patch file that Red Hat provides for the current version of FC5.

It takes some knowledge to extract the policy sources from an `src` RPM. You can always use the primary reference policy (as described previously) rather than the Red Hat packages. It will also install and build usable policies on FC5.

# B

# Participation and Further Information

## In this chapter

This appendix identifies where to look for past, current, and future information and discusses how to participate in the development of SELinux and SELinux policies. As with any current technology, SELinux is still evolving, and staying abreast is important.

## B.1 The SELinux Mail List

The best place to find out about SELinux development and to ask questions is the SELinux mailing list. To subscribe to the SELinux mailing list, send a message to the following address:

```
majordomo@tycho.nsa.gov.
```

Put *subscribe selinux* as the body of the message. You can find more information about the mailing list on the *National Security Agency* (NSA) Web site:

```
www.nsa.gov/selinux/
```

Note that although the site refers to it as a "Developers List," new people are welcome, and the discussions extend to many SELinux subjects. There are archives of the mailing list both at NSA's Web site and at the following site:

```
http://marc.theaimsgroup.com/?l=selinux&r=1
```

## B.2 The Annual SELinux Symposium

Since 2004, an annual conference has been held as a platform for exchanging ideas and presenting new developments and applications of SELinux. The conference is held in the Baltimore, Maryland/Washington, D.C. area at the end of February or the beginning of March. The Web site for the symposium is at this address:

```
www.selinux-symposium.org/
```

The Web site contains information about the upcoming conference and electronic versions of past presentations.

## B.3 The NSA

The NSA Web site, www.nsa.gov/selinux/, is one of the best places to find information. You can find many of the original architecture papers, some of which have been updated, more current papers, and pointers to the upstream versions of current packages and libraries. There are also pointers to the SELinux mailing list, an FAQ, and other items of interest such as a list of major features that need to be done.

## B.4 Tresys Technology

The Tresys Technology Web site contains many useful and informative pages. You can access the main page at this address:

```
www.tresys.com/selinux/
```

This page links to information on the SeTools package, information on the Tresys SELinux policy course (including up-to-date versions of all the slides), a current object class, and a permissions information page similar to Appendix C, "Object Classes and Permissions." This site also include information about Tresys' enhancements to SELinux, such as conditional policy, loadable modules, reference policy, an SELinux policy development and integration IDE, and the SELinux policy server.

## B.5 Open Source Projects

The following are links to some SELinux-related projects. These open source projects welcome and encourage community participation and contribution. Be aware, however, that because of the nature of open source projects, they might have moved by the time this book is published.

**Main SELinux**—http://sourceforge.net/projects/selinux

**Reference policy**—http://serefpolicy.sourceforge.net

**SELinux policy management infrastructure (SELinux policy server and loadable modules)**—http://sepolicy-server.sourceforge.net/

## B.6 The SELinux IRC Channel

There is an SELinux IRC channel. Use your favorite IRC chat client, point to irc.freenode.net, and join  #selinux. It is a fairly active channel, and there is usually a knowledgeable person around willing to answer any questions you might have. Features, bug fixes, and enhancements are often discussed here before they migrate to the mailing list.

## B.7 The Fedora Core Site

Red Hat maintains a large site where you can find everything from ISO images of all the Fedora releases and RPM packages to loads of documentation on Fedora and SELinux. The main site is here:

```
http://fedora.redhat.com/
```

This site is considering a switch to a new home:

```
http://fedoraproject.org/
```

The new site currently has a wiki site set up with lots of useful information. Red Hat/Fedora also maintains several Fedora Core-specific mailing lists, a list of which you can find here:

```
http://fedoraproject.org/wiki/Communicate
```

This list includes a Fedora SELinux mailing list that you can join from this page:

```
www.redhat.com/mailman/listinfo/fedora-selinux-list
```

## B.8 Hardened Gentoo

Hardened Gentoo was one of the first Linux distributions to include SELinux. Hardened Gentoo has excellent documentation on SELinux and documentation on how to integrate other security packages into an SELinux-Gentoo system. The main Hardened Gentoo page is here:

```
www.gentoo.org/proj/en/hardened
```

A page on this site is specifically for SELinux.

## B.9 Other Related Security Information

The following are resources that are not SELinux-specific but may be of interest. The *Linux Security Module* (LSM) mailing list discusses kernel developments related to the LSM. The LSM is how SELinux hooks into the Linux kernel. You can join the LSM mailing list from this site:

`http://mail.wirex.com/mailman/listinfo/linux-security-module`

An audit framework was added in the Linux 2.6 kernel series that greatly extends Linux audit capabilities. You can join the Linux audit discussion mailing list here:

`www.redhat.com/mailman/listinfo/linux-audit`

Several SELinux/Linux Common Criteria evaluations are ongoing at the time of this writing. For the current status of those evaluations, refer to the following Web site:

`http://niap.nist.gov/cc-scheme/`

The page contains links to "Validated Products" that have passed evaluation and "Products in Evaluation."

# C

# Object Classes and Permissions

**In this chapter**

This appendix provides a detailed summary and listing of all object classes and permissions supported by the kernel at the time of this writing. Be aware that object classes and permissions are occasionally changed and added. Some object classes and permissions listed are no longer used. They remain defined primarily for compatibility reasons. Their use in a policy would have no effect on a system with an up-to-date kernel. You can find a maintained list of object classes and permissions at www.tresys.com/selinux. You can also use the National Security Agency (NSA) technical report "Implementing SELinux as a LSM," available at www.nsa.gov/selinux/info/docs.cfm.

## C.1 Common Permission Sets

Some object classes share sets of permissions. These permission sets are defined as *common permissions* and are assigned a common permission identifier in the policy. They are then "inherited" by kernel object classes when the common permission identifier is assigned to the class. Thus, they are "common permissions" defined for multiple class definitions. Allowing the same permission sets for multiple object classes make using multiple object classes in a single policy rule possible. See Chapter 4, "Object Classes and Permissions," for more information on how object classes and permissions are defined.

Note that it may be a bit confusing in that the identifiers used for common permission sets are also the identifiers used to name some kernel object classes. For example, there is a common set of permissions called "file," and there is a kernel object class also called "file," which inherits the common "file" permissions. The common permission and object class namespaces are separate, and the common permission `file` and the object class `file` are distinct entities; be careful not to confuse the two.

In the following tables, we list the three common permissions and their permissions sets that are currently used by the kernel. The three common permission sets are as follows:

- `file`    Common permissions used by filesystem object classes
- `socket`    Common permissions used by various socket classes

- `ipc`   Common permissions used by System V *interprocess communication* (IPC) classes

**TABLE C-1**
**Common Permissions File**

| Permission | Description |
|---|---|
| append | Append to object's contents (that is, opened with O_APPEND flag). |
| create | Create new object of this class. |
| execute | Execute the object. |
| getattr | Get attributes for object, such as access mode (for example, stat, some ioctls). |
| ioctl | ioctl(2) system call requests on the object not addressed by other permissions. |
| link | Create hard link to object. |
| lock | Set and unset object's locks. |
| mounton | Use object as a mount point; typically used for dir object class. |
| quotaon | Allow file to be used as a quota database. |
| read | Read the object's contents. |
| relabelfrom | Change the object's security context from the existing type. |
| relabelto | Change the object's security context to the new type. |
| rename | Rename any hard links to the object. |
| setattr | Change attributes for object such as access mode (for example, chmod, some ioctls). |
| swapon | Deprecated, allowed the object to be used for paging/swapping space. |
| unlink | Remove hard link (delete the file if no other hard links are present). |
| write | Write the object's contents. |

TABLE C-2
Common Permissions socket

| Permission | Description |
| --- | --- |
| accept | Accept a connection to the socket. |
| append | Write or append socket file contents. |
| bind | Bind name to the socket. |
| connect | Initiate connection from the socket. |
| create | Create new socket file. |
| getattr | Get file attributes for socket file, such as access mode (for example, stat, some ioctls). |
| getopt | Get socket options. |
| ioctl | I/O control system call requests on the socket not addressed by other permissions. |
| listen | Listen for connections to the socket. |
| lock | Set and unset socket file locks. |
| name_bind | Use port or file; for AF_INET sockets, defines a relationship between a socket object and its port number; no longer applied to UNIX domain sockets (post Linux Security Module [LSM]). |
| read | Read data received from socket. |
| recv_mesg | Permission required for a socket to receive a message from a port. |
| recvfrom | Currently unused (a legacy of older network checks). |
| relabelfrom | Change the socket's security context from the existing type. |
| relabelto | Change the socket's security context to the new type. |
| send_msg | Permission required to send a message from a socket to a port. |
| sendto | Send data to UNIX domain sockets. |
| setattr | Change file attributes for socket file, such as access mode (for example, chmod, some ioctls). |
| setopt | Set socket options. |
| shutdown | Shutdown connection. |
| write | Write or append to the socket. |

**TABLE C-3**
**Common Permissions** `ipc`

| Permission | Description |
|---|---|
| `associate` | Get the ID of an IPC object. |
| `create` | Create an IPC object. |
| `destroy` | Destroy an IPC object. |
| `getattr` | Get IPC object attributes. |
| `read` | Read or receive data from an IPC object. |
| `setattr` | Change IPC object attributes. |
| `unix_read` | Read; required by IPC operations. |
| `unix_write` | Write or change; required by IPC operations. |
| `write` | Write, send message, or change the value of an IPC object. |

## C.2 Object Classes and Defined Permission Sets

The following tables show all the kernel object classes and the permissions defined for each object class. These permissions correspond to permissions required by the kernel's LSM hooks and are used as the object class/permission specifications in policy statements. Each object class's permission table lists any inherited/common permissions first and then any permissions that are unique to that class. The classes are grouped alphabetically within the following four categories:

- File related      Object classes relating to filesystem objects
- Network/socket    Object classes associated with network access or sockets
- IPC      System V IPC object classes
- Miscellaneous    Other object classes not in the previous three categories

### C.2.1 File-Related Object Classes

File-related object classes represent many of the system objects that are familiar to a Linux user. Almost all of them inherit the common file permission set. Some classes also have unique permissions that either relate specifically to SELinux operations or are extensions that were added to the normal Linux permissions (for example, a permission to add a file to a directory). The object classes in this group are listed in Table C-4.

TABLE C-4
Summary of File-Related Object Classes

| Object Class | Description | Permission Definitions |
|---|---|---|
| blk_file | Block files | Table C-5 |
| chr_file | Character files | Table C-6 |
| dir | Directories | Table C-7 |
| fd | File descriptors | Table C-8 |
| fifo_file | Named pipes | Table C-9 |
| file | Ordinary files | Table C-10 |
| filesystem | Filesystem (that is, an actual partition) | Table C-11 |
| lnk_file | Symbolic links | Table C-12 |
| sock_file | UNIX domain sockets | Table C-13 |

TABLE C-5
blk_file **Permissions**

| Permissions | Description |
|---|---|
| file common permissions | See Table C-1. |

TABLE C-6
chr_file **Permissions**

| Permissions | Description |
|---|---|
| file common permissions | See Table C-1. |
| entrypoint | Added only to make execmod permission index map to the same index as the file execmod permission (see execmod). |
| execmod | Added to allow certain applications to make executable mappings of character device memory. |
| execute_no_trans | Added only to make execmod permission index map to the same index as the file execmod permission (see execmod). |

**TABLE C-7**
`dir` **Permissions**

| Permissions | Description |
|---|---|
| `file` common permissions | See Table C-1. |
| `add_name` | Add a hard link (name) to the directory (for example, creating or moving a file into a directory). |
| `remove_name` | Remove a hard link from the directory (for example, remove or move a file from a directory). |
| `reparent` | Change directory's parent directory. |
| `rmdir` | Remove the directory object. |
| `search` | Needed to find an object contained in the directory or for a directory object in the path to another object. Does not allow directory listing, which is controlled by `read`. |

**TABLE C-8**
`fd` **Permissions**

| Permissions | Description |
|---|---|
| `use` | Permission to use the file descriptor (for example, reading or writing to a file descriptor inherited from another process). Appropriate permissions on the underlying object are still required. (For example, successfully reading from a file using a file descriptor requires use permission on the `fd` object and read permission on the file object.) |

**TABLE C-9**
`fifo_file` **Permissions**

| Permissions | Description |
|---|---|
| `file` common permissions | See Table C-1. |

TABLE C-10
`file` **Permissions**

| Permissions | Description |
|---|---|
| `file` common permissions | See Table C-1. |
| `entrypoint` | File can be used as the entry point of a domain via a domain transition. |
| `execmod` | Make execute a file mapping that has been modified by copy-on-write. |
| `execute_no_trans` | Execute the file in the calling process' domain (that is, without a domain transition). |

TABLE C-11
`filesystem` **Permissions**

| Permissions | Description |
|---|---|
| `associate` | Allow file-related object classes with given types to be stored on the filesystem. |
| `getattr` | Needed to `statfs` a filesystem. |
| `mount` | Needed to mount the superblock of a filesystem. |
| `quotaget` | Get quota information. |
| `quotamod` | Modify quota information. |
| `relabelfrom` | Used to control context mounts. |
| `relabelto` | Used to control context mounts. |
| `remount` | Change filesystem mount flags. |
| `transition` | Deprecated permission from pre-LSM SELinux, not used. |
| `unmount` | Unmount. |

TABLE C-12
`lnk_file` **Permissions**

| Permissions | Description |
|---|---|
| `file` common permissions | See Table C-1. |

**TABLE C-13**
sock_file Permissions

| Permissions | Description |
|---|---|
| `file common permissions` | See Table C-1. |

## C.2.2 Network and Socket Object Classes

Network and socket object classes represent network resources and sockets. They include the classes for all types of network socket objects, from raw IP sockets to specialized Netlink sockets. This group also includes the classes and permissions for network interfaces and nodes. Almost all these object classes inherit the common permission `socket`. The object classes in this group are listed in Table C-14.

**TABLE C-14**
Summary of Network and Socket Object Classes

| Object Class | Description | Permission Definitions |
|---|---|---|
| `association` | Represents an IPSec security association. | Table C-15 |
| `key_socket` | Sockets that are of protocol family PF_KEY, used for key management in IPSec. This class was created to distinguish PF_KEY sockets from general sockets. | Table C-16 |
| `netif` | A network interface. A domain must have the appropriate permissions on a netif object to send and/or receive packets on an interface. The domain must also have the same permissions for a node object (see node class), and if the domain is using a UDP or TCP socket, it must also have the corresponding tcp_socket/udp_socket permission (that is, *_send_msg or *_recv_msg) on the TCP/UDP socket object. | Table C-17 |
| `netlink_ audit_socket` | A netlink_audit_socket object is a netlink socket connection to the audit service. The socket is used to list/add/delete filter rules, get/set status, and so on. | Table C-18 |

*continues*

TABLE C-14 (continued)
Summary of Network and Socket Object Classes

| Object Class | Description | Permission Definitions |
|---|---|---|
| netlink_ dnrt_socket | Netlink socket to control DECnet routing. | Table C-19 |
| netlink_ firewall_socket | Netlink socket to create userspace firewall filters; copy packets from kernel, send accept or reject packet verdict to kernel. | Table C-20 |
| netlink_ ip6fw_socket | Netlink socket to create IPv6 userspace firewall filters. | Table C-21 |
| netlink_kobject _uevent_socket | Netlink socket to send kernel event notifications to userspace (for example, processor temperature detection). | Table C-22 |
| netlink_ nflog_socket | Netlink socket to receive Netfilter logging messages in userspace. | Table C-23 |
| netlink_ route_socket | Netlink socket to control and mange network resources such as the routing table and IP address from userspace. | Table C-24 |
| netlink_ selinux_socket | Netlink socket that receives userspace notification messages on SELinux events (for example, policy load, enforce mode toggle, and Boolean change). | Table C-25 |
| netlink_socket | Netlink socket to control all Netlink sockets for which there is not yet a specific SELinux class defined. | |
| netlink_ tcpdiag_socket | Netlink socket to monitor TCP connections. | Table C-27 |
| netlink_ xfrm_socket | Netlink socket to get, maintain, set IPsec parameters such as security associations, security policies, and security parameter indexes. | Table C-28 |

| Object Class | Description | Permission Definitions |
|---|---|---|
| node | Represents a host IP address or range of addresses. A domain must have send or receive permission on a node object to send or receive data on a particular IP address. The domain must also have send or receive permission on the network interface object associated with the address (see netif class). If the domain uses a UDP or TCP socket, it must also have the corresponding tcp_socket/ udp_socket permission (that is, *_send_msg or *_recv_msg) on the socket object. | Table C-29 |
| packet_socket | Raw sockets where the protocol is implemented in userspace. The packets for this type of object are sent at OSI Layer 2. A domain must also have the NET_RAW capability permission to use a packet_socket object. | Table C-30 |
| rawip_socket | IP sockets that are neither TCP nor UDP. | Table C-31 |
| socket | Any socket type for which there is no specific class defined for its protocol family. SELinux, as of policy version 19, defines socket classes for the following protocol families: unix, inet, inet6, netlink, packet, and key. | Table C-32 |
| tcp_socket | A TCP socket. A domain also needs tcp_recv and/or tcp_send on both the associated node and netif objects to receive/send packets (in addition to the recv_msg/send_msg permission on the tcp_socket object). | Table C-33 |
| udp_socket | A UDP socket. A domain also needs udp_recv and/or udp_send on both the associated node and netif objects to receive/send packets (in addition to the recv_msg/send_msg permission on the udp _socket object). | Table C-34 |
| unix_dgram_ socket | IPC datagram sockets on a local machine. The socket allows for passing credentials (PID, UID, and GID) for authentication. If any of the credentials are not the same as the process,' the process (that is, its domain) must also have the sys_admin, setuid, and/or setgid capability, respectively. | Table C-35 |

TABLE C-14 (continued)
Summary of Network and Socket Object Classes

| Object Class | Description | Permission Definitions |
|---|---|---|
| unix_stream_ socket | IPC stream sockets on a local machine. The socket allows for passing credentials (PID, UID, and GID) for authentication. If any of the credentials are not the same as the process,' the process (that is, its domain) must also have the sys_admin, setuid, and/or setgid capability, respectively. | Table C-36 |

TABLE C-15
association **Permissions**

| Permissions | Description |
|---|---|
| recvfrom | Receive packets using an IPSec security association. |
| sendto | Send packets using an IPSec security association. |

TABLE C-16
key_socket **Permissions**

| Permissions | Description |
|---|---|
| socket common permissions | See Table C-2. |

TABLE C-17
netif **Permissions**

| Permissions | Description |
|---|---|
| rawip_recv | Receive raw IP packet via the network interface. |
| rawip_send | Send raw IP packet via the network interface. |
| tcp_receive | Receive TCP packet via the network interface. |
| tcp_send | Send TCP packet via the network interface. |
| udp_recv | Receive UDP packet via the network interface. |
| udp_send | Send UDP packet via the network interface. |

**TABLE C-18**
`netlink_audit_socket` **Permissions**

| Permissions | Description |
|---|---|
| `socket common permissions` | See Table C-2. |
| `nlmsg_read` | Used to get the audit system status. |
| `nlmsg_readpriv` | List all auditing rules. |
| `nlmsg_relay` | Send userspace audit messages to the kernel audit system. |
| `nlmsg_write` | Used to set audit system parameters. |

**TABLE C-19**
`netlink_dnrt_socket` **Permissions**

| Permissions | Description |
|---|---|
| `socket common permissions` | See Table C-2. |

**TABLE C-20**
`netlink_firewall_socket` **Permissions**

| Permissions | Description |
|---|---|
| `socket common permissions` | See Table C-2. |
| `nlmsg_read` | Not used. |
| `nlmsg_write` | Write control message to firewall. |

**TABLE C-21**
`netlink_ip6fw_socket` **Permissions**

| Permissions | Description |
|---|---|
| `socket common permissions` | See Table C-2. |
| `nlmsg_read` | Not used. |
| `nlmsg_write` | Write control message to firewall. |

TABLE C-22
`netlink_kobject_uevent_socket` **Permissions**

| Permissions | Description |
|---|---|
| `socket` common permissions | See Table C-2. |

TABLE C-23
`netlink_nflog_socket` **Permissions**

| Permissions | Description |
|---|---|
| `socket` common permissions | See Table C-2. |

TABLE C-24
`netlink_route_socket` **Permissions**

| Permissions | Description |
|---|---|
| `socket` common permissions | See Table C-2. |
| `nlmsg_read` | Read kernel routing table. |
| `nlmsg_write` | Write routing information to routing table. |

TABLE C-25
`netlink_selinux_socket` **Permissions**

| Permissions | Description |
|---|---|
| `socket` common permissions | See Table C-2. |

TABLE C-26
`netlink_socket` **Permissions**

| Permissions | Description |
|---|---|
| `socket` common permissions | See Table C-2. |

**TABLE C-27**
`netlink_tcpdiag_socket` **Permissions**

| Permissions | Description |
|---|---|
| `socket` common permissions | See Table C-2. |
| `nlmsg_read` | Request kernel TCP parameters. |
| `nlmsg_write` | Currently unused. |

**TABLE C-28**
`netlink_xfrm_socket` **Permissions**

| Permissions | Description |
|---|---|
| `socket` common permissions | See Table C-2. |
| `nlmsg_read` | Request IPsec configuration data. |
| `nlmsg_write` | Set IPsec configuration data. |

**TABLE C-29**
`node` **Permissions**

| Permissions | Description |
|---|---|
| `enforce_dest` | This permission is deprecated. It was used in an extended socket API in previous versions of SELinux. |
| `rawip_recv` | Receive raw IP packet from the node. |
| `rawip_send` | Send raw IP packet to the node. |
| `tcp_receive` | Receive TCP packet from the node. |
| `tcp_send` | Send TCP packet to the node. |
| `udp_recv` | Receive UDP packet from the node. |
| `udp_send` | Send UDP packet to the node. |

**TABLE C-30**
`packet_socket` **Permission**

| Permissions | Description |
|---|---|
| `socket` common permissions | See Table C-2. |

**TABLE C-31**
`rawip_socket` **Permissions**

| Permissions | Description |
|---|---|
| `socket` common permissions | See Table C-2. |
| `node_bind` | Ability to bind to a node. |

**TABLE C-32**
`socket` **Permissions**

| Common Permissions (socket) | Description |
|---|---|
| `socket` common permissions | See Tablte C-2. |

**TABLE C-33**
`tcp_socket` **Permissions**

| Permissions | Description |
|---|---|
| `socket` common permissions | See Table C-2. |
| `acceptfrom` | Deprecated, not used. |
| `connectto` | Deprecated, not used. |
| `name_connect` | Connect to a specific port number. |
| `newconn` | Deprecated, not used. |
| `node_bind` | Ability to bind to a node. |

**TABLE C-34**
`udp_socket` **Permissions**

| Permissions | Description |
|---|---|
| `socket` common permissions | See Table C-2. |
| `node_bind` | Ability to bind to a node. |

**TABLE C-35**
`unix_dgram_socket` **Permissions**

| Permissions | Description |
|---|---|
| `socket` common permissions | See Table C-2. |

**TABLE C-36**
`unix_stream_socket` **Permissions**

| Permissions | Description |
|---|---|
| `socket` common permissions | See Table C-2. |
| `acceptfrom` | Deprecated, not used. |
| `connectto` | Connect to server socket. |
| `newconn` | Deprecated, not used. |

## C.2.3 System V IPC-Related Object Classes

System V IPC-related object classes are for those resources that support System V IPC objects such as message queues, semaphores, and shared memory. Most of these classes inherit the common permission `ipc`. The object classes in this group are listed in C-37.

**TABLE C-37**
**Summary of IPC-Related Object Classes**

| Object Class | Description | Permission Definitions |
|---|---|---|
| `ipc` | Deprecated; no longer used. | Table C-38 |
| `msg` | Messages within a message queue. | Table C-39 |
| `msgq` | Message queues. | Table C-40 |
| `sem` | Semaphores. | Table C-41 |
| `shm` | Shared memory segment. | Table C-42 |

**TABLE C-38**
`ipc` **Permissions**

| Permissions | Description |
|---|---|
| `ipc` common permissions | See Table C-3. (Note that `ipc` object class is no longer used.) |

TABLE C-39
msg **Permissions**

| Permissions | Description |
| --- | --- |
| receive | Remove a message from a queue. |
| send | Add a message to a queue. |

TABLE C-40
msgq **Permissions**

| Permissions | Description |
| --- | --- |
| ipc common permissions | See Table C-3. |
| enqueue | Put a message onto a queue. |

TABLE C-41
sem **Permissions**

| Permissions | Description |
| --- | --- |
| ipc common permissions | See Table C-3. |

TABLE C-42
shm **Permissions**

| Permissions | Description |
| --- | --- |
| ipc common permissions | See Table C-3. |
| lock | Lock/unlock page(s) in memory. |

## C.2.4 Miscellaneous Object Classes

The remaining object classes are primarily system control and management object classes. Most of the permissions are usually those reserved for the root user on a non-SELinux system and generally would be limited to selected trusted domains in SELinux. Most object classes are one or a fixed number of instances. (That is, you cannot create object instances of these classes like you can with file or socket classes.) The object classes in this group are listed in Table C-43.

TABLE C-43
Summary of Remaining Miscellaneous Object Classes

| Object Class | Description | Permission Definitions |
|---|---|---|
| capability | Privileges that are implemented as capabilities in Linux. These capabilities represent the typical "root" privileges. In SELinux, each process has a single instance of this object class that has the same type as the process itself. In SELinux, to use a capability defined in the kernel, the process domain type must be allowed the associated permission for the capability object class for the type of the process.<br><br>Note that the capabilities grant privileges with respect to standard Linux; the Linux check (either for the capability or superuser) and the SELinux check are orthogonal. (That is, both are required; neither is sufficient alone.) | Table C-44 |
| passwd | A userspace class that represents the password and shadow files. The permission checks are enforced in the passwd program (although the access information is held in the kernel policy). | Table C-45 |
| pax | Pax security objects. Pax is a separate Linux security mechanism that may be integrated with SELinux. | Table C-45 |
| process | Each process itself is an object of class process and must have permission to its own type (or other process types) to perform certain actions with regard to the target process. | Table C-46 |
| security | The SELinux security server. There is only one instance of this object class. | Table C-47 |
| system | The system. Any system-level privileged functions not covered by the capability or the security object classes are embodied in the system object. There is only one instance of this object class. | Table C-48 |

TABLE C-44
`capability` **Permissions**

| Permissions | Description |
|---|---|
| `audit_control` | Allows the process to change auditing rules. Set login UID. |
| `audit_write` | Allows the process to send audit messsages from userspace. |
| `chown` | Allows the process to change file ownership on a system where users are restricted to only changing group ownership. |
| `dac_override` | Allows the process to ignore discretionary access controls including access lists. The capability does not include the access covered by `linux_immutable` (see below). |
| `dac_read_search` | Allows the process read and search permission on all files and directories regardless of their DAC settings except for access covered by `linux_immutable` (see below) or where not permitted by SELinux permissions. |
| `fowner` | Allows the process to access a file when the file owner is not the same as the process' user ID. Other security checks (that is, DAC and MAC) are still in effect. |
| `fsetid` | Allows the process to set the group ID of a file where the group ID does not match that of the process. |
| `ipc_lock` | Allows the proceses the capability to lock non-shared and shared memory segments. |
| `ipc_owner` | Allows the process to ignore IPC ownership checks. |
| `kill` | Allows the process to send a kill signal to a process owned by a different user. |
| `lease` | Allows the process to take leases on a file. A lease allows a process to be notified when another process accesses the file that a lease's file descriptor refers to. |
| `linux_immutable` | Allows the process to change `S_IMMUTABLE` and `S_APPEND` file attributes on supporting filesystems. |
| `mknod` | Allows the process to create character and block device nodes. |
| `net_admin` | Allows the process a variety of trusted network permissions such as configuring network interfaces, firewall settings, and routing tables. (See `/usr/include/linux/capabilities.h` for full list). Appropriate SELinux permissions remain in effect. |

| Permissions | Description |
|---|---|
| net_bind_service | Allows the process to bind TCP/UDP sockets to ports below 1024 or bind to ATM VCIs below 32. |
| net_broadcast | Allows the process to send network broadcasts and listen to incoming multicasts. |
| net_raw | Allows the process to create and use non-TCP/UDP sockets. Appropriate SELinux controls are still in effect. (That is, the process must also have appropriate permissions on a packet_socket or rawip_socket). |
| setgid | Allows a non-root process to set its group IDs. |
| setpcap | Adds or removes the process' capability from another process' capability set. Note that the use of an added capability must still be allowed in the policy. |
| setuid | Allows a non-root process to set its real and/or effective IDs. |
| sys_admin | This capability allows the process many "standard" administrative functions. Some of these are: configuring syslog, setting the domain and host names, turning swap on or off, accessing and configuring of various devices (for example, IDE, SCSI, and do on), and setting the encryption key for a loopback filesystem. See /usr/include/linux/capability.h for the complete list. |
| sys_boot | Allows the process to reboot the system. |
| sys_chroot | Allows the process to use the chroot(2) call. |
| sys_module | Allows the process unrestricted kernel modification capability including, but not limited to, loading and removing kernel modules. Allows modification of kernel's bounding capability mask. |
| sys_nice | Allows the process to change priority of other processes. Also allows the process to change the scheduling algorithm used by any process. |
| sys_pacct | Allows the process to modify process accounting. |
| sys_ptrace | Allows the process to ptrace(2) another process. |

*continues*

TABLE C-44 (continued)
`capability` **Permissions**

| Permissions | Description |
| --- | --- |
| sys_rawio | Allows the process to use `ioperm(2)` and `iopl(2)` as well as the capability to send messages to USB devices via `/proc/bus/usb`. |
| sys_resource | Allows the process to change various system resources: quota limits, reserved `ext2` filesystem space, `ext3` journaling mode, IPC message queue size restrictions, control of interrupts from real-time clock, change maximum number of consoles, and change maximum number of keymaps. |
| sys_time | Allows the process to set system time and to set the real-time clock. |
| sys_tty_config | Allows the process to configure tty devices. Allows `vhangup(2)` call on a tty. |

TABLE C-45
`passwd` **Permissions**

| Permissions | Description |
| --- | --- |
| chfn | Change `finger` information for a different user (that is, the string in the `passwd` file for an account; commonly the user's real name). |
| chsh | Change login shell for a particular account. |
| crontab | Permits a `cron` job to be run as a different user than the user who submitted the job. |
| passwd | Update a different user's password. |
| rootok | Allow update if the user is root and the process has the `rootok` permission. |

**TABLE C-46**
pax **Permissions**

| Permissions | Description |
| --- | --- |
| emutramp | Emulate gcc trampolines (a technique for implementing nested functions) so that they will work with pax. |
| mprotect | Protects the modification of a task's address space. |
| pageexec | Paging-based, non-executable pages. |
| randexec | Randomize the mappings of an executable not built with relocatable code. |
| randmmap | Randomize mappings in a task's address space for an executable with relocatable code. |
| segmexec | Segmentation-based, nonexecutable pages. |

**TABLE C-47**
process **Permissions**

| Permissions | Description |
| --- | --- |
| dyntransition | Allows a process to dynamically transition to a new context. This capability is tied in with the setcurrent capability; both are required for a process domain transition. The ability of a process to change from one domain to another is extremely dangerous because it violates the principle of label tranquility for a process. It creates a real potential for unintentional granting of access. |
| execheap | Make the heap executable. |
| execmem | Make executable an anonymous mapping or private file mapping that is writable. |
| execstack | Make the process stack executable. |
| fork | Fork into two processes. |
| getattr | Get attributes of a process through the /proc/[pid]/attr directory. |
| getcap | Get Linux capabilities allowed for this process. |
| getpgid | Get Process Group ID of process. |
| getsched | Get priority of process. |
| getsession | Get session ID of process. |

*continues*

TABLE C-47 (continued)
`process` **Permissions**

| Permissions | Description |
|---|---|
| `noatsecure` | Disable secure mode environment cleansing. Allows process to disable secure mode feature of `glibc` on `execve(2)`. |
| `ptrace` | Trace program execution of parent or child. |
| `rlimitnh` | Inherit process resource limits from parent process. |
| `setcap` | Set Linux capabilities allowed for this process. |
| `setcurrent` | Set the current process context. This is the first permission checked when a process tries to perform a dynamic domain transition. The dyntransition capability is also required. |
| `setexec` | Override the default context for the next `execve(2)`. Allows a process to set the context of a program it execs to something other than the default context. (The context must still be a valid context for the domain of the new process.). |
| `setfscreate` | Allows a process to set the context of an object created by the process to something other than the default context. |
| `setpgid` | Set Process Group ID of process. |
| `setrlimit` | Change process hard resource limits. |
| `setsched` | Set priority of process. |
| `share` | Allow state sharing with cloned or forked process. |
| `sigchld` | Send `SIGCHLD` signal. |
| `siginh` | Inherit signal state from parent process. |
| `sigkill` | Send `SIGKILL` signal. |
| `signal` | Send a signal other than `SIGKILL`, `SIGSTOP`, or `SIGCHLD`. |
| `signull` | Test for existence of another process without sending a signal. |
| `sigstop` | Send `SIGSTOP` signal. |
| `transition` | Transition to a new context on `execve(2)`. |

TABLE C-48
security **Permissions**

| Permissions | Description |
|---|---|
| check_context | Allows a domain to check with the security server to see whether a context is valid within the current policy. |
| compute_av | Ask the security server to compute an access vector given a source/target/class using the selinuxfs interface. |
| compute_create | Retrieve a labeling decision on a new object. |
| compute_member | Ask the security server to compute a polyinstantiation membership decision through the selinuxfs interface. |
| compute_relabel | Allows a domain to use the selinuxfs interface to compute a relabeling decision. |
| compute_user | Allows domain to use the selinuxfs interface to retrieve a user's reachable SIDs. |
| load_policy | Load the security policy. This completely changes the kernel policy being enforced, and flushes the current access vector cache (AVC) so that all future access decisions are made against the new policy. |
| setbool | Allows a domain to set policy Boolean values. The domain also needs permissions on the Boolean file (that is, based on the label of the Boolean file). |
| setcheckreqprot | Set if SELinux will check original protection mode or modified protection mode (read-implies-exec) for mmap/mprotect. |
| setenforce | Change the enforcement state of SELinux to either permissive mode or enforcing mode. The kernel may be built to not allow this capability. |
| setsecparam | Set kernel AVC tuning parameters. |
| compute_user | Allows domain to use the selinuxfs interface to retrieve a user's reachable SIDs. |
| compute_relabel | Allows a domain to use the selinuxfs interface to compute a relabeling decision. |
| compute_create | Retrieve a labeling decision on a new object. |
| compute_av | Ask the security server to compute an access vector given a source/target/class using the selinuxfs interface. |

*continues*

TABLE C-48 (continued)
`security` **Permissions**

| Permissions | Description |
|---|---|
| compute_member | Ask the security server to compute a polyinstantiation membership decision through the selinuxfs interface. |
| setenforce | Change the enforcement state of SELinux to either permissive mode or enforcing mode. The kernel may be built to not allow this capability. |
| check_context | Allows a domain to check with the security server to see whether a context is valid within the current policy. |
| load_policy | Load the security policy. This completely changes the kernel policy being enforced, and flushes the current access vector cache (AVC), so that all future access decisions are made against the new policy. |
| setbool | Allows a domain to set policy Boolean values. The domain also needs permissions on the Boolean file (that is, based on the label of the Boolean file). |
| setsecparam | Set kernel AVC tuning parameters. |
| setcheckreqprot | Set if SELinux will check original protection mode or modified protection mode (read-implies-exec) for mmap/mprotect. |

TABLE C-49
`system` **Permissions**

| Permissions | Description |
|---|---|
| avc_toggle | No longer used (see setenforce permission in the security object). |
| bdflush | Deprecated, not used. |
| ichsid | Deprecated, not used. |
| ipc_info | Get info for IPC objects. |
| nfsd_control | Deprecated, not used. |
| syslog_console | Allows domain to enable and disable logging to the console and to set the level of syslog messages sent to the console. |
| syslog_mod | Perform syslog operation other than those operations controlled by syslog_read or syslog_console permissions. |
| syslog_read | Allows domain to retrieve the last kernel messages sent to the log and the size of the log buffer. |

# D

# SELinux Commands and Utilities

**In this chapter**

In this appendix we provide an introduction to some of the available SELinux tools. These tools include utilities for policy analysis, policy writing, policy generation, SELinux system management, and more. We indicate where to find the tools and, in the case where a tool is not included with a distribution, we provide the most current repository on the Internet.

## D.1 System Utilities

Distributions that support SELinux include a number of core utilities and programs that are usually present on any SELinux-enabled system. In this section, we present the programs included with *Fedora Core 4* (FC4). *Red Hat Enterprise Linux version 4* (RHEL4) and FC5 will have mostly the same core system utilities. We have mentioned many of these utilities throughout this book.

### D.1.1 Policy Tools

The policy tools are directly related to the SELinux policy, and writing and managing policies:

*checkpolicy(8)*      This is the SELinux policy compiler. It transforms a complete SELinux policy into a binary version that the kernel can load. It can also be used to debug a policy in that it can mimic some of the capabilities of the SELinux security server. No special permissions are needed to run this program if you are experimenting/debugging a policy outside of the official policy directory (that is, /etc/selinux/).

*load_policy(8)*      This utility loads a binary policy file into the kernel. To successfully load a policy in enforcing mode, the user must run the command in a domain that has the load_policy permission. (See the security object class in Appendix C, "Object Classes and Permissions").

*setsebool(8)*      This command sets current and persistent values for policy Boolean variables. See Chapter 9, "Conditional Policies." This command requires setbool permission for the security class *and* read/write permission to the Boolean files themselves.

*togglesebool(1)*     This command toggles the current value of SELinux Booleans. The same permissions as the `setsebool(8)` command are required.

*setenforce(8)*     This command changes the mode of SELinux between enforcing and permissive modes. The domain in which the command is run must have the `setenforce` permission for the `security` object class.

*audit2allow(1)*     A command that takes *access vector cache* (AVC) audit denial messages (usually from the system log file) and outputs allow rules that, if included into the policy, permit the actions that were denied. This command is commonly used to generate a rough first draft type of policy for an application. The man page describes the weaknesses of this approach and some of the other problems with developing policy this way.

*audit2why(1)*     Attempts to provide a reason for AVC audit denial messages by comparing them with the rules in the policy. This is most useful for identifying constraint violations.

*ausearch(8)*     Although not explicitly an SELinux command, this command does some basic interpretation of audit messages and can pull out just AVC messages with the `-m avc` option. It is part of the new Linux audit framework package and is included in the updated audit RPM for FC4 4, Update 2 for RHEL4, and FC5.

## D.1.2 SELinux Status Information

These utilities return information about SELinux. They do not change or affect the operation of SELinux in any way:

*avcstat(8)*     Displays statistics and counters for various AVC actions (for example, the number of cache hits).

*getenforce(8)*     Returns a string indicating the current mode of SELinux ("permissive" or "enforcing").

*selinuxenabled(1)*     Specifically designed for shell scripts to be able to determine whether SELinux is enabled or disabled (as opposed to permissive/enforcing mode).

| | |
|---|---|
| *getsebool(8)* | Returns the active value of one or more SELinux Boolean values. It returns "active" if the Boolean is true, and "inactive" if the Boolean is false. |
| *sestatus(8)* | A program that returns various status information about SELinux, such as the enforcing mode, the current policy version and name, and the status of the Booleans. |

## D.1.3 Security Context Labeling

These programs relate to managing security context labeling for objects. They are generally administrative commands that require enough privilege to relabel file-related objects. Some systems have a specific SELinux policy for the commands to ensure that only approved domains may run them with full privileges. In most cases, the commands must be run in a domain with `relabelto/relabelfrom` permissions on the source and target security contexts, and must meet any relevant `validatetrans` constraints. The new security context must also be a valid triplet (that is, user/role/type) for the currently loaded policy.

| | |
|---|---|
| *chcon(1)* | Changes the security context, or part of the security context, for file-related object classes (for example, ordinary files and directories). |
| *fixfiles(8)* | A utility that relabels any number of filesystem objects. Its default behavior is to relabel all mounted filesystems that support SELinux labeling unless they were mounted with the `context mount` option. It automatically determines the file security context specifications to use for the labeling. |
| *restorecon(8)* | A labeling utility similar to `fixfiles(8)` except that it is suited more for relabeling individual files or directories. |
| *setfiles(8)* | The original system relabeling utility. It is similar to `fixfiles(8)`. The main difference is that it requires a file context specification file as an argument along with at least one path name. |
| *genhomedircon(8)* | A script for generating the correct file context specification files for users' home directories. |
| *matchpathcon(8)* | This command returns the default security context for a path based on the active policy's file context file. |

## D.1.4 Security Context Changing Utilities

These command are used to start new processes with specific SELinux security contexts. The initiating domain type must have appropriate permission to allow a domain transition to the new type:

*newrole(1)*  This command creates a new shell running with a new security context. The user may specify a new role and/or type. If the system is a *multilevel security* (MLS) or *multicategory security* (MCS) system, a security level may also be specified. If only a role is specified then the default type derived for that role is used. The current user's password must be entered for the command to succeed.

*runcon(1)*  Similar to `newrole(1)` except that it requests that a specified command is run with a different security context. A combination of user/role/type/level may be requested instead of a full security context.

*run_init(8)*  Runs an `initrc` script using the security context found in the current policy's `contexts/initrc_context` file. This command is usually used to restart system services so that they end up in the intended domain.

## D.1.5 SELinux Modified Commands

The following commands are standard Linux commands that have been modified for SELinux to provide additional SELinux-related features:

*dir(1)*  Additional arguments that list security contexts in various formats

*find(1)*  Options to use security contexts as a search criteria and an output format

*install(1)*  Options to preserve security contexts (when copying) or use specified security contexts (when creating)

*killall(1)*  Adds an option to kill all processes with a specified security context

*ls(1)*  Additional arguments that list security contexts in various formats

*mkdir(1)*  Adds an option to specify the security context for a new directory

*ps(1)*  Adds an option to display the security contexts of processes *pstree(1)*    Adds an option to display the security contexts of processes

*stat(1)*     Adds an option to display the security context

*vdir(1)*     Additional arguments that list security contexts in various formats

*sudo/sudoedit(8)*    Adds options to specify a role and type to run the command in

## D.1.6 Policy Module Manual Pages

There are a series of manual pages written to help administrators with the SELinux aspects of various "standard" Linux services and utilities. Usually the manual pages describe the effects of the particular policy module on that specific service. There is also a manual page describing SELinux in general and the use of Booleans:

| | |
|---|---|
| *booleans(8)* | General information on how to use SELinux Booleans |
| *selinux(8)* | General information on SELinux |
| *ftpd_selinux(8)* | Information on how SELinux affects the FTP daemon |
| *httpd_selinux(8)* | Information on how SELinux affects the Web server |
| *kerberos_selinux(8)* | Information on SELinux and Kerberos |
| *named_selinux(8)* | Information on SELinux and the name daemon |
| *nfs_selinux(8)* | Information on how to use NFS with SELinux |
| *rsync_selinux(8)* | Information on SELinux and the rsync daemon |
| *samba_selinux(8)* | Information on SELinux and resource sharing with a Samba server |
| *ypbind_selinux(8)* | Describes how to configure SELinux to permit NIS its required network privileges |

## D.2 SETools Suite

Tresys Technology has a long standing suite of tools for analyzing and debugging SELinux policies. These tools are open source and are usually included in any Linux distribution that supports SELinux. The latest version of the tool suite and its source code is available from www.tresys.com/selinux.

All the source packages contain help files explaining how to use the tools and their features. All the tools are based on common policy library, `libapol`, also included in the setools package.

*apol*
This is the SELinux policy analysis tool we use throughout this book. It accepts either a `policy.conf` file or a compiled binary policy file. It is able to parse almost all versions of SELinux policy. `Apol` allows complicated rule searches and has several powerful automated analysis modules that perform such things as information flow and domain transition analyses.

*sediff*
A utility to semantically compare two policies. It can compare source policies, binary policies, or a combination of both. It can be run from the command line or with a GUI front end. (Both `sediffx` or `sediff -X` bring up the GUI.)

*seaudit*
A tool to browse and analyze SELinux audit messages. The tool will operate directly on the target system in real time or it can be used to analyze off-loaded log files. It not only has extended filtering capabilities, but it also provides an analysis tie-in with the policy that was on the source system. It can save filter configurations or views and can generate both text and HTML reports.

*seaudit-report*
A command-line tool that processes audit logs and generates reports in HTML and plain text. The reports are based on `seaudit` views (that is, saved filter specifications).

*sechecker*
A command-line tool that performs various quality checks on a policy file (binary or source). It includes a template for generating custom checks. The goal is to provide a tool that can examine an SELinux policy for common problems and weaknesses.

*secmds*
A collection of command-line tools that examine various information on an SELinux policy. The collection includes the following:

> *seinfo*
> Provides general information about a given policy file (source or binary).
>
> *sesearch*
> Performs `apol`-like rule searches on a given binary or source policy.

| | |
|---|---|
| *findcon* | A command to search for files and directories with a specific security context. The search can be limited to a specific object class. |
| *replcon* | A command similar to findcon, but with the added feature of allowing a partial or whole replacement of the security context. |
| *indexcon* | Generates a database file of all of the labels of files and directories on the system, or, if specified, a directory. The database file can be used with the file contexts analysis function of apol or searchcon. |
| *searchcon* | Searches through a file context database generated by indexcon using user specified criteria. |

## D.3 Other SELinux Tools

A number of other tools are being developed by various organizations. These tools are available as open source projects. They are in various levels of development and primarily aimed at aiding in the development or generation of SELinux policy.

*Polgen/Slat* (*www.mitre.org/tech/selinux/*) Tools developed by the MITRE Corporation. Polgen can be used to automatically generate policy. Slat performs information flow analysis between types.

*SLIDE* (*http://sourceforge.net/projects/selinux-ide*) A new open source project by Tresys Technology to develop an *integrated development environment* (IDE) that covers all aspects of SELinux policy development. The goal is to provide a single environment to develop, modify, analyze, and test SELinux policies.

*Virgil* (*http://sourceforge.net/projects/sepolicy-virgil*) A policy generation tool developed by IBM. It is a utility that generates SELinux policy automatically through a GUI. It is designed to provide a quick and easy policy for services where there is not yet a developed policy.

*seedit* (*http://sourceforge.net/projects/seedit*) A policy editor originally developed by Hitachi Software. It provides a Web-based GUI for generating new policy statements. It attempts to ease the development of policy by generalizing some of the policy details and providing a point-and-click interface.

# Index